GEORGE RUSSELL (Æ)
AND THE NEW IRELAND, 1905–30

To Louise

George Russell (Æ) and the New Ireland, 1905–30

NICHOLAS ALLEN

FOUR COURTS PRESS

Set in 10 on 13 point Janson for
FOUR COURTS PRESS LTD
7 Malpas Street, Dublin 8, Ireland
e-mail: info@four-courts-press.ie
and in North America
FOUR COURTS PRESS
c/o ISBS, 5824 N.E. Hassalo Street, Portland, OR 97213.

A catalogue record for this title
is available from the British Library.

ISBN 1–85182–691-2

Printed in England
by MPG Books, Bodmin, Cornwall

Contents

Acknowledgements

My first thanks are to Michael Allen, for his faith, and Terence Brown, for his care. I am indebted to them both. Edna Longley, Eamonn Hughes and Hugh Magennis gave early encouragement at Queen's University Belfast. Nicholas Grene, Eiléan Ní Chuilleanáin, John Scattergood, Eve Patten, Gerald Dawe and Ian Campbell Ross offered a warm welcome to Trinity College Dublin whose generosity still sustains. Dáire Keogh found this book its proper home. Roy Foster, Warwick Gould, John Kelly, Norman Vance, Kevin Whelan and Trevor West gave freely of advice, encouragement and support, for which I am very grateful.

I thank Grant Allardyce, Vanessa Buchanan, Rhyall Gordon, Elena Prieto, Keith and Catherine Sweeney for their long-held friendship; Jim Shanahan, Shane Mawe, Niall Mac Suibhne and Gearóid Ó Maoilmhichíl for their relief from the world of letters; Philip McGowan, Patrick Kilmartin, John Duncan, John Sweeney, Aaron Kelly, Catherine Morris; Eamonn Cantwell, Aileen Douglas, Nicholas Daly, Noreen Doody, Julie Anne Stephens and the School of English, Trinity College Dublin; Joe Clery, Robert Welch, Mary Shine Thompson, Pauric Travers, Crónán Ó Doibhlin, Mary Henry; Margaret Kelleher, Luke Gibbons, Seamus Deane, Alan O'Day, Shane Murphy, Patrick Walsh, Clare Hutton, Maurice Walsh, Sean Moore, Conor MacCarthy, Michael McAteer, Malcolm Ballin, Diana Beale; Seona MacRaimonn, Barbra Smith Morris and Mary Balthrop for such pleasant summer distraction; Katie Keogh and the Irish Seminar of the University of Notre Dame; Hélène Conway, Miriam Broderick, Dermot Campbell, Sue Norton and the School of Languages, the Dublin Institute of Technology; Ciaran Brady and the Department of Modern History, Trinity College Dublin; John Fairleigh, Liviu Cotrau, Adrian Radu, Tudor Balinisteanu, Daniel Darvay and the staff and students of the University of Babes-Bolyai, Romania; James Rodgers and Thomas Dillon Redshaw of the *New Hibernia Review*; Maurice Bric, Eda Sagarra and the Irish Research Council in the Humanities and Social Sciences; James Quinn and James McGuire, gentlemen employers.

Colin Smythe has long worked to secure Russell's posthumous reputation; his sponsorship of research and publication is testimony to a generous imagination. I am extremely grateful for his kind permission to quote from George Russell's published and unpublished works. I owe much to the scholarship of Alan Denson, John Eglinton, Monk Gibbon, Peter Kuch and Henry Summerfield. I hope this book upholds their tradition of enquiry. Kate Targett made available the Plunkett Foundation archives, Oxford, with much grace and good humour. I thank Hilary Pyle and the National Gallery of Ireland; Rose Byrne, Paul Doyle, Eileen Birch, Tony Carey, Charles Benson, Stuart Ó Seanóir, and the staff of Trinity College Dublin Library; Noel Kissane and the staff of the National Library of Ireland; Liz Forster and the Hugh Lane Municipal Gallery; the staff of Queen's University Belfast and British Libraries. To Michael Adams and Martin Fanning of Four Courts Press, I express my gratitude through George Wither's dedication; 'an honest Stationer (or Publisher) is he, that exerciseth his Mystery (whether it be in printing, binding or selling of Books) with more respect to the glory of God and the publik advantage than to his own Commodity & is both an ornament & a profitable member in the civill Commonwealth'. My thanks also to Martin Healy, Ronan Gallagher and Anthony Tierney.

'Self-portrait by George William Russell (1903)' is reproduced by permission of Russell and Volkening as agents for the estate of George Russell. I am thankful to Dixon Gaines for his help. The Board of Trinity College Dublin, the Council of Trustees of the National Library of Ireland, the Plunkett Foundation, the British Library and the Society of Authors, on behalf of the George Bernard Shaw estate, gave permission to quote from manuscript material in their holdings. The research and writing of this book were conducted with the generous aid of a Government of Ireland Postdoctoral Fellowship in the Humanities and Social Sciences, a Trinity Trust and Assocation Award, assistance from the School of English, Trinity College Dublin, a Government of Ireland Postgraduate Fellowship and a Trinity College Dublin Award.

This book would not have been written without the love, patience and support of my mother, father and brother, Ann, George and Nigel. I am blessed by their belief. My grandparents are a continous presence; William and Esther McCreight, George and Beatrice Allen, each have a place in the world of these pages. I thank Mr and Mrs H.T. Deacon and the Kidney family, Barry, Jane, Mark, John and Emmett, for their warm welcome. To my wife Louise I offer this work in all love and happiness.

The divine vision

George Russell edited two journals, the *Irish Homestead* and *Irish Statesman*, every week for twenty-five years, writing columns, commissioning work and entertaining visitors at his Dublin office in the Plunkett House at 84 Merrion Square. His room was at the top of this tall Georgian building's high stairs; 'It's like going to see God', said Walter de la Mare.[1] Russell sat behind a large desk covered in manuscripts, papers and poems, the walls around him painted with weird figures of his own imagination, symbols that suggested the occult aspect of his mind, human shapes crowned with stars of spiritual royalty. Hybrid animals patrolled the free spaces, the backgrounds of flower and leaf a pastoral relief from the individual intensity of the vision. We can find every one of Russell's interests in his office, painting, prose, and poetry, the occult and the practical. It was from here he wrote the majority of his journalism, looking out over the roofs of Dublin to the mountains beyond, the city and country both in his view, as they were in his work.

The Plunkett House was named in honour of Russell's lifelong colleague and sponsor, Horace Plunkett, founder in 1894 of the Irish Agricultural Organisation Society (IAOS).[2] Russell edited the organisation's weekly journal, the *Irish Homestead*, from 1905 to 1923. Its pages featured editorial comment, news from around the world, rural science and propaganda of Irish intellectual and material development. The cultural revival found solid root in this 'pig's paper', George Russell the focus, as editor, of every major controversy of the period. To look at Russell in this light, as an intellectual and editor, is to create a new sense of his writing and the culture he addressed. The intellectual awakening in Ireland of the late nineteenth and twentieth centuries took many forms, economic, political, and social, as well as literary. Book editions alone will not help us understand this. We need, instead, to look at new sources of material, at painting, journals, letters, pamphlets and posters, across new fields of enquiry, agriculture, anarchism, industry and the environment. We will find a literature

---

1 Austin Clarke, *A penny in the clouds*. 57.   **2** For an illuminating life of Plunkett, see Trevor West's *Horace Plunkett: co-operation and politics*, a crucial study complementary to any of George Russell, Plunkett's close associate and friend. Plunkett's sponsorship of Russell's work was continued by Trevor West's unfailing, generous support of this project.

engaged with more than a bare struggle between art and religion in Ireland, as so often portrayed, the intellectual classes we discover responsible to more than an abstract ideal of pure nationality. The range of George Russell's encounters, intellectual and personal, with James Connolly, Eamon de Valera, Kevin O'Higgins, Patrick Pearse, Franklin Roosevelt, George Bernard Shaw, H.G. Wells, and even Gandhi, suggests the variety of this life. He remained accessible throughout. Frank O'Connor remembered Russell at work as

> a big, burly north of Ireland Presbyterian with wild hair and beard and a pipe hanging from his discoloured teeth. He usually sat well back in his chair, beaming benevolently through his spectacles, his legs crossed, and his socks hanging down over his ankles. Sometimes in an earnest mood he leaned forward with his two fat hands on his knees, his head lowered as he looked at you over the specs, giving his appearance almost an elfin quality. He was an extraordinarily restless, fidgety man, for ever jumping up to find some poem he was about to print (usually lost in the heap of papers, prints and manuscripts in his desk) or some book he was reviewing.[3]

Such energy drove Russell to his task, the near endless writing of his weeklies added to by collections of poetry, prose and political agitation. The variety of his work made him influential contacts. The *Irish Homestead* and *Irish Statesman* were recognised as important organs of public opinion. Contributors included, over time, Padraic Colum, James Joyce, Alice Milligan, Sean O'Casey, Liam O'Flaherty, Standish O'Grady and William Butler Yeats. Of the rising generation, Frank O'Connor and Sean O'Faolain were frequent contributors to the *Irish Statesman*, their knowledge of Russell's business good apprenticeship for their involvement with the *Bell*. John Boyd and John Hewitt looked to Russell for inspiration. Patrick Kavanagh walked from Monaghan to Dublin to see him. George Bernard Shaw called the *Irish Homestead* 'the best weekly paper of its kind in the world', predicting, correctly, that 'Some day its back numbers will be treasured like Addison's Spectator and Steele's Tatler'.[4] Russell, in Shaw's words, edited the paper 'for a dock labourer's wages'.[5] 'It contains', he wrote, 'always from one to three first rate political and social articles, followed by instructions how to keep bees or conduct continuous cropping or what not'.[6] 'When the paper is out for the week, Russell goes home and paints pictures'.[7]

This man of many abilities, George William Russell, was born on 10 April, 1867, in Lurgan, Co. Armagh, the son of Thomas Elias Russell, a clerk, and

---

3 F. O'Connor, *My father's son*. 29. 4 G.B. Shaw, 'How Shaw and Russell met', British Library, (cited subsequently as BL) ms 50562/213-15. 5 Ibid. 6 Ibid. 7 Ibid.

Marianne Russell. One of three children, he attended the local Model School from 1867 until his father accepted a position in Dublin in 1878 from Robert Gardiner, a family friend and partner in an accountancy firm. Russell's education continued at the Metropolitan School of Art. Here he met another outsider, W.B. Yeats, in 1884. As conventional members of the Church of Ireland, Russell's family must have little expected a son with the strange gifts he possessed. Yeats found a visionary in *The celtic twilight* of 1893, Russell a gateway to a 'great Celtic phantasmagoria whose meaning no man has discovered, nor any angel revealed'.[8] But Russell was also distant, 'unknown, obscure, impersonal',[9] qualities beyond the young Yeats' power of description. It took a later memory, of 1922, for Yeats' revelation of Russell's character in youth. Of their time at art school, Yeats wrote, Russell

> had been almost unintelligible. He had seemed incapable of coherent thought, and perhaps was so at certain moments. The idea came upon him, he has told me, that if he spoke he would reveal that he had lost coherence; and for the three days that the idea lasted spent the hours of daylight wandering upon the Dublin mountains that he might escape the necessity for speech. I used to listen to him at that time, mostly walking through the streets at night, for the sake of some stray sentence, beautiful and profound, amid many words that seemed without meaning; and there were others, too, who walked and listened, for he had become to, I think, all his fellow-students sacred, as the fool is sacred in the East.[10]

The complexity of Russell's relationship with Yeats has been the subject of some consideration.[11] As young men they shared enthusiasms, from Madame Blavatsky's Theosophy to Shelley's poetry, two loves that were, typically, to consume Russell more obsessively than Yeats. As he grew older, Russell encased himself in familiar forms, the habits of his conversation as fixed as the images of his poetry. But assumed form was the protection of a fragile mind. As Yeats observed with harsh precision, Russell's 'voice would often become high and lose its self-possession during intimate conversation'.[12] But 'the moment the audience became too large for intimacy, or some exacting event had given formality to speech, he would be at the same moment impassioned and impersonal'.[13] Russell's character was consciously elusive. His only fragment of auto-

8 W.B. Yeats, *The celtic twilight*. 25. **9** Ibid. 20. **10** W.B. Yeats, 'More memories', *London Mercury*, July 1922. 284. **11** Peter Kuch's *Yeats and Æ* examines the early, antagonistic friendship. Competition between Russell and Yeats intensified as each projected a different version of Revival authority, through parallel, but divergent, career phases. Russell's invention of what he perceived to be a relevant version of Yeats in the 1920s surfaces later in this book. Russell was finally reconciled to an idea of Yeats he could accept as personally tenable in his last years, as discussed in the conclusion. **12** William Butler Yeats, 'More memories', *London Mercury*, July 1922. 286. **13** Ibid.

biography, 'The sunset of fantasy', is less record than reinvention. Russell's home life takes up little of his correspondence. His two posthumous biographers, John Eglinton and Henry Summerfield, each failed to resolve the dilemma of Russell's character.[14] He is to both saint and oddity, a myriad-minded man whose interest is, finally, his strangeness. George Moore found Russell a spectre in *Hail and farewell*. To Moore, Russell existed 'rather in one's imagination, dreams, sentiments, feelings, than in one's ordinary sight and hearing, and try as I will to catch the fleeting outlines, they escape me; and all I remember are the long, grey, pantheistic eyes that have looked so often into my soul and with such a kindly gaze'.[15] Among Moore's portraits, Russell is 'the least living, and that is the pity. He does not silhouette as Yeats does'.[16] George Bernard Shaw found it equally difficult to identify Russell in September 1908:

> I met Russell for the first time as a man lost in the desert might catch sight amazedly of another figure on the naked horizon. To be exact, I was one day in the Dublin National Gallery, one of the best in Europe of its size, and therefore less populous than Connemare (*sic*) or Timgad, when lo! A man! Presently I pulled up before a lovely little modern picture. The master who painted it had suppressed its name, not in modesty, but because he found that he could get fully a hundred times for his work by adopting the name of Correggio. The man came over to have a look at it too; and, at once, without preliminaries, we entered into intimate conversation as if we had known one another all our lives. When I mentioned the incident afterwards I was told 'Oh, that must have been George Russell'; and when he mentioned it he was told 'Oh, that must have been Bernard Shaw'. But we had both known without being told, though I never said, like H.M. Stanley when he met Livingstone in an only slightly more probable place, 'Mr Russell, I presume'; nor did Æ dream of going through that ceremony with Mister Shaw.[17]

James Joyce had arrived on Russell's doorstep unannounced at midnight in August 1902 to discuss poetry and the occult, Russell later arranging for three of Joyce's short stories, collected in *Dubliners*, to be published in the *Irish Homestead*, then under the editorship of H.F. Norman, in 1904. But Joyce's vision of Russell in *Ulysses* is again indistinct. 'Æ, what does that mean? Initials perhaps. Albert Edward, Arthur Edmund, Alphonsus Eb Ed El Esquire'.[18] Æ, as Joyce knew, was the name Russell took after submitting a work as 'Aeon' to a printer

---

14 John Eglinton's *A memoir of Æ* is a useful, if detached, introduction to Russell's life. Henry Summerfield's *That myriad-minded man* is an invaluable factual resource for the new scholar. I owe each author a debt of gratitude. 15 G. Moore, *Ave*. 160. 16 G. Moore, *Vale*. 243. 17 G.B. Shaw, 'How Shaw and Russell met', BL ms 50562/213–15. 18 J. Joyce, *Ulysses*. 158.

of the journal *Lucifer* in 1888. The devil, as ever, is in the detail and the last two letters were dropped. To Joyce, memorably, Russell's speech was 'The ends of the world with a Scotch accent. Tentacles: octopus. Something occult: symbolism. Holding forth'.[19] Sean O'Casey, bitter over Russell's management of the *The silver tassie* controversy, remembered Russell as equally vague. Russell was a painter with a palette 'typical of himself, indistinct, uncertain, to allow him to outspread a vision of thinly-tinted dreams. He splashed on the dove-grey, the light blue, and the pink, that coloured his empty heaven and his emptier earth, symbols of his own vague mind, vapouring everything in nature within lilac and pink and dove-grey so as to fit them into the tinselled universe conceived in the mirage of his own ancestral self'.[20]

Russell's friends, as his enemies, stressed his unworldliness. George Moore, again, was ironic. To him, 'Æ's life is in his ideas as much as Christ's' as 'his wife has never tried to come between him and his ideas'.[21] Others were more reverent. Darrell Figgis, author of *Æ: a study of a man and a nation*, of 1916, doubted the propriety of sharing knowledge of Russell's life with the wider world.[22] Charlotte Elizabeth MacManus evoked a prophet of hidden power.

> Mr Russell came to see me one evening. His face was half covered by his beard into which flowed his long dark hair on each side. He was big, with round shoulders. He wore glasses over eyes busied with the external things of life. So you thought for a moment. The outer look, however, was but another pair of glasses, and I soon caught gleams of the inner eyes, the third sight, which was more enlarged than the aid the glasses bestowed. To that sight, external things had drawn back, or served as mediums through which could be seen other countries and people, none of them in an ether so vast and unmapped that thought sought in vain for boundaries, in which in moods of abstraction or on mountain heights – in rarer atmosphere – the third sight visualized forms and scenes that might have dwelt in and been part of eternity. For Mr Russell has the gift of vision, as Blake had the gift, and Swedenborg and Ezekiel.[23]

19 Ibid. **20** S. O'Casey, *Autobiographies*. 171. **21** G. Moore, *Vale*. 243. **22** Figgis wondered if 'The profoundest parts of a life are not its deeds but the long and slow preparations of personality necessary to those deeds; and these are untellable. Partly they are so because to seek to expound in round terms what were originally compounded of adventures, hesitancies, much incertitude and a slow dawning of light, mixed pitifully with bright illuminations and blackest despair, is to turn the facts of living into the lie of print; but also by what is implied in the modern making of books. Publicity has become a prohibition. Books are not published, as proclamations are supposed to be, for those whom it may concern, but for every curious eye to greet; and the result, however honesty may deplore it, has been a tighter drawing of the curtains about the secrets of the soul.' *Æ: A study of a man and a nation*. 13-14. Russell, suitably, was embarrassed by Figgis' work. **23** C.E. MacManus, *White light and flame*. 53.

Raghavan and Nandini Iyer found Russell, in retrospect, a full-born mystic. Despite a youth 'cramped by a rigid educational system that ran contrary to his generous impulses', Russell's 'profound compassion for all human beings prevented' his 'mysticism from being purely subjective or self-indulgent'.[24] More entertaining is Robert Bernard Davis' *George William Russell (Æ)*. A man of 'gentle and humble nature',[25] Russell is a new Christ. 'Though Russell', Davis writes erroneously, was

> born in Northern Ireland, he became one of the most powerful voices in the entire country. Neither Catholic nor Protestant, his inherent spirituality made him respected by many Catholics and Protestants. A nationalist, but not a revolutionary, his sincerity and objectivity in matters of politics caused him to be trusted by all parties, and by English statesmen as well. In the terrible days of the Anglo-Irish War he was one of those who pleaded for moderation and sanity. He was a leader of the Irish Renaissance, with great accomplishments in arts and letters, and was also a force in the development of the Irish cooperative movement, the cause sponsored by the Irish Agricultural Organisation Society. As we read of him in the prime of his life, during the period from 1913 to 1923, it seems that he was everywhere at once, performing great deeds for his country and for the entire world.[26]

This is comic. But Davis' analysis hides a serious problem. Russell was born in an Ireland undivided, but his character, like that of the island of his birth, is under partition. Critics have not yet reconciled that split which Yeats perceived in Russell's character between the private and the public, between the occult and the practical, between the individual and the national. Russell's work is lost to this failure, his poetry invisible, his prose unrecognisable, his painting in the vault. His best writing was contained in the *Irish Homestead* and *Irish Statesman*, two journals difficult to access and overwhelming in their weekly output, the affairs of the day over three decades mingled with opinion on literature and art. But a study of that work suggests a new sense of George Russell and the culture in which he wrote. The Literary Revival has typically been understood to be a cultural development directed by Yeats. Its dominant context is the evolution of Irish nationalism from Parnell to Pearse. Its controversies follow plots as familiar as Synge's *Playboy of the western world*, from the disputes over the 1798 centenary commemorations to the fallout from George Moore's scandalous *Hail and farewell*, post 1911. But we are misled if we follow Irish literature by these

---

24 R. and I. Iyer, *The descent of the gods*. 1.   **25** R.B. Davis, *George William Russell ('Æ')*. 19.   **26** Ibid. 20.

dates. We should rather set ourselves to a more fragmentary practice, our mobile terms of reference informed by events whose genesis and effects are fugitive and diffuse, the constant motion of political manoeuvre and the draft version of first published poems. As editor of the *Irish Homestead* and *Irish Statesman*, George Russell was master of the fleeting argument, a controversialist whose opinions cultivated Irish, British and American opinion across society. This book exposes Ireland of the late nineteenth and early twentieth centuries as a multiple site of conflicting interests, a nation, then state, where anarchism, co-operation, labour and capital fought for recognition through pamphlets, periodicals, news-sheets and weeklies.

The defining standards of Irish cultural achievement should be removed from anthology editions to a changing landscape whose topography is defined by the failing magazine, the censored text and intercontinental event. Irish culture of the first three decades of the twentieth century is, by this standard, a necessary failure. Established writers stand upon the detritus of a public culture that encouraged participation across all the scales of advantage. George Russell's journal work is a series of conversations held with contemporaries on a variety of subjects. To recognise the importance of event to thought is, at the same time, to reintroduce a number of fundamental moments to their pivotal place in Irish culture. The First World War and Russian Revolution are peripheral to many analyses. The development of industry and technology are equal strangers to cultural debate, the time-worn image of religious conflict between peoples leading, irrevocably, to deadening, and misleading, descriptions of atavistic Independence. The reader of Russell's work will find a different world, an Ireland of intense practical development and concerted industrial propaganda. The great monument to this Ireland might be the power station on the Shannon River, and not the General Post Office. The new Ireland of this book's title is a place of polemic, a nation and state whose borders are contested by rival literatures, the fugitive press of now fading pages still in full life, the editorial rushed to a printers (as was the *Irish Homestead* every Thursday evening) in embrace with the advertisement, letters and poems that follow.

Russell began his own literary career as a member of this commercial world as a clerk in the drapery firm of Pims, where he worked for seven years from 1890. He published his first poetry collection, *Homeward songs by the way*, in 1894, and contributed a wide variety of miscellaneous work to esoteric journals. Russell's first published essay was a co-written article with Charles Johnson, the son of a northern Irish Member of Parliament, in the *Theosophist* of 1887. Russell further contributed to the *Irish Theosophist* and its successor, the *Internationalist*, which he also co-edited. William Blake's influence rests on much of this work, Yeats having compiled, with E.J. Ellis, an edition of Blake's work in 1893, a work with which Russell was familiar.[27] Russell cited passages from Blake's *The marriage of heaven and hell* throughout his life and shared Blake's belief that the material world is but a shadow of spiritual reality. In consequence, individuals (or more precisely poets) who can see, as Russell put it, 'through the glimmering deeps', are blessed, the savants in possession of a future vision that might, with due effort, unveil itself in glory. This book is founded in a fascination with this aspect of Russell's visionary capacity, not as evidence of sainthood but as a suggestion of radicalism, Russell's Theosophy a doctrine of empowerment that combined with his sense of nationalism to create, in his writings, a prophetic voice that assumed cultural and political authority.

Russell was a Theosophist for his near entire adult life. Theosophy was, according to its founder H.P. Blavatsky, a Russian *émigré*, 'not a religion' but a reconstitution of philosophical thought on spirituality 'as old as thinking man'.[28] The first branch of the Theosophical Society had been formed in the United States of America in 1875, its founders a Colonel Olcott, William Q. Judge and Blavatsky herself. Theosophy's first appearance in the Dublin literary scene is traced by John Eglinton (the pseudonym of William Kirkpatrick Magee, a sceptic in the employment of the National Library of Ireland) to a discussion held at the home of Trinity English Professor Edward Dowden in the late 1880s. Dowden would not have touched 'the Theosophy Movement with a long pole',[29] but Yeats, whose father was a friend of Dowden, was undeterred and read aloud from A.P. Sinnett's *Esoteric Buddhism*.[30] Russell formed a concrete association with Theosophy when he moved into the lodge of the Dublin Theosophical Society at 3 Upper Ely Place in 1891, where one of his companions was Eglinton's brother, Malcolm Magee. The society held regular lectures on Friday evenings and published the *Irish Theosophist* on a press that Edward Pryse had imported from London.[31] Theosophy's foundation text was Blavatsky's *The secret doctrine*, first published in 1888. A strange work, *The secret doctrine* is a sprawling, often incoherent, account of the genesis of human religion. An entire world is contained within its pages, its occult history complete with theories of reincarnation and divination. It is a book that could not, perhaps, have been written outside the second half of the nineteenth century. *The secret doctrine* is a tempting illusion, its apparently comprehensive detail hiding subtle inadequacies.

Blavatsky herself was greatly ambitious for her 'new Genesis',[32] its post-Darwinian foundation myth a grand synthesis of the systematic methodology of

---

27 Yeats' publication of Blake's works, co-edited by E.J. Ellis, was announced in the *Irish Theosophist* in October 1892. An extract from Blake's 'There is no natural religion', taken from Yeats' edition, was published in the journal, facing Russell's 'The hour of twilight'. See *Irish Theosophist*, 15 Mar. 1893. 59. **28** H.P., Blavatsky, *The secret doctrine*. xxxvi. **29** K.R. Ludwigson, *Edward Dowden*. 45. **30** J. Eglinton, *A memoir of Æ*. 11-13. **31** Russell respected Pryse, an American Theosophist resident in the Dublin Lodge in the 1890s, throughout his life. Yeats dismissed Pryse as an 'American hypnotist' in his *Autobiographies*. 237. **32** H.P. Blavatsky, *The secret doctrine*. vii.

Victorian science with the spirituality that the material practice of such science typically displaced. The book was, however, only to be understood as 'new' in so far as it reconstituted some ancient, unitary philosophy. *The secret doctrine* aimed to establish 'three fundamental propositions'.[33] The first asserted the existence of 'An Omnipresent, Eternal, Boundless, and Immutable PRINCIPLE on which all speculation is impossible' because it 'transcends the power of human conception and could only be dwarfed by any human expression or similitude'.[34] Blavatsky pictures deity as an absence, its immensity impossible to render imaginatively. In the unknowable, Blavatsky finds the indestructible, a belief system immune, as already suggested, from the sceptical inquiries of scientific materialism. Here, Blavatsky states, is a faith unshakeable. One of many points in *The secret doctrine* where the text shows itself to be more concerned with the contemporary than the eternal, Blavatsky's revolutionary appeal was her ability to conceive of a secret history self-evident when properly perceived.

The secret doctrine is in this respect analogous to *On the origin of species* in its revelation of a truth previously unsuspected by a general readership.[35] Blavatsky had no comparable method to that of Darwin but both rely, each in their separate manner, on observation and abstraction. In Russell's case, to understand his interest in Theosophy one must also recognise his lifelong interest in science, his obsession with atomic physics evident even in the last years of the *Irish Statesman*. This is not to claim for Theosophy a rational basis that it does not have. But there is no doubt that *The secret doctrine* affected a part of the public imagination, small perhaps in size, already conditioned to accept the outlandish as fact. For who in the early nineteenth century would have imagined the simian basis of the human race? As few, one might suspect, as later became initiates of Theosophical lodges. Like a scientific manual, *The secret doctrine* is full of technical phrases, a further attraction to a mind like Russell's, seduced as it was by the power of the arcane. Blavatsky, for example, imagined that 'The Eternity of the Universe' existed '*in toto* as a boundless plane'.[36] This plane is governed by the 'absolute universality of that law of periodicity, of flux and reflux, ebb and flow, which physical science has observed and recorded in all departments of Nature'.[37] Science and nature are in concert, 'natural law' dominant as a force, which, like the seasons, must be adhered to. Complementary to the corporate

---

33 Ibid. 14. **34** Ibid. 14. **35** Scientists did approach an understanding of evolution before Darwin. Jean Baptiste Lamarck (1744-1829) first had the idea that acquired traits are inheritable. Erasmus Darwin (1731-1802), Charles' grandfather, published his *Zoonomia or the laws of organic life* between 1794 and 1796. The elder Darwin argued that species modified their physical stature over time to adapt to the natural environment. Alfred Russell Wallace (1823-1913) evolved a theory of natural selection independently of Charles Darwin. His 1855 essay 'On the law which has regulated the introduction of new species' directly influenced the author of *On the origin of species*. **36** H.P. Blavatsky, *The secret doctrine*. 16. **37** Ibid. 17.

authority inscribed in such natural order, Blavatsky's final law was the assertion of 'The fundamental identity of all souls with the Universal Over-Soul, the latter itself being an aspect of the Unknown Root'.[38] This 'Unknown Root' is complementary to the indescribable being of Blavatsky's first principle. The relationship between 'soul' and 'Over-Soul' necessitates in turn the 'obligatory pilgrimage of every soul – a spark of the former – through the Cycle of Incarnation (or "Necessity") in accordance with Cyclic and karmic law'.[39] The idea of 'necessity' is fundamental to any understanding of Russell's career. Not only does it provide an insight into the increasingly authoritarian stances of his later prose but it also creates the bedrock for his prophetic voice. To speak with the knowledge of history is critical to a literary self-perception that imagines itself to be gifted with foreknowledge. Russell's hope of an avatar throughout his career, the arrival in Ireland of a spiritual saviour, is easily mocked but his and Yeats' sense of historical determinism lent tremendous power to their version of Irish cultural nationalism.

The highest ideal in *The secret doctrine* is to reintroduce a 'Golden Age vibration' to the present, 'to ameliorate the collective predicament of mankind'.[40] The golden age was a period of consciousness without material form, the high point of a cyclic decline to silver, bronze and our present iron age. This is our predicament, an age that 'began over 5,000 years ago and will last altogether for a total of 432,000 years'.[41] It is 'characterised by widespread confusion of roles, inversion of ethical values and enormous suffering owing to spiritual blindness'.[42] In face of this, Blavatsky believed that 'action must be performed, or the frame of things within which the individual can seek salvation will fall apart'.[43] The allusions to salvation and private responsibility are, again, typical of wider Victorian discourse. Bizarre as the attraction to Blavatsky's doctrine might seem to the modern mind, such devotion to the public ideal of private action suggests the relative centrality of Theosophy to particular modes of Victorian expression.[44]

Russell's mind was further rooted in the nineteenth century with his love for the work of Standish O'Grady. The author in 1878 and 1880 of a seminal two-volume *History of Ireland*, O'Grady was a graduate of Trinity College Dublin, where he excelled at oratory and essay writing. O'Grady was the son of a Church of Ireland clergyman at Castletown Berehaven. His rural childhood landscape haunts his history, the geography of his early surroundings marking the contours of his study. To O'Grady, 'The bardic literature of Erin stands alone, as distinctly

38 Ibid. **39** Ibid. **40** Ibid. 18. **41** Ibid. **42** Ibid. **43** Ibid. 44. **44** Literary evangelism was a phenomenon common to the nineteenth century. T.W. Heyck observes of the period that 'Shelley's ideal of the poet as "a nightingale, who sits in darkness to cheer his own solitude with sweet sounds" was diluted by Evangelical earnestness and the gospel of work into the ideal of the prophetic man of letters, who like Carlyle preached and warned in broad sunlight directly to the middle class'. *The transformation of intellectual life in Victorian England.* 193. See also S. Collini, *Public moralists: political thought and intellectual life in Britain.*

and genuinely Irish as the race itself, or the natural aspects of the island. Rude indeed it is, but like the hills which its authors peopled with gods, holding dells of the most perfect beauty, springs of the most touching pathos'.[45] O'Grady was called to the Bar in 1872 but devoted most of his energy to literary criticism in the *Gentleman's Magazine* and leader writing for the Dublin *Daily Express*. He was also author of adventure novels, notably the *Flight of the eagle* and the *Chain of gold*.[46] O'Grady was originally unionist. His support for the ascendancy weakened as he despaired of its survival. A pugnacious journalist, O'Grady became proprietor of the *Kilkenny Moderator* in 1898 to popularise his own views on the Irish literary and political situation. When this title failed due to a libel action, O'Grady founded the weekly *All Ireland Review*, published from 1900 to 1906. A quirky, eccentric publication, O'Grady's journal included poetry by Russell, prose by Yeats and serial notes on the Irish language.[47] O'Grady's editorials, frequent letters from the likes of John Pentland Mahaffy and Lady Gregory, and a dispute between Russell and William Sharp on the virtues of Celticism, gave the *All Ireland Review* an admirably cantankerous character. O'Grady's prose owed much to Thomas Carlyle.[48] Constructed in the narrative style of a novel, the first volume of O'Grady's *History of Ireland* is an imaginative rendering of ancient Irish texts. Composed in forty-eight separate chapters, each of a length to encourage the attention of a casual browser, each section boasts a dramatic title, such as 'At the ford', 'Plot' and 'Ah Cu!' To a readership familiar with MacPherson's *Ossian* and Walter Scott, O'Grady's attempt to label his work 'history' was understood to be no more than the feint of a clever stylist. O'Grady tried to counter this appearance of a lack of high seriousness in his work, his second volume adopting the scholarly apparatus of footnotes to his text. But O'Grady was unable to temper a grand style: 'These heroes and heroines', he wrote, 'were the ideals of our ancestors, their conduct and character were to them a religion, the bardic literature was their Bible'.[49]

45 S. O'Grady, *History of Ireland*. I. 39-40.   **46** *The chain of gold* was published in London by Fisher Unwin in 1895, *The flight of the eagle* by Lawrence and Bullen in 1897. Both were romantic adventures, much in the nature of Robert Louis Stevenson's *Treasure island* and *Kidnapped*, published in 1883 and 1886 respectively. It is interesting to note the school audience that reprints of O'Grady's work were to inspire under the Free State, the Talbot Press republishing his work in illustrated editions throughout the 1920s.   **47** See for example Russell's poem 'Dana', *All Ireland Review* (cited subsequently as *AIR*), 26 May 1900. 5. Also Yeats' 'A postscript to a forthcoming book of essays by various writers', *AIR*, 1 Dec. 1900. 6. Irish language items were published nearly every week.   **48** The grandiloquent manner of O'Grady's *History of Ireland* imitates Carlyle's flourish, especially in *On heroes, hero-worship, and the heroic*. Carlyle's subject was the effect of the heroic on society. His suggestion was that heroes were ciphers for divine inspiration, conduits of the divine, an idea taken up by O'Grady in his depiction of Cuchulain. As Carlyle put it, 'All things that we see standing accomplished in the world are properly the outer material result, the practical realisation and embodiment, of Thoughts that dwelt in the Great Men sent into the world: the soul of the whole world's history, it may justly be considered, were the history of these'. 3.   **49** S. O'Grady, *History of Ireland*, I.vii.

Russell first met O'Grady in 1895. Already captivated by Blavatsky, Russell discovered in O'Grady's theory of epic literature a connection between his inner life and Irish historical experience. O'Grady, quite unknowingly, provided Russell with the medium by which he might express his occult vision of Ireland in terms acceptable to an audience definite in its national convictions. O'Grady wrote his history to inspire an ideal of heroic action in his caste, the Anglo-Irish. To do so he created the Ulster hero Cuchulain as a standard of Irish behaviour, to the degree that the *History of Ireland* is, like Homer's *Iliad*, dominated by one character's fate.[50] (O'Grady did use classical models for sections of the text and his treatment of Cuchulain's character is clearly intended to inspire.)[51] A mute hero who rarely, if ever, speaks, Cuchulain stands in the *History of Ireland* as a sign, a warning to the Protestant landlords of Ireland during the late 1870s to respond to the Land League crisis. Cuchulain's void character was, however, the basis of his attraction to Russell and his nationalist contemporaries. Capable of fulfilment by radical nationalist sentiment, Cuchulain became an epic being of political mythology, his new life an instruction to Ireland to recover an ancient past that was in reality a fiction of the late nineteenth century. Appropriately, a sense of epiphany attends Russell's memory of his conversion to O'Grady's epic. Russell felt restored to a birthright lost in the fracture of Irish history. After O'Grady's death in 1928, Russell remembered himself before O'Grady as

> a man who, through some accident, had lost memory of the past, who could recall no more than a few months of new life, and could not say to what songs his cradle had been rocked, or by what woods and streams he had wandered. When I read O'Grady I was as a man who suddenly feels ancient memories rushing at him, and knows he was born in a royal house, that he had mixed with the mighty of heaven and earth and had the very noblest for companions. It was the memory of race that rose up within me as I read, and I felt exalted as one who learns he is among the children of kings.[52]

Russell's sense of mission was common to British intellectuals of the late nineteenth and early twentieth centuries. Russell's Irish nationalism may mark

50 Bernard Knox, in his 'Introduction' to Robert Fagles' *Iliad*, notes that 'Homer's great epic poem has been known as "The *Iliad*" ever since the Greek historian Herodotus so referred to it in the fifth century B.C. But the title is not an adequate description of the contents of the poem, which are best summed up in its opening line: "the rage of Peleus's son, Achilles"'. 3. Similarly, O'Grady's *History of Ireland* figures national destiny as Cuchulain's fate. **51** In *The story of Ireland*, Dathi is 'buried on the right bank of the Shannon in a great mound. His warriors set up a tall pillar over the mound and held funeral games around it'. 39. In the twenty-third book of the *Iliad*, 'Funeral games for Patroclus', 'all the woodcutters hoisted logs themselves-/ ... and they heaved them down in rows along the beach/ at the site Achilles chose to build an immense mound/ for Patroclus and himself'. 563. **52** G. Russell, 'A tribute', *Standish James O'Grady: the man and the writer*. 63-4.

his difference in political sympathy from many of his contemporaries, but his compound interests in poetry, the occult and social organisation identify Russell as an Edwardian intellectual, albeit of Irish provenance. Edward Carpenter, for example, had little problem integrating the arcane with the political. Like Russell, Carpenter, a Cambridge graduate, vegetarian and anarchist, was a devotee of Blavatsky. Carpenter also shared some of Russell's friends, mutual acquaintances including George Bernard Shaw and the journalist H.W. Nevinson.[53] In a further synchronicity, Carpenter lectured on co-operation to English Theosophical societies. Carpenter's autobiography, *My days and dreams*, is a register of the wide variety of experience that formed a radical, late Victorian intellect. Carpenter lists Blavatsky's Theosophical Society alongside the Democratic Federation, the Society for Psychical Research, the Vegetarian Society and the anti-vivisection movement as preparation by his generation 'for the new universe of the twentieth century'.[54] Russell took his place in this world as editor of the *Irish Homestead*, a journal of progressive conviction and broad interest. Audiences for such publications across Ireland and Britain varied enormously, from a few dozen to thousands. In England, the Fabians, a society of social reformers under the direction of the Webbs and George Bernard Shaw, conducted their media campaigns in the *New Age*, a journal edited by Russell's contemporary and friend, A.R. Orage. Orage, like Carpenter, was possessed of a range of interests similar to Russell. Like Russell, Orage too has suffered from posthumous neglect, a pity when one considers the clarity of his criticism. The *New Age* was a vigorous vehicle for Orage's evolving belief in the suitability of guild socialism for the equitable organisation of the English working classes. A keen reader of Russell's mystical text *The candle of vision*, Orage also wrote ably on James Joyce and John Eglinton.[55]

We can now begin to see a George Russell very different from the vague abstraction that hides behind Æ, a man very much of his time and place. Russell was an intellectual, the core of whose beliefs demanded commitment to the world. Theosophy promised destiny and the long fight to spiritual renewal. It engaged with the public through periodical and pamphlet propaganda, Blavatsky's *The secret doctrine* the master document for initiates. The movement's proselytising energy attracted Russell, a north of Ireland Protestant by birth, with a family feeling for evangelism. Theosophy in Ireland was further attractive to the young and the marginalized as it was radicalised by local condition. Its first promise, the spiritual refuge of the bourgeoisie from the demoralising effects of Darwinian theory, proved brief respite. But Blavatskty's idea of the world in an iron age took different meaning in Ireland than it did elsewhere.

---

53 E. Carpenter, *My days and dreams*. 246-7.   **54** Ibid. 240.   **55** See A.R. Orage, *Selected essays and critical writings*.

Britain was the world's great industrial power and Ireland its servant. Freedom was figured as struggle, an individual stand, as Cuchulain at the Gap of Ulster, or George Russell on Bray pier, shouting to the wind of the return of the gods to bemused Sunday walkers. Standish O'Grady later claimed to be surprised at the effect his writing had on the revival generation. But his heroic ideal of ancient Ireland confirmed Russell's belief that humanity was conduit to the divine. The divine sought outlet and Russell imagined Ireland most suitable. It had a core of initiates ready to accept the fantastic and a rural people still close to the earth, the wellspring of all occult. Russell found in O'Grady the evidence that gods walked the earth in the heroic period, possessing Cuchulain to greater deeds. In all Russell's poetry the positive will works through the individual person, transfiguring the normal to the superhuman, from Prometheus to Pearse. This world of the unknown was not always easily summoned. George Moore enjoyed his Boyne valley cycle with Russell in *Hail and farewell*, but Finn would not sortie from Slievegullion, the ancient hero afraid, no doubt, of the two Presbyterians who shadowed our pair throughout.

Russell sought revelation always in his poetry, but the relation of the real to the abstract caused him increasing anxiety. His first collection, *Homeward songs by the way*, published in 1894, is self-assured (that he even wrote poetry was by chance; not knowing whether prose or poems were the best form by which to express his thought, he asked his fellows in the lodge for advice. Poetry, they responded). Dedicated to Charles Weekes, Russell's lifelong friend, *Homeward songs by the way* is prefaced by Russell's comments on his labour. 'I moved', he wrote, 'among men and places, and in living I learned the truth at last. I know I am a spirit, and that I went forth in old time from the Self-ancestral to labours yet unaccomplished; but filled ever and again with homesickness I made these songs by the way'.[56] Life is, at this point, subordinate to Russell's mind. But the confidence by which he expresses his discovery of the truth does not survive in Russell's second collection, *The earth breath*, of 1897. A growing self-reflection evolved from Russell's closer relationship with Yeats, to whom the volume is dedicated. The poetry is now melancholic.

> Homeward I go not yet; the darkness grows;
> Not mine the voice to still with peace divine:
> From the first fount the stream of quiet flows
>   Through other hearts than mine.
>
> Yet of my night I give to you the stars,
> And of my sorrow here the sweetest gains,

---

56 G. Russell, *Homeward songs by the way*. vii.

> And out of hell, beyond its iron bars,
> My scorn of all its pains.[57]

Russell was, by the year of *The earth breath*'s publication, on the cusp of a new life, leaving Pim's for employment in the IAOS in 1897. Founded by Horace Plunkett in 1894, the IAOS was dedicated to industrial and social improvement of the rural classes. It met with much mistrust. Nationalist politicians suspected Plunkett's unionism; his membership of the Dunsany family, education, at Eton and Oxford, and landowning wealth separated him from the new nation. But Plunkett's physical frailty, his thin frame in constant pain in later life from an x-ray burn maladministered in 1916 by a Harley Street doctor, belied a mental strength. The IAOS promoted co-operative aid between farmers and townspeople. It promoted the belief that rural Ireland, at first, would only gain economic strength by mutual aid, farmers bonding their power of purchase and consumption together. To effect this, Plunkett faced every disadvantage. Constitutional nationalists distrusted his motives, fearing improvement of social conditions would distract popular opinion from the national question. Traders throughout Ireland attacked the IAOS as detrimental to their business. Plunkett made mistakes. His criticism of the Catholic Church in *Ireland in the new century* of 1904 was never forgotten. But he persevered and was rewarded with increasing membership of the IAOS north and south, with official approval of his policies after Independence in the Irish Free State. Russell was Plunkett's partner throughout. The two sometimes disagreed but never split. Russell was employed first to organise rural banks. He travelled the west of Ireland, occasionally depressed by the distance and weather, and spoke to farmers' meetings of the benefits of co-operation. He was recalled to Dublin in 1898 to work in the Dublin office of the organisation and began to write reviews for Plunkett's newly acquired paper, the *Daily Express*. The *Irish Homestead*, official organ of the Irish co-operative movement, was at this time edited by H.F. Norman. Russell took responsibility for the 'Celtic Christmas' *Irish Homestead* annuals, sold as a special edition and containing much of his writing. His fire for the coming work illuminates 'The earth breath', a word painting of rural divinity after Millet.

> From the cool and dark-lipped furrows
>   breathes a dim delight
> Through the woodland's purple plumage
>   to the diamond night.
> Aureoles of joy encircle
>   every blade of grass

---

57 G. Russell, *The earth breath*. 9.

Where the dew-fed creatures silent
	and enraptured pass.
And the restless ploughman pauses,
	turns and, wondering,
Deep beneath his rustic habit
	finds himself a king;
For a fiery moment looking
	with the eyes of God
Over fields a slave at morning
	bowed him to the sod.
Blind and dense with revelation
	every moment flies,
And unto the mighty mother, gay, eternal, rise
	all the hopes we hold, the gladness,
Dreams of things to be.[58]

Land and people are divine, the holy island of Ireland the access point to a spiritual life that communities divorced from the earth cannot access. Britain, developed and industrial, is the invisible guest at this pastoral, Russell using his poetry to clear imaginative space free of foreign influence. Like the western states of the American poet Walt Whitman, whom Russell revered always, Russell looked to the reclaimed territory of the Irish peasant as a root for his imagination. Russell projected what he believed to be a manageable programme for Irish renewal, urban and rural, throughout the *Irish Homestead* and *Irish Statesman*, based on local community and small-scale industry. The commitment such work required still troubled him in *The earth breath*. Russell wrote with some doubt, but no humility, of an angel's epitaph to his career in 'Epilogue'.

He has built his monument
With the winds of time as strife,
Who could have before he went
Written on the book of life.

To the stars from which he came
Empty handed, he goes home;
He who might have wrought in flame
Only traced upon the foam.[59]

For all his anxiety, Russell found himself in the quotidian. The major work of his career was as editor and journalist, his finest poems those of the moment,

58 Ibid. 11.   59 Ibid. 94.

his best prose polemic. Self-awareness of this fact grew with his increased social standing. Yeats had long identified Russell's leadership potential, first as a key figure in Dublin Theosophy. But Russell became something more as the new century turned. He married Violet North, an English occultist, in 1898. He had children, his two surviving sons, Brian and Diarmuid, born in 1900 and 1902. He began to host Sunday night gatherings from 1900 at his house in Coulson Avenue, Rathgar, with his near neighbours Maud Gonne and Constance Markievicz. He imported the doctrine of co-operation from the fields to art. *The divine vision*, of 1904, suggests the collaborative effort of a poet engaged with the world. Russell's 'Comrades in the craft', to whom the volume was dedicated, were Tom Keohler, Susan Mitchell, George Roberts, James Starkey, Susan Varian and Elizabeth Young, most of whom contributed to Russell's 1904 anthology, *New songs*. Of these six, George Roberts was a founding member of the publishing house of Maunsel and Company, and James Starkey we will meet again as the editor of the *Dublin Magazine*, under the pseudonym of Seumas O'Sullivan. Russell's relationship with Susan Mitchell is the most complicated. His editorial assistant to the *Irish Homestead* and the *Irish Statesman*, Mitchell is often supposed, but not yet proved, to have been Russell's lover. The status of their affection is unclear; but certainly the depth of Russell's despair at her death in 1926 suggests uncommon affection.

In 1904, Russell's gathered strength made him combative. There is definite change, from the regretful to martial, between *The earth breath* and *The divine vision*. Russell is now intent to act, his experience of Ireland beyond the metropolis and his widening social circle both prompting 'A farewell' to previous doubt.

I am fired by a Danaan whisper of battles afar
    in the world,
And my thought is no longer of peace, for
    banners in dream are unfurled,
And I pass from the council of stars and of
    hills to a life that is new:
And I bid to you stars and you mountains a
    tremulous long adieu.

I will come once again as a master, who played
    here as child in my dawn.
I will enter the heart of the hills where the gods
    of the old world are gone.
And will war like the bright Hound of Ulla
    with princes of earth and of sky.

> For my dream is to conquer the heavens and
> battle for kingship on high.[60]

Here is the George Russell of this book, a man fighting for a new Ireland of his own mind's eye. It is an Ireland of constant controversy, of pamphlet and periodical attacks, of a fugitive press that flares up and fades, of agricultural, labour and social relations debated through media long lost to the general reader. The cultural movements in Ireland from 1890 to 1930 were fragmentary, shifting phenomena. The best way to address them is through the media of their first expression, through the *Irish Homestead*, *Irish Statesman*, *Sinn Féin* and *Tomorrow*. From here we can trace their engagement with, and effect on, the cultures of Europe and the world, their readers' pages containing letters from Australia to India, their reviews conduits to developments in thought from Bergson to Einstein. This book is itself a revival, in miniature, of an author and a culture that we have neglected. It portrays an editor, journalist, prose writer, poet and painter in the full light of his engagement with the broad spectrum of Irish cultural and political life, from anarchism to nationalism, from literature to science. This book gives some sense of these hidden Irelands, blooms with petals now pressed tight between dusty pages of crumbling journals. It promotes understanding of a culture vital and polemical, idealistic and imaginative. It presents George Russell, over four decades and more, as a centre of intellectual energy, his place in a new Ireland restored.

---

60 G. Russell, *The divine vision.* 38-9.

1 / Deep foundation: 1905–12

George Russell was appointed editor of the *Irish Homestead* in August 1905. A weekly journal established to support the (IAOS), the co-operative movement founded by Sir Horace Plunkett in 1894, the *Irish Homestead* was a nineteenth-century-style miscellany, with editorial notes, news, domestic and international, agricultural information and reviews. Its first issue was published on 9 March 1895 under the editorship of Thomas Finlay, a Jesuit priest, scholar and co-operator, at a price of one penny. True to Plunkett's belief that industry required imagination, the *Irish Homestead* maintained a twin interest in material and intellectual development, with advertisement for cream separators and the poetry of Christina Rossetti, recently deceased.[1]

Ecumenical in his interests, Plunkett meanwhile courted the Literary Revival through contact with W.B. Yeats, who spoke to the IAOS annual conference at the Antient Concert Rooms on 3 November 1897. Yeats' words were revealing. 'The thinkers of antiquity', he spoke, 'thought that the tilling of the soil and the hoarding of cattle were the true foundation of the State, and surely it is better to live among hills and fields than in dark cities and filthy factories.'[2] The wilful romanticism of Yeats' vision of rural life should not deter our recognition of his identification of the co-operative movement with the foundation of a new state. Here, a quarter century before independence, we have Yeats laying a corner stone to an ambitious project, a union between culture and industry that would replace the fractured consensus of Irish politics post-Parnell. For

> Those who were working at Irish literature and at purely intellectual things were, just so far as they were really idealists, able to value a practical movement just like the present one. There is no greater fallacy than the common fallacy that the idealist despised practical movements. How could he despise them? Would not all his own work be fruitless unless all

---

1 Early funding of the *Irish Homestead* was unorthodox. Horace Plunkett extracted £3000 for agricultural co-operation from Sir Henry Cochrane on 1 April 1897 with the promise that Plunkett would use his influence to obtain a baronetcy on Cochrane's behalf. £1000 of this was diverted to the *Irish Homestead*. Nepotism has rarely served a better end. Plunkett diaries.   2 'An eventful conference', *IH*, 6 Nov. 1897. 742.

kinds of practical work, all kinds of practical movements went on about him?[3]

Yeats showed his appreciation for the co-operatives by suggesting they employ Russell. Partly driven by concern for his friend's increasingly intense visions, Yeats thus made one of his most important interventions in Irish life. By persuading Russell to join the IAOS, he provided a channel for his contemporary's sometimes wild evangelism.[4] Plunkett first met Russell on 19 November 1897; Plunkett's diary describes him as 'a £60 a year clerk in Pim's'.[5] A 'poet, mystic, theosophist', Plunkett thought Russell would 'be a success'.[6] After Russell departed Dublin to organise rural banks in 1897, the editorship of the *Irish Homestead* was transferred to J.K. Montgomery before Russell's fellow Theosophist, H.F. Norman, took the post in August 1900. Norman was sympathetic to the Gaelic League and was keen to reciprocate Yeats and company's interest in the co-operatives, announcing that the *Irish Homestead* would 'keep abreast of the literary movement in Ireland' as 'business alone can neither make a nation great nor a newspaper attractive. Besides business, there must be imagination, beauty and humour.'[7]

Norman introduced the themes that Russell later advanced in his creation of the *Irish Homestead* as the most consistently creative organ of cultural and industrial opinion in Ireland of the first two decades of the twentieth century. Development, education, the foundation of libraries and the need for technical instruction were all subjects that Russell, like Norman, addressed with enthusiasm. Norman, however, lacked Russell's credentials with the cultural revival, a movement that enamoured Plunkett in the years prior to Russell's appointment. Plunkett attended the first production of Russell's play *Deirdre* in August 1903; 'rarely', he wrote in his private diary, 'have I seen more beautiful acting'.[8] He toured a Glens of Antrim feis organised by Joseph Biggar in June 1904 and, with all the patrician bearing of his caste, declared it 'a day to be remembered', with '5000 there, I daresay, and not a drunken man'.[9] Immediate to Russell's appointment he lunched at Mount Trenchard with Bertrand Russell, Douglas Hyde, Alice Stopford Green and Roger Casement. He found these last two 'so predominantly anti-English' that there could be 'nothing constructive in them'.[10] Russell, however, was a man of hidden enthusiasms, an adept of secret societies; he could deliver the revival's energy to Plunkett's own programme for national rejuvenation in the *Irish Homestead*. Russell brought his full personality to the journal. He had by 1905 already served a useful apprenticeship in the co-opera-

3 Ibid.   4 Roy Foster suggests that Yeats encouraged Russell's 1897 enlistment in the co-operative movement as a means to root his imagination in a more circumspect version of reality. See R. Foster, *W.B. Yeats*. 185–6.   5 19 Nov. 1897, Plunkett diaries.   6 Ibid.   7 'Ourselves', *IH*, 16 Nov. 1901. 758.   8 22 Aug. 1903, Plunkett diaries.   9 30 June 1904, Plunkett diaries.   10 30 July 1905, Plunkett diaries.

tive movement. Travelling the length and breadth of Ireland, he promoted himself as the intellectual abroad. We can see him in a group photograph of IAOS organisers in the *Irish Homestead* of April 1903, present at an official congress. Surrounded by gents in bowler hats, Russell stares out with full beard and artisan's cap, every inch the artist among the workers. He held a special position in the movement as agent between ideal and reality, praising in his conference speech the co-operatives'

> spirit of human feeling and of faith in the progress of humanity. He had often wondered at the marvellous way in which the movement had been kept living when it seemed as if its funds had come to an end, and it appeared as if the powers which guide the destinies of man had carried the faith on which they had been working, and made it a working capital at the Bank (loud applause).[11]

The *Irish Homestead* was first published to support Plunkett's ambitions for co-operation. Russell's genius was to make this task intrinsic to a commentary on Irish life. Realising a potentially huge readership among the rural classes of Ireland, Russell set out to make his mark. Criticising co-operative societies that did not regulate their affairs efficiently, he combined the rhetoric of self-help with a belief in the inevitable advantage to be gained from scientific efficiency. By this he manipulated the motivating language of Ireland's two major political movements to the benefit of his own cause; nationalists demanded home control of industry while unionists insisted that manufacture could not survive outside an empire that realised business' best interests. So Russell manoeuvred the *Irish Homestead* as circumstance demanded, in a public space cleared of the detritus of past failures. 'The young Ireland of fifty years ago grew into this old Ireland which is so futile', but 'we trust that the young Ireland of to-day will do better, and help to gently bundle the people who promise much and do nothing into the limbo, where all futilities and humbugs go in the long run.'[12] Russell scanned the columns of the *Cork Examiner*, the *Irish Peasant* and the *Longford Leader* for any negative reaction to his project. He also knew, from his days as a rural organiser, of the importance of the clergy to his ambitions. It is often supposed, mistakenly, that Russell was antagonistic to all organised religion on account of his Theosophical beliefs. His early editorship of the *Irish Homestead* does not bear this presumption out as fact. The journal was careful to praise clerical support where it was given and to name churchmen who had achieved significant success in their parishes. So we find Thomas Finlay, himself a secretary of the IAOS, credited as founder of the Home Industries Society, and a

11 'The organisers' dinner', *IH*, 25 April 1903. 341.   **12** 'The laziness of elected persons', *IH*, 2 Sept. 1905. 654.

Father Maguire with stewardship of co-operative development in Dromore, Co. Tyrone.[13]

By 1906, Russell placed a vision of the ideal life before the co-operatives. For co-operation was never, in the pages of the *Irish Homestead*, a purely economic theory. Yes, the foundation of productive, mutually supporting societies was the first aim. But the desire to improve living standards partnered a belief that survival was no longer the minimum standard. It is perhaps no coincidence that the IAOS was founded but three years after the Parnell split; co-operation was a mutual enterprise that promoted union of interest between its members. As the new Ireland fought free from faction, the *Irish Homestead* dedicated itself to questions beyond the immediate, to problems of culture, education and literacy. These last were previously the preserve of the leisured classes. Russell sought to change this. 'When land purchase has been completed', he wrote,

> and the great families who, however inadequately, kept up the tradition of a cultured class in Ireland, are gone, as they will go for the most part – for families with wealth untied to local possessions will inevitably gravitate to other countries – what kind of a country will it be from the intellectual point of view? There are no bookshops in Ireland outside Dublin, Belfast, Cork, Derry, Limerick, and perhaps one or two other towns. In other countries the peasant has his library. We in Ireland must try not to lose all interest in the higher thought or culture of the world. In the democracy of the future every man must be his own duke.[14]

Russell set the *Irish Homestead* to teach the new Ireland its potential. He did this through art, economics and literature. Since late 1905 the journal had published a series of paintings by the nineteenth-century French painter Millet. The first was a reproduction of *The sower* in October that year, accompanied by an essay to explain the painting's meaning. Painted in 1850, *The sower* shows a young peasant walking downhill from left to right. In his left hand he steadies a bag of seed wrapped over his shoulder. His right hand sows. The entire effect is of a modern colossus, the subject huge in the foreground against the shadowy trees of far perspective. The painting symbolises the peasant's epic quality and his mastery of the earth's cycles. In mid-nineteenth-century France it was viewed by radical critics as a liberation of the working man to the rights he was due.[15] In Ireland some fifty years later we find the native rural classes inspired to

13 'Irish clergymen and Irish civilisation', *IH*, 7 Oct. 1905. 753–4.   14 'Village libraries', *IH*, 31 Mar. 1906. 242.   15 In the 1850s 'radical critics like Castagnary and Thoré-Burger, defending Millet and Courbet, claimed that the tradition of naturalism which stemmed from 17th-century Holland was one that spoke for individualism and for democratic values, rather than for government and religious authority. This attitude was surprisingly widespread, and pitted paintings of

emulate the primal achievement of their French model. Rural depopulation was a problem to both France and Ireland, the workers migrating to the cities in one and sailing abroad in the other. To portray the peasant as master of his own fate was in its context revolutionary, Russell showing the rural labourer as connected to a reality basic to any Irish revival. For Millet's

> figure has more of the elemental strength of some physical force – the wind, the spring rains, the passing of the seasons – than any other exponent of the changing and less durable rights of man. Such a man, employed in such a labour, we feel to be among human beings, the prime and most authentic embodiment of cosmic energy. It is he who traps that energy nearest to its source, the stream of whose abundance he is the prime recipient, fertilising the whole field of human activities.[16]

We know of Russell's passion for revelation. We can see it here revealed in physical action, a suggestion of force that echoes through Russell's subsequent career as propagandist of figures diverse as James Connolly and Terence Mac-Swiney. There follows in the *Irish Homestead* a reproduction of a second work by Millet, the drawing of *The shepherdess*, completed in 1855.[17] This picture shows a young girl, shawled and leaning upon a long stick, looking at the ground before a small rise upon which her sheep graze behind her. The image is peaceful and iconic, the shepherdess lost in thought as she meditates oblivious to her surrounds. *The shepherdess* informed Russell that humanity's connection to the living earth was the substance of its future well-being. But Russell was not interested in the creation of the Irish peasant as an icon of primitive virtue. He was concerned instead with the link between Irish rural life and the advance of the modern world. By absorbing the belief that they formed the link between past and future, Irish co-operators ensured a stable, national evolution towards modernity.

To support this Russell created an image of the co-operatives as allies to other advanced intellectual movements in Ireland. These other bodies were driven, appropriately given Russell's appreciation of Thomas Carlyle, by great men of vision. First, was the Gaelic League. 'Douglas Hyde, for example, is an excep-

rural life and landscape against paintings of religious and historical subjects. In practical terms, this meant the identification of values of individual choice, freedom, and plein-air methods with artistic freedom, and the identification of traditional beaux-arts subjects and studio methods with official approbation.' In Robert Herbert et al, *Jean-François Millet*. 11. Russell's own paintings bear witness to this rural radicalism; the peasant landscapes that now seem vague and formless then formed a connection between the country and modernity that we now cannot see. **16** 'Art and the sower', *IH*, 14 Oct. 1905. 754. **17** 'The romance of agriculture', *IH*, 4 Nov. 1905. 803. Russell used unusual methods to promote the excitements of rural life; this same issue reproduces a photograph of the Creevelea derby, a race between young men on donkeys.

tional man. Other people talked about nationality. He has induced thousands of people to be Gaelic in their speech and manner of life.'[19] Second, the national theatre. Russell disliked the image of the Irish peasant put forward in John Millington Synge's *Playboy of the western world* but was willing to credit Yeats with being 'an exceptional man'.[20] 'We may like or dislike the Irish dramatic movement on Mr Yeats's lines, but he did the creative work, and we hold it is better to have done something good or bad than to have merely held an idle or empty dream which came to nothing.'[21] Synge is often credited with producing the first vital image of the Irish peasant on stage. But there is nothing more real in his depiction of Mayo than there is in Russell's image of the countryman after Millet. Both Synge and Russell trade icons in competition over the future direction of Irish cultural, and by implication, national, even industrial, development. For the workers of any future state would come from the countryside. To be assimilated to a modernising project without destabilising it, the Irish peasant had to be trained to new standards of self-expression and perception. The swearing and womanising in Synge's work was simply inappropriate to Russell's model of efficiency. To regulate this unrolling vision of the future, Russell in turn suggested a new role for Anglo-Ireland. Every man might be duke of his own kingdom but there could be no harm if he were taught the laws of fealty by old masters. To Russell,

> Rural Ireland, now rapidly becoming an Ireland of small proprietors, requires three things. It requires better methods in farming, better methods in business, and a more intellectual and brighter social life. The County Committee of Agriculture, the IAOS and its co-operative associations, are working at the economic side of the problem, while the Gaelic movement, with numberless less-known associations, are working on the social side.[22]

Russell's motivation was to place the *Irish Homestead* and the co-operative movement at the vanguard of Irish intellectual development. Outside commentators recognised this fact; the English journalist Sydney Brooks, a columnist for the *Daily Mail* and the *Morning Post*, published a comparison of co-operation, the Gaelic League and Sinn Féin in a 1907 book entitled *The new Ireland*. All three shared a determination to redefine Irish cultural and practical life in terms that Russell identified with the poetry of the young Padraic Colum. *Wild earth*, Colum's first collection, shows Russell's definite influence. Its range of rural sub-

19 'The position of Sir Horace Plunkett', *IH*, 6 April 1907. 261.   **20** Ibid.   **21** Ibid.   **22** 'The future of the Irish aristocracy', *IH*, 1 Feb. 1908. 82.

jects might be taken from Millet as 'The plougher's first lines trade on the reader's visual sense, "Sunset and silence! A man: around him earth/ savage, earth broken" '.[23] 'A drover' invokes a reality that is entirely the American poet Walt Whitman's;

> O! the smell of the beasts,
> The wet wind in the morn;
> And the proud and hard earth
> Never broken for corn.[24]

The *Irish Homestead* praised *Wild earth* extravagantly.

> Padraic Colum is the first Irish poet who has chosen to write of the common life. He has not gone, like W.B. Yeats, to fairyland for inspiration, nor taken any obscure light of the soul to mean the light of the world. He has not looked down on his people like Mr Synge and the writers of his school, to whom life is only a subject for art. He has not looked up to them, unwittingly idealising all his characters, like so many sentimentalists, who write as if every Irish peasant was only a little lower than the angels. Padraic Colum is in love with the normal. He feels with truth that there is a substance of more noble poetry in the daily average than in the exceptions. He walks among the people, accepting them for what they are, in the same way Whitman, Burns, and the great masters of everyday life, the rarest of all sentiments in literature.[25]

Here we have Yeats and Synge the fantasists, with Colum Christ-like in acceptance of normality's flawed potential. The submerged, and longstanding, competition between literary factions that surrounded Russell and Yeats exposes itself here, as each promotes a true idea of national life. Russell supported a variety of writers adjacent to his co-operative project throughout his career, a fact that earned Yeats' scorn in 'To a poet, who would have me praise certain bad poets, imitators of his and mine'. Important to Russell in the first decade of the twentieth century were Colum, George Birmingham (the pen name of the Reverend J.O. Hannay whose position as a Church of Ireland clergyman ensured his writings on behalf of the IAOS were doubly treasured) and James

---

23 P. Colum, *Wild earth*. 1.   **24** Ibid. 4.   **25** 'Notes of the week' (cited subsequently as 'NOTW') *IH*, 14 Dec. 1907. 972.   **26** All three benefited from Russell's patronage. See for example, 'NOTW', *IH*, 11 Jan. 1908. 23. 'NOTW', *IH*, 4 Sept. 1909. 720. Macmillan published James Stephens due to Russell's direct intervention. See letter from Russell to Sir Frederick Macmillan of 27 October 1911,

Stephens.[26] James Joyce also contributed to the *Irish Homestead* between 1904 and 1910, despite his later dismissal, not even original, of it as the 'pig's paper'.[27] Russell himself used the journal to educate his affiliates in the radical potential of select poetry. The comparison of Padraic Colum to Walt Whitman is not incidental. For Whitman was the artistic stimulus to any social development that Russell envisaged. *Leaves of grass* was first published in Britain in 1868 and Whitman corresponded with Edward Dowden, bane of Yeats' later *Autobiographies*, throughout the 1870s. Whitman's poetry enjoyed a controversial popularity and *Leaves of grass* was temporarily withdrawn from the library shelves of Trinity College Dublin. Russell first read Whitman in the late 1880s and one of his first polemical essays, 'Priest or hero?', published in the *Irish Theosophist* in 1897, was prefaced with a quotation from the American writer.[28] Whitman was the model of the national poet to which Russell aspired, his poetry a spur to Russell's proposed development of the Irish mind. With a recent Russian revolution in mind, Russell observed that

> All the unrest over Europe, the revolutions and peasant uprisings are attempts of despairing humanity to bring about some happy and secure form of life. We should not leave to the new races the work of regeneration. We should sing for ourselves the song which the pioneer poet of New Worlds made for his race:
>
> > Have the elder races halted? Do they droop and end
> > Their lesson,
> > Wearied, over there beyond the seas?
> > We take up the task eternal, and the burden and the
> > Lesson,
> > Pioneers, O Pioneers!'[29]

Russell's rhapsody imagines Ireland as a space free from the trammels of its past history. It is a territory open to new investigation, to reinvigoration and the creation of new ideals of national association. Whitman's work provides the model for an Ireland refreshed from bitterness, self-aware and capable of creating its own identity. The *Irish Homestead* felt that 'There is in Ireland at present an atmosphere akin to that described by Whitman, in that exquisite poem when he describes, after the Civil War in the United States, the untying of the last tent ropes, the wind blowing fresh over the fields and prairies with infinite vistas

Denson typescript. 200.   **27** Joyce published 'Song' from *Chamber music* in *IH*, 17 Sept. 1910. 785. Russell previously arranged publication of Joyce's 'The sisters' and 'Eveline' in the *Irish Homestead* on 13 August 1904 and 10 September 1904 respectively. H.F. Norman and not Russell, as many scholars mistakenly suggest, was then editor.   **28** See G. Russell, 'Priest or Hero?' *Irish Theosophist*, 15 April 1897. 127–31. *Irish Theosophist*, 15 May 1897. 148–52.   **29** 'Agricultural communities', *IH*, 30 Dec. 1905. 950.

revealed in every direction.'[30] To a country crippled by congested districts and paralysed the previous decade by parliamentary struggle in the wake of Parnell, Whitman's message of post-traumatic recovery was powerful. As the *Irish Homestead* reminded its readers, 'It must be remembered that Whitman is an American, a member of a race upon whose soaring ambitions the terror of age-worn conventions is powerless to cast its malefic shadow.'[31]

Other movements than co-operation were equally desperate to liberate Ireland from its disabling past. Sinn Féin, founded by Arthur Griffith, himself an admirer of Russell, advocated a programme, extreme by its contemporary standards, of total indigenous control of Irish affairs. This was more than the *Irish Homestead*, pledged to independence from political association, could explicitly support. Padraic Colum was a regular contributor to the *Sinn Féin* weekly that appeared under Griffith's editorship from 1906. One of his major contributions was a series of articles on Walt Whitman. Colum's appreciation of the American poet stresses his radical potential; to Colum, 'Whitman is consciously the poet of his age, the poet of our world, the modern world. Whitman is consciously the interpreter of a movement – that movement for the emancipation of the individual which we call Democracy.'[32] Democracy was the shared standard of *Sinn Féin* and the *Irish Homestead*, its terms negotiable through the subterranean contacts each journal shared with the other.

Russell had given early, and favourable notice of his Sinn Féin contemporaries in a rousing editorial to promote self-help among his readers. 'Now there is a new movement', he wrote in January 1906, 'springing up in Ireland, with whose political aims we cannot deal, as they are not our business, but it has adopted a Gaelic motto, which, being roughly paraphrased, means, "Let us look after ourselves". We are heartily in agreement with this spirit.'[33] And with the substance too, if truth be told. Russell had subscribed to Griffith's movement from 1905.[34] He also preserved a strong dislike of Sinn Féin's direct antagonist, the dominant nationalist Irish Parliamentary Party, barely hidden in the *Irish Homestead*. Goaded by the equal antipathy that John Dillon and T.W. Russell held for the IAOS, Russell positioned the co-operative movement to independence from orthodox nationalism and unionism; the result was a self-help credo that was Sinn Féin in essence. *Sinn Féin* in turn supported Russell's personal ambition. It positively reviewed an exhibition of Russell's painting and evinced similar literary tastes to the *Irish Homestead*, praising Whitman and Birming-

---

30 'National action required', *IH*, 10 Feb. 1906. 101–2.　**31** Diarmuid, 'Walt Whitman', *IH*, 24 Feb. 1906. 146.　**32** P. Colum, 'Walt Whitman – I', *Sinn Féin*, 8 June 1907. 3.　**33** 'Let us look after ourselves', *IH*, 20 Jan. 1906. 41.　**34** Griffith acknowledged Russell's subscription when he was still editor of the *United Irishman*, the journal that preceded *Sinn Féin*, in a letter dated 16 Dec. 1905. Griffith was 'exceedingly glad of your letter, for you are one of the men whose good opinion I sincerely value'. National Library of Ireland (cited subsequently as NLI) ms 10872.

ham. Connection between Russell and his radical nationalist contemporaries was assumed by their readership; a reader asking for a copy of Colum's *Wild earth* in a Dublin bookshop was offered Russell's *The earth breath* by mistake.[35] Perhaps the Theatre of Ireland production of Russell's play *Deirdre* at the Abbey Theatre in December 1907 suggests the closest link between Russell and Griffith. *Sinn Féin* warmly welcomed the play, archly observing that Russell 'has naturally and easily in his play "Deirdre" struck freely the note of heroic simplicity which Mr Yeats has been striving at all his playwriting life to attain to', having 'so far failed'.[36] Yeats' sin of commission for Synge's *Playboy of the western world* was still fresh in Griffith's memory. A ferocious controversialist, Griffith was not to be crossed and Yeats' comeuppance was the rival promotion of Russell's genius. Beyond this personal antagonism, the cast list for *Deirdre* is revealing. On stage were Seamus O'Sullivan, playing Fergus, the Countess Markievicz as Lavarcam and Maire nic Shuiblaigh as Deirde. All three had impeccable national credentials and their participation in Russell's play was public recognition of the vital position its author, the editor of the *Irish Homestead*, held in Irish intellectual life.

Russell managed his public editorship of the *Irish Homestead* carefully while he conducted a radical private life. Aware that readers antagonistic to the economic pretensions of the co-operative movement monitored his every word, he allowed his nationalist sympathies to emerge only by implication from the subjects that he addressed. Self-help was the key phrase of his editorial engagement, his practical ideal of the co-operative movement all the while developing a potential state within a nation, an administrative, cultural and economic body incipient to the new Ireland that might emerge. Russell largely avoided traditional controversies over home rule or union, both potentially disastrous to the social consensus that he tried to create through the *Irish Homestead*, by a redefinition of Irish sovereignty. Independence was not to Russell in the gift of Westminster, or indeed College Green. Freedom was a state of mind common to all the great cultures of human history. Appropriately, Russell attended a Sinn Féin demonstration in the company of his wife, Violet Russell, on the night of Monday 23 March, 1908 to hear

> Mr Bulmer Hobson, of Belfast, who ... was loudly cheered, and emphasised the doctrine of self-reliance. Ireland had relied on British Liberalism and British Toryism – and now it was time to rely upon itself. They stood for an independent Ireland, and they would sink all differences in the love of Ireland and the determination to make it free and prosperous.
>
> The Chairman then put the resolution. 'All in favour of it', he said, 'will say "Aye".' A mighty shout of 'Aye' made the vast room tremble.

35 'Wild earth and its tamers', *Sinn Féin*, 21 Dec. 1907. 3.   **36** 'The theatre of Ireland', *Sinn Féin*, 21 Dec. 1907. 3.

'Against', continued the Chairman, 'will say "no".' 'Carried unanimously', said Mr Sweetman amidst a tempest of cheers.[37]

Even allowing for *Sinn Féin*'s enthusiasm for its own point of view, we can well imagine Russell taking his place in the crowded room and cheering loudly for Hobson's motion. Russell developed the substance of such support to a new understanding of co-operative potential shortly after in the *Irish Homestead*.

> Athens, Sparta, Corinth, and other places much more famous than Ireland, and quite as world-famous as England, worked the mine of humanity within areas as small as County Cork, and got more human wealth out of them than has ever been got before or since. When things are worked on too large a scale with central control, there is no freedom of development, and without perfect freedom to develop the result is mediocrity. If we are told, 'You are a citizen of the universe', we are only mildly elated, and we hardly see our way to institute changes for the better in its administration. But if we were living in the independent Kingdom of Sligo, we would feel it was not beyond the power of one man to influence its destinies and help to set it on the path of rivalling Athens or Sparta. The smaller the community, the better the human results.[38]

Patrick Kavanagh, writing some thirty years after this, is credited with the invention of the theory of the parish and the universe, of the local being the necessary first point from which all meditations on the general proceed. Here we have Russell, whom we know Kavanagh admired enough in his early adulthood to walk to Dublin to visit, argue exactly that a local society could be the first stage in the creation of a new Irish order. Russell's Atlantic Sparta, with citizens created to participate in a society on the fringes of the Western seaboard, encroached to the heart of Yeats' imaginative territory. His ideal of rural community combines a number of ideas then current to Irish cultural nationalism: economic and social self-determination, the ideal west of Ireland and the need to instruct subjects of the British Empire to Irish citizenship. Russell's projection follows what Padraic Colum, writing in *Sinn Féin*, called Walt Whitman's

> advice to States ... 'Produce great personalities, the rest follows'. Whitman would have the ideal poet absorb the life of his country; he would have him absorb the world's masterpieces in art and literature, he would have him absorb art and metaphysics, knowing that the true poet would soon rid himself of what is accidental and fantastic, finding life all around him.[39]

37 'The hosting of Sinn Féin', *Sinn Féin*, 28 Mar. 1908. 2.   **38** 'NOTW', *IH*, 11 April 1908. 283.
39 P. Colum, 'Walt Whitman – IV', *Sinn Féin*, 29 June 1907. 4.

Russell proposed the merger of national life with art in the publication of his long poem, 'On behalf of some untraditional Irishmen', in *Sinn Féin* of November 1908. This work is Russell's attempt to create synthesis of the forces that surrounded him, his call to the hoplites of an Irish Sparta. Its publication coincided with Arthur Griffith's own appraisal of the absolute suitability of co-operation to the Sinn Féin cause. As background, there had been bitter dispute over institutional funding for the IAOS from the Department of Agriculture and Technical Instruction since 1906. Parliamentary Party functionaries mistrusted the IAOS on two counts; first they considered Horace Plunkett to be a unionist whose stated desire for national improvement through self-help in agriculture was cover for an attempt to influence the rural nationalist majority that supplied much of their vote. Second, the Parliamentary Party had strong links to country traders, with John Dillon one of the largest. Its newspaper, the *Freeman's Journal*, attacked the IAOS, unfairly, as a trading body that did not deserve Government support to disadvantage its competitors. The result of such active distrust was the suspension of the government grant to the IAOS in 1908. Griffith was pleased at this outcome; the IAOS, he wrote, 'is now an absolutely independent Irish organisation, self-governing, self-reliant, and self-supportive – Sinn Fein in agriculture'.[40]

Russell published his appeal 'On behalf of some untraditional Irishmen' simultaneously. It starts, unsurprisingly, with an attack on his Parliamentary Party antagonists. 'They call us aliens/ we are told,/ Because our wayward visions stray/ From that dim banner they unfold.'[41] The poem has two movements, the first a definition of orthodox Irish nationalist history as moribund, the second a call to arms. Throughout, Russell combines an aesthetic Calvinism sceptical of false icons and images with a pseudo-Imperial appeal to rally to self-help's flag. The battle is joined between those enslaved to dead symbols, now void of meaning in the twentieth century, and those dedicated to future vision, the poem a conflict between received and projected forms of Irish identity. The first movement ends with the speaker's mocking those who

> ... would have us join their dirge,
> The worship of an extinct fire,
> In which they move beyond the verge
> Where races all outworn expire.
> The worship of the dead is not
> A worship that our hearts allow,
> Though every furious shade was wrought
> With thorns above the brow.[42]

---

40 *Sinn Féin*, 14 Nov. 1908. 2.   **41** G. Russell, 'On behalf of some untraditional Irishmen', *Sinn Féin*, 14 Nov. 1908. 3.   **42** Ibid.

There is anger here unusual to Russell's work, even if the religious inflection is familiar from his Theosophical writings, themselves controversial. Attacks on constitutional nationalism were standard fare of radical nationalist newspapers and journals. Harsh criticism helped differentiate *Sinn Féin* from the *Freeman's Journal* and mutual abuse was an accepted form of business. But Russell takes the poem in a new direction. We could say that Irish political poetry of the period typically followed one trajectory: criticism of the established consensus followed by its unfavourable comparison to some forgotten, tragic or neglected, to the author's mind, national figure. Charles Parnell was a particular favourite. Russell, with his years' experience rousing the unwilling to work for Theosophical and co-operative societies, issued a different appeal, his poem a recruiting call to an army whose terms of engagement were not yet set:

> We are less children of this time
> Than of some nation yet unborn
> Or empire in the womb of time.
> We hold the Ireland in the heart
> More than the land our eyes have seen,
> And love the goal for which we start
> More than the tale of what has been.
> The generations as they rise
> May live the life man lived before,
> Still hold the thought once held as wise,
> Go in and out by the same door.
> We leave the easy peace it brings;
> The few we are will still unite
> In fealty to unseen kings
> Of unimaginable light.[43]

It is standard to wonder the effect that Yeats' writing had on the genesis of Irish revolution. Russell's contribution to the cause has been less considered. This peaceable, pipe-smoking co-operator who believed, we are told, in the common unity of humankind would not, all assume, advocate violence. The evidence suggests otherwise. 'On behalf of some untraditional Irishmen' is the perfect recruitment poem. It gives an image of stale life before conflict and argues for action to reinvigorate reality. There is an ideal to fight for, that Ireland of the heart, and a dismissal of 'easy peace' that would recur in English poetry on the outbreak of the First World War. The fealty we owe to unseen kings is suitably ambiguous, appealing to the Gaelic romanticism of *Sinn Féin* readers like

43 G. Russell, 'On behalf of some untraditional Irishmen', *Sinn Féin*, 14 Nov. 1908. 3.

Patrick Pearse. A revival of ancient Irish society was a long held aim of an influential section of cultural and political activists, making the idea of Kingship less archaic than it now appears. The poem finishes:

> We would no Irish sign efface,
> But yet we would as gladly hail
> The first-born of the Coming Race
> As the last splendour of the Gael,
> No blazoned banner we unfold:
> One charge alone we give to Youth,
> Against the sceptred myth to hold
> The golden heresy of truth.[44]

Russell was, we know, editor of the *Irish Homestead*, a Theosophist, author of *Deirdre*, a play that impressed advanced nationalist Ireland, a poet and prose writer. The one impulse that drove all his interests was a personal sense of non-conformity. It emerges here at the end of a patriotic poem that tries to raise an army of the mind and causes the great failure of 'On behalf of some untraditional Irishmen' to build on the force of sentiments established before its final lines. It is as if Russell, just at the moment of most pressure, backs away from the implications of his writing. Not ready yet to break an easy peace, he calms the situation with opaque sentiment. This is a poetic weakness; but it tells us something of Russell's psychology, of a man who had the insight of vision but not always the courage of conviction.

In this he is not unusual. But Russell's obsession with individual struggle was the positive motivation to much of his life's work. Radicalised by the end of the first decade of the twentieth century by constant struggle on behalf of the IAOS against government departments that refused funding and support to a co-operative project that worked for the benefit of all citizens, Russell developed a growing respect for continental anarchism. Readers' attention had been called to the importance of the 'great Russian thinker, Prince Kropotkin' as early as October 1905.

> A traveller through the far sundered regions of many sciences, he has laid the accumulated treasures of his wanderings before the door of the farm-stead, which he recognises as the pivot of civilisation. We know no one before who has ever invested agriculture with such a halo of romance. Who that reads his book, 'Fields, Factories and Workshops', can again doubt that the labour of the fields is capable of gratifying all the tastes and faculties of the most cultivated humanity?[45]

44 Ibid.   **45** Diarmuid, 'The romance of agriculture', *IH*, 21 Oct. 1905. 770.

Prince Peter Kropotkin was born in Russia in Moscow in 1842 and was educated at a St Petersburg military academy. He then served as an officer in a Cossack regiment in eastern Siberia, an area from which he took many of his observations of natural and social life.[46] Adjutant to the regional governor, he became increasingly disaffected with imperial bureaucracy. Leaving the army in 1867 he spent a period in Switzerland studying the International Workingmen's Association. Arrested after his return to Russia he was imprisoned before his escape, eventually, to England, in 1876. He published three major works, *The conquest of bread*, *Fields, factories, and workshops*, and *Mutual aid*. The first does not seem to have entered Russell's mind. The second two were major influences on his thinking. Kropotkin had a simple, but revolutionary, premise, that human relations are governed by the desire for mutual aid over competition. Full of the practical knowledge that Russell, from his youthful reading of Emerson and Thoreau, so appreciated, Kropotkin evangelised the need for a revised understanding of capital relations.[47]

Fields, factories and workshops was published in English in 1899. It questioned the generally held belief that national economies were most efficient when dedicated to specific types of production. Individual countries, Kropotkin argued, should not dedicate themselves specifically to agriculture or industry. This point was well taken by Russell; he was conscious of the damage that Ireland's rural subsistence had caused during the famine. Kropotkin combined his call for diversity in production with an appeal for 'integrated education',[48] whereby students would learn science and handcrafts from earliest childhood. Such teaching would 'give the society the men and women it really needs'.[49] Creation of the ideal character is a recurrent motif in Kropotkin and Russell's writing. Culture is ever the instrument to achieve civilisation; Kropotkin offered the moral, of mutual aid, that might underpin the literature of a new economy. Each village or rural commune would pursue small-scale industry and agriculture, operating as self-dependent, to as large a degree as possible, fiefs. Writers' pleas for rural utopia have been common since before Southey and Coleridge; but Kropotkin's commune, like Russell's vision of the co-operative Kingdom of Sligo, combined ethics with science in a manner impossible since Darwin's theory of evolution had upset the balance of divine creation. 'Modern knowledge', Kropotkin wrote,

---

46 A two-part account of Kropotkin's life was published in the *Irish Homestead*. See Eugene Basaroff, 'Peter Kropotkin – his life and work', *IH*, 7 Dec. 1912. 999–1000. Eugene Basaroff, 'Peter Kropotkin – his life and work', *IH*, 14 Dec. 1912. 1023–4.   **47** Russell had read Emerson by October 1887. See H. Summerfield, *That myriad-minded man.* 26. For comments on Thoreau see Diarmuid, 'Thoreau', *IH*, 17 Feb. 1906. 126–7.   **48** P. Kropotkin, *Fields, factories and workshops.* 7. **49** Ibid.

has another issue to offer the thinking men. It tells them that in order to be rich they need not take the bread from the mouths of others, but that the more rational outcome would be a society in which men, with the work of their own hands and intelligence, and by the aid of the machinery already invented and to be invented, should themselves create all imaginable riches. Technics and science will not be lagging behind if production takes such a direction. Guided by observation, analysis and experiment they will answer all possible demands ... But they guarantee, at least, the happiness that can be found in the full and varied expression of the different capacities of the human being, in work that need not be overwork, and in the consciousness that one is not endeavouring to base his own happiness on the misery of others.[50]

Fields, factories and workshops set the basis for Kropotkin's social strategy. He proposed further refinements in *Mutual aid: a factor of evolution*, published in English in 1902. The evolutionary subtitle to Kropotkin's book is important. Co-operation is, to Kropotkin, both a moral imperative and a scientific fact. Evolutionary theory post-Darwin tended, according to the author of *Mutual aid*, to stress competition between species. This, Kropotkin felt, was a culturally biased reading, the intelligentsia of the second half of the nineteenth century informed as much by perceptions of industrial society as they were by close observation of nature. Kropotkin was deeply affected by the mutual aid he saw at work in the extremes of climate he travelled in Siberia. He found that people, when pushed to the limit, instinctively helped one another survive. Kropotkin understood evolution as something different from biological adaptation; his history is based on social interaction, with empirical science providing his methods of observation. He presents his readers with an account of human development that reached its apogee in the guilds and fraternities of medieval Europe. All were crushed by that great disaster, the formation of the modern state, which bound citizens to abstract concepts of fidelity and justice, rather than ties of personal affection.

Russell no doubt could see himself in Kropotkin's description of late-nineteenth-century voluntary organisation: 'All these associations, societies, brotherhoods, alliances, institutes, and so on, which must now be counted by the ten thousand in Europe alone' are 'so many manifestations, under an infinite variety of aspects, of the same ever-living tendency of men towards mutual aid and support'.[51] Co-operation, Sinn Féin, the Gaelic League and a plethora of other committed reformers all fell under the penumbra of Kropotkin's theory. Russell was captivated by such broad rhetoric, his mind well accustomed to the

50 Ibid. 274–5.   **51** P. Kropotkin, *Mutual aid*. 284.

Theosophist Madame Blavatsky's far-flung speculations. The ancient city-states so beloved by Russell in his co-operative propaganda were likewise to Kropotkin 'the periods when institutions based on the mutual-aid tendency took their greatest developments' and 'the periods of ... greatest progress in arts, industry and science'.[52]

Russell took up Kropotkin's anarchism with enthusiasm in the *Irish Homestead*. After a protracted dispute over the spoliation of butter in transport by an English railway company, he remarked with exasperated wit that, faced with a bureaucracy that denied all responsibility, he felt a strong sympathy 'for hasty people like anarchists, dynamitards, and terrorists, who take the law into their own hands, and who blow themselves and their enemies into eternity at the same time'.[53] He put Kropotkin's policy of self-help in commerce to practical effect in August 1908 when he chaired the newly founded Sinn Féin Co-operative People's Bank after helping the institution to 'carry out the business of banker and Bill Discounter, and of Dealer in Stocks, Shares, Bonds, Debentures and other Securities to assist in the development of Irish industries'.[54] Russell's passion for independent activity fed into a general distrust of the state mechanism in Ireland that, while published in the *Irish Homestead* as co-operative propaganda, was entirely *Sinn Féin* in aspiration. In Ireland

> The affection of the people for the State is greater with us than with any other people in Europe. The State is a fetish. It is supposed to be omnipotent, to do everything. The devotion to it and the trust in it is touching. Every now and then, just as the Negro kicks his fetish, we howl and kick at the State; but we soon renew our supplications and ask it to start industries, to capitalise them, to lend money, to give money, and all the while to have untold millions of our own money lying in deposit in savings and joint-stock banks. We want to bring back self-reliance in these matters. It will be good for us in every way, publicly and privately that we cannot, in the one breath complain about the Irish administration, and ask for more assistance and more money.[55]

The creation of a co-operative citizen would, according to Russell, be evidence of true 'social evolution'.[56] It would lead the Irish from the fractious nineteenth to the modern twentieth century without fear of the working-class revolution that threatened British industry. Co-operation in the *Irish Homestead* is the bridge between the ancient and modern whose foundation Kropotkin laid.

52 Ibid. 296.   **53** 'NOTW', *IH*, 19 Jan. 1907. 45.   **54** 'The Sinn Féin bank', *Sinn Féin*, 22 August 1908. 2.   **55** 'The opening of Irish money-bags', *IH*, 2 Feb. 1907. 81.   **56** 'Science and the problem of rural life', *IH*, 12 Sept. 1908. 736.

A later generation of nature observers has raised doubts as to whether this supposed competition for food or life within each species is really the dominant factor in evolution. They have discovered mutual aid support everywhere in nature, and many think now that this co-operation between members of a same species is a far more formidable factor in the maintenance of life and in promoting progress to a higher type than the keen competition which the earlier scientists declared as the chief cause of development ... The thoughtful patriot knows that it is by the most complete development of co-operation in the national life that that life can preserve itself best. This is so if nature has any lesson for us or religion any meaning. If we fail to carry out this law then the Irish Celt must go.[57]

Russell wrote these comments the same week that British suffragettes of the Women's Social and Political Union asserted their right to full participation in national life by protest at the House of Commons. Miners also were active in pressing their claim from the start of the twentieth century and their efforts would culminate in the formation of a triple alliance of dockers, miners and railwaymen. The British political landscape was also changed by the formation of the Labour Party in 1906 as Liberals and Tories tried to adapt in response to the new reality of a widened, and increasingly disaffected, franchise. The first major result was the National Insurance Act of 1911. Russell, like many counterparts on the left wing of British labour, was against this development. He argued that any increase in the state was a decrease of individual freedom and that any benefit it promised was offset by the dependency on bureaucracy it ensured. Russell, with his belief in the socially transformative powers of the co-operative movement and his negative experience of department antagonism to the IAOS, fought any growth of the British state, memorably comparing national insurance to H.G. Wells' *Invisible man*, feeding surreptitiously off the poorest families.[58] He also felt, like many nationalists, that Ireland should learn Britain's lesson and regulate the growth of its industrial base.

Socialism, not anarchism, had emerged as the great doctrine of industrial reform in Britain. But the Irish media and political élite were strongly against it. Newspapers like the *National Democrat*, publicly committed to Irish socialism, were fugitive and badly funded. Publications critical of socialism were in the great majority. The *New Ireland Review*, a Jesuit publication contributed to by Father Thomas Finlay, wrote regularly of the falsehoods that socialist agitators offered as salvation to their audience.[59] Finlay himself delivered a report to the

---

57 'The salt which preserves a race', *IH*, 17 Oct. 1908. 837–8.   58 'The prodigal son', *IH*, 28 Oct. 1911. 845.   59 See for example the Revd R. Fullerton, 'Socialism and religion', *New Ireland Review*, Oct. 1909. 95–102. Fullerton was venomous: 'by falsehood and calumny, and lying promises which they are hopelessly incapable of fulfilling, socialist demagogues are endeavouring to find favour

IAOS convention of December 1909 in support of the co-operatives as a remedy to the ills that socialism tended across the Channel. The *Irish Homestead* reassured its readers that 'All that the organisation of industry by the State, the special ideal of Socialists, can do to affect economics, can be done in rural districts
much more effectively and economically by agricultural co-operation.'[60] Russell
kept in touch with the progress of continental reform through the pages of
English journals like the *Co-operative News*. The industrial socialist congress of
1910 had urged its members to join co-operative movements in their home
countries to unite them in federations. Russell mocked that

> Karl Marx himself, if born in Ireland, could not advance socialism one
> inch here. Henry George would have died of grief if he had lived in
> Ireland. The persuasive Mr Wells would have found all his sweetness and
> light wasted. Our one furious Irish Socialist, Bernard Shaw, showed what
> a quick intelligence he has by using Ireland simply as a pleasure ground
> on his holidays without attempting the vain task of trying to spread
> Fabian ideas. He keeps his Socialism for soft and yielding countries like
> England. We are so certain that we will take no harm from Socialists that
> we welcome any there are here into the co-operative movement in the
> belief that it will be for their good to help in something practical.[61]

The socialist should 'come in from out of the cold. He will be as welcome as any
Nationalist, Unionist, Orangeman, or Sinn Feiner; the more variety in life there
is the better.'[62] Co-operation by this standard is the social bond that will drive
Ireland to efficient modernity, free from fear of social unrest. But Russell's ironic dismissal of Marx, George, Shaw and Wells from Irish political life hides a real
interest in the development of the continental left since before 1905. His problem was ever the state. It was never, or rarely, socialism in a form that was self-
dependent. Russell was aware of the contribution that Shaw and the Webbs had
made to the scientific analysis of social conditions. He knew that the 'methods
of English Fabians, Trade Unions, and Labour members have been so successful' that they 'had an effect on Socialists in Europe, and the doctrine of social
revolution is gradually becoming a doctrine of evolution by stages'.[63] Instead of
'building barricades', labour found itself in 'sympathetic alliance with all kinds
of popular organisations. Of these the co-operative societies are the most
important, and the last move of Socialism in Europe is to seek to make the co-
operative organisations a kind of basis for a Fabian party of social expansion and
reconstruction of society.'[64]

with the labouring classes, whose condition renders them liable to fall into the sway of cunning mis-
chief-makers'. 101. **60** 'The antidotes to socialism', *IH*, 18 Dec. 1909. 1017. **61** 'NOTW', *IH*,
10 Sept. 1910. 752. **62** Ibid. **63** 'Co-operation at home and abroad', *IH*, 21 Jan. 1911. 41. **64**
Ibid.

Russell found the synthesis of popular movements attractive; Kropotkin had after all prophesied in *Mutual aid* that the growth of voluntary organisation was evidence of co-operative evolution. Russell was also trained to look at the emergence of phenomena on a global scale by his Theosophical learning. Russell chose this moment of increased solidarity, of the potential union between co-operation and forms of advanced socialism, to introduce argument on behalf of rural labour to the *Irish Homestead*. The neglected layer beneath the level of the small farmer upon which the IAOS concentrated, the landless rural worker was vulnerable to infrequent work, poor pay and worse education. In a new departure, Russell suggested that the 'labourer should also be invited to become member of rural stores, and so be given any advantages which co-operation can afford. The true co-operative spirit tries to take in everybody.'[65] There was, as ever, a political dimension to such goodwill. For

> The more we read of the real facts about what industrial nations like the English, the more certain do we feel that Ireland ought to concentrate in rural development as the means by which our people will grow most prosperous, live happiest, and be freest from the wild scenes which have made London and Liverpool seem as if revolution and civil war had broken out on their streets.[66]

It is a pleasant irony that England, and not Ireland, struggling over the passage of home rule bills and imminent paramilitary action, should be the disruptive state the *Irish Homestead* chastises. Imaginative leadership, it seems, might still redeem Ireland. Commentators other than Russell shared this opinion. Standish O'Grady, the author of the two-volume epic *History of Ireland* that prompted revival writers like Russell to the first appreciation of a national literature, entered a correspondence in the *Irish Homestead* in February and March 1910 that outlined his own personal plans for the development of Ireland's industrial and intellectual potential. Under the serial title 'The first Irish commune of the new order', O'Grady set out his ideal of rural resettlement. In his first letter of 5 February, O'Grady proposed himself as the centre of a new society that he hoped to promote. He felt 'compelled to act temporarily as a rallying point and nucleus'.[67] Like the biological cell he imagines, O'Grady's communes were to be 'creative and reproductive, shedding forth continually replicas of themselves'.[68] Communards were to come from the urban bourgeoisie, the office clerks and shop assistants of Dublin with the education to realise that the life they lived was not the ideal. O'Grady ties into ideas general to Irish cultural nationalism, of

65 'Co-operation and the problem of rural labour', *IH*, 27 May 1911. 406.   66 'Ireland and industrialism', *IH*, 19 Aug. 1911. 646.   67 S. O'Grady, 'The first Irish commune of the new order', *IH*, 5 Feb. 1910. 109.   68 Ibid.

heroic self-sacrifice, of imitation of the ancient Gaelic clan system and of vision of a pure future. 'I see here', ended O'Grady in his first letter, 'an expanding vista of things greater and more glorious than were ever dreamed of on the earth before.'[69] O'Grady was himself a convert to Whitman's poetry before Russell and there is strong suggestion here of *Leaves of Grass* and the prose work, *Democratic vistas*, of promises of a heavenly future.

O'Grady, addressing Russell as editor of the *Irish Homestead*, felt that he might 'speak for you too, though you are hidden somewhat to-day behind the mask of the HOMESTEAD',[70] thus hinting at Russell's covert passions, of anarchism, the occult and Sinn Féin self-help. But Russell would not be taken in. In the first place he was already spokesman of a successful rural movement that would instil the ideas of voluntary communism to which O'Grady aspired. Further he observed that Jean-Baptiste Godin, a philanthropist who built a foundry to support workers he attracted before transferring control of the enterprise to them, had already established such a commune at Guise in France.[71] Even in Ireland, a similar project was reported in Sir John Keane's construction of a bacon factory at Cappoquin. An IAOS sympathiser, Keane proposed to transfer his shares to a co-operative society in due course. Russell showed his enthusiasm for the project by the publication of a series of gory photographs in the *Irish Homestead* that take the reader mercilessly though the production process.[72] But Russell would not act for O'Grady. He did continue, out of deference, to publish O'Grady's letters, even as his mentor grew increasingly argumentative. By the second letter, O'Grady's ideal grew beyond a new plantation of Ireland. His aim now was to

> Declare that in the midst of all the place-hunters and money grubbers of Ireland that men can be rich without money and wealthy without ever seeing a pound, and that armed with this faith, and having first conquered themselves, a mere handful of Irish boys and girls might go forth to conquer Ireland, and through Ireland, conquer the world, and end, for all time, the dominion of the infernal Trinity, Morloch, and Belial and Mammon.[73]

Russell was, understandably, worried for his friend's sanity. His upset must only have been half that of the bemused Miss Smithson of 35 Kildare Street to whom volunteers were directed to apply. Russell tried to calm his wayward leader. He criticised O'Grady's description of Irish greed in a corrective that might also serve for Yeats' dismissal of the small merchant in 'September 1913'; 'Most of

69 Ibid.   **70** Ibid.   **71** 'A rural commune', *IH*, 5 Feb. 1910. 99–100.   **72** See 'Bacon factory at Cappoquin', *IH*, 29 Feb. 1908. 170–2. Photographs are reproduced in *IH*, 4 July 1908. 534.   **73** S. O'Grady, 'The first Irish commune of the new order', *IH*, 12 Feb. 1910. 130.

the people', Russell felt, 'whom Mr O'Grady thinks are grubbing for money are in all truth working for family as best they know how, for love, or some of the other idealisms which Mr O'Grady has a respect for'.[74] Russell continued to counsel patience as O'Grady's letters arrived. He knew that O'Grady, 'like all poets, likes the exceptional men, and writes for them'.[75] But the social reformer, in Russell's experience, thought 'humanity ... the hero' and exhibited 'infinite patience and understanding of the human failings which cause delay'.[76] O'Grady paid no attention, now addressing Russell's audience as his own. His volunteers would

> see – those who have been at all affected by the so-called Irish literary revival – that it is a tremendous descent from the life of the champions of the Red Branch and of the ruddy-complexioned, valiant warriors and writers whose camp was on the Hill of Allen, and whose captain was that very open-air hero called Finn, men who actually worshipped the Sun and the Wind and the good Earth. We worship them no more, and the more is the pity.[77]

We are now in the extremes of fantasy and Russell knew it, restricting himself to correction of O'Grady's wilder statements, many of which came from the parallel letters that O'Grady was submitting to the *Irish Peasant* at the same time he wrote to the *Irish Homestead*.[78] But what is interesting in O'Grady's mania is the collage of ideas that his letters evidence. There is a colonial sense of growth to his belief that communes will spread across the face of the earth; there is also a very late-nineteenth-century British ethic of physical fitness and regimentation, also appropriated in Ireland by Patrick Pearse at St Enda's school. All this feeds on a fear of urban revolution, the stimulus to all O'Grady's letters on communal life. His anxieties are revealed when he urges the Irish, like the Boers before them, to depart for new land.

> You know, as well as I do, that the soon-coming destruction of our modern civilization will begin in the great towns. Lord Macauley, in his later period, saw that clearly; so did Carlyle, so did Ruskin; and many others. I have been for years, studying, considering, and pondering over these things, including, amongst them in my very serious survey, Socialism, Socialistic legislation, all the schemes and nostrums of all the reformers

74 'NOTW', *IH*, 12 Feb. 1910. 123.   **75** 'NOTW', *IH*, 26 Feb. 1910. 164.   **76** Ibid.   **77** S. O'Grady, 'The first Irish commune of the new order', *IH*, 26 Feb. 1910. 108.   **78** O'Grady's correspondence was carried on in the *Irish Peasant* from 5 Feb. 1910 to 16 April 1910. His proposals were met with some scepticism; the *Irish Peasant*'s letters' pages major debate centred on the suitability of horse-racing as a pastime for the new commune.

and humanitarians, and my final conclusion, arrived at, not yesterday, or the day before, may be summed up in one short word – 'Trek'.[79]

The image of a race freed from enslavement, whether real or imagined, is as old as the escape from Egypt. By raising the ghost of the Boer trek O'Grady tries to bring his new commune to the modern world. Carlyle and Ruskin had attempted this the previous century, but with little success. Carlyle's *Past and present* argued for the rural welfare of workers while Ruskin founded a Guild of St George in 1878 that aimed to transform unused countryside to productive agriculture. O'Grady cast himself in line of the prophets and waited for his commune to form. But despite the collection of over one hundred signatories prepared to join him, O'Grady's project never materialised. The abstract Ireland of space free from capital contamination was a powerful image of attraction to the romantically minded; but, as Russell remarked, even Robinson Crusoe did not have to pay taxes.[80]

The problem then was to find a social model that could adapt to the demands of modernity, of industry regulated by culture. Russell did this in the *Irish Homestead* by the vigorous promotion of the co-operative ideal and the creation of an image of the world before his readers as a fast-moving, ever evolving mass that needed national energy to sustain it. He noticed 'science encroaching everywhere in the world' and felt that 'Ireland must key itself up and get the same kind of electric life and energy which the new countries like Japan or USA have within them'.[81] Belfast was the one city that might match its contemporaries but Russell wondered how 'to turn our sleepy rural population into vigorous, progressive and intellectual farmers'.[82] He had tried before to rouse his readership by the reproduction of inspirational speeches by Theodore Roosevelt on behalf of 'The man who works with his hands'.[83] But the new world demanded a range of skills that might only be found in the specially gifted. Russell mused that

> Da Vinci painted some of the greatest pictures of the world, but he was also the greatest scientist in his time; he discovered the circulation of the blood before Harvey, invented flying machines, built fortifications, made engines of war, and in fact, as without modesty, but with perfect truth, said: 'I can do anything as well as any man living'. Goethe, the greatest poet of Europe at the beginning of the last century, was also a distin-

79 S. O'Grady, 'The first Irish commune of the new order', *IH*, 5 Mar. 1910. 190. The image of the 'trek' held a minor place in Irish nationalist imagination; a postcard advertising the Theatre of Ireland production of Russell's *Deirdre* at the Abbey of December 1907 is illustrated with hundreds of ancient Irish warriors on the march. NLI ms 35/454/3. **80** 'Back to the land', *IH*, 11 Mar. 1911. 90. **81** 'NOTW', *IH*, 11 Mar. 1911. 185. **82** Ibid. **83** 'The man who works with his hands', *IH*, 10 Aug. 1907. 631–3. 'The man who works with his hands', *IH*, 17 Aug. 1907. 653–5.

guished scientist, and the universality of Shakespeare's genius has compelled a great many people to believe, knowing the prodigality of the well-fed mind, that he must have done other things as well, and they have imputed Bacon's works to him.[84]

So

National problems are not solved when looked at only from the angle of political vision or from the point of view of the unionist or the social reformer; national problems have to be walked round and round as the sculptor walks round and round his work to see that it looks well from any point of view.[85]

Passages like these are the joy of the *Irish Homestead*, its editor trawling his office encyclopaedia for information assembled in an entirely idiosyncratic fashion in support of an original principle. Russell's visual sense, sharpened by practice as a painter, further adds to the image of society as a sculpture not yet complete. His call for redefinition of national problems, of constitution, culture and development, was prompted by the publication of the first issue of the *Irish Review* the month previous. Its editor, Padraic Colum, aided by a coterie that included Mary Colum, Patrick Pearse, Thomas MacDonagh and Joseph Mary Plunkett, billed their project as 'A monthly magazine of Irish literature, art and science',[86] illustrating ambition to match that of Russell. The editor of the *Irish Homestead* was aware of the *Irish Review* before it was published and wrote to John Quinn in praise of its potential.[87] In an echo of the *Irish Homestead*, the first editorial declared that

The Irish Review has been founded to give expression to the intellectual movement in Ireland. By the intellectual movement we do not understand an activity purely literary; we think of it as the application of Irish intelligence to the reconstruction of Irish life. Science and economics will claim an interesting share of attention as our people progress towards the control of their resources. The Irish Review is prepared to give space to these interests as well as to the activities displayed in art, literature and criticism.[88]

A series of essays by Russell on 'The problem of rural life' form the backbone of the *Irish Review* throughout 1911. Many sentiments there found first expression in earlier editorial and leading comment in the *Irish Homestead*; there are

84 'NOTW', *IH*, 8 April 1911. 266.   **85** Ibid. 266–7.   **86** For an account of the *Irish Review*'s conduct see Mary Colum, *Life and the dream*. 157–9.   **87** Letter from Russell to John Quinn, 13 Feb. 1911. Denson typescript. 191.   **88** 'The Irish Review', *Irish Review*, March 1911. 1.

for example familiar remarks on the necessity to reverse rural depopulation and an amusing series on the incapacity of drunken public servants, all part of advanced nationalist criticism of inefficient Irish placemen. Russell's next contribution was an illustration to accompany Standish O'Grady's essay on the Dorian race of prehistoric Greece. Called 'The dark place in the wood' it illustrates two children, a boy and girl, walking through a forest at night lit only by background fairy light.[89] It seems that Russell was in search of illumination towards the end of 1911 as Ireland lurched towards a home rule crisis. His poem, 'Children of the king', published in the *Irish Review* of November 1911, wonders what reconciliation might be possible between conflicting elements of national life.

> Ah, did the Red Branch on the battlefield
> See such a love, all magical, revealed,
> Passing in combat? Did they recognise
> Kinships with Tirnanoge in flashing eyes
> What lovely brotherhood the foe concealed?
>
> … Could you and I but of each other say,
> From what a lordly house we took our way,
> And to what Hostel of the Gods we wend,
> Oh, would we anticipate the end?
> Oh, would we not have Paradise to-day?[90]

The creation of heaven on earth was increasingly difficult in Ireland of late 1911. The confidence of the year before had dissipated as nationalist and unionist fought each other over self-government. Labour unrest all the while threatened to make the problem immaterial. Russell's remedy was to publish *Co-operation and nationality*, a primer to mutual aid in society, in February 1912. Flouting the convention of editorial modesty, Russell introduced the book to his readers in the *Irish Homestead*, used as they were to his bouts of 'bad temper and petulance'.[91] An uneven text that the *Irish Review* compared to an indistinct Impressionist painting,[92] *Co-operation and nationality* is a strange union of Fabian social report, complete with figures and statistics, nationalist polemic and mystic rapture. Displaying elements of classical appreciation, archaeology, epic history and an interest in feminism, the book's diffuse concerns betray its genesis in the *Irish Homestead* of the seven years before its publication.[93] Arranged over twenty short chapters the text is barely one hundred pages long. But it is

89 G. Russell, 'The dark place in the wood', *Irish Review*, Sept. 1911.   **90** G. Russell, 'Children of the king', *Irish Review*, Nov. 1911. 430.   **91** 'NOTW', *IH*, 10 Feb. 1912. 110.   **92** 'Reviews', *Irish Review*, March 1912. 51–4.   **93** Summerfield notes that 'More than a third of this work consisted

Russell's first sustained attempt, during the home rule crisis, to outline his vision of Irish society.

That territory lay in a mental geography between Ireland and the United States, a country whose image is constantly invoked. The America to which Russell refers is not the cluster of east-coast urban centres to which the emigrant Irish were in the main attracted, but the rural America of open prairie. It is an America of plain ground, the imagined territory once again of Whitman and Emerson. To Russell, 'It is not the work which is done which excites Whitman, but the work which is yet to be done – the long vistas and the yet unbridled close.'[94] The ideal of free space obsessed Whitman, the long, effusive lines of his poetry in part an attempt to populate the clearing that Emerson, in a fit of high romanticism, promised the American poet:

> Thou true land-lord! sea-lord! air-lord! Wherever snow falls, or water flows, or birds fly, wherever day and night meet in twilight, wherever the blue heaven is hung by clouds, or sown with stars, wherever are forms with transparent boundaries, wherever are outlets into celestial space, wherever is danger, and awe, and love, there is Beauty, plenteous as rain, shed for thee, and though thou shouldest walk the world over, thou shalt not be able to find a condition inopportune or ignoble.[95]

Yeats for one was suspicious of the power of simple annunciation and later regretted the influence that Emerson and Whitman held over Russell's youth.[96] But the occult deficiencies of Emerson's transcendentalism, crucial to Yeats' disquiet, were of secondary importance to the author of *Co-operation and nationality*. Emerson imagined a physical territory blessed of spiritual potential. This belief, translated by Whitman to popular idealism, was critical to that section of the Irish revival associated with Russell. Provided with an imaginative territory clear of the binds of class and religious association, Russell was able to picture a new nation, dependant for its existence on the scope of his intellectual commitment. In *Co-operation and nationality*, Russell uses his cleared space to conceive of his ideal 'social order', an order composed, like Emerson's American scholar, of three qualities, 'economic development', 'political stability' and a 'desirable social life'.[97] The success of this new medium depended on Russell's ability to

of passages from his leading articles and "Notes of the Week" incorporated with only the slightest variations ... Much of the book is written in the vigorous, natural and often witty language of Æ's *Homestead* articles, sliding easily, without any obtrusive transition, into a more impassioned style'. *That myriad-minded man*. 139–40. **94** G. Russell, *Co-operation and nationality*. 32. **95** R. Emerson, 'The poet', *Ralph Waldo Emerson*. 214–15. **96** In his *Autobiographies*, Yeats wondered what Russell 'would have been had he not met in early life the poetry of Emerson and Walt Whitman, writers who have begun to seem superficial precisely because they lack the Vision of Evil'. 246. **97** G. Russell, *Co-operation and nationality*. 36.

present its attraction coherently in *Co-operation and nationality*. Russell's desire for economics to appeal to the popular reader lends his prose a curious quality. Its moral argument against the evils of capitalist individualism is interspersed with conversational reflections on the nature of being:

> Sometimes one feels as if there were some higher mind in humanity which could not act through individuals, but only through brotherhoods and groups of men. Anyhow, the civilisation which is based on individualism is mean, and the civilisation built on great guilds, fraternities, communes and associations is of a higher order. If we are to have any rural civilisation in Ireland it must spring out of co-operation.[98]

Russell's insistence on the importance of fraternity to Irish civilisation is notable. Embedded in Russell's theory is a cult-like fascination with secret organisation and the ordination of superior intellect. This interest is obscured by Russell's insistence on a generally inclusive rhetoric but is exposed in the language of racial superiority that infects his vision of the Irish future. To return again to America, so often in this text the template for a projection of the Irish nation's future, Russell predicts that a 'great civilisation' will yet arise.

> What Whitman called their 'barbaric yawp' may yet turn into the lordliest speech and thought, but without self-confidence a race will go no further. If Irish people do not believe they can equal or surpass the stature of any humanity which has been upon the globe, then they had better all emigrate and become servants to some superior race, and leave Ireland to new settlers who may come here with the same high hopes as the Pilgrim Fathers had when they went to America.[99]

The disturbingly impersonal aspect to Russell's thought, the celebration of territory over people, is an early indication of the basis on which Russell later offered his support to the Free State when its sovereignty was challenged during the civil war. Setting himself against former friends, Russell's prime imperative after the separation of the six northern counties was to maintain an ideal of Ireland able to sustain itself alone from the power centre of Dublin. Before partition, Ireland as a whole is figured as the holy city in *Co-operation and nationality*. Russell's concept of nationhood is at one with his belief in its divine origin. William Blake exhibited similar faith to Russell in 'Jerusalem'. Blake's radicalism was a spur to Russell's own empowerment, his work a key to *Co-operation and nationality*'s agricultural nationalism. Russell remembered 'an English poet' who wrote

98 Ibid. 44.   **99** Ibid. 84.

I will not cease from mental fight,
Nor shall my sword sleep in my hand
Till we have built Jerusalem
In England's green and pleasant land.[100]

Blake's 'Jerusalem' is commonly associated with the British labour movement. But Russell's radical presumption was that land itself was the basis of his plan for national regeneration, Ireland the Eden of his future reform. The irony of England's appearance as a blueprint for Irish nationalism is apparent. But critical to Russell's identification with Blake is his personal assumption of responsibility for creating the new Jerusalem in Ireland's 'green and pleasant land'. This is exactly the point where co-operation and nationality meet, land previously the preserve of Irish agriculture now the cradle of a new humanity. Blake's vision provides the bridge by which Russell's national and economic interests contact his epic imagination. Ireland is transported into a new era, its history baptised to a new tradition. The nation can leave behind its 'thousand years of sorrow and darkness' to enjoy 'as long a cycle of happy effort and ever-growing prosperity'.[101] Its people enter a world between the material and abstract:

> The country people carry quietly about with them, unknown to themselves, divine powers and tremendous destinies, as children predestined to greatness carry, unknown to themselves or others, powers that will make beauty or stormy life in the world hereafter.[102]

Russell blesses co-operation, a huge movement of agricultural reform, with a guiding destiny. *Co-operation and nationality* is a rhapsody on Ireland's economic and spiritual potential. 'We have', Russell wrote, 'all that any race ever had to inspire them, the heavens overhead, the earth underneath, and the breath of life in our nostrils. I would like to exile the man who would set limits to what we can do.'[103] Inspired by epic, as history and religion, and preceded by O'Grady and Blavatsky, Russell imagined himself as the precursor to a new order, the avatar himself, his insight the guarantee of change. So Russell dedicates *Co-operation and nationality* to 'those who are working at laying deep the foundations of a new social order'.[104] There is a missionary zeal to Russell's prose, the adventure into the remote depths of the Irish mind reminiscent of Victorian missions to the 'dark continent', Africa. Russell, however, found the remote depths of humanity closer to hand. The anarchist of the first seven years of the *Irish Homestead* was faced with the uprising of a revived human spirit in the labour and revolutionary disputes that racked Ireland from 1913. Russell always felt that great

100 Ibid. 86. **101** Ibid. 95–6. **102** Ibid. 102. **103** Ibid. 96. **104** Ibid.

future battles would be fought over social and not national organisation. In the year and more following publication of *Co-operation and nationality*, his prophecy appeared true. In Dublin's crucible of poverty-inspired social militancy we find Russell at his most radical, the anarchist advocate of social reform confronted with violence.

2 / National beings: 1913–17

George Russell was established by 1912 as a pivot about which influential opinion on Irish culture and politics turned, at home and abroad. He was editor of the *Irish Homestead*, a journal that addressed a co-operative movement that had by November that year a membership of 970 societies and an annual turnover of two and three quarter million pounds.[1] He was one of the most established of revival writers, published by Macmillan and with a readership in Ireland, Europe and the United States.[2] Popular with the rising generation of Irish writers, with George Birmingham, Padraic Colum and James Stephens, he occupied a place of central authority that Yeats, by his Cuala Press publication of *The green helmet and other poems* in 1910, was felt to have discarded. To the *Irish Review*, 'Mr. Yeats has become aristocratic, not merely in his intellectual attitude, but in his political convictions.'[3] 'This aristocratic bias goes with something that has come into the poet's spirit – the consciousness of haughty isolation.'[4]

For Russell too 1913 was a year of new beginnings and old ideas reconsidered. Both Yeats and Russell were preoccupied with the foundations of Irish culture. Yeats found solace in Anglo-Ireland. Russell turned to the life immediately around him, his conscience raised by newspaper boys who hawked labour papers as he walked from the *Irish Homestead* offices in Merrion Square to catch the tram home to Rathgar.[5] 'The city', a poem published in the last issue of the *Irish Review* to be edited by Padraic Colum in July 1913, sets the reader in a twilight whose coming darkness is the future unknown.

> What domination of what darkness does this hour,
> And through what rejoicing, winged, ethereal power,

1 Statistics in 'The annual report of the IAOS', *IH*, 16 Nov. 1912. 921–2. 2 Russell met Sir Frederick Macmillan in 1903. Macmillan held sole rights to Russell's poetry from 1913, in which year they published *Collected poems*. Correspondence between the two men is collected in the Macmillan archive, British Library. 3 'The green helmet and other poems', *Irish Review*, April 1911. 101. 4 Ibid. Yeats responded to such criticism with the ironic 'At the Abbey theatre', *Irish Review*, Dec. 1912. 565. The poem asked Douglas Hyde to 'Impart to us – / We'll keep the secret – a new trick to please'. Hyde responded the next month with 'An answer to Mr Yeats' poem, "In the Abbey theatre"', *Irish Review*, Jan. 1913. 561. This episode is mentioned in R. Foster, *W.B. Yeats*. 455. 5 'NOTW', *IH*, 13 April 1912. 290.

O'erthrown, the cells opened, the heart released from fear?
Gay twilight and grave twilight pass. The stars appear
O'er the prodigious, smouldering, dusty city fare.
The hanging gardens of Babylon were not more fair
Than these blue flickering glades, where childhood in its glee
Re-echoes with fresh voice the heaven-lit ecstasy.[6]

Yeats had found himself on a city pavement before and wished for transport to the 'Lake isle of Innisfree'. Russell remained rooted in the urban, the locus of national rejuvenation no more castles in the west, but now the streets of Dublin, where 'Heaven hath no lordlier court than earth of College Green'.[7] The speaker wonders

... is it paradise
To look on mortal things with an immortal's eyes?
Above the misty brilliance the streets assume
A night-dilated blue magnificence of gloom
Like many-templed Nineveh tower beyond tower,
And I am hurried on in this immortal hour.
Mine eyes beget new majesties: my spirit greets
The trams, the high-built glittering galleons of the streets
That float through twilight rivers from galaxies of light.[8]

The poem ends in revelation, as 'I walk in Dublin town',

The fiery rushing chariots of the Lord are there,
The whirlwind path, the blazing gates, the trumpets blown,
The halls of heaven, the majesty of throne by throne,
Enraptured faces, hands up-lifted, welcome sung
By the thronged gods, tall, golden-coloured, joyful, young.[9]

As a high finale this last cannot be matched, the speaker lost to personal ecstasy. The poem rests divine authority in urban Ireland. The Irish writer, it suggests, need look no longer to the country as ground for the ideal citizen. The city workers, 'Those dark misshapen folk ... not all ignoble',[10] can take their place in future society. James Connolly, labour organiser and revolutionary, noted the lack of attention the Literary Revival gave the worker in an essay to the *Irish Review*, now under the militant editorship of Joseph Mary Plunkett, in October 1913. Connolly's Ireland was, memorably, a place of 'wonderful charity and singularly little justice'.[11] Due to the obsession with home rule

---

6 G. Russell, 'The city', *Irish Review*, July 1913. 228.   7 Ibid. 229.   8 Ibid.   9 Ibid.   10 Ibid.
11 J. Connolly, 'Labour in Dublin', *Irish Review*, Oct. 1913. 385–6.

all the literary elements of society, those who might have been, under happier political circumstance, the champions of the downtrodden Irish wage labourer, or the painstaking investigators of social conditions, were absorbed in other fields, and the working class left without any means of influencing outside public opinion. As a result, outside public opinion in Dublin gradually came to believe that poverty and its attendant miseries in a city were things outside of public interest, and not in the remotest degree concerned with public duties, or civic patriotism.[12]

Russell answered Connolly's call; expecting urban revelation he watched the development of workers' organisation in Dublin throughout 1913. James Larkin, head of the Irish Transport and General Workers' Union (ITGWU), had been instrumental with Connolly in the consolidation and expansion of his union among the Dublin working classes. Russell regarded Connolly as 'a really intellectual leader'.[13] But the trade unions had formidable opponents. William Martin Murphy, a local magnate, in particular tried to stop union agitation among his tram workers. These workers struck in retaliation in horse show week of August 1913. Thereafter James Larkin called a protest meeting at which he was arrested and so started the eight-month Lock-Out of Dublin workers by a confederation of city employers. Russell and Connolly found themselves sharing a platform to petition for Larkin's release at a demonstration at the Royal Albert Hall in London on the first of November 1913. Larkin was duly freed twelve days later despite his sentence of seven months imprisonment.[14] Russell could barely take credit for the effect of his speech. He did not project his voice from the stage, with the result that a large portion of the audience could not hear him.[15] But Russell was explicit in his criticism of Dublin employers, mocking a race of capitalists who imagined they were 'superhuman beings'.[16] Subversively, he maligned the actions of police who had, he suggested, 'set upon and beaten'[17] workers at the command of Dublin's merchant élite. Russell's speech is remarkable in its consistent connection of the apparatus of civil government to the interests of industry and its placement of both in opposition to the democratic rights of organised labour. He damned the attitudes of those, including the vocal archbishop of Dublin, William Walsh, who forcibly halted the temporary fostering of locked-out workers' children with sympathetic families in England and the north of Ireland:

12 Ibid. 387. 13 G. Russell, 'How to protect ourselves from the peace that threatens us', *Better Business: a Quarterly Journal of Agricultural and Industrial Co-operation*, I:1, Oct. 1915. 22. 14 Details of this dispute can be read in W. Ryan, *The Irish labour movement from the 'twenties to the present day*. 214–33. 15 H. Summerfield, *That myriad-minded man*. 163. 16 G. Russell, 'A plea for the workers', *The Dublin strike*. 1. 17 Ibid.

You see, if children were even for a little out of the slums, they would get discontented with their poor homes, so a very holy man has said. Once getting full meals, they might be so inconsiderate as to ask for them all their lives.[18]

Russell continued his attack with reference to Larkin's incarceration. The employers, he imagined, were attempting to sound the depths of human poverty. Only Larkin had the courage to interrupt 'their interesting experiments towards the evolution of the underman and he is in gaol'.[19] The state is portrayed, as Russell was so fond of writing, echoing Nietzsche, as the coldest of all cold monsters. Russell himself was sure who should be imprisoned in Larkin's place: 'If our Courts of Justice were courts of humanity, the masters of Dublin would be in the dock charged with criminal conspiracy'.[20] For the 'greatest crime against humanity is degradation',[21] a degradation that first afflicts those in service of the state. Russell accuses the instruments of civil and political authority (the police, the judiciary, the owners of capital and the representatives of organised religion) of unconscious action. They are, in this state, outside Irish national evolution. Dehumanised, the police become 'wild beasts that kill in the name of the state'.[22] Even the Ancient Order of Hibernians, an organisation that stopped children of the locked out being sent to Liverpool, become 'wild fanatics who will rend' the workers 'in the name of God'.[23]

Russell's speech caused fury in the *Freeman's Journal* and the *Leader*. Both criticised Russell's involvement in an English socialist demonstration as evidence of his secret anti-Irish sympathies.[24] Their antagonism was longstanding, the *Freeman's Journal* a veteran of controversy between the Irish Parliamentary Party and the IAOS, and the *Leader*, edited by D.P. Moran, a journal previously sympathetic to the co-operatives but turned against Plunkett since the anticlerical remarks of *Ireland in the new century* in 1904. Moran had worked with the *Freeman's Journal* in a campaign to relieve the IAOS of its government subsidies, a dispute only settled in the co-operatives' favour in 1913. Russell's Albert Hall speech was therefore the perfect opportunity for his opponents to question the co-operative movement's national motives. The *Freeman's Journal* observed of the IAOS that

Mr. Russell, almost as much as Sir Horace Plunkett, stands in the public eye for that organisation. Are the members of the I. A. O. S. in agree-

---

18 Ibid.   **19** Ibid. 2.   **20** Ibid.   **21** Ibid.   **22** Ibid. 3.   **23** Ibid.   **24** The *Freeman's Journal* of Monday, 3 November 1913, reported that the 'meeting applied itself in the main to denunciation of the priests of Dublin and threats against the regular leaders of the Labour movement'. 6. The *Leader* noted on the same date that 'Some English Socialists are only too glad to exploit the sorrows of Dublin for their own purposes. The Mr. Russell, who calls himself A.E., has been to the Big Brother and made Johnny Bull laugh'. 299.

ment on this occasion with their industrious spokesman? Will the society assume any responsibility for the campaign? That is a question which the Irish public, without distinction of Party would like to have answered immediately.[25]

Plunkett was silent throughout the controversy and Russell survived in his post as editor of the *Irish Homestead*. Russell was fortunate that criticism of his Albert Hall appearance was limited mainly to that section of the Irish press already known to be antagonistic to his opinions. *Sinn Féin* and *Irish Freedom* remained loyal to an old ally.[26] The readership of the *Irish Homestead* was reluctant to sacrifice its editor to their opponents' interests. But Russell's militant speech did betray the scale of economic realignment he considered from behind the mask, as O'Grady had earlier put it, of the *Irish Homestead*. In a letter of clarification written after his speech, Russell expressed himself in moderate language but maintained that violence was the inevitable product of social discontent. Significantly, the letter was published in the London *Times* as Irish papers refused to print it.[27] In it Russell suggested his sole dedication to the evolutionary development of Irish society. But there were limits to his pacifism. Russell wanted stability but was

> not with those who wish to bring about in Ireland a peace of God without any understanding, and I and all free spirits will fight with all our power against the fanatics who would bludgeon us into their heaven, to bow to their savage conception of a deity. The deity of the infuriated bigot, call him by what holy name they choose, is never anything but the Old Adversary.[28]

The devil takes many forms and he is embodied here in the Irish political and economic establishment. Russell searched for a divine light in the working classes of Dublin and his concern for them brought James Connolly's close

25 *Freeman's Journal*, 3 November 1913. 6. **26** Arthur Griffith's *Sinn Féin* offered a national solution to a class problem, suggesting to workers that they find freedom through the 'nation and not outside of it'. In an unlikely revelation, labour would 'regain all they have lost since the black shadow of foreign rule fell upon their country and struck down that civilisation of our Gaelic ancestors in which Capital prayed on Labour a blessing on each work undertaken and Labour gave the blessing in token of the satisfaction with the recompense'. 'Sinn Féin and the labour question', *Sinn Féin*, 25 Oct. 1913. 3. *Irish Freedom*, the journal that contained Patrick Pearse's monthly notes 'From a hermitage', expressed its 'desire to regard the whole question from the national point of view and not from the exclusive point of view of any class or party within the nation'. It did offer some succour to Russell in its belief 'that the only solution to the issue between capital and labour is the co-operative solution'. 'Capital and labour', *Irish Freedom*, November 1913. 5. **27** See the unsigned introductory note to the letter in *The Dublin strike*. 7. **28** G. Russell, 'An appeal to Dublin citizens', *The Dublin strike*. 8.

attention. Connolly was born in Edinburgh in 1868; he then spent time as 'a tramp, navvy, and pedlar, eventually settling down for a time in Glasgow'.[29] He also lived in Dublin and America before his appointment as Ulster district secretary and organiser of the ITGWU in 1911. During this period he was involved in a successful strike in Belfast on behalf of firemen and sailors against the Shipping Federation.[30] W.P. Ryan further credited him with the improvement of dockworkers' conditions in the city. Connolly came to Dublin in 1913 to work under Larkin, a relationship that was often fractious. Connolly devoted his time to the increasingly militant agitation of Dublin's workforce, his assumption of control of the Irish Citizen Army (ICA) typical of his radical motivation.[31] Known as the 'runaway army' after an early clash between some of their number and the Royal Irish Constabulary (RIC) in 1913, their later actions proved how ill deserved their nickname was. Their detachment at the Royal College of Surgeons in 1916 was one of the last of the rebel units to surrender, five days after the start of the Easter Rising. Connolly's development of the ICA is evidence of his shared belief with Russell in political self-sufficiency. Both Connolly and Russell, by their involvement with union and co-operative respectively, created parallel institutions within the state, designed primarily to defend their members' interests.

The mutual drive to encourage workers to adopt either method of mutual aid ensured rivalry between the two movements. During 1913, Russell described trade unionism as 'an imperfect form of co-operation'.[32] Co-operation between workers and producers in rural areas had allowed its adherents to 'save a stage in the process'[33] of capital transactions in order that co-operators might 'divide among ourselves what that stage formerly cost us'.[34] In contrast, trade unionists were, according to Russell, 'weak individuals who have not brought their organisation to its full and perfect state'.[35] Trade unionism was, to Russell, a complement of, rather than an alternative to, capitalist economics.[36] Union subscribers were thus unable to 'dispense with their employer'.[37] Workers could only 'cut down ... profits a little'[38] and prevent an employer from 'exploiting them so much as he would if he dealt with them singly'.[39] In contrast,

---

29 W. Ryan, *The Irish labour movement.* 146. **30** Ibid. 193–4. **31** Connolly's association of the ICA with militant nationalist organisations such as the Irish Volunteers and Irish Republican Brotherhood was not entirely popular with its members. Sean O'Casey, for example, resigned as secretary of the movement in protest. See A. Mitchell, *Labour in Irish politics 1890–1930.* 68. **32** 'Co-operation and trade unionism', *IH*, 21 June 1913. 509. **33** Ibid. **34** Ibid. **35** Ibid. **36** Russell's opinion of trade unionism was similar in this respect to Arthur Griffith's wider prescription of socialism in *Sinn Féin*; 'I deny', Griffith wrote, 'that Socialism is a remedy for the existent evils or any remedy at all. I deny that Capital and Labour are in their nature antagonistic – I assert that they are essential and complementary the one to the other.' 'Sinn Féin and the labour question', *Sinn Féin*, 25 Oct. 1913. 2. **37** 'Co-operation and trade unionism', *IH*, 21 June 1913. 509. **38** Ibid. **39** Ibid.

The co-operative state is like to the kingdom of Heaven in the parable. All are invited voluntarily to fulfil the law of their own being, which is to be sociable, brotherly, and friendly. If they will not listen, nature will still have its way and its laws will be enforced by a multitude of bureaucrats carrying out orders, and there will be weeping and gnashing of teeth.[40]

Connolly responded to Russell's considerations in *The re-conquest of Ireland*, published in 1915, devoting the eighth chapter to the question of 'Labour and co-operation in Ireland'. Connolly's comparison of the two movements stressed their common experience of disadvantage. As Connolly remarked, the co-operatives had encountered 'no more bitter enemies than the political representatives of the Irish people, regardless of their political colour'.[41] Likewise, the ITGWU had little support in 1913, with almost the entire Irish press and political establishment ranged against them.[42] Connolly is further mindful of his experiences in the Lock-Out when he writes of the 'beneficent activities of the co-operative societies'[43] during the dispute. The co-operatives' supply of food left 'such an impression upon the minds of the workers of the Dublin Labour Movement' that he expected many new societies to be formed 'under the auspices of that movement'.[44] The potential union between labour and the co-operatives was not restricted to Ireland. Russell reported favourably in 1913 on a conference held between the British Labour Party, which had nearly fifty seats in the House of Commons, the trade union movement and the English co-operatives.[45] Russell described the meeting as an industrial augur, hoping that it would 'come to be regarded in future years as the most important political event in the century'.[46] The conference proposed to combine parliamentary agitation for workers' rights with a policy of strike action if suitable legislation was not forthcoming. But he was sceptical of party organisation. Any successful constitutional reform ceded to labour would be a 'soup of their own tails disguised in flavour to make it appear to be composed of their employers'.[47]

In preference, Russell concentrated his attention on the potential of industrial action. In preparation for any strike that might occur, the unions would

40 'The parable of labour', *IH*, 20 Sept. 1913. 779.   **41** J. Connolly, *Labour in Ireland: labour in Irish history: the re-conquest of Ireland*. 315.   **42** Robert Lynd's introduction to Connolly's *Labour in Ireland: labour in Irish history: the re-conquest of Ireland* suggests that in 1913 Connolly 'had the intellectuals and the poor on his side, but he had all the Press and all the parties against him'. xxi.   **43** J. Connolly, *Labour in Ireland: labour in Irish history: the re-conquest of Ireland*. 320. The Irish Agricultural Wholesale Organisation (IAWS), an offshoot of the IAOS, provided credit for those unemployed during the dispute. The ever jaundiced Moran was prompted to ask: 'Is there a deal here? ... now the IAWS are getting a big slice of business ... Some of the Hairy Fairies weren't born yesterday.' *Leader*, 1 Nov. 1913. 276. 'Hairy Fairy' was a name given to Russell because of his beard and occult interests.   **44** Ibid. 320.   **45** 'A momentous conference', *IH*, 15 Feb. 1913. 121–3.   **46** Ibid. 121.   **47** Ibid. 123.

invest their subscriptions in a co-operative movement that would supply union members engaged in industrial action. 'War', he wrote, 'will not be declared so readily' on labour if employers know their 'enemy is well provisioned and can hold out for a indefinite period'.[48] Connolly responded in print to Russell's 1913 article on the English conference two years later. He did not share Russell's hope that an understanding between co-operators and the unions would result in a period of stability, perhaps because Connolly had himself prepared for rebellion since the start of the war.[49] Connolly did agree with Russell that unions should help co-operatives by purchasing 'the products of the agricultural co-operative societies in time of industrial peace'.[50] All this created a bond of mutual interest, a union that would see co-operatives provision workers during the future revolution that Connolly predicted. The 'workers', Connolly claimed, would thus 'enjoy their credit in time of war'.[52] Once again Connolly sees the co-operatives as a useful tool in his struggle. The IAOS was an obvious ally, firmly established in rural Ireland as it was by its development of farmers' productive efficiency. Connolly felt that the co-operatives could heal the 'latent antagonism between town and country',[53] which had existed 'almost throughout all historic periods'.[54] As a socialist he favoured his own methods to put

> an end to that antagonism by bringing the advantages of the city to the toiler in the country; Mr. Russell foresees, however, a co-operation in which the city and the country shall merge in perfecting fraternal methods of production and distribution.[55]

Connolly had starker intentions for rural producers than Russell's ideal of fraternity. Connolly suggested that rural co-operators might provide the bedrock from which the urban workers could work their revolutionary ends:

> Thus when to the easily organised labourers of the towns is added the immense staying power of the peasantry ... the Party of Labour which will thus manifest itself will speak out with a prophetic voice when it proclaims its ideal of a regenerated Ireland – an Ireland re-conquered for its common people.[56]

48 Ibid. 122.   **49** See for example Connolly's comments in *Forward*, 15 Aug. 1914: 'Is it not clear as the fact of life itself that no insurrection of the working class, no general strike, no uprising of the forces of Labour in Europe could possibly carry with it or entail a greater slaughter of Socialists than will their participation as soldiers in the campaigns of the Armies of their respective countries?' Collected in *A socialist and war 1914–1916*, ed. P. J. Musgrove. 2.   **50** J. Connolly, *Labour in Ireland: labour in Irish history: the re-conquest of Ireland*. 323.   **51** Ibid.   **52** Ibid.   **53** Ibid. 331.   **54** Ibid.   **55** Ibid.   **56** Ibid. 325.

Connolly, unsurprisingly, is optimistic of the revolutionary potential of rural and urban Ireland. He assumes that farmers who have collaborated together as co-operators will collaborate with revolutionary workers. Since Russell had to warn his readers in 1913 not to say anything political at their co-operative meetings for fear of disruption,[57] Connolly's proposition was unlikely. He put too much faith in 'Mr. George Russell, the gifted editor of the *Irish Homestead*'[58] when he accepted at face value 'that the overwhelming proportion of Irish farmers employ no labour but generally work their own farms'.[59] This made Connolly sure that the farmers would not be 'hostile to the claims of labour'.[60] He accepted as fact this part of Russell's propaganda on behalf of the co-operatives, a propaganda aimed at lifting co-operators from complacency. Indeed Russell was driven to criticise farmers during the Lock-Out for attitudes they held towards the labour they did employ:

> We find some farmers hinting that they will give in now labour is necessary for the harvest, but once let that be over and they will have their turn for stopping work. What, then, if next year they have no labour at all?[61]

Connolly and Russell were in closer agreement in their belief that Europe was vitally important to Ireland. The ideal of 'Europe' as the basis of a moral constituency with relevance to Irish experience was frequent in both men's writings. After Connolly's execution in May 1916 Russell immediately asked if 'we ... in this distracted country' are 'thinking as Europeans and citizens of the world?'[62] On the outbreak of war Connolly wrote in the *Irish Worker* that if 'the working classes of Europe, rather than slaughter each other for the benefit of kings and financiers' decide 'to erect barricades all over Europe' then 'we should be perfectly justified in following such a glorious example'.[63] Connolly viewed the war as an opportunity, almost as a prerogative, and had established Ireland's right to rebel in response to unrest on the continent in *Labour in Ireland*, first published in 1910.

Here Connolly presented the rebellions of 1798 and 1848 and the growth of fenianism as Irish movements inspired by Europe. 1798 was an Irish expression of the tendencies embodied in the First French Revolution'.[64] 1848 throbbed in sympathy with the democratic and social upheavals on the continent of Europe and England' to make 'Fenianism a responsive throb in the Irish heart to those

---

57 G. Russell, 'The policy of strikes and batons', *IH*, 6 Sept. 1913. 737–8. 58 J. Connolly, *Labour in Ireland: labour in Irish history: the re-conquest of Ireland.* 321. 59 Ibid. 60 Ibid. 61 'The policy of strikes and batons', *IH*, 6 Sept. 1913. 738. 62 'Lessons from the war', *IH*, 10 June 1916. 353. 63 W. O'Brien, 'Introduction', *Labour and Easter week: a selection from the writings of James Connolly.* 2–3. 64 J. Connolly. *Labour in Ireland: labour in Irish history: the re-conquest of Ireland.* 208.

pulsations in the heart of the European working class which elsewhere pro-duced the International Working Men's Association'.[65] Connolly connects the landmark struggles of Irish nationalism to a wider class conflict. It is his attempt to legitimate socialism in Irish terms – a movement criticised by Rus-sell as an unsuitable growth for Irish soil.[66] Connolly's analysis of European events provides him with access to a history of 'common exploitation' which would make 'enthusiastic rebels out of a Protestant working class' and 'earnest champions of civil and religious liberty out of Catholics'.[67] Connolly's clever inversion of the stereotypes of 'rebellious Catholic' and 'liberty-loving Protes-tant' suggests that rebellion and the pursuit of liberty are common acts in pur-suit of social justice.

But even though Connolly and Russell disagreed on the best structural alter-native to the state in which they found themselves, their common aim was, according to Connolly, 'to combat capitalism and finally to supplant it'.[68] In this struggle the labour leader promised Russell the 'constant support of every friend of progress in Ireland'.[69] Connolly located in Russell's rhetoric an acknowledgement of a common enemy, capitalism. Russell was indeed critical of Dublin's business elite during the 1913 Lock-Out, with most of his bile reserved for those also involved in the refusal to set up Hugh Lane's gallery.[70] They became, by lack of culture, symbols of Ireland's isolation from the rest of Europe, agents of the unconscious become animal in their ignorance: 'The "practical men" of Dublin came out against the waste of money on such things as art. These ignorant donkeys ... who call themselves "business men" ... do not seem to realise that half of the backwardness of Ireland in industry is due to its neglect of and contempt for the arts.'[71]

Russell sets these individuals apart from the Irish civilisation he hopes to cre-ate, although he stops short of offering a radical method for their disposal: 'The Lord may forgive them for their work because no patriotic Irishman ever could.'[72] If the arts were to be the signal expression of the Irish intellect, then the ambitions of those who ignored them were illegitimate. Culture, for

65 Ibid.   **66** 'NOTW', *IH*, 5 April 1913. 273.   **67** J. Connolly, *Labour in Ireland: labour in Irish history: the re-conquest of Ireland.* 216.   **68** Ibid. 331.   **69** Ibid.   **70** In *The life of W. B. Yeats* Terence Brown notes that Lane 'had generously offered to the city a collection of paintings (including work by French Impressionists, then less universally regarded as they subsequently became), provided the municipal authorities would earmark funds for a suitable gallery. By 1912, despite some move-ment in that direction by the municipal authorities, Lane was losing all patience. A subscription fund was established to augment what the public purse would provide. A sense began to get abroad that the whole scheme was an act of Ascendancy condescension to Dublin's citizenry ... By the autumn of 1913 Lane had withdrawn his offer and the bequest seemed lost to the city forever'. 201. A further account of Lane's plans, architectural and visual, including a gallery across the Liffey at the 'Halfpenny' footbridge, can be read in Roy Foster's *W. B. Yeats.* 478–83.   **71** 'NOTW', *IH*, 6 Sept. 1913. 740.   **72** Ibid. 740.   **73** J. Connolly, 'A war for civilisation'. *Labour and Easter week: a selection from the writings of James Connolly.* 90.

Russell, was the cipher by which Irish social and economic realignment might be imagined. This is the site of Russell's divergence from Connolly, despite the latter's adoption of the language of high culture to confer legitimacy on the class struggle. To Connolly 'labour alone in these days is fighting the real *war for civilisation*'.[73] So the 'capitalist class' was the 'natural enemy of ... national culture'.[74] Connolly committed himself to revolution while Russell, more cautious, wrote for change through the *Irish Homestead* and, increasingly, his poetry.

Russell lacerated contemporary society in *The gods of war*, published privately for the author in 1915.[75] We are lucky in this to still have a single copy in proof form with the author's own undated corrections; its fourteen poems share one theme, the effect of conflict on Russell's contemporary world. The tone is various. The elegiac 'Continuity' wonders if 'the ruins shall be made' into 'some yet more lovely masterpiece'. 'Battle ardour' in contrast is frenzied, with its picture of a 'mighty hunter' that tramples 'to dust the cities of our pride'. The disturbed nature of this collection convinced Russell, as the editor of the *Irish Homestead*, not to submit it for general publication. His poetry allowed him to express his concerns in terms different from his journal articles. The title poem, 'Gods of war', addresses Christ; 'How wanes thine Empire, Prince of Peace!' it laments, as the 'ancient gods their powers increase' and 'thine own anointed ones/ Do pour upon the warring bands/ The devil's blessing from their hands'. Russell implicates the clergy with the war effort (many indeed had blessed British troops before they were shipped across the English Channel) to stress their partiality. They are linked to the governments of Europe as if they have made a pact with an ancient, maleficent power ('This is the Dark Immortal's hour'). Russell's speaker looks outside the bounds of established authority for his inspiration to ask 'Who dreamed a dream mid outcasts born/ Could overthrow the pride of kings?' The 'dream' is a symbol in Russell's poetry of power coming into being; imagination, and not material production, is the force that first drives society.

The dove of Christ spreads 'its gold and silver wings' to nest 'in flame/ In outcasts who abjure his name'. The dove, symbolic of peace, finds a new home in the company of rebels. It sits phoenix-like in the fire of industrial unrest to rise upon the victory of the workers. It is further symbolic of the imagination that drives the labour leaders. Russell had used the image of a bird to symbolise the expression of labour's discontent before. In 1913 'Labour, long voiceless

---

74 J. Connolly, 'A continental revolution'. *Labour and Easter week: a selection from the writings of James Connolly*. 42.   **75** Russell first collected the poems that comprise *The gods of war* in one volume in September 1915. One hundred copies of the text were made and circulated among Russell's friends and admirers. The copy from which I take the following quotations is collected unbound and unpaginated in the NLI. Thus there are no page references available for the lines referred to.

... found a voice'[76] in the cries of a 'stormy petrel'.[77] The bird 'who has just set Dublin in a blaze, has told us that he feels a divine mission to awaken discontent. To that we can have no objection.'[78] It is not clear in the 'Gods of war' whether the workers will triumph: 'O outcast Christ, it was too soon/ For flags of battle to be furled/ While life was still at the hot noon'. The establishment of labour's cause as an extension of the will of a universal divinity suggests that European, as well as Irish, contexts, inform Russell's poetry. In *The gods of war* as a whole the national movement in Ireland becomes a passing, if not invisible, player in the wider theatre of conflict. The last poem of the collection, 'Apocalyptic', is a case in point. The poem's first stanza acknowledges the social dislocation that the war caused and laments the passing of a world that the speaker formerly knew:

> Our world beyond a year of dread
> Has paled like Babylon and Rome,
> Never for all the blood was shed
> Shall life return to it as home.

All will change utterly: 'No peace shall e'er that dream recall;/ The avalanche is yet to fall'. The poem is a prophecy of doom to come. Russell predicted in the *Irish Homestead* that the end of the war would merely signify a massive outbreak of labour trouble as millions of demobilised men were put back into society, having made the greatest of sacrifices without any reward.[79] Peace would in reality be a 'battlefield', a 'grave/ Either for master or for slave'. In preparation for this conflict the speaker chooses sides. It will 'be better to be bold/ Than clothed in purple in that hour'. The speaker relishes the possibility of making his voice a mouthpiece for resistance. His readers are advised to laugh 'with disdain' if the 'black horse's rider reign,/ Or the pale horse's rider fire/ His burning empire'. These agents of the apocalypse are robbed of symbolic force as they bring destruction only to those 'who have made of earth' their 'star'. The audience that the speaker addresses is destined for a higher fate as they have proved their spiritual worth by suffering:

> only those can laugh who are
> The strong Initiates of Pain,
> Who know that mighty god to be
> Sculptor of immortality.

---

76 G. Russell, 'The parable of labour', *IH*, 20 Sept. 1913. 777.   **77** Ibid.   **78** Ibid.   **79** 'Economy of production', *IH*, 15 July 1916. 437–8.

The speaker sees a coming battle between master and slave necessary to the freedom of humanity, that 'last test which yields the right/ To walk amid the halls of light'. The image of the war as a test was common among English poets in the early years of the war.[80] Many welcomed it as a chance to prove the value of their generation but few envisaged it as a preparation for a wider struggle. The war to end all wars was to Russell the omen of a revelation only yet partially perceived.

A sense of new beginning is evident in Russell's final publication of 1915, *Imaginations and reveries*. A collection of twenty-four pieces of prose and drama, the text is a retrospective of Russell's political and occult interests since the 1890s. Perhaps the most popular of Russell's works included in *Imaginations and reveries* is *Deirdre*, first performed with Yeats's *Cathleen ni Houlihan* in 1902.[81] Also reproduced is the fiercely evangelical essay, 'Hero in man'.[82] The author's preface to *Imaginations and reveries* is revealing of Russell's state of mind at the end of 1915. Russell admitted that his personal desire for contemplation could not silence a 'conscience' that 'would not let me have peace unless I worked with other Irishmen at the reconstruction of Irish life'.[83] But

> To aid in movements one must be orthodox. My desire to help prompt-ed agreement, while my intellect was always heretical. I had written out of every mood, and could not retain any mood for long. If I advocated a national ideal I felt immediately I could make an equal appeal for more cosmopolitan and universal ideals. I have obeyed my intuitions wherev-er they drew me, for I felt that the Light which is within us knows bet-ter than any other the need and the way.[84]

Russell found his way in the spring of 1916 to Edward MacLysaght's home in Co. Clare to spend the Easter weekend with him.[85] He left Dublin on Good

---

80 See for example Rupert Brooke's poem 'Peace' or Laurence Binyon's 'The fourth of August': 'We step from days of sour division/ Into the grandeur of our fate'. Cited from *Up the line to death*. 7.   **81** *Deirdre* is Russell's adaptation of the legend of Naisi's love for Deirdre and its tragic conse-quences for the Red Branch of Ulster. The play ends with the death of its two main char-acters. Russell wrote the play to inspire heroic self-abnegation in Ireland at the beginning of the twentieth-century. As the Ulster king Concubar suggests, 'Deeds will be done in our time as mighty as those wrought by the giants who battled at the dawn; and through the memory of our days and deeds the gods will build themselves as eternal empire in the mind of the Gael.' *Imaginations and reveries*. 207. *Deirdre* and *Cathleen ni Houlihan* were first produced on 2 April 1902.   **82** 'Hero in man' is an 1897 treatise on human suffering. Russell argues that our ability to conquer pain is evi-dence of a divine trait. 'All knowledge', Russell suggests, 'is a revelation of the self to the self, and our deepest comprehension of the seemingly apart divine is also our furthest inroad to self-knowl-edge; Prometheus, Christ, are in every heart; the story of one is the story of all; the Titan and the Crucified are humanity.' *Imaginations and reveries*. 145.   **83** G. Russell, *Imaginations and reveries*. ix. **84** Ibid. ix–x.   **85** H. Summerfield, *That myriad-minded man*. 177.

Friday, 21 April 1916, hearing the first news of unrest in the city when he tried to return to it on Tuesday 25 April. Russell reached the capital on 26 April, a Wednesday. He entered a city confused. James Stephens, in his account of Easter Week, recalled meeting one man 'who spat rumour as though his mouth were a machine gun'.[86] This individual claimed variously that:

> the Germans had landed in three places ... the whole city of Cork was in the hands of the Volunteers ... German warships had defeated the English ... the whole country was up, and the garrison was outnumbered by one hundred to one.[87]

Surprised, Russell, like nearly everyone else, had to rely on his knowledge of Dublin prior to the insurrection to write about it in the aftermath. Russell's first report in the *Irish Homestead* on the Rising appeared on 13 May 1916. This edition contained three issues as earlier publication was made impossible by the destruction in Easter Week of the *Irish Homestead*'s office; anyway, as Russell wryly remarked, 'if it had been published it would not have been read'.[88] This time lapse perhaps accounts for the fact that 'The hope that remains', the leading *Irish Homestead* article of 13 May, spends only its first four lines concentrating specifically on 'one of the most tragic episodes in Irish history'.[89] Russell's response was to identify the Rising as the latest expression of grievances long identified by the *Irish Homestead*. The Rising was in Russell's opinion the logical expression of the working classes' discontent with their conditions,[90] a portent of the 'social revolution many people fear'[91] and a timely warning that labour was undefeated from 1913.[92] Russell further remarked that if 'journalists and politicians' did not 'discover some humanity in themselves, and try to understand those whom they have attacked for so many years' then 'they will keep Ireland in hostile camps for generations to come'.[93] His hope lay in the 'average man', 'a more intellectual and humane being than the people ... on platforms, in Parliament and the Press'.[94]

Russell spent the main body of 'The hope that remains' promoting the co-operative movement as the only 'camp of reconcilement'[95] in which the Irish people could escape the burden of their past. They had been 'separated by tradition for centuries'; it was now time to 'unite upon some common ground'.[96] Russell accused journalists of partisanship, using the rebellion as an opportunity to lodge 'in court as evidence in support of their contentions the ruins of the

86 J. Stephens, *The insurrection in Dublin*. 32. **87** Ibid. 32–3. **88** 'NOTW', *IH*, 13 May 1916. 286. **89** 'The hope that remains', *IH*, 13 May 1916. 285. **90** Ibid. **91** 'NOTW', *IH*, 10 June 1916. 354. **92** 'NOTW', *IH*, 13 May 1916. 287. **93** Ibid. **94** Ibid. 286. **95** Ibid. 285. **96** Ibid.

city of Dublin'.[97] Russell's criticism of the press reaction to the rebellion is relevant to his sympathy for Connolly. For the *Irish Independent*, the newspaper
owned by William Martin Murphy, organiser of the employers' Lock-Out in
1913, was in 1916 the only Irish paper to call explicitly for the execution of the
labour leader;[98] proof, if it were needed, of the bitter legacy the trade dispute
left among all sections of Dublin society.

Russell was distraught at Connolly's loss. In prison, the labour leader had
told his wife to contact Russell so that the editor of the *Irish Homestead* could
arrange for the female members of the family's safe passage to the United
States. Connolly's son was to remain in Ireland for his education. Russell obliged and set up a fund that raised £101 on their behalf. Contributors included
Russell, H.F. Norman, Edward MacLysaght and Plunkett.[99] He then obtained
permission from General John Maxwell, the British officer commanding, for
the Connolly family's passage in the third week of June 1916. The British
authorities revoked this license, as they feared the family would be used as propaganda against them in America. Russell, who had been on holiday in Clare
when he thought the matter settled, was enraged. He wrote to Shaw:

> I have been made very sad and angry since I came back as I found the
> military authorities here have withdrawn the permission given to Mrs
> Connolly to go to America. It seems that they believe she would be
> exploited in the States & regretted their consent & withdrew it.
> Personally if I shot a man on behalf of the state I would take the conse-
> quences and not be afraid of what his wife might say & have said about
> her ... I will try to see that she is kept going here until the authorities
> relent and let the poor woman earn her living where she likes ...
> Plunkett is ill in London and there is nobody I know here with any influ-
> ence and he did his best. Ireland is in a damnable condition and these
> fool politicians are making it worse. I wish you would cease being a dis-
> ciple & come over here as the Irish Avatar. The country wants a leader,
> the job of leading the Irish race is vacant. Will you apply?[100]

---

97 Ibid.   **98** In his introduction to the 1917 edition of Connolly's *Labour in Ireland: labour in Irish
history: the re-conquest of Ireland*, Robert Lynd wrote that 'The *Irish Independent* – alone among nationalist papers, I think - warned the Government against clemency as a peril. In the result Connolly was
taken out and shot.' xxv–xxvi.   **99** The full list of donors and the amounts given were as follows: Dr
Tobin, £10, The O Mahony, £5, Per Father Aloysius, £5, Rank Martin, £2/2, Rt Hon M. F. Cox,
£2/2, D. O'C. Miley, £1/1, Anon, £0/5, Father O'Brien, £0/10, Christian Brothers Belfast, £1, Anon
(per GWR), £1, E. MacLysaght, £1, H. F. Norman, £1, A G. R. Volunteer, £2, T. Kennedy, £1,
George Russell, £10, Sir Horace Plunkett, £20, G. Bernard Shaw, £38. This made a total of £101.
Shaw papers, BL ms 50548/190. Dr Tobin attended the wounded Connolly in captivity.   **100** G.
Russell to G. Bernard Shaw, 1 August 1916. Shaw papers, BL ms 50548/185–7.

Shaw declined. National recovery was a task left to Russell's first prose publication after the Easter rising, *The national being*, in September 1916. Started two years before, in March 1914, *The national being* was a discourse on Russell's esoteric sense of Irish nationality in a period of abnormal social and economic conditions. Composed of twenty chapters, the central premise of *The national being* is that Ireland possesses a distinct national identity that must be nurtured to ensure the future success of its civilisation. Written in a generally measured style, *The national being* combines mysticism with economics to create a compelling vision of Ireland's potential. Unsurprisingly, the text is also deeply concerned with the First World War and its relevance to the Irish situation, the institution of home rule suspended from the outbreak of the conflict. The war, a disaster for European culture in general, casts a long shadow over *The national being*'s deliberations. The strikes and social disorder that Russell commented on weekly in the *Irish Homestead* become portents in *The national being* of a global realignment of spiritual and political order. The text is Russell's reading of the signs that foretell apocalypse, his prose an offering to the gods of war that he addressed poetically in 1915.

The visionary aspect of Russell's ambition is inscribed in *The national being*'s first pages. 'Hercules', Russell wrote, 'wrestled with twin serpents in his cradle',[101] just as the young Ireland struggled with the ideologies of unionism and nationalism. *The national being* is, like the *Iliad* and *Odyssey*, partly instructional in nature, a text meant, to 'reveal character … and the will which is in it'.[102] The ideal character that Russell presents to his reader is national and not individual. Economics and politics are the substance of its material constitution. Its national soul is occult, the divination of Ireland's character the responsibility of its intellectual class. Delayed at birth, the urgent need of the state's delivery was evident to Russell from the outbreak of revolutionary violence in Dublin. Russell accordingly dedicates himself in *The national being* to an 'imaginative meditation' upon the thought that 'the State is a physical body prepared for the incarnation of the soul of a race'.[103]

After two introductory chapters, Russell's meditation exposes itself to be primarily economic propaganda for the Irish co-operative movement. Co-operation was, as we have seen, the basis of Russell's ideal social organisation. By providing each class of the nation's producers and consumers with an interest in the products of their trade the national interest would be bound by common concern. Russell's vision of the co-operative commonwealth in *The national being* differs little from that espoused in the *Irish Homestead* over the ten years previous. Organised around small-scale co-operative societies, each division of the movement was responsible for its members' entire well being. Patronising to a

---

101 G. Russell, *The national being*. 2.   **102** Ibid. 3.   **103** Ibid. 2.

degree, Russell presents the reader with the typical Irish character whose lot will be improved by the working of the co-operative miracle. Named Patrick, the character Russell describes is a rural smallholder. Co-operation is the cement of his individual life as it 'connects with living links the home, the centre of Patrick's being, to the nation, the circumference of his being'.[104]

Within this circle of national association, *The national being* considers Ireland's cultural condition. There is, surprisingly, less confidence in Ireland's achievement in this sphere. Russell declares himself dissatisfied with post-revival literature and calls upon his contemporaries to reinstate a sense of wonder in their audience. The author's criticism of Irish literature is, in part, a pose, his declaration of the superiority of classical culture a common feature of polemic. But, in September 1916, the date of the *The national being*'s publication, Russell's literary prescriptions take on a novel political context:

> In ancient Ireland, in Greece, and in India, the poets wrote about great kings and heroes, enlarging on their fortitude of spirit, their chivalry and generosity, creating in the popular mind an ideal of what a great man was like; and men were influenced by the ideal created, and strove to win the praise of the bards and to be recrowned by them a second time ... in great poetry ... It is the great defect of our modern literature that it creates such few types. How hardly could one of our public men be made the hero of an epic.[105]

Russell's readership might have been surprised to read this passage five months after the Easter Rising, when Pearse's heroic vision of Cuchulain inspired him to die for an Irish republic alive only to his imagination. Russell's contemporary Yeats composed his response to the rebellion, 'Easter 1916', in the late summer and autumn of that year, in the same period in which *The national being* was first published.[106] Yeats' poem tried to capture the Rising's sacrificial integrity by its incantatory effect, his need, as Yeats put it, to 'write it out in a verse'.[107] 'Easter 1916' is, as Terence Brown has suggested, Yeats' attempt to ascribe a numerological pattern to the process of history.[108] *The national being* is less subtle a construction but is certainly schematic. The text is part of Russell's attempt to reconstitute a unitary national body from the disparate limbs of its political factions. To achieve this Russell must first contain the influence of revolutionary Irish nationalism. A bold move in light of the effect that the executions had on public opinion, Russell determines that

104 Ibid. 27.   **105** Ibid. 13–14.   **106** Brown notes that 'It is not certain when this poem was composed. It is dated September 25 in the typescript which was used in 1917 to print 25 copies ... we can assume it was much on his mind through the summer and early autumn of 1916.' *The life of W. B. Yeats*. 228.   **107** W. Yeats, 'Easter 1916'. *Yeats's poems*. 288.   **108** For Brown's reading of the

Few of our notorieties could be trusted to think out any economic or social problem thoroughly and efficiently. They have been engaged in passionate attempts at the readjustment of the superficies of things. What we require more than men of action are scholars, economists, scientists, thinkers, educationalists, and littérateurs, who will populate the desert depths of national consciousness with real thought and turn the void into a fullness.[109]

Russell's allusion to passion is, in retrospect, Yeatsian, a forewarning of the 'passionate intensity'[110] that marks the negative aspect of 'The second coming'. As figured here by Russell, intellectual reason is passion's antidote, the poet a citizen of the ideal republic that *The national being* proposes. Curiously, for a text published in its immediate aftermath by an author who knew, among others, James Connolly, Thomas MacDonagh and Patrick Pearse, the uprising itself merits only a footnote in *The national being*.[111] The simple explanation for this omission is that Russell had completed the manuscript for *The national being* before the Easter Rising occurred. Neither was Russell, in contrast to Yeats, an inveterate reviser of his work. But more revealing of Russell's attitude to the Easter Rising was his observation in the *Irish Homestead* that the rebellion was an outbreak of national fever at a time of European sickness. *The national being* dedicates more than half its space to the description of the national body and Russell admits to it no risk of contagion. Russell's deliberate myopia as regards the uprising in *The national being* is an act of decontamination, his political anatomy of the Irish soul conducted in an environment sterile of revolutionary infection. Russell's republicanism is that of the enlightenment, his senate a 'National Assembly'[112] after the French model. But Russell's discussion of the free rights of the Irish citizen distracts the reader from the reality of Ireland's imperial association. *The national being*, as Russell freely acknowledges at the end of the text, never discusses 'the relations of Ireland with other countries'.[113] Ireland is in this sense a country of Russell's imagination, a state of mind but not reality.

The first twelve chapters of *The national being* present the reader with what in contrast seems to be a concrete, rational analysis of the Irish economic situation. Each chapter discusses a particular class or problem – the condition of farmers, agricultural labourers and the urban working class are all considered.

---

poem see *The life of W. B. Yeats*. 229–36.   **109** G. Russell, *The national being*. 5.   **110** W.B. Yeats, 'The second coming'. *Yeats's poems*. 294.   **111** Referring to the general argument made by *The national being*, Russell observed that 'Since this book was written Ireland has had a tragic illustration of what is urged in these pages'. 135. It seems likely that *The national being* was already in proof copy by the time the Easter Rising occurred. Yeats was in good company among Irish writers unaware of the imminent rebellion.   **112** G. Russell, *The national being*. 120.   **113** Ibid. 150.

Sectional interest divided class from class. Russell, naturally, proposes a co-operative economic solution to their problems. If classses recognised their interdependence, then the nation would be bound to a stable, undivided entity; all, in fact, that Ireland was not in September 1916. Russell however was hopeful for his plans. At the end of the twelfth chapter, the narrator reflects on 'what we have come to'.[114] He considers that co-operation means more

> than a series of organizations for economic purposes. We hope to create finally, by the close texture of our organizations, that vivid sense of the identity of interest of the people in this island which is the basis of citizenship, and without which there can be no noble national life.[115]

The alternative is distressing. The body of the national being, like the human body after which it is ordered, will malform. 'Hardly', Russell suggests, do Irish nationalists know if an independent Ireland would 'be deformed if it survived'[116] its birth. In *The national being* only strong intellectual order can stop social miscarriage. Appropriately, *The national being* contains a blueprint for civic conscription, a method whereby Irish citizens might participate in the practical nurture of their nation. Russell compares such recruitment to the experience of conscript soldiers in the battlefields of France. But as Russell considers the combatants' motivation an occult sense of his national plan emerges:

> Men in a regiment have to a large extent the personal interests abolished. The organization they now belong to supports them and becomes their life. By their union with it a new being is created. Exercise, drill, manoeuvre, accentuate that unity, and *esprit de corps* arises, so that they feel their highest life is the corporate one; and that feeling is fostered continually, until at last all the units, by some law of the soul, are as it were in spite of themselves, in spite of the legs which want to run, in spite of the body which trembles with fear, constrained to move in obedience to the purpose of the whole organism expressed by its controlling will; and so we get these devoted masses of men who advance again and again under a hail more terrible than Dante imagined falling in his vision of the fiery world.[117]

Russell's 'controlling will' is revealing. Such a force motivates the soldiers and overcomes their physical reaction to it. It is the impetus to an advance that,

---

114 Ibid. 97.   **115** Ibid. 97–8.   **116** Ibid. 1.   **117** Ibid. 138.

as Russell suggests, approaches the mouth of hell. The standard precepts of social organisation in early twentieth-century Europe are powerless before such arcane national expression. Politicians, regents and soldiers alike are slaves to an order invisible to material social analysts. In *The national being*, the First World War, that 'great tragedy of Europe', was

> brought about, not by the German Emperor, nor Sir Edward Grey, nor by the Czar, nor any of the other chiefs ostensibly controlling foreign policy, but by the nations themselves. These men may have been agents, but their action would have been impossible if they did not realize that there is a vast body of national feeling behind them that is not opposed to war.[118]

The apocalypse that Russell considers is the product of misdirected national will. Russell suggests to the reader the existence of an *animus* similar to that *daemon* perceived by Yeats in 'The second coming'.[119] Russell reminds of Yeats regularly throughout *The national being*; now the First World War 'is wrecking our civilizations, is destroying the body of European nationalities, the spirit is freer to reshape the world nearer to the heart's desire'.[120] *The land of heart's desire* was a Yeats play of 1894 and an invocation of a faery other-world beyond the realm of everyday sense. A 'poignantly fantastical'[121]work as Brown describes it, *The land of heart's desire* is invoked by Russell in *The national being* as evidence, again, of the power of compulsion. Yeats' play is the story of a peasant woman tempted away to the land of faery by a child who is allowed to enter her family home. The mysterious child calls the woman, Mary Breen, to her by a force of will:

> You shall go with me, newly-married bride,
> And gaze upon a merrier multitude.
> (White-armed Nuala, Aengus of the Birds,
> Fiachra of the hurtling foam, and him
> Who is ruler of the Western Host,
> Finvara, and their Land of Heart's Desire,)
> Where beauty has no ebb, decay no flood,
> But joy is wisdom, time an endless song.
> I kiss you and the world begins to fade.[122]

---

118 Ibid. 153–4.   **119** Yeats' speaker feels that 'surely some revelation is at hand;/ Surely the Second Coming is at hand./ The Second Coming! Hardly are these words out/ When a vast image out of *Spiritus Mundi/* Troubles my sight'. Famously, the vision is of a 'rough beast, its hour come round at last'. 'The second coming', *Yeats's poems*. 294–5.   **120** G. Russell, *The national being*. 129.   **121** T. Brown, *The life of W.B. Yeats*. 20.   **122** W.B. Yeats, 'The land of heart's desire'. *Collected plays*.

Yeats' passage is the perfect aesthetic complement to Russell's political vision in *The national being*. The world into which Mary Breen enters is a world ordered by an occult knowledge, a wisdom that transcends time and the natural order of perception. Mary Breen is compelled to enter this alternative dimension by the call of the child to her house. Equally, the subjects of the Ireland that *The national being* addresses will be compelled to enter its new order by its revelation of a perfect vision before them. The co-operative movement, Russell's material equivalent of Yeats' faery land, exercises its seductive will on the Irish population. The only danger to this gradual revelation of Russell's social order was an Irish revolution, such as that presaged by the Easter Rising. A disruption of *The national being*'s vision, the Rising upsets the natural balance of Russell's co-operative state, much as the 'Hearts with one purpose alone' trouble Yeats' 'living stream'[123] in 'Easter, 1916'. Russell declared himself in *The national being* to be a 'friend of revolt if people cannot stand the conditions they live under, and if they can see no other way'.[124] His caution concerned the

> danger in revolution if the revolutionary spirit is much more advanced than the intellectual qualities which alone can secure the success of the revolt. These intellectual and moral qualities – the skills to organize, the wisdom to control large undertakings, are not natural gifts but the products of experience. They are evolutionary products.[125]

We are at the crux of Russell's revolutionary dilemma. Russell, for all his sympathy for Connolly and cohorts, is solicitous of the power of the natural revelation that revolution interrupts. His national being has a will of its own, its agency unlimited in comparison to that of its subjects. In this context, Pearse and Connolly were precipitate in their action, the Easter Rising a misguided attempt to call into being a nation not yet fully ordered. As Russell puts it in *The national being*:

> There are no nations to whom the entire and loyal allegiance of man's spirit could be given. It can only go out to the ideal empires and nationalities in the womb of time, for whose coming we pray. Those countries of the future we must carve out of the humanity of to-day, and we can begin building them up within our present empires and nationalities just as we are building up a co-operative movement in a social order antagonistic to it. The people who are trying to create these new ideals in the world are outposts, sentinels, and frontiersmen thrown out before the armies of the intellectual and spiritual races yet to come into being.[126]

69.   **123** W.B. Yeats, 'Easter, 1916'. *Yeats's poems*. 288.   **124** G. Russell, *The national being*. 80. **125** Ibid. 80–1.   **126** Ibid. 156.

Russell's adepts in *The national being* are the spiritual corollary of the volunteer units, with Russell's ideal Irish nation as distant from reality in 1916 as the republic that Pearse summoned to his presence in Sackville Street. The end of *The national being* recovers the revolutionary legacy of Irish nationalism that was lost, so Russell thought, to the firing squad. The text's final two chapters summon a vision of Ireland that invokes its sacred character. In part an attempt by Russell to adapt the Literary Revival to the demands of the modern state, with the practice of science and of industry, *The national being* commits itself to a future evolved beyond the vision of any of Russell's republican contemporaries. *The national being* is a generally accessible introduction to Russell's cultural and economic ideals. It is one of his least obscure books and occupies an important place in the canon of the Literary Revival as Russell's exploration of the possibilities of a new Ireland. But for all its pragmatism *The national being* is, finally, Russell's spiritual contract with the Irish nation:

> If the spirit of man has likeness to Deity, it means that if it manifests itself fully in the world, the world too becomes a shadowy likeness of the heavens, and our civilization will make a harmony with the diviner spheres … Then arise the towers, the temples, the cities, the achievements of the architect and engineer. The earth is tapped of its arcane energies, the very air yields to us its mysterious powers. We control the etheric waves and send the message of our deeds across the ocean.[127]

As Ireland settled for a brief period between the Easter Rising and the conscription crisis of 1918, *The national being*'s prescriptions retained some possible currency. Russell's evolutionary optimism was heightened by the announcement of the formation of a national assembly to discuss the possibility of home rule in May 1917. The Irish Home Rule Convention was held in Regent House, Trinity College Dublin, from 25 July 1917 to 5 April 1918. It was formed to enable Irish political parties, unionist and nationalist, to reach agreement over the status of Irish government before the end of the First World War. The British administration was faced with an enormous task of reconstruction after the end of a conflict whose outcome was still uncertain. Imperial reorganisation was complicated by the suspension of an increasingly outmoded 1914 Irish Home Rule Act on the statute books. The Irish Parliamentary Party, architects of this earlier settlement, no longer represented the full range of Irish nationalist opinion after the Easter Rising; proof of this was Eamon de Valera's election for Sinn Féin to East Clare in June 1917. To enjoy any claim to legitimacy, delegates to the Irish Convention had to be selected from outside the tra-

---

127 Ibid. 172–3.

ditional consensus. Accordingly, fifteen places were reserved for delegates with specific economic, political and social skills.[128]

Russell set himself to attend. He gathered his ideas in 'Thoughts for a Convention', published in three consecutive instalments in the *Irish Times* from 26 May 1917. Russell's choice of newspaper seems at first an odd one. The *Irish Times* was unionist and antagonistic to any nationalist demands associated with what it perceived to be the extremism of the 1916 Rising. But, as the paper's accompanying editorial note suggested, while 'We take no responsibility for Mr. Russell's opinions, many of which we are unable to accept … It is important that, on the eve of this National Convention, Irish Unionists should have an understanding of the various currents of Nationalist opinion which this Memorandum affords.'[129] Russell was popularly understood to be a fair analyst of his opponents, a quality that may have commended him to the *Irish Times*. But equally likely was Horace Plunkett's influence with the paper, an influence that contributed to Russell's publication as the privileged voice of ecumenical Irish nationalism.[130] Whatever the case, Russell constructed his thoughts in a twenty-four point memorandum of three definite sections: the ideals of the Irish parties, the limits of the necessary relationship with Britain and the possible scope of future reform.

Russell dealt first with Irish unionism. Southern unionists had survived centuries of Irish life to become closely associated with their neighbours by intermarriage and assimilation. Yet 'they still retain habits, beliefs, and traditions from which they will not part'.[131] Northern unionists 'form a class economically powerful. They have openness and energy of character, great organising power, and a mastery of materials, all qualities invaluable in the Irish state.'[132] The cliché of northern Protestant practical ability is familiar but it is important to note Russell's recognition of their virtue in context of an Irish state. This is critical to his approach to both his memorandum and to the Irish Convention. The Irish nation required heroes of Promethean stature, men, preferably, who sacrificed themselves to the ideal of a future state. With that state in reach, the hero is obsolete. What Ireland must then have, Russell suggests, are the tools of material as well as moral progress. His great dilemma is to associate this industrial impulse with national, rather than global or imperial, economics. As

128 The standard account of the assembly is R.B. McDowell. *The Irish Convention 1917–18*. Records of the Convention can also be found in P. Buckland, *The Anglo-Irish and the new Ireland 1885–1922, passim*, and T. West, *Horace Plunkett: co-operation and politics, an Irish biography*. 157–76. **129** *Irish Times*, 26 May 1917. 4. **130** John Healy edited the *Irish Times* from 1907. The British government released 120 republican prisoners involved in the 1916 Rising from jail on 16 June 1917 as a sign of its good faith to the Convention. The *Irish Times* was dissuaded from too critical an editorial response to this development by Plunkett's personal plea to Healy. See R.B. McDowell, *The Irish Convention 1917–18*. 102. **131** G. Russell, 'Thoughts for a Convention', *Irish Times*, 26 May 1917. 4. **132** Ibid.

Russell observes, Ulster unionists 'consider that security for industry and freedom for the individual can best be preserved in Ireland by the maintenance of the Union, and that the world spirit is with great Empires'.[133] We have two fundamental aspects of a future Irish identity exposed here. Ulster unionists suggest that Ireland can remain part of the Empire and involve itself in economic expansion. Sinn Féin, according to Russell's memorandum, rather believed

> that the Union kills the soul of the people; that empires do not permit the intensive cultivation of human life, that they destroy the richness and variety of existence by the extinction of peculiar and unique gifts and the substitution therefore of a culture which has its value mainly for the people who created it.[134]

With the twin poles of his argument established, Russell spends little time in his consideration of the Irish Parliamentary Party, still by 1917 the major constitutional force. Referred to as the 'Middle party',[135] constitutional nationalists are left to the previous century, having achieved 'land reform and security of tenure'.[136] The reader cannot doubt that their time has passed. Russell continues to wonder what Ulster 'could not do as efficiently in an Ireland with the status and economic power of a self-governing Dominion as they do at the present? Could they not build their ships and sell their manufacture and export their linens?'.[137] To argue this point in 1917 is to argue that an independent Ireland would not be the agriculturally dominated state that northern unionists negatively predicted. Furthermore, Russell's idea of an Irish economy independent of land holding suggests a belief that future Irish citizens might require a new identity in a state separate from the demands of nineteenth-century rural reform. Russell argues for a new Ireland in the final passage of his memorandum with a sceptical audience very much in mind. Irish members of

> The brotherhood of Dominions ... would be inspired as much by the fresh life and wide democratic outlook of Australia, New Zealand, South Africa, and Canada, as by the hoarier political wisdom of Great Britain. Does that not indicate a different form of Imperialism from that which they hold in no friendly memory? It would not be Imperialism in an ancient sense, but a federal union of independent nations to protect national liberties, which might draw into the union people hitherto unconnected to it, and so beget a league of nations to make a common international law prevail. The allegiance would be to common principles which mankind desire, and would not permit the dominance of any one

133 Ibid.   134 Ibid.   135 Ibid.   136 Ibid.   137 Ibid.

race. We have not only to be good Irishmen, but good citizens of the world.[138]

We are at a crucial point in Russell's intellectual development. He admits the deficiencies of British imperialism but it is hard not to see in his assimilative vision of universal law a similar impulse to govern and incorporate. Russell struggles here to combine the terms of imperial and national association. His compromise is to rewrite the standard language of Irish nationalism in order to incorporate northern business to the new state. Capital development was the new engine of Irish secular civilisation. Allied to it are the rational self-disciplines of industry and science. Russell now prompted the London *Times* to acknowledge his devotion to national life. The *Times* announced Russell's 'brilliant analysis of the present state of parties in Ireland'.[139] His memorandum 'has been read with keen intent by Irishmen of all parties and has produced a sequel which must be regarded as a far from negligible factor in the political situation'.[140] This sequel was James Douglas' submission to the *Irish Times* on 1 June 1917 of a list of individuals in support of Russell's memorandum. Fed to the *Times* the day before its publication in Dublin, this document was designed for maximum media effect. Its signatories expressed their general agreement with Russell but reserved the right to differ on unspecified points. Edmund Curtis, George Gavan Duffy, Nugent Everard, Alice Stopford Green, Sir John Griffith, Douglas Hyde, Lord Mounteagle and, most significantly to the *Times*, the archbishop of Dublin, William Walsh, were among the notables listed, a spontaneous upsurge of support that had been planned since at least the month before.[141]

A laudatory letter to the *Irish Times* from Horace Plunkett praised the 'tone and temper'[142] in which Russell handled 'the whole magazine of Irish controversy'[143] and hoped that Russell's memorandum would be widely read. Russell next submitted a private letter to the same newspaper from George Bernard Shaw, whose permission he had to publish it. Shaw argued that Russell's preference for imperial federation was impossible; Russell prefaced Shaw's letter

---

138 Ibid.   **139** 'Thoughts on Irish settlement', *Times*, 31 May 1917. 8.   **140** Ibid.   **141** Letters to Maurice Moore from Alice Green in April and May 1917 show that the signatories Moore hoped to attract to his initial memorandum form the main body of supporters for Russell's 'Thoughts for a Convention' in the *Irish Times*. See NLI ms 10561/10573. Archbishop Walsh's inclusion was most surprising because Russell had attacked his social conservatism during the 1913 Lock-Out in 'A plea for the workers', published in his 1913 pamphlet *The Dublin strike*. Walsh attended the Convention as a nationalist delegate. Of the others, Edmund Curtis was a Trinity historian, George Gavan Duffy the solicitor for the executed Roger Casement, Sir Nugent Everard a retired soldier, Alice Stopford Green a nationalist historian resident in London, Sir John Griffith the retired Chief Engineer of Dublin Port and Commissioner of Irish Lights, Douglas Hyde the first President of the Gaelic League and Professor of Modern Irish in University College Dublin, Lord Mounteagle an ex-unionist peer and a friend of Plunkett.   **142** *Irish Times*, 31 May 1917. 4.   **143** Ibid.

with the observation that his general idea 'was much more akin to that Council of Dominions suggested by General Smuts in a recent speech than to the scheme of federation advocated by Mr Joseph Chamberlain'.[144] Irish politics had two other trajectories beyond the dominions. Radical nationalists looked to America for democratic salvation and unionists relied on Britain to secure their rights. To Russell, dominion status offered both acknowledgement of national difference and security of association. Such settlement was anathema to Sinn Féin. When the constitution of the Irish Convention was finally ratified the separatist party refused to take the five seats offered it. This left the assembly in a potential bind. Its supporters could no longer argue that it represented all shades of Irish opinion, political and economic, to create consensus. Sinn Féin's disquiet arose not only from what it considered to be its under-representation but also from its absolute demand for Irish independence. Its hopes rested on the peace conference it hoped would follow armistice, with the rights of small nations asserted.

Of the fifteen delegates then invited to attend by Henry Duke, the chief secretary for Ireland, George Russell and Edward MacLysaght were chosen as representatives of the advanced nationalist position. Russell was asked to join the Convention on 12 July 1917. Russell wrote immediately to MacLysaght to ask if he too would accept his invitation. MacLysaght contacted Sinn Féin and made sure that it privately supported his acceptance.[145] When it was made clear that Sinn Féin would appreciate an inside view of the Convention, MacLysaght accepted and Russell, in apparent innocence of such intrigue, followed suit. Throughout his entire term as a Convention delegate, MacLysaght reported regularly to Sinn Féin in the person of Eoin MacNeill. Russell took his place alongside MacLysaght, William Martin Murphy and Horace Plunkett in an

---

144 *Irish Times*, 1 June 1917. 3. In a speech delivered to a banquet of the houses of parliament in his honour on 15 May 1917, Smuts suggested the formation of an imperial council to co-ordinate the post-war Empire. To Smuts, 'the British Empire, or this British Commonwealth of Nations, does not stand for unity, standardization, or assimilation, or denationalization; but it stands for a fuller, a richer, and more various life among all the nations that compose it. And even nations who have fought against you, like my own, must feel that they and their interests, their language, their religions, and all their cultural interests are as safe and as secure under the British flag as those of the children of your household and your own blood'. Cited from W. Hancock and J. Van Der Poel, eds., *Selections from the Smuts papers: volume three June 1910–November 1918*. 512. This speech was widely reported in the contemporary press and no doubt influenced Russell's redefinition of imperial relations at the end of his 'Thoughts for a Convention'. Joseph Chamberlain had been Secretary for the Colonies under Lord Salisbury and worked for closer relations within the Empire before he lost power with the Conservative Party in 1906.   145 Before replying to Duke's invitation, MacLysaght 'made sure that the Sinn Féin leaders approved of my accepting. It was agreed that it would be advisable to have someone in the Convention who was in sympathy and in close touch with Sinn Féin and so could act as a sort of liaison member but still could not be regarded in any sense an official representative of the party'. E. MacLysaght, *Master of none*. Unpublished autobiography, NLI ms 4750/viii–4.

assembly whose members included fifty-two constitutional nationalists, twenty-four Ulster unionists, nine southern unionists, six labour delegates and two liberals, besides a sprinkling of advanced nationalists and independent thinkers like John Pentland Mahaffy.[146] The first meeting of the assembly was held at Regent House, Trinity College Dublin, on 25 July 1917.[147] It was opened by a speech from Duke that ended with an unfortunate quotation from Cicero to never lose faith in the republic. MacLysaght's ironic cheers did nothing to soothe loyal members' irritation.[148]

The Convention's first task was to select a chairman and here Russell repaid his lifelong debt to Plunkett handsomely. The select committee appointed to elect a chairman had agreed on Lord Midleton's candidate Southborough when Russell threatened to raise the matter on the floor of the Convention if Plunkett were not afforded the honour. Under pressure from John Redmond, Midleton withdrew his candidate and Plunkett was elected unopposed.[149] The Convention then debated through August which forms of self-government were appropriate for assembly discussion. Delegates were overwhelmed with huge amounts of documents, memoranda, precedents and statistics to inform them of the full range of legislative possibilities both within and without the British Empire. MacLysaght himself remembered interminable rounds of lunch and dinner, all designed by Plunkett to encourage co-operation between members outside normal party bounds. This was an intelligent strategy but there was from the beginning little hope of settlement, the Ulster unionists unwilling to compromise when they already possessed an assurance from Lloyd George that, whatever the outcome, the north of Ireland would not be coerced into a settlement it found disagreeable.

Plunkett knew by early October 1917 that southern unionists would accept a home rule compromise and so their northern brethren remained the major obstacle. Russell himself was appointed on 11 October 1917 to a select committee of nine members of the Convention asked to report on a basis for general agreement, the thought being that concentrated attention on detailed matters was best directed by a representative selection of delegates. Russell's co-members were Hugh Barrie, Joseph Devlin, Lord Londonderry, Lord

---

146 R.B. McDowell, *The Irish Convention 1917–18*. 100. Mahaffy was Provost of Trinity College Dublin from 1914 to 1919. He kept a diary of the Convention's proceedings and made notes of other delegates' speeches. He 'profoundly disagreed' with Russell, especially on matters of national education. See Trinity College Dublin (cited subsequently as TCD) mss 2986–2987/178–204. **147** The press were not allowed to publish details of the workings of the Irish Convention once it started sitting. Neither were speeches formally recorded in an attempt to encourage delegates to state freely held opinions. Details of Convention business in the pages following derive mostly from TCD ms 2986–7, especially Item 177, Horace Plunkett's secret dispatch, 'The Irish Convention, confidential report by the chairman to His Majesty the King'. **148** E. MacLysaght, Master of none. Unpublished autobiography, NLI ms 4750/viii-6/7. **149** R.B. McDowell, *The Irish Convention 1917–18*. 104.

Midleton, William Martin Murphy, the Most Reverend Patrick O'Donnell, then bishop of Raphoe, Hugh Pollock and John Redmond.[150] Russell found the process of committee work entirely disagreeable; he remarked to MacLysaght that working for settlement with the stubborn Barrie was degrading. There was disappointment when the committee ended in deadlock over the issue of fiscal autonomy, which the nationalists desired, as opposed to fiscal union, which the unionists demanded. The committee composed a draft of its findings by 15 November 1917 and Russell signed an appendix that stated the minimum economic requirements of an Irish dominion; Russell, Redmond, the bishop of Raphoe and Devlin all thought it essential that Ireland raise and collect its own taxes, control its foreign trade and be guaranteed of no disadvantage in the British market. The final words of their appendix suggest again the limits to which the definition of an Irish nation was stretched by the necessity of material reorganisation; 'We regard',[151] they wrote, 'Ireland as a nation, an economic entity. Governments exist to foster the economic interests of their peoples. Self-government does not exist where those nominally entrusted with affairs of government have not control of fiscal and economic policy.'[152] It is hard to imagine a definition of Ireland further removed from the epic inspiration of most Irish nationalist literature and propaganda of the early twentieth century.

Russell grew increasingly frustrated with the Convention as October passed to November. Plunkett in fact warned him of his conduct in committee in early November; MacLysaght later remembered Russell's absolute disillusion with the lack of what he perceived to be any Ulster unionist good faith in attempting a compromise that would avoid partition.[153] A major development was Lord Midleton's secret November 1917 'Memorandum of southern unionists', circulated among delegates to suggest that 'We are ready, if the Irish parliament be constituted as proposed with fair representation of the minority and other effective safeguards which are in our view essential, to concede to it control of internal taxes, administration, legislation, judicature and police'.[154] Midleton's clever

---

150 Hugh Barrie was Unionist MP for North Londonderry; Joseph Devlin was Irish Parliamentary Party MP for west Belfast; Lord Londonderry was a Conservative MP recalled from service with the Royal Horse Guards to serve at the Convention; Lord Midleton was leader of the southern unionists; William Martin Murphy was an industrialist and owner of the nationalist *Irish Independent*; Patrick O'Donnell had been closely connected to the Irish Parliamentary Party but was critical of the 1916 executions and sympathetic to Sinn Féin; Hugh Pollock was a businessman nominated to the Convention to represent the Belfast chamber of commerce; John Redmond was MP for Waterford and leader of the Irish Parliamentary Party until his death during the Convention on 6 March 1918. **151** Item 70, TCD ms 2986–7/70, fol 21. **152** Ibid. **153** MacLysaght recalled that 'In November Æ considered resignation and writing to Lloyd George a letter (to be published) in which he would state how the Ulster Unionists with the former's pledge in their pockets sat and jeered at all efforts to compromise knowing their safety to block everything'. Master of none. Unpublished autobiography, NLI ms 4750/viii–7. **154** TCD ms 2986/73, fol 2. Item 73.

use of the word 'internal' qualifies his enthusiasm for the scope of Irish home rule but he does at least acknowledge such a project's legitimacy. The next major submission to the Convention was the formal submission of Russell's committee's findings on 18 December 1917. With the Convention's absolute failure to make any compromise between unionist and nationalist demands it is no coincidence that Russell's next move was to publish the next day an inflammatory open letter in the *Irish Times*. As a preface to a poem, 'To the memory of some I knew who are dead and who loved Ireland', in praise of Ireland's dead from the First World War and the Easter Rising, Russell observed 'The modern Irish are a race built up from many races who have to prove themselves for the future'.[155] 'We are a new people',[156] he wrote, 'and not the past, but the future, is to justify a new nationality'.[157]

But what did the future hold? Russell considered himself the prophet of a nation as yet unveiled. He had warned delegates of the consequences of their failure to recognise this new era in his very first speech to the Convention. Plunkett reported that 'if failure followed our deliberations',[158] Russell 'felt that he could "hear the whistle of bullets in the street; see the gutter filled with blood while the souls of young men part prematurely into the wisdom of their God protesting against the Convention and its want of wisdom" '.[159] His warning ignored, he stormed into Plunkett's office on the last day of December 1917 furious at a lack of progress. The same month he wrote to MacLysaght that the Convention was bound to fail, as it was unrepresentative of Irish opinion; but he would 'not withdraw unless there was a ghost of a chance of it [the Convention] doing any good'.[160] Russell's retreat to a world of spectres suggests something of his withdrawal from the blunt reality of Convention politics. He was absent from the sittings of the ninth and tenth of January but reappeared on the fifteenth to be listed by Plunkett as a member of the advanced nationalist caucus that centred around Russell, the bishop of Raphoe and William Martin Murphy. A critical moment was MacLysaght's resignation on 22 January 1918. Russell soon made what was to be his own last speech to the Convention before he too resigned on 1 February 1918. Russell, in Plunkett's words,

> gratefully acknowledged the sacrifice of feeling made by the Southern Unionists and would have accepted their proposals had Ulster come in. Failing that essential of a settlement, which would ensure the setting up of an all-Ireland parliament, he could not accept a compromise which meant 'a bow to God and a wink to the devil'. He longed for an end to political agitation in the interest of the Arts and civilisation, and for the

155 'The new nation', *Irish Times*, 19 December 1917. 6.   **156** Ibid.   **157** Ibid.   **158** H. Plunkett, 'The Irish Convention, confidential report by the chairman to His Majesty the King'. 154.   **159** Ibid.   **160** A. Denson, ed., *Letters from Æ*. 134.

friendship of England in order to end demoralising racial animosities. Above all, he wanted to throw upon Ireland the responsibilities of self-government before the socialistic and revolutionary ideas now rampant in Russia had, as they inevitably would, developed to be vast. 'There is going to be wild weather through the world, and we want an Irish captain and an Irish crew in command of the Irish ship.'[161]

Russell's naval metaphor was well chosen as his prediction of social disturbance was aimed directly at the Ulster unionist delegates, fond as they were of the Belfast shipyards as symbol of their success. Plunkett reports this speech in a spirit of melancholy, depressed at Russell's withdrawal from the Convention.[162] But Russell's words were a coded threat. Only two weeks before his final convention speech, the *Irish Homestead* predicted apocalypse. The first two seals were broken in 1789 in France and in 1917 in Russia. Russell felt the next rupture was imminent.

> We are only on the outskirts of that commotion, but we will not escape from it, though as we are not, except in North-East Ulster, a highly industrialised people the most revolutionary effects will in all possibility not be felt here. The revolutionary ideas will, we believe, affect the great city populations and must in turn affect the rural populations, especially due to the determination of workers in towns that there must be no profiteering in foodstuffs.[163]

Russell conveniently ignores the urban centres of Dublin, Cork and Galway to concentrate on Belfast as the centre of industrialisation and of contagion. Open to the world's goods, Belfast was also open to the world's ideas, and socialism, like linen, travels to its most suitable market. Russell's experience of Ulster unionism had evidently persuaded him that the Belfast working classes were as frustrated as he was himself. His final gift to the northern leaders was the threat of a revolution that would make nonsense of their claims to industrial protection within the empire. He left Plunkett on better terms, unwilling to offend a

---

161 H. Plunkett, 'The Irish Convention, confidential report by the chairman to His Majesty the King'. 5–6.   **162** Plunkett declared himself 'distressed' at Russell's 'proposed withdrawal' from the Convention. He hoped that Russell would accompany the convention to meet the British cabinet in London in early February 1918. Russell responded, 'The Sinn Feiners were right in their intuitions from the first. If I had followed my intuition from the first I would have remained away also. A man must be either an Irishman or an Englishman in this matter. I am Irish.' Cited from A. Denson, ed. *Letters from Æ.* 136–8. Russell's memory was as faulty as his faith in intuition if he obscured his early enthusiasm for the Convention. His experience of the assembly soured him to any further participation in representative politics; he was to turn down an invitation from William Cosgrave to join the Free State Senate in 1922.   **163** G. Russell, 'NOTW', *IH*, 12 January 1918. 19.

man who was both his proprietor at the *Irish Homestead* and a close friend. Russell kept his letter of resignation confidential from the press but stated his belief that the new Irish nationalism inspired by the Easter Rising was akin to a religion among Irish youth. The rebellion had unleashed a national feeling that could not be countermanded; 'any government established', he wrote, 'which does not allow this national impulse free play will be wrecked by it'.[164] There was little immediate sign of such possible accommodation; Edward Carson arrived in Belfast to advise Convention unionists the same day Russell resigned and the *Irish Times* published a bullish editorial that condemned what it perceived to be bullying Sinn Féin election tactics.[165]

The Convention stuttered on until 5 April 1918 when it adjourned without agreement. Miss Lily Power was the greatest immediate beneficiary of its failure, winning a competition by Paterson's matches in the *Irish Independent* to guess the nearest number of Convention sittings. She predicted forty-seven, four off the actual total of fifty-one. But world circumstance changed rapidly by 1918 and even Miss Power could not guess the effect of the Russian Revolution and the end of European war on Ireland. What remained constant was Russell's apocalyptic vision of the future. Russell also anticipated social disharmony on the demobilisation of conscript armies at the end of the First World War. Fired by the portent of these great changes, Russell returned to public expression in the *Irish Homestead*, ever a refuge for his thoughts. But Russell could not ignore his active political instincts for long. Pushed by the end of the decade to a defence of his co-operative ideal Russell became, as the decade closed with an Anglo-Irish war, a nationalist radical by even his own previous standard.

---

164 H. Plunkett, 'The Irish Convention, confidential report by the chairman to His Majesty the King'. 4   **165** The *Irish Times* criticised what it perceived to be the Duke administration's inability to suppress Sinn Féin sedition during a South Armagh by-election. *Irish Times*, 2 February, 1918. 6.

3 / World circumstance: 1917–21

George Russell's resignation from the Irish Convention in February 1918 disappointed Plunkett.[1] But signs of his discontent with the assembly were apparent throughout December 1917. The same month saw Russell again use the *Irish Times* to publish his reflections on the Irish situation, just as he had with his 'Thoughts for a convention'. But there are great differences between Russell's December letter, 'The new nation', and its predecessor. 'Thoughts for a convention' was published to secure Russell's nomination to a senatorial body. 'The new nation', with its postscript, the poem 'To the memory of some I knew who are dead and who loved Ireland', proclaimed Russell's belief in a new Ireland subsequent to that conceived of in Plunkett's Convention. Aware that the assembly had failed to create pan-Irish consensus, Russell rewrote the terms of Irish controversy to create aesthetic unity where none could exist politically.

'The new nation' first reflects that Christmas is a time of truce between enemies. Proposing to use this period of quietened emotion to consider Ireland's future, Russell first admitted the intractability of Ireland's political problem. Unionism and nationalism were the constant themes of a dispute that would not be solved even by partition. Separation itself was 'no settlement, because there is no geographical limitation of these passions'.[2] Russell attempted to negotiate Ireland's political situation rather by a redefinition of the terms of Irish nationality. Inspired by the season of the nativity, Russell announced the birth of a new race. 'We have been told', he wrote, 'that there are two nations in Ireland.'[3] This is 'not true to-day' as the union of 'Saxon and Celt which has been going on for centuries is now completed'.[4] So Russell determined the existence of 'one Irish character', that of 'a new race'.[5]

This was a bold claim and Russell's basis for it is hardly less surprising. He admitted the distress of Ireland's colonial experience but suggested that it revived both the indigenous and invading peoples. Russell found the 'invasions

---

1 In a letter to Russell dated 6 Feb. 1918, Plunkett acknowledged that 'while your resignation may be a very serious blow to the Convention in Ireland, in England, and perhaps most of all in America, I am using what I can sincerely say of your character, intellect and knowledge to bring it home to the Government that they must deal seriously, radically and immediately with the situation'. Denson typescript. 332.   2 G. Russell, 'The new nation', *Irish Times*, 19 Dec. 1917. 6.   3 Ibid.   4 Ibid.   5 Ibid.

of Ireland and the Plantations, however morally unjustifiable, however cruel in method ... justified by biology'.[6] Furthermore, the 'invasion of one race by another is nature's ancient way of reinvigorating a race'.[7] Russell's evidence for this in modern times was Pearse's rebellion against British power in Ireland, motivated by his half-English parentage.[8] Whatever the scientific merit of Russell's biological theory it does, in December 1917, illustrate the depth of his disillusion with the consensual process of the Irish Convention. Russell saw in its irresolution the inertia of a dying culture. He found that

> Mr. Flinders Petrie, in his 'Revolutions of Civilisation', has demonstrated that civilisation comes in waves, that races rise to a pinnacle of power and culture, and decline after that, and fall into decadence, from which they do not emerge until there has been a crossing of races, a fresh intermingling of cultures. He showed in ancient Egypt eight such periods, and after every decline into decadence there is an invasion, the necessary precedent to a fresh ascent with reinvigorated energies.[9]

Sir William Matthew Flinders Petrie was born at Greenwich, London, on 3 June 1853. The son of a distinguished family, his maternal grandfather died in exploration of Australia and Tasmania in service of the Royal Navy. He travelled to Egypt to begin work on the great pyramid at Giza in 1880 and uncovered pottery fragments at Naukratis and Daphnae that proved these Egyptian sites to be trading posts of the ancient Greeks. His most famous find was the Meneptah Stele, unearthed at Thebes in 1896. Meneptah was King of Egypt from 1214 to 1204 BC and his stele contains the earliest discovered reference to Israel. Professor of Egyptology at University College London in 1892, Petrie was knighted in 1923. He was author, in 1911, of the book that attracted Russell's interest above, *The revolutions of civilisation*. Working from his analysis of cultural change in the ancient world, Petrie attempted to chart the rate of global human progress. To this end he created a timetable for cultural development and decline, with periods of growth followed by retrenchment and, finally, destruction. Petrie was a scholar of the period of high empire, his belief secure in the scientific method and unmatched resources of his discipline. Finding himself gifted with a wider, more schematic, knowledge of antiquity than any of his forbears, Petrie was moved to ask in *The revolutions of civilisation* if we can

> extract a meaning from all the senseless turmoil and striving, and success and failure, of these thousands of years? Can we see any regular struc-

6 Ibid. 7 Ibid. 8 Russell noted that 'Pearse himself, for all his Gaelic culture, was sired by one of the race he fought against. He might stand as the symbol of the new race which is springing up'. 'The new nation', *Irish Times*, 19 Dec. 1917. 6. 9 Ibid.

ture behind it at all? Can we learn any general principles that may formulate the past, or be projected on the mists of the future?[10]

Petrie's book suggests that failure is inscribed in the success of any human culture. Humanity declines when it becomes too comfortable and must be shocked into a new sense of itself; the barbarian invasions of the Roman Empire, for example, were the predictable outcome of earlier Roman hegemony. Russell further learnt from Petrie that race conflict between indigenous and invading races was inevitable in the first stage of civilisation and that in the second stage, union between the two former antagonists was possible.[11] In 'The new nation', Russell casts the Irish Convention and its adherents as the immobile standards of an old order, their glory decayed. They will be superseded by a new Irish race, forged from the conflict between Gael and planter since the sixteenth century, long matured in silence to be announced in the Easter Rising. The rebellion is the first act of patriotism on behalf of a new nation, comparable in honour to the death of Irish constitutional volunteers in the First World War. Much to the disgust of the *Irish Times*,[12] Russell felt that 'No one has more to give than life, and, when that is given, neither Nationalist nor Imperialist in Ireland can claim moral superiority for the dead champions of their cause'.[13]

As postscript, 'The new nation' has a poem, 'To the memory of some I knew who are dead and who loved Ireland'. An extended version of an earlier work, 'Salutation', which dealt only with the Irish rebellion, 'To the memory of some I knew' has seven stanzas, the first six of which speak alternatively of the Easter Rising and the great war. The seventh attempts in literature the political miracle of reconciling the differing opinions of the previous six. The premise of 'To the memory of some I knew' is that both republicans and Irish volunteers in service of the crown shared the same motivation, patriotism. Patrick Pearse is the first subject. Despite the speaker's declaration that Pearse died for a 'dream, not mine',[14] his sacrifice yet managed to turn 'life's water into wine'.[15] This image

---

10 W. Petrie, *The revolutions of civilisation*. 2.   **11** Petrie argued that 'The rise of a new civilisation is conditioned by an immigration of a different people. That is to say, it arises from a mixture of two different races. That effect of mixture cannot take place all at once. There are barriers of antiquity, barriers of creed, barriers of social standing, but every barrier to race-fusion gives way in time, when two races are in contact'. *The revolutions of civilisation*. 128.   **12** The *Irish Times* printed Russell's letter because he 'is a member of the Irish Convention, and the views of members of that body, whether wise or foolish, have more than a personal importance; and because we wish to state, clearly and promptly, the attitude of all Irish loyalists to his appeal for what we may describe as a moral amnesty'. That attitude was, understandably, negative. Russell's opinions were 'not held by the ... Irishmen who have died in Flanders and Gallipoli. To most of them Mr. Russell's appeal ... is inexpressibly painful.' 'The only way', *Irish Times*, 19 Dec. 1917. 4.   **13** G. Russell, 'The new nation', *Irish Times*, 19 Dec. 1917. 6.   **14** Ibid.   **15** Ibid.

of communion, with its presentation of wine as the blood of Christ, made possible by death, is central to the poem's meaning. Death is the shedding of the physical self in pursuit of a higher spiritual consciousness. The fact that life is given up voluntarily is sanction to the ideal left behind. Pearse's final dream was an independent Irish republic. With Pearse dead, the speaker revises this ideal: 'my spirit rose in pride,/ Refashioning in burnished gold/ The image of those who died'.[16] The speaker leaves us with a totem, speechless in its golden casket. Russell makes individuals addressed in the poem icons for his new race, their violence understood symbolically to be a stimulus to Ireland's intellectual development.

The second stanza marks the death of Alan Anderson, son of R.A. Anderson, secretary of the IAOS. He fell on the 'fields of France as undismayed'[17] by death as Pearse in Dublin. The speaker insists that Anderson died content with the 'thought of some thing for Ireland done'.[18] This ideal 'lured' him to his death on the 'long heroic barricade'.[19] Russell's description of the trenches as an 'heroic barricade' is a romantic fudge. In order to elevate Anderson's death to a symbolic level Russell is, ironically, forced to ignore the horrific reality of his last moments. The same is true of the poem's third stanza addressed to Thomas MacDonagh, another executed leader of the Rising. MacDonagh's 'high talk'[20] is transformed after the rebellion. It 'grew/ To nobleness by death redeemed'.[21] At this point the poem's rhetoric is on the verge of collapse. The power of speech becomes meaningless before MacDonagh's execution: 'Life cannot utter words more great/ Than life may meet by sacrifice'.[22] Rhetoric is exposed as the route to a symbolic dead end as 'high words were equalled by high fate'.[23] The speaker acknowledges this development but his recognition of violence and death as powers equal to dialogue and discussion sets a dangerous precedent. Frightened by such a possibility, he retracts. Those Irishmen who fought in the European war 'proved by death as true as they [the rebels],/ In mightier conflicts played your part,/ Equal your sacrifice may weigh'.[24] The speaker's use of 'may' is a crucial qualification to his argument that both conflicts will occupy an equal part of the Irish imagination. The speaker becomes defensive, asserting 'That other Ireland did you wrong/ Who said you shadowed Ireland's star'.[25] But poetic unity is, finally, impossible. It becomes the speaker's duty to provide the dead of the First World War with 'laurel wreath' and 'song',[26] the slain silent beneath the poet's valediction. Pearse and MacDonagh share the same fate, heroic in death and amenable to eulogy because of their silence. The only individual blessed by Russell with a future is Connolly, the emissary of a hope that 'lives on age after age', that 'Earth with its beauty might be won/ For labour as

16 Ibid.   17 Ibid.   18 Ibid.   19 Ibid.   20 Ibid.   21 Ibid.   22 Ibid.   23 Ibid.   24 Ibid.
25 Ibid.   26 Ibid.

a heritage'.[27] Cast as Christ, Connolly triumphs over death, to be evangelised by the speaker. Importantly, Connolly is credited with closure in the poem, to 'cast the last torch on the pile'.[28]

Of all the icons created in 'To the memory of some I knew', Connolly is the only one associated with any vital force. Immediately after the Rising, the *Irish Homestead* knew that 'a hundred other streams fed the revolt, streams of history, culture, politics, etc., but this group of dissatisfied labour held the inflammatory spark which set fire to all'.[29] Connolly is the keeper of the flame and by sacrifice ensures its persistence. Of all the dead who 'put life by with a smile', Connolly remains 'my man'.[30] The speaker's identification with Connolly weakens the final stanzas. The speaker's address is vague ('You, too, had Ireland in your care,/ Who watched o'er pits of blood and mire') and idealized (battlefields become 'Wild forests, magical, of fire').[31] Those killed in the war are simply the 'gallant dead'[32] as if their very number defies the speaker to deal in anything but platitudes.[33] Finally, the speaker lays a wreath for William Redmond 'on your clay'.[34] Russell was prescient in his assignment of constitutional Irish nationalism, in the form of William Redmond, to history, for John Redmond's Irish Parliamentary Party collapsed under Sinn Féin pressure in the 1918 election. In contrast, neither Connolly's execution nor burial is mentioned in 'To the memory of some I knew'. The speaker promises instead that 'One river, born from many streams' will 'Roll in one blaze of blinding light'.[35] United behind Connolly the torchbearer, Irish nationalism was bound to a social awareness its adherents, in the form of the Irish Parliamentary Party, had previously neglected. In context of Russell's intellectual development to 1917, 'To the memory of some I knew' marks a significant progression. It reiterates Russell's sympathy for Irish labour and declares Connolly as Russell's avatar, a precursor of the new order whose cultural edifice would be constructed by sympathetic intellectuals.

Freed meanwhile from his responsibilities at the Irish Convention, Russell spent the majority of 1918 at work on *The candle of vision*. Published in November of that year, the book is part an autobiographical account of Russell's early life and part prophecy. Divided into twenty separate chapters, *The candle of vision* was one of Russell's better-selling books.[36] Its first section treats of Russell's youth and manhood and is the closest that Russell ever came to writing sus-

---

27 Ibid. **28** Ibid. **29** G. Russell, 'NOTW', *IH*, 26 Aug. 1916. 537. **30** G. Russell, 'The new nation', *Irish Times*, 19 Dec. 1917. 6. **31** Ibid. **32** Ibid. **33** For a record of Irish involvement in the British Army in the First World War see T. Johnstone, *Orange, green and khaki, passim*. **34** G. Russell, 'The new nation', *Irish Times*, 19 Dec. 1917. 6. **35** Ibid. **36** In a letter to Charles Weekes of 7 Feb. 1919, Russell confessed to be 'rather astonished about the Candle going into a third edition. I expected to sell about 500. I would have made the book twice the size but I got scared, though I think now I might have gone on'. Denson typescript. 347.

tained reflection on his early experience.[37] After three chapters *The candle of vision* becomes a more general dissertation on the nature of perception, the origin of human language and the relation of matter to spirit. But the text's dominant theme is Russell's fascination with the nature and exercise of authority. Chapters on meditation, poetry or vision all lead to a similar conclusion, that

> What we are alone has power. We may give up the outward personal struggle and ambition, and if we leave all to the Law all that is rightly ours will be paid. Man becomes truly the Superman when he has this proud consciousness. No matter where he may be, in what seeming obscurity, he is still the King, still master of his fate, and circumstance reels about him or is still as he, in the solitude of his spirit, is mighty or humble.[38]

It is hard not to read these lines in light of Russell's experience of the Irish convention in the year and more previous. Russell's frustration at the failure of the assembly to acknowledge the relevance of Sinn Féin to the contemporary situation bred in him the belief that change, if it were to occur at all, would have to happen at an individual level. To effect this transformation, Russell constructed *The candle of vision* as a psychological primer, written to equip the reader with skills for adequate self-perception. Meditation is prescribed as the primary means to enlightenment. With its practice

> We learn our hitherto unknown character. We did not know we could feel such fierce desires, never imagined such passionate enmities as now awaken. We have created in ourselves a centre of power and grow real to ourselves. It is dangerous, too, for we here fling ourselves into the eternal conflict between spirit and matter, and find ourselves where the battle is hottest, where the foemen are locked in a death struggle.[39]

The candle of vision was written to help us see; the truth that Russell wishes to illuminate is that literature has a sacred duty of more immediate relevance to Ireland than party organisation. Russell wonders if, after due self-consideration, we would

> fully come to ourselves, [and] be like those beings in the Apocalypse full of eyes within and without? Would we, in the fulness of power, act

---

[37] One of Russell's early personal joys was his friendship with Yeats: 'I had just attempted to write in verse when I met a boy whose voice was soon to be the most beautiful voice in Irish literature ... The occurrence of our personalities seemed mysterious and controlled by some law of spiritual gravitation, like that which in the chemistry of nature makes one molecule fly to another.' *The candle of vision*. 16–17. **38** G. Russell, *The candle of vision*. 17–18. **39** Ibid. 22–3.

through many men and speak through many voices? Were Shakespeare and the great masters unconscious magi, blind visionaries, feeling and comprehending a life they could not see or who, if they saw, thought it was their own creation …?[40]

This passage reiterates a recurrent theme in Russell's writing: the idea that literature is a medium for occult force. His interest in Shakespeare is of great importance to this section of *The candle of vision*. By connecting Shakespeare to prophecy, Russell suggests that in troubled times the artist can perceive in advance a disturbance of the material world. In periods of disruption a writer can divine the dominant spiritual force behind physical reality, the trembling, as it were, behind the veil. Russell was inspired to this idea by the Romantic poet Shelley, whose *Prometheus unbound* permeates *The candle of vision*.[41] First published in 1820, *Prometheus unbound* was Shelley's adaptation of Aeschylus' *Prometheus bound*. The substance of the original myth was that Prometheus the Titan was condemned to suffer punishment by Zeus because of his gift to humankind of fire and the arts. For this the titan was bound to a rock for an eternity before being plunged into an abyss. Shelley alludes to this fate as his hero, unbroken,

> … would fain
> Be what it is my destiny to be,
> The saviour and strength of suffering man,
> Or sink into the original gulf of things.[42]

Shelley's play differs from that of Aeschylus in that Prometheus is unbound from his rock while Jupiter, who is Zeus in Greek myth, is overcome by the mysterious figure of the Demogorgon. As a symbol of the oppressed, Prometheus is, to Shelley, an embodiment of a republican energy that promises humanity a new dignity. The Demogorgon, an embodiment of an original primal god, alive before Olympian or Titan, ends the play with a refrain suitable to an Ireland in recovery after 1916.

> To defy power which seems omnipotent;
> To love, and bear; to hope, till Hope creates

---

40 Ibid. 52–3.   **41** Shelley is mentioned twice in *The candle of vision*. 'We are overcome', Russell writes, 'when we read Prometheus Unbound, but who, as he reads, flings off the enchantment to ponder in what state was the soul of Shelley in that ecstasy of swift creation[?]' *The candle of vision*. 27–8. Later Russell wonders if second sight is the substance of 'Poetry or fantasy. It has visited thousands in all ages and lands, and from such visions have come all that is most beautiful in poetry or art. Their forms inhabited Shelley's cloudland.' *The candle of vision*. 169. **42** P. Shelley, *Prometheus unbound*. 107.

From its own wreck the thing it contemplates;
Neither to change, nor falter, nor repent:
This, like thy glory, Titan, is to be
Good, great and joyous, beautiful and free;
This is alone Life, Joy, Empire, and Victory.[43]

Shelley's resolution is boldly idealistic. But to have given the gods such radical voice, Russell felt Shelley to be under divine influence. Shelley had, Russell
thought, divine sanction for his vision. He had created a holy book, just as Russell hoped to in *The candle of vision*.[44] Shelley's hero, Prometheus, is furthermore
a combination of suffering, nobility and triumph, each of which attributes
appealed to Russell as ideal aspects of Irish character. Russell's mind was drawn
to archetypes and Prometheus was especially attractive in the connection he
offered between art and the masses, between individual heroism and the general population. Shelley acknowledged that *Prometheus unbound* was more than
entertainment.

> The great writers of our age are, we have reason to suppose, the com-
> panions and forerunners of some unimagined change in our social con-
> dition, or the opinions which cement it. The cloud of mind is discharg-
> ing its collected lightning, and the equilibrium between institutions and
> opinions is now restoring, or about to be restored.[45]

Russell had a more disturbed, and in the immediate sense, less optimistic
vision than Shelley. But both believed that the artist had a gift to motivate the
collective consciousness of his audience. Russell chose to stimulate Irish perception by devoting a central section of *The candle of vision* to the description of
an apparition of 1897. In a letter to Yeats of June that year, Russell had
described an avatar who lived in a cottage in Sligo, 'middle-aged' with 'a grey
golden beard and hair (more golden than grey), face very delicate and absorbed.
Eyes have a curious golden fire in them, broad forehead.'[46] Russell, like Yeats,
to whom he first told of his experience, was thrilled with the possible arrival of
a celtic avatar. Recalling that time in *The candle of vision* Russell remembered
that 'I was meditating about twenty-one years ago in a little room, and my med-

---

43 Ibid. 233.   **44** Russell wrote in the preface that 'These retrospects and meditations are the
efforts of an artist and poet to relate his own vision to the vision of the seers and writers of the
sacred books.' *The candle of vision*. vii-viii.   **45** P. Shelley, *Prometheus unbound*. 41.   **46** H. Summerfield, *That myriad-minded man*. 78. Coincidentally, the figure of Russell's vision bears a
remarkable resemblance to an individual described in Whitman's 'I sing the body electric'.
Whitman's speaker relates a man 'of wonderful vigour, calmness, beauty of person' and celebrates 'The shape of his head, the pale yellow and white of his hair and beard, the/ immeasur-
able meaning of his black eyes, the richness and breadth of his/ manners'. *Leaves of grass*. 124.

itation was suddenly broken by a series of pictures which flashed before me.'[47] Now in its twenty-first year, Russell's vision has attained its majority and Russell reveals the full extent of its potential significance for the first time in *The candle of vision*.

The vision has four parts. The first is familiar from correspondence between Russell and Yeats in the late 1890s. It records Russell's imagination of a figure descended from the sky to an unspecified rural district, 'broad and noble in type, beardless and dark-haired'.[48] The avatar was of great physical presence, having a face 'in … breadth akin to [that] of the young Napoleon, and I would refer both to a common archetype'.[49] Never one for self-restraint, Russell describes his second vision as the appearance of 'a woman with a blue cloak around her shoulders, who came into a room and lifted a young child upon her lap, and from all Ireland rays of light converged upon that child'.[50] Russell's revelation is, up to this point, predictable. Its first character might be one of the magi appearing before the second vision's nativity scene. The Christ-like associations of the child are obvious, with the mother dressed in the blue so favoured by iconographers of the virgin mother. Heaven's light sanctifies the scene. The vision attains power only in its latter sequence:

> I was brought from Ireland to look on the coronation throne at Westminster, and there sat on it a figure of empire who grew weary and let fall of sceptre from its fingers, and itself then drooped and fell and disappeared from the famous seat. And after that in swift succession came another scene, and a gigantic figure, wild and distraught, beating a drum, stalked up and down, and wherever its feet fell there were sparks and the swirling of flame and black smoke upward from burning cities.[51]

In a letter of July 1918 to St John Ervine, Russell had claimed that *The candle of vision* would 'finally make it impossible for me to take part in politics in Ireland as it is full of religious heresies'.[52] The adoption of the virgin and Christ to Russell's own personal doctrine was certainly unorthodox. But Russell's suggestion that *The candle of vision* would end his political career was misleading; it promised instead to re-position him as an independent radical after the failure of the Irish Convention. Disillusioned with the legislative process, Russell established his new status as outcast prophet, much in the Old Testament man-

---

47 G. Russell, *The candle of vision*. 97.   **48** Ibid. 99.   **49** Ibid.   **50** Ibid.   **51** Ibid.   **52** Denson typescript. 338.   **53** *The candle of vision* has two Bible quotations on its title page. The first is from Proverbs: 'The spirit of man is the Candle of the Lord.' The 'Candle of the lord' was the text's original title until Russell discovered that another book published by Macmillan shared the same title. See the Denson typescript. 339. The second quotation, appropriately, is from Job: 'When this candle shined upon my head and by His light I walked through darkness.' *The candle of vision*. iii.

ner.[53] He predicted the arrival of a saviour and interpreted his vision of 1897 as a premonition of the Messiah's imminent birth:

> All that I could make of the sequence was that some child of destiny, around whom the future of Ireland was to pivot, was born then or to be born, and that it was to be an avatar was symbolised by the descent of the first figure from the sky, and that before the high destiny was to be accomplished the power of empire was to be weakened, and there was to be one more tragic episode in Irish history.[54]

Russell has a powerful sense of Irish salvation. In biblical tradition prophets proved themselves unmoved by popular condemnation. Russell likewise speaks as an individual who has renounced the responsibility of collective decision-making to speak from the margins of Irish culture. His message is simple. The Irish are a blessed race and their nation is held, not by the British Empire, but in trust of a higher spiritual sanction. Conflict and martyrdom are, in turn, two necessary aspects of national rejuvenation. Written immediately before the outbreak of the Anglo-Irish war, it is tempting to think that what Russell perceived in his vision was less the coming of an Irish Christ than an acknowledgement of the determination of a relative minority to achieve independence. Elements of Russell's faith did coincide with certain articles of Irish revolutionary theory. Russell, like many Irish republicans in the period, made a fetish of heroic leadership. *The candle of vision* was written in the period when Pearse, and to a lesser degree Connolly, were first elevated to secular sainthood.[55] Russell concluded the report of his own premonition in optimism: 'I look everywhere in the face of youth, in the aspect of every new notability, hoping before I die to recognise the broad-browed avatar of my vision'.[56] This most readable of all Russell's books ends with inspiration. *The candle of vision* demands participation from its readers, whose duty it is to make 'this world into the likeness of the Kingdom of Light'.[57] The temptation is to read Russell's religious rhetoric as evidence of innocent aspiration. But his evangelism was deeply rooted in his awareness of material conditions contemporary to the publication of his text. *The candle of*

54 G. Russell, *The candle of vision*. 100. **55** Pearse's posthumous public standing was secured partly by the wide edition of his works in the years immediately after his death. Padraic Colum and E.J. O'Brien for example edited *Poems of the Irish Revolutionary Brotherhood: Thomas Mac-Donagh, P.H. Pearse (Padraic MacPiarais), Joseph Mary Plunkett, Sir Roger Casement* in July 1916. A second edition was published in America just four months after the executions took place, evidence of early sympathy for the rebels. Pearse also had his *Poems* issued in Dublin by Maunsel in 1918. Maunsel reissued Connolly's works in 1917. Connolly was a favourite subject for dedications from Irish revolutionary authors; Aodh de Blacam addressed *Towards the republic* 'To the Irish Democracy in Memory of James Connolly'. np. **56** G. Russell, *The candle of vision*. 101. **57** Ibid. 169.

vision, it will be remembered, was issued at the end of October 1918, less than a month before the end of the First World War. As Europe considered its post-war dispensation, Russell suggested sympathy for socialism in his desire to reverse established social orders. Appropriately, *The candle of vision* leaves us with a continent of 'fierce things made gentle, and timid things made bold, and small made great'.[58]

'The coming of trusts', Russell's first editorial after the armistice was signed, clearly identifies Russell's post-war antagonists.[59] The 'old world empires are ending', he wrote, to be replaced by a 'new world' whose influence would derive from 'economic and industrial'[60] strength. These powers aimed to control national resources, not territory. With this in mind, Russell warned that 'these forces ... are bestowing some attention to Ireland, and ... may upset our efforts to secure an Irish control over Irish industry and agriculture'.[61] If national assets were dominated by foreign competition then Irish people would be reduced to working 'for others and relinquishing to them the profitable part of ... business and retaining for themselves the bare pittance as allowed as necessary for sub-sistence'.[62] Russell generally argued that the achievement of Irish political inde-pendence without adequate economic development was pointless; it would sim-ply exchange oppressors. Accordingly he warned that trusts would be more than happy to 'leave us our spiritual ideals, because they will have our material cash, which is their political ideal'.[63] Russell felt it would be 'quite possible for Ireland to be an independent Republic and ... be economically enslaved by for-eign capitalists'.[64] The immediate context for Russell's antagonism to corporate capitalism in the *Irish Homestead* was the end of the First World War. But Rus-sell had another event in mind when he agitated for a redefinition of Irish eco-nomics. The Russian Revolution of the year previous had left a definite mark on his mind, not least because he interpreted it to be a continental echo of the Easter Rising.[65]

Russell wrote a speech in praise of the revolution in November 1918; it was to be delivered at a meeting at the Dublin Mansion House but was never read.

---

58 Ibid. 174.   **59** The 'trust' policy that Russell here refers to is the conglomeration of for-merly competing companies into one capital entity to dominate a market. Russell probably has the American corporate model in mind, thus his use of the word 'trust' to describe such monop-oly companies.   **60** G. Russell, 'The coming of trusts', *IH*, 16 Nov. 1918. 749.   **61** Ibid.   **62** Ibid. 750.   **63** G. Russell, 'Going on or going under', *IH*, 7 Dec. 1918. 798.   **64** Ibid.   **65** Russell's first report on the Russian Revolution appeared in the *Irish Homestead* in May 1917. He immediately compared it to the Easter Rising which had been to him an economic rebellion 'on a smaller scale'. Russell explicitly connected the aspirations of the Russian to the Irish work-ing classes. To Russell the events in Russia were evidence of the fact that 'Nature has a way of ensuring that no one section of humanity can for long remain indifferent to any other section without being disagreeably reminded of its existence'. G. Russell, 'Preparedness', *IH*, 26 May 1917. 386. Tsar Nicholas II abdicated on 2 March 1917. The Bolshevik coup took place on 24

Russell sent it instead as a letter to William O'Brien, the treasurer of the ITGWU.[66] This was printed in the *Voice of Labour*, a journal edited by Cathal O'Shannon, in November 1918. O'Shannon was born in Randalstown in Co. Antrim and had contributed the 'Northern notes' to James Connolly's paper, the *Workers' Republic*.[67] He had worked in Belfast and Cork, as an official of the ITGWU, and from March 1918 became the editor of the *Voice of Labour*, to be followed after its suppression by the *Watchword of Labour*. Although enthusiastic about Ireland's right to national self-determination, O'Shannon, like Russell, was less convinced of the integrity of Irish constitutional politics.[68] Like Connolly before him, O'Shannon shared an international perspective with Russell in his Irish political analysis; the substance of O'Shannon's friendship with Russell in the disturbed period after 1916 was their mutual interest in continental socialism. In his letter to O'Brien, Russell applauded the 'heroic efforts ... being made to organise Russia, to build up a new social order on democratic and co-operative lines'.[69] He argued that although the leaders of the revolution had been 'Marxians' the mass of the people 'with ideals of life begotten in the Mirs and their co-operative movement, desired a social order combining more freedom with democratic solidarity'.[70] The co-operative societies enjoyed a further advantage as they were the only organisation to survive the revolution with an extensive practical knowledge of democratic business. To Russell, they were in a position to direct Russia's future; 'the Revolution, through their guidance, is tending to make of Russia a vast network of co-operative industrial and agricultural societies'.[71] The creation of such synergy involved devolution of power, with 'central government ... more and more delegating the work of production and distribution'[72] to the societies.

O'Shannon described the letter as 'the voice of the most western hailing the most eastern people of Europe'.[73] It is surprising that this self-proclaimed 'Irish Bolshevik'[74] should support Russell's ideas. Russell after all advocates the practical seizure of revolutionary ideals by the co-operative movement. However,

November in Petrograd.   **66** William O'Brien was born in 1881 and died in 1968. A trade union activist, he helped found the ITGWU in 1909. O'Brien was prominent in the 1918 campaign against conscription in Ireland and in the 1920s became a Dáil representative for Dublin South City and Tipperary.   **67** C. Greaves, *The Irish Transport and General Workers' Union*. 147.   **68** Just four months before the 1918 general election, O'Shannon warned his readers to 'Beware the cloven hoof, whether it be wrapped in Orange or in Green. Red is Labour's colour.' 'The workers' republic', *Voice of Labour* (cited subsequently as *VoL*), 31 Aug. 1918. 395. Russell contributed on several occasions to the *Voice of Labour*. He did not 'believe the workers will get anything out of Parliaments before they have got the best out of themselves'. For labour to appeal to the legislature for help was 'like a lion looking to a mouse to get it out of the trap ... the mouse as a rule prefers the lion in the trap'. 'Paths to the co-operative commonwealth', *VoL*, 1 May 1919. 2.   **69** G. Russell, 'Æ on the new order in Russia', *VoL*, 23 Nov. 1918. 497.   **70** Ibid.   **71** Ibid.   **72** Ibid.   **73** Ibid.   **74** C. Greaves, *The Irish transport and general workers' union*. 216.

O'Shannon saw the co-operatives as a useful tool to be used in the creation of an ideal state. They offered the workers an environment potentially free from exploitation as shareholders in their own enterprises. In addition, the societies could also offer themselves as a useful ally during periods of industrial unrest. A strike at Ballina in 1919 proved the point. During the dispute, the town's principal traders organised a blockade of strikers who in turn appealed to a Dublin co-operative society to help them. The society did so, backed by a financial guarantee from the executive of the ITGWU, and went so far as to open a co-operative store in Ballina for the duration of the strike. O'Shannon reported joyfully that 'co-operation has raised the siege and proved itself an indispensable ally of the fighting trade union movement'.[75] Such an understanding had been proposed before; Connolly and Russell had both touched upon the matter in their writings. It was, to an extent, an alliance created by necessity; the unions especially needed the guarantee of supplies during any long and protracted strike action. In the *Voice of Labour* itself, Russell outlined the most vivid expression of the possible outcome of an alliance between labour and the co-operative societies. In the May Day issue of 1919 he wrote that

> When the unions have a monopoly of labour they control the most important asset in the country. That is the organisation of the army. Second comes the co-operative store. That is the organisation of the commissariat. When the army is recruited and the commissariat in order then the campaign can begin.[76]

Russell's militant language was accompanied by a qualification of his earlier belief that Ireland needed social evolution and not revolution; evolution now needed to be 'urged on as rapidly as is consistent with safety'.[77] His vagueness is suggestive. It would be difficult to know when the limits of safety were reached and in a climate of widespread industrial agitation it would be difficult to stop violence escalating. Prepared by *The candle of vision*, Russell adapted comfortably to the role of socialist prophet. His words were regularly taken up by O'Shannon, who had located with Russell a common enemy in the agents of 'autocracy in industry'.[78] O'Shannon re-printed editorials from the *Irish Homestead* in full and suggested that if he were a millionaire his first task 'would be to send all over Ireland a fleet of aeroplanes scattering broadcast in leaflets Æ's editorials'.[79] He even took to using sentences from Russell's texts as banner headlines above the *Voice of Labour*'s 'Co-operative notes'.[80] Thus Russell was tem-

---

75 C. O'Shannon, 'Ballina in blockade: co-op. comes to the rescue', *Watchword of Labour*, 13 Dec. 1919. 1.   76 G. Russell, 'Paths to the co-operative commonwealth', *VoL*, 1 May 1919. 2.   77 Ibid.   78 Ibid.   79 Quoted from O'Shannon's introduction to 'Paths to the co-operative commonwealth', *VoL*, 1 May 1919. 2.   80 See for example the quotation from Russell ('Our

porarily elevated to the position of Desmoulins and Connolly, both of whose revolutionary maxims were printed throughout the paper. Russell and O'Shannon were willing to sideline their immediate differences in the name of a common cause, an attack on established capital. They were able to do this by leaving the terms of their understanding vague enough that each could take what they wanted from the other's comments. Thus O'Shannon could write that labour was 'at one, on broad and general grounds at least, with the best of the pioneers of co-operation whom we know in Ireland'.[81] Implicitly referring to Russell, he wrote that these 'pioneers may prefer to call their goal a Co-operative Commonwealth, and Labour may prefer to call it the Workers' Republic'[82] but

> in the long run it will be found that they and we are travelling towards the same City of Lights, and indeed that some of us are travelling towards it by the same road, although we may not always be in sight of each other.[83]

O'Shannon's counter-claim to Russell's own ambitions for labour have the further merit of sly humour. O'Shannon and Russell were not always in sight of each other because O'Shannon was on the run from the RIC. Neither did Russell contribute to the *Watchword of Labour*, a paper regularly suppressed by the government. O'Shannon's interpretation of the meaning of the 'Co-operative Commonwealth' illustrates the flexibility of the terms by which he and Russell both expressed their beliefs. This was not an attribute unique to these two writers. Elsewhere in the *Watchword of Labour*, O'Shannon showed that his workers' republic could be adapted to complement the ideals of Sinn Féin. The six ITGWU candidates nominated to the 1920 Dublin municipal election 'stand for the Republic; and that Republic the Irish Republic; and that again the Workers' Republic'.[84]

This is the point where Sinn Féin's drive for Irish autonomy coincided with both labour and co-operative ambitions. Sinn Féin, militant labour and the co-operative movement shared the common interest of economic re-organisation in the revolutionary period. We have seen that Russell's economic ideas complemented certain political aspirations of Sinn Féin from its inception; their mutual stress on the need for Irish self-determination, whether economic or political, is the most obvious. This suggests that the co-operative movement, despite its inability to ally itself to any one political movement, could be

task is truly to democratise civilisation') placed above the 'Co-operative notes', *VoL*, 29 June 1918. 313. This quotation is taken from *The national being*. 60. **81** C. O'Shannon, *VoL*, 29 Nov. 1919. 2. This was a double issue dedicated to the question of 'Ireland and co-operation'. **82** Ibid. **83** Ibid. **84** C. Greaves, *The Irish Transport and General Workers' Union*. 258.

manoeuvred to adapt to circumstance. Russell did remind his readers in the *Irish Homestead* that, as committed co-operators, they should 'keep continually before them the idea that whatever be the means adopted, a particular kind of civilisation is the object'.[85] But his acknowledgment that 'nations cannot exist on raids alone'[86] suggests the reality of militant separatism and its role in the foundation of an Irish state. Russell hints at this further as he writes that 'we should have a national economic policy, to be pursued energetically through the day, however and in what adventures the nights of the idealists be spent'.[87] Russell's separation between the events of the night and day is telling. The 'national economic policy' is allowed to stand clear and unimpeachable in the light of scrutiny while the darkness that follows covers a rebellion that might make a theory of national policy practice. Light and darkness are, of course, both part of the same day.

The British administration in Ireland was not ignorant of this fact. No less a person than the Chief Secretary for Ireland, Sir Hamar Greenwood, described Russell as an extreme advocate of Sinn Féin in the House of Commons in 1920.[88] There was justification to his accusation. Russell was not a member of Sinn Féin but his range of personal and intellectual contacts with advocates of radical nationalism was evident.[89] Implicit in Russell's call for the transfer of industry and agriculture to a system of co-operative organisation was the assumption that an increased measure of democracy would result for the labouring classes. This is the major reason for O'Shannon and Russell's mutual regard. Contact between the two was disrupted by O'Shannon's arrest in 1920. He was released after going on hunger strike[90] but the authorities must have been aware of Russell's contributions to the *Voice of Labour* and his consistent support of the Russian Revolution. They paid the paper close enough attention to suppress it the day after it published an advertisement of the Dáil's

85 G. Russell, 'NOTW', *IH*, 10 April 1920. 256.   86 Ibid.   87 Ibid.   88 Greenwood's attack on Russell is recorded in Summerfield's *That myriad-minded man*, 202. Greenwood was appointed Chief Secretary for Ireland in April 1920 and was the last person to hold the post. Greenwood, unsurprisingly, was unable to contain the Irish situation and Lloyd George announced the Anglo-Irish truce without his Chief Secretary's consent on 11 July 1921.   89 It is important to realise how Russell's rhetoric might have appealed to Sinn Féin. Aodh de Blacam, a Sinn Féin propagandist without official party position, wrote to the *Irish Homestead* in 1920 to urge 'Gaels' to 'study the possibilities of the co-operative movement as a means to liberate Irish-Ireland from its economic bonds'. De Blacam remarked further that 'Anglicisation and capitalism have progressed together. To restore democracy in economics is clearly the first step to liberating Irish culture.' 'The gaeltacht v. co-operation', *IH*, 21 Feb. 1920. 130. De Blacam's enthusiasm for co-operation suggests that Russell had manoeuvred the movement into an enviable position. Russell could afford to leave propaganda on behalf of national self-determination and the political achievement of an Irish republic to Sinn Féin. At the same time he enjoyed the implicit understanding of a portion of his readership in the *Irish Homestead* that his attacks on capital were made on behalf of that other political struggle.   90 C. Greaves, *The Irish Transport and General Workers' Union*. 264–5.

National Loan on 20 September 1919.[91] Greenwood, so often imperceptive in his reading of the Irish situation, might in Russell's case have had a point.

Official censure soon became military threat as crown forces mounted raids on rural co-operatives in 1920 in retaliation for guerrilla attack by republican volunteers. The first report in the *Irish Homestead* of assaults made by soldiers on co-operative societies appeared on 5 June 1920. Russell was caught unawares.[92] His officially apolitical agricultural organisation should have been safe from reprisals, despite the campaign of political assassination being carried out in the countryside around it. Russell was so confident of the movement's security that the week before the first attack he praised the efforts of his 'countrymen' who were 'by whatever roads, turnings and indirections, moving steadily towards the creation of a civilization and social order which will be democratic and co-operative'.[93] He did not imagine that co-operative societies would suffer because of revolutionary activity. Accordingly, Russell's first reaction to the destruction of three creameries in Tipperary was mild. He lamented the fact that they had been damaged by 'persons whose official functions are to prevent anything of the kind taking place' but would make 'no comment' until a 'statement is made ... to clear the persons accused or to give reparation for the wrong done'.[94]

The matter rested until the start of August, by which time nine more creameries had been attacked. Russell's response was robust and polemical. However, instead of presenting the co-operative societies as innocent victims of the Anglo-Irish war, Russell again exposed his radical sympathies by locating their plight in context of an international struggle. Russell felt that the 'centre of power' in European society was shifting 'from legislatives and so-called representative assemblies to the great economic organisations of capital and labour'.[95] The state had so far allied itself to capital as the element 'most powerful'[96] in the body politic. Parliament was 'ready to execute' capital's 'wishes, as it realises that the consciousness of power has shifted from itself to the new organisations'.[97] Since Russell had earlier declared the co-operative movement to be against the individual ownership of industrial capital, the attacks on the

91 Sinn Féin inaugurated the first Dáil of the Irish republic on 21 January 1919. Cathal Brugha was elected first President due to the imprisonment of Eamon de Valera, Eoin MacNeill the Finance Minister, Michael Collins the Home Affairs Minister, George Noble Plunkett the Foreign Affairs Minister and Richard Mulcahy the National Defence Minister. De Valera was elected President in April 1919 after his escape from Lincoln Jail. The first Dáil functioned under extreme stress as a revolutionary alternative to the British administration in Ireland.   **92** Co-operative societies had however been accused of revolutionary activity before. Sir Frederick Shaw of the Irish Game Protection Society claimed in 1909 that creameries were distributing arms. Russell denied this strongly. See 'NOTW', *IH*, 8 May 1909, 370.   **93** G. Russell, 'Co-operative land purchase', *IH*, 29 May 1920. 399.   **94** G. Russell, 'NOTW', *IH*, 5 June 1920. 420.   **95** G. Russell, 'NOTW', *IH*, 7 Aug. 1920. 591.   **96** Ibid.   **97** Ibid.

movement in Ireland signalled a change in labour relations in Europe as a whole. 'Extra Parliamentary action', he wrote, 'is becoming more common, and we are in for an era of direct action in politics and economics.'[98] Having offered the *Irish Homestead*'s readership this analysis of the reasons for attacks on their property, Russell remarked cryptically that 'We have thrown out these suggestions because we know that the HOMESTEAD is read not only by farmers but also by some labour leaders.'[99] He is, in other words, urging labour to support the co-operatives in a joint plan of direct action; Russell suggests that the attacks on co-operative creameries could, in theory at least, be answered by direct action from farmers and labour. What form this action would take is not specified, but it is important to realise that if co-operatives did organise to retaliate economically against crown forces they would simultaneously be fulfilling a revolutionary Sinn Féin objective.

The co-operatives, labour and the nationalist movement travelled a narrow path in 1920. The *Irish Homestead*, for example, carried a strike notice on behalf of the Irish Labour Party and Trade Union Congress for two weeks at the end of July. This called upon readers of the *Irish Homestead* to support nearly one thousand railwaymen who had been locked out of work for refusing to operate trains for transport of munitions and soldiers. It stressed that 'This is not a Railwayman's fight, nor a Trade Unionist's fight – it is the Nation's fight – IT IS YOUR FIGHT!'[100] Labour's appeal to the national sentiments of Russell's readership partially obscures the fact that their call for solidarity between co-operators and workers reiterates Russell's previous call for support from labour. With attacks on creameries increasing it was possible that such a union might be forced upon all sides. But regardless of whether the appeal for solidarity was made in nationalist or economic terms, the net result would have been the same, open insurrection.

Russell meanwhile used the *Irish Homestead* to report on the attacks on societies. He observed that soldiers' rage was a result of having to operate 'in a country where so many people are hostile to them and life has been taken'.[101] Russell expressed his anger in irony; there was 'no evidence at all, nor could there be, to show that the creamery wrecked the barracks'.[102] Despite his apparent moderation, Russell could not help but compare the attacks to the destruction of an earlier Irish industry. He warned the government that the 'suppression of the woollen industry in Ireland by Act of Parliament, long ago, has left bitter enough memories without adding to that the destruction of the dairy industry'.[103] Russell called for the government to take responsibility for its soldiers' behaviour; if it did not do this then 'future historians of Ireland'[104] would

---

98 Ibid. **99** Ibid. 594. **100** Irish Labour Party and Trade Union Congress, 'Munitions of war', *IH*, 24 July 1920. 568. See also *IH*, 31 July 1920. 588. **101** G. Russell, 'Rain and ruin', *IH*, 14 Aug. 1920. 606. **102** Ibid. **103** Ibid.

interpret the attacks on the creameries 'as instances of the same policy surviving from century to century'.[105] Russell was keen to stress the co-operatives' independence from trouble around them. At the same time he was not averse to appropriating the vocabulary of Irish nationalism with his suggestion that colonial economics caused the destruction of the woollen industry. Russell cleverly distanced the co-operatives from the actual mechanics of political action while benefiting, when he had to, by appeals to their 'national' stature within Ireland. As the attacks increased, the distance between politics and co-operation narrowed. Russell continued to argue that the creameries were the property of innocent civilians. But their destruction meant that if 'the committee of a creamery whose premises are wrecked meets at all' then 'its very first activity in regard to its own existence must of necessity make it have a strong political bias'.[106] With the possibility that the co-operative movement as a whole could be destroyed, both Russell and Horace Plunkett appealed to an English audience direct.

Their joint campaign started through the offices of Plunkett, who tried to make the government take responsibility for the destruction of creameries by initiating a claim for damages. Plunkett's correspondence with Greenwood, the Chief Secretary of Ireland, was published in the *Irish Homestead*.[107] Russell generally treated the government's replies with disdain, even when Greenwood promised Plunkett that he would personally ensure that the campaign of reprisals against the co-operatives would stop. His promises, to Russell, seemed 'to be as vain as Sir Neville Macready's sermon to the troops on the iniquity of reprisals'.[108] He felt that neither official was able to provide security for the movement and tried instead to influence his British co-operative counterparts to agitate on his behalf.

The start of this new phase of Russell's media campaign began in September 1920 when he reported on the annual co-operative congress in Great Britain, just then held in Preston. A pamphlet condemning the outrages in Ireland was circulated to conference delegates. In the *Irish Homestead* Russell urged his English counterparts to come quickly to their aid 'or there will only be a bitter memory of co-operation in many counties in Ireland'.[109] He further argued that the soldiers who carried out the attacks in Ireland might be transferred to England at a later date. This is evidence indeed of the particular benefits of Russell's international perspective of the Anglo-Irish conflict. By raising the possibility of class struggle Russell plays for sympathy from a constituency that might otherwise be antagonistic. To stress his point, Russell prophesied that the 'training

104 Ibid. 607.   105 Ibid.   106 G. Russell, 'The burning of co-operative creameries', *IH*, 28 Aug. 1920. 642.   107 This correspondence starts in *IH*, 28 Aug. 1920. 646.   108 G. Russell, 'The world we are living in', *IH*, 4 Sept. 1920. 658.   109 G. Russell, 'NOTW', *IH*, 25 Sept. 1920. 710.

in wrecking co-operative enterprises here may fit men for executing similar work in Great Britain in labour struggles in the future'.[110] He did this because he sensed a natural affiliation between the interests of labour and the co-operative movement in both countries; 'we believe', Russell wrote, 'that labour in Great Britain regards the co-operative stores as its commissariat department'.[111] Russell reminded his readers that 'in a fierce struggle between capital and labour' there could be nothing 'more natural ... than the wrecking of stores or factories which supplied labour with the necessaries of life'.[112] Russell played upon the anxieties of the congress constituency and warned that democratic industrial interests in England might be attacked after the success of reprisals in Ireland. Russell's appeals were made in the immediate context of a miners' strike in Great Britain, a dispute not long settled.[113] In a climate of British industrial unrest, the spectre of the state attacking labour was real indeed. Such events strengthened Russell's argument and led him to point out that the government should award damages to the creameries. If they did not, the 'same atrocities may arise in England if a Government, controlled by capitalism, finds it convenient to elude enquiry'.[114] This argument was not original. Karl Marx had suggested that Ireland suffered first what was later visited on England, and Erskine Childers warned in 1919 that the military were trained to break strikes throughout the United Kingdom.[115]

Russell was an adroit media manipulator. He realized the need to address public opinion beyond co-operation. The London *Times*, under the editorship of Wickham Steed, was antipathetic to reprisals. It accused Lloyd George's government of a foolish Irish policy that prompted violent reaction. Powers for the Restoration of Ireland Act were promulgated in the House of Commons in September 1920. To the *Times* this was 'a confirmation of bankruptcy in statesmanship'.[116] Russell seized the opportunity of dissent within the English print media in a letter to the *Times* of 23 August in protest at the destruction of three creameries at Castleiney, Loughmore and Killea. To Russell, 'reprisals, if we are to hold to the hard justice of the Mosaic law, should be on those who committed the acts complained of. It is not justice in any sense to wreck a creamery because barracks have been burned.'[117] But, since assurance was given of creameries' security,

> six times the number of cooperative societies have had their premises wrecked. Either the British Government in Ireland has control over its subjects, or it does not want to control them, or those in authority were

110 Ibid. 111 Ibid. 112 Ibid. 113 For a report see 'NOTW', *IH*, 11 Sept, 1920. 674–8. 114 G. Russell, 'NOTW', *IH*, 25 Sept. 1920. 710. 115 E. Childers, *A strike-breaking army at work*. 1919. 116 *Times*, 23 Aug. 1920. 11. 117 *Times*, 23 Aug. 1920. 6.

so indolent that no steps were taken. We are left to assume either incompetence, malignancy, or indifference.[118]

Russell asked the editor of the *Times* to 'use the powerful influence' of his 'paper to draw attention to the operation of a most dangerous policy in Ireland'.[119] Russell's letter would have received attention even in moderate times; he was respected in England as an Irish commentator since his humbling of Rudyard Kipling during the Home Rule crisis in 1912.[120] But his criticism of Liberal government policy was all the more urgent as the republican Lord Mayor of Cork, Terence MacSwiney, starved himself to a slow death in Brixton Prison. MacSwiney had been arrested for holding a Sinn Féin meeting in Cork city hall. The same issue of the *Times* that carried Russell's letter in defence of the co-operatives also published a short note recording that the Mayor's sister, Mary MacSwiney, had been refused leave by the Home Secretary, Edward Shortt, to see him. With his hunger strike Terence MacSwiney became a symbol of Irish resistance to English oppression. But he was important as more than a martyr to the Irish; he gave definite form to English unease over Irish policy, an unease developed over the previous year in large circulation newspapers like the *Times*, the *Manchester Guardian*, the *Daily Mail* and *Daily News*.[121] The *Times* urged MacSwiney's immediate release:

> the LORD MAYOR OF CORK has stirred imagination and pity. Argument on the merits of his case has become subordinate to those sentiments which the dramatic spectacle of a man confronting death for the sake of an ideal were certain to evoke in a Christian people. ALDERMAN MACSWINEY, a man whose name was unknown outside his own city, will, if he dies, take rank with FITZGERALD, with EMMET, and with TONE in the martyrology of Ireland – his memory infinitely more eloquent and infinitely more subversive of peace than he himself could ever be. Already the mood of Ireland has found expression in an impassioned sonnet from one of her greatest poets which we print to-day.[122]

The poem was Russell's 'Brixton prison: August 31, 1920' and it is one of his finest. Published beneath the above editorial it reflects on Russell's belief in the divinity of the human will:

118 Ibid. **119** Ibid. **120** Russell's 'Open letter to Rudyard Kipling' was published in the *Daily News* on 15 April 1912, three days after Kipling's subversive 'Ulster: 1912', an incitement to unionist violence in defiance of home rule. Mary Colum later remembered that Russell's criticism 'was such a reproof and on such a large-minded plane that Kipling's reputation as a writer was shaken, even unjustly shaken'. *Life and the dream*. 171. **121** Maurice Walsh has written a brilliant introductory study of English newspaper coverage of Ireland in 'British correspondents and the Anglo-Irish war 1919–1920'. Unpublished MRES thesis, Goldsmith's College, 2000. **122** *Times*, 2 Sept. 1920. 11.

See, though the oil be low, more purely still and higher
The flame burns in the body's lamp! The watchers still
Gaze with unseeing eyes while the Promethean will,
The Uncreated Light, the Everlasting Fire,
Sustains itself against the torturers' desire
Even as the fabled Titan upon the hill.
Burn on, shine here, thou immortality, until
We too have lit our lamps at the funereal pyre;
Till we too can be noble, unshakeable, undismayed:
Till we too can burn with the holy flame, and know
There is that within us can triumph over pain,
And go to death alone, slowly and unafraid.
The candles of God are already burning row on row,
Farewell, Lightbringer, fly to thy heaven again.[123]

It is strange to think that MacSwiney read this sonnet in his cell before he died on 27 October 1920. It celebrates a triumph of will that appeals, as the *Times* knew, to spiritual values above sordid politics. It is everything that critics felt British government policy in Ireland was not: humane, ideal and self-aware. Its publication date does however undo its façade of universal sympathy as the poem bids farewell to an individual not yet dead, in an attempt to force a future that must occur. 'Brixton prison' is a calculated, if impassioned, attempt to make political capital for Irish separatism from Terence MacSwiney's hunger-strike. It may still be sincere. But Russell, caught unawares by Connolly's sacrifice four years before, was not to be deceived again. 'Brixton Prison' places MacSwiney in the Promethean tradition of suffering to which Irish separatists that Russell favoured were elevated. MacSwiney, it appears, must follow his fate. The poem is as carefully orchestrated as the funeral, with its Irish volunteer guards and a pipe band that played 'Good-bye to Cork' in procession from St George's Catholic Cathedral at Southwark to Euston Station, that paraded the streets of London.[124] The only thing shocking in all this is the British establishment's propaganda collapse in response, a surrender only explained by internal instability and a weakness inherited from the end of the First World War.

Russell appealed again 'to the British people'[125] in 'A plea for justice', first published in the *Irish Homestead* on 18 December 1920. Having found the official system of courts in Ireland to be inadequate for the purpose of convicting those responsible for reprisals, Russell relied on the British people's 'sense of fair play to judge between Irish co-operators and the Government'.[126] Russell

---

123 *Times*, 2 Sept. 1920. 11.   **124** *Times*, 29 Oct. 1920. 9.   **125** G. Russell, 'A plea for justice', *IH*, 18 Dec. 1920. 900.   **126** Ibid.

immediately refuted the Chief Secretary's accusation that the societies were 'centres of revolutionary propaganda'.[127] He repeated the warning that he had already made to British co-operators; the British people would 'lay up a hell for themselves in their own country'[128] if they did not exert pressure on the government to institute an inquiry into the attacks. It is ironic that Russell, acting as spokesman for an organisation which had been condemned by a British official as a focus for revolutionary activity, should further appeal to the British tradition of parliamentary democracy to vindicate himself. By their actions the police and soldiers were 'tearing up all the safeguards of justice won through centuries of struggle'.[129] Again he warned 'there are too many interests minatory to democracy in power to allow them the advantage of such precedents'.[130] It is interesting to note the measured tones of Russell's voice in 'A plea for justice'. There is no mention of 'labour' or 'capital' although both words appear frequently in the *Irish Homestead*. Russell, it seems, could not prejudice the co-operative case to the general British public by a petition in language that might be associated with socialism. But he remained blunt: 'It may be', he ended, 'we Irish are scoundrels, but if we are let us be tried openly for our crimes.'[131] Russell puts his appeal to 'fair-mindedness'. He was astute to do so; the standard of decency was the substance of most English newspapers' critique of the reprisal policy.[132] Sir Hamar Greenwood had insisted up to this point that individual co-operative societies should take their claims for damages to the courts. Russell knew well that the submission of evidence and witnesses to these courts was almost impossible in Ireland due to intimidation. Indeed many Irish courts had ceased to function effectively after they were superseded by a rival judicial system instituted by the Dáil in 1919. Russell's alternative to Greenwood's proposition is that the British people act as the jury for the case that he presents. In doing so he makes the same allusions to 'fairness' and 'reason' that a barrister might make to a jury. Within this rhetorical framework he can accuse without the burden of proof required by law. The strength of Russell's propaganda is that it looks impartial but is definitely committed.

Russell's appeal to the English people was supported in early January 1921 in Westminster by a delegation of MPs from the Co-operative and the Labour parties.[133] They met the Chief Secretary in order to petition the government on

---

127 Ibid. **128** Ibid. **129** Ibid. **130** Ibid. **131** Ibid. **132** Maurice Walsh notes that 'Coverage of this new war of reprisals was marked by a profound shift in how the story of the troubles in England was framed by the British correspondents. The main threads of explanation up to then – despair over disorder, optimism about the possibility that some compromise could be reached by reasonable men on both sides and a desire of the reform of the Irish administration – were all distilled to a question of the legitimacy of the British government's methods in Ireland'. 'British correspondents and the Anglo-Irish war 1919–1920'. Unpublished MRES thesis, Goldsmith's College, 2000. 29. **133** The Co-operative Party was formed in 1917 and had one member elected to parliament in December 1918. See G.D.H. Cole, *A history of the Labour*

behalf of Irish co-operatives. Greenwood promised the MPs that attacks on co-operatives would cease, but it was a promise that the Chief Secretary must have known he was unqualified to keep.[134] Russell reported that this Joint Parliamentary Committee would agitate on Ireland's behalf but doubted 'whether those who at present sit in the seats of the mighty are not at enmity with all democratic movements'.[135] He regarded the government's inability to stop reprisals as a prelude to a military campaign in Britain which would 'enfeeble' labour movements 'to make way for trusts and big business on capitalist lines'.[137] Accordingly Russell relied on his own propaganda and published *A plea for justice* as a pamphlet to be distributed widely. Russell urged Irish co-operators to 'send copies ... to persons they trade with in Great Britain and to point out the effect of this policy on unemployment there'.[138] There 'they are thinking of little else than unemployment, and in so far as the plight of Ireland bears upon unemployment then the plight of Ireland will receive attention'.[139]

To supplement this media drive in Britain a new column was started in the *Irish Homestead* on the 15 January called 'Notes from overseas'. It was supposed to report foreign events of interest to the journal's readership. Since Russell's weekly 'Notes and comments' already covered this territory, it is obvious that the column's real purpose was to supplement the Irish co-operative movement's propaganda efforts in England. 'Notes from overseas' first reported the visit of a representative commission of the British Labour Party to Ireland. On its return to Britain the commission organised 'meetings at eighty great centres of population'[140] to raise public awareness of the Irish co-operatives' plight. The rallies enjoyed the joint support of the Co-operative Party, and MPs from both groups addressed audiences 'specifically with the subject of the attacks on the Irish societies'.[141] The next weeks brought some comfort to Russell and his readers as resolutions in favour of Irish co-operators were passed regularly and unanimously at meetings.[142] The campaign organised by the Co-operative and Labour Parties reached its climax with a mass meeting at London's Albert Hall on 15 February 1921. Unfortunately for propaganda the 'metropolitan press practically boycotted the meeting'.[143] The only published reports appeared in the *Daily Herald*, a radical labour paper whose editor, George Lansbury, had published articles in the *Voice of Labour*, and the *Co-operative News*, both of whose readership might already have been sympathetic to the Irish co-operators' case.

Party from 1914. 83   **134** Greenwood's assurance was reported in 'NOTW', *IH*, 8 Jan. 1921. 20–4.   **135** Ibid. 24.   **137** Ibid.   **138** G. Russell, 'NOTW', *IH*, 22 Jan. 1921. 53.   **139** Ibid. **140** 'Notes from overseas', *IH*, 15 Jan. 1921. 56.   **141** Ibid.   **142** See for example 'Notes from overseas', *IH*, 29 Jan. 1921. 72–4.   **143** 'Notes from overseas', *IH*, 26 Feb. 1921. 136.

The Labour Party commission, whose visit to Ireland led to the rally, had meanwhile published the results of its inquiry into the destruction of a creamery at Ballymaceligott. The commission refuted the official version of events that claimed soldiers were shot at from the creamery premises. It did 'not believe there was any ambush'.[144] To Russell, the findings of this body, which included a retired general and three sitting MP's in its number, was proof of the justice of his cause; 'After all',[145] he wrote, they 'are all Englishmen, and ... not likely to weigh the balance of judgement against themselves and their own country'.[146] Russell's bitterness is suggestive of a nationalism increasingly extreme; his angry anti-government polemic revived old audiences. Sinn Féin reproduced Russell's pamphlet, *The inner and the outer Ireland*, in Ireland in July 1921, after its first publication in the American *Pearson's Magazine*, edited by Frank Harris, in May of that year.[147]

The inner and the outer Ireland asks two questions; what is the cause of the 'Irish trouble'[148] and why has it continued? The simple answer to the first question is that the 'Irish people want to be free'.[149] To the second, they 'feel in themselves a genius which has not yet been manifested in a civilisation'.[150] Russell argued that the ancient Greeks achieved greatness because they 'externalised their genius'[151] in 'a society with a culture, arts and sciences peculiar to themselves'.[152] So the Irish people rebel by virtue of a 'biological and spiritual necessity'.[153] Such 'necessity' drives antagonism towards their rulers, not content with the 'character in which British statesmen would mould them'.[154] The introduction of a racial element to Russell's analysis of the Irish struggle is signal of a general change in attitude towards violence that the previous two years had conditioned. Russell wonders whether violence is 'good or evil',[155] a question that led him to contrast the 'moralist'[156] with the 'artist'[157] in his character. The 'moralist' found 'race hatreds ... abhorrent'.[158] The 'artist' 'delights in varieties of culture and civilisation, and ... tells me it is well worth some bloodshed to save the world from being "engirded with Brixton"'.[159] It is clear that the 'artist' has won Russell's affections as he celebrates the power of the Irish race; 'in spite of all the proddings of British bayonets the people born in Ireland will still be Irish'.[160] Russell extends this durability to the distant past. The Irish character has remained unchanged for centuries and the widespread use of English 'has but superficially modified Irish character ... Gaelic culture still inspires all that is best in Irish literature and Irish life'.[161] This from a writer who

---

144 G. Russell, 'NOTW', *IH*, 5 Feb. 1921. 86. **145** Ibid. **146** Ibid. **147** *The inner and the outer Ireland* is reprinted in full in the section that describes Russell in Harris' 1927 book *Latest contemporary portraits*, a text that also contains essays on Shaw, Wilde and Yeats. **148** G. Russell, *The inner and the outer Ireland*. All page numbers refer to the 1921 Talbot Press edition. 4. **149** Ibid. **150** Ibid. **151** Ibid. **152** Ibid. **153** Ibid. 5. **154** Ibid. **155** Ibid. **156** Ibid. **157** Ibid. **158** Ibid. **159** Ibid. **160** Ibid. **161** Ibid.

showed no inclination to learn or promote the Irish language; Russell's call for 'Gaelic' is merely convenient to the introduction of his main point. For the 'last great champion of the Gaelic tradition was Padraic Pearse, who led the astonishing enterprise of Easter Week, 1916'.[162] Pearse 'made his soul out of the heroic literature of the Gael'.[163] His actions led Russell to think of 'Standish O'Grady, an earlier prophet of the Gaelic tradition'.[164]

O'Grady was, we know, the inspiration of much of Russell's early work.[165] Russell gains access to Pearse by connection to O'Grady. But in doing so he does not mention Pearse in a literary context, even though this is the most obvious link. Russell was aware of Pearse's writings.[166] But he preferred to stress that Gaelic literature affected Pearse internally; it created his 'soul'. Russell saw the same condition in other 'political rebels'[167] he knew. They were 'determined' and had overcome the Irish 'power of sympathy and understanding' which previously 'made them politically weak'.[170] The 'oppression of the last six years ... has strengthened the will'.[171] Russell sensed in Ireland a triumph of force over speech; political activists are 'so little given to speech that it is almost impossible to find among Sinn Feiners an orator'.[172] Russell knew his subject. Ernie O'Malley, a volunteer during the war of independence, remembered of his service that he 'lived on a mountain top where there was no need for speech, even. I felt an understanding, a sharing of something bigger than ourselves, and a heightening of life.'[173] Russell commented on this condition recurrently. If force of will dominates, a voice must be found to articulate desire. Russell is once more the prophet. He ends *The inner and the outer Ireland* with a self-assumption of the national character, trying only 'to interpret the mood of my countrymen rather than to express my own feelings'.[174] Russell is the conduit for the national will, the medium of divine inspiration. His occult perception of Irish national motivation expresses itself in political prose but remains, for all that, arcane. Russell interprets Irish nationality and takes responsibility to speak to the wider world of his nation's cares. *The inner and the outer Ireland* was then followed in September 1921 by another appeal to a British audience with the publication of *Ireland and the Empire at the court of conscience* in the *Manchester Guardian*.[175] In this, Russell's occult sense of Irish nationality did not confuse his political instinct. *Ireland and the Empire* was issued in the middle of Treaty nego-

---

162 Ibid.　163 Ibid.　164 Ibid.　165 In 'A tribute by Æ', published in 1929, Russell wrote of O'Grady's *History of Ireland* that no other book had ever 'excited my imagination more than Standish O'Grady's epical narrative of Cuculain'. *Standish James O'Grady*. 63.　166 The *Collected works of Pearse* were reviewed in *IH*, 14 July 1917. 522–5. Pearse had 'a purity of spirit which is rare in any literature'. 525.　167 G. Russell, *The inner and the outer Ireland*. 9.　170 Ibid.　171 Ibid.　172 Ibid.　173 E. O'Malley, *On another man's wound*. 53.　174 G. Russell, *The inner and the outer Ireland*. 15.　175 The *Manchester Guardian* and the *Times* were newspapers praised in O'Malley's *On another man's wound* for making 'discord in the general chorus of

tiations between Michael Collins and Lloyd George; the pamphlet was Russell's stake in the creation of a new post-Treaty Irish identity; it immediately sold over 5000 copies when published by the Talbot Press.[176]

The formal model for *Ireland and the Empire* is John Mitchel's *Jail journal*. Mitchel, transported to the prison hulk *Bermuda* in 1848, recorded an imaginary dialogue in his cell between Ego, his conscience, and Doppelganger, an accuser. Ego defends Mitchel's radicalism as born of love of Ireland. Doppelganger denies it as hatred of England. Ego responds, 'I hold that now, and for fifty years back, the best friend to the British nation is simply he who approves himself the bitterest enemy to their government, and to all their institutions, in Church and State. And thus I claim to be, not an enemy, but a friend, of England; for the British people are what *I* call England'.[177] The dialogic format of question and answer, accusation and rebuttal, allows Mitchel to air extreme opinion through the privileged voice of Ego, more politically conscious and confident than Doppelganger, the shadow that concedes of Ego 'I do begin to be of his opinion'.[178] Ego's ideal is of co-operative resistance to atrocity across imperial possessions, 'the reeky shanks and yellow chapless skulls of Skibbereen' and 'the ghosts of starved Hindoos in dusky millions'.[179] Ego is Jacobin, preaching 'wherever you see a greedy tyranny (constitutional or other) grinding the faces of the poor, join battle with it on the spot – conspire, confederate, and combine against it, resting never till the huge mischief come down, though the whole "structure of society" come down with it'.[180] Russell fought his own battle against injustice in *Ireland and the Empire*, writing, unlike Mitchel who was stranded in the private frustration of prison and failed rebellion, from a public position of influence.

After a brief introductory passage, the text consists of a dialogue between two opposing voices in the 'House of reason'. Each voice represents a different element of Irish nationalist opinion, the second more extreme than the first. Russell described his work as an attempt to explain to the British people why there was such uncertainty in Ireland over how to respond to the proposed settlement; he felt compelled to 'break silence on behalf of these millions' who faced 'an agony of conscience'.[181] Russell is again national spokesperson, on this occasion transfigured almost to an embodiment of the nation itself. He takes his

newspapers which made the most of gunmen shooting troops in the back'. 270. **176** The managing director of the Talbot Press wrote to Russell on 26 Jan. 1922: 'My dear "Æ", I have now got a statement of the last pamphlet, "Ireland and the Empire". The first 5000 went very quickly, and in October we printed another 5000, which are still in our hands. This reprint was a publishing gamble, and the luck went against us. However, the sale of the first lot cleared the expenses on the second lot, with £10 over, and an equitable arrangement would, I think, be to send you a cheque for Five Guineas, and if the balance are of any use to you, you may have them without charge.' Talbot Press archive, National Archives (cited subsequently as NA) MS 1048/70/85. **177** John Mitchel, *Jail journal*. 83. **178** Ibid. 93. **179** Ibid. 86. **180** Ibid. 92. **181** G. Russell, *Ireland and the Empire*. 2.

'own doubts, hesitations, and ponderings as typical of the mood of the majority of my countrymen'.[182] He presents these feelings so that 'what underlies acceptance or rejection may be known to others as it is to ourselves'.[183] The division between the two voices of *Ireland and the Empire* is at first easy to sustain. The first represents Sinn Féin before 1916. Even limited freedom will allow future generations of Irish people to be grafted on to the 'Gaelic root', an improvement on the present generation who were 'perverted ... in youth by concepts alien to the Irish nature'.[184] This argument foreshadows Arthur Griffith's argument in the Treaty debate of January 1922 that the agreement's terms were no more final than his was the last generation of Irishmen. Both the first voice and Griffith share a gradualist approach to a redefinition of Irish identity. The second voice is impatient. It argues that 'The national genius cannot inspire if we first give allegiance to the spirit of empire',[185] anticipating de Valera's refusal to take the oath of allegiance to the crown and sit in the Free State Dáil. This voice stresses a point that Russell earlier made in *The inner and the outer Ireland*, that the Irish are compelled to rebel against Britain by 'biological and spiritual necessity'.[186] The first voice criticises the second for its dogmatism; 'You speak ... like those impossible people who will have all or nothing'.[187] It mocks the hopes of the second voice which it claims expects 'Great Britain to allow complete independence because of a revulsion of feeling which has taken place suddenly within four or five years'.[188] It rationally asserts the depth of 'cultural and economic ties'[189] which bind a majority of the population in north-east Ireland to Britain.

It is at this point, where the first voice is at its most logical, that Russell's attachment to the second voice reveals itself. It argues that the 'insurrection of Easter Week was based on human intuition and not human reason'.[190] It was, in empirical terms, an irrational act. In Theosophy this is exactly how divinity achieves human agency.[191] The rebellion is sanctified by 'Pearse and his companions' sounding 'the last trumpet of the Gael'.[192] Pearse achieves resurrection, raising the 'dead ... from the graves of fear, unbelief or despair, and out of a deep sense of identity ... they reeled after the shepherds who called'.[193] The second voice is now privileged to recite almost verbatim one of Russell's central defences of the co-operatives, that they were a social organisation ideally suited to the Irish way of life. Under the Empire, 'The evolution of a more democratic and humane social order in Ireland would be hampered unless we were free to adopt any trade policy and industrial system to which our interests and our natural humanity may dispose us.'[194] The first voice replies pointedly that

182 Ibid. 3.   **183** Ibid.   **184** Ibid. 4.   **185** Ibid. 5.   **186** Ibid.   **187** Ibid. 7.   **188** Ibid. 8.
189 Ibid.   **190** Ibid.   **191** H. Blavatsky, *The secret doctrine*. xxxvi.   **192** G. Russell, *Ireland and the Empire*. 9.   **193** Ibid.   **194** Ibid. 10–11.

to adopt a 'national theory of economics'[195] would be to risk partition, as Northern industrialists feared a potential bias towards the agricultural South in an Irish assembly. The second voice has no adequate reply to this charge and can only suggest that 'at some crisis' in the future the inhabitants of Ulster will find 'unsuspected depths in their being'.[196] The first voice dismisses this 'intuition or surmise'.[197] It asks if the second voice is prepared to risk the partition of Ireland in pursuit of its 'whole demand'.[198] The second voice resorts to racialism; it cannot imagine that the 'conscience of the world will permit the extermination of a white race because it refuses to acknowledge the sovereignty of another people'[199] (the implication being of course that the world would be quite happy if this were to happen to others). Such argument is extreme and irrational but illustrates, with great vulgarity, what Russell stressed as the importance of 'world circumstance'[200] to Ireland at the end of *The inner and the outer Ireland*.

Both pamphlets suggest the possibility of outside intervention in the Anglo-Irish conflict. This did not need to be military. It could relate to a change in world economics whereby England would be unable to maintain its dominions. So at the end of *Ireland and the Empire* Russell imagines an Ireland freed by the 'mills of God'[201] which 'come at last in their grinding to the British Empire as they came to the Roman Empire ... and other empires whose sins and magnificence have sunk far behind time'.[202] Russell's language is that of the apocalypse as the second voice has final say: 'It might be better for us to face one final ordeal and have the terror over than leave such an agony for our children.'[203] It desires the sacrificial release that 'Brixton Prison', Russell's poem for Terence Mac-Swiney, desired. The pretence that the second voice is separate from that of Russell's own in the introductory section of *Ireland and the Empire* finally collapses. But in its conclusion the second voice moves beyond summary of previous argument to introduce a new element to the text. It promises resolution of Ireland's political problems by a redemptive spiritual awakening. The 'deciding factor' as to acceptance of a settlement will be a measurement in the 'scales' of justice in a 'transcendent sphere'.[206] 'The will of Heaven will be in our resolve.'[207]

Russell's belief in the divinity of the Irish nation was soon tested. The Anglo-Irish Treaty passed the Dáil by a narrow majority on 7 January 1922. After the Provisional Government took office Russell was finally confronted with the reality of an Irish state. His theory of nationality developed over the previous thirty years had to adapt to a new dispensation. To complicate matters further, civil war broke out when a section of Sinn Féin refused to accept the Treaty. Russell was immediately confronted with the possible failure in its first year of

---

195 Ibid. 11.   196 Ibid. 13.   197 Ibid. 15.   198 Ibid.   199 Ibid.   200 G. Russell, *The inner and the outer Ireland*. 15.   201 G. Russell, *Ireland and the Empire*. 15.   202 Ibid.   203 Ibid. 16.
206 G. Russell, *Ireland and the Empire*. 16.   207 Ibid.

existence of a state whose arrival he had long awaited. For a man who saw independence as the opportunity to release a wave of 'pent-up intellect and idealism'[208] this was a grievous prospect. To avoid it Russell redefined his sense of nationality. Russell, sympathetic to revolutionary nationalism pre-independence, was a writer of very different sensibilities post-1922.

---

208 G. Russell, 'The new era', *IH*, 17 Dec. 1921. 842.

4 / Interpreters: 1922–3

George Russell's *The interpreters* was published in November 1922, just one month before the first ever sitting in December of the Executive Council of the Irish Free State. Ten months only had passed since the Dáil voted to accept the Anglo-Irish Treaty on 7 January 1922, but much had changed. Eamon de Valera had resigned as Dáil President, his successor Arthur Griffith was dead and a civil war that lasted from June 1922 until April 1923 wracked the country. Fought between pro- and anti- Treaty factions, the conflict was bitter.[1] Russell supported the Treaty side. Published at a critical time in the history of the Irish state, *The interpreters*, Russell's major prose work of the 1920s, proposes a new, politically decisive, relationship to be formed between intellectuals and the Free State.

The interpreters is a political fantasy in which six main characters, imprisoned in a cell, debate the fundamentals of revolutionary doctrine. The book is set in a future century in which airships dominate the earth on behalf of a global imperial power, so echoing Standish O'Grady's pseudonymous novel of 1900, *The queen of the world*. A strange imagination of life in the twenty-second century, O'Grady's novel is an adventure to a failing world empire.[2] Power is concentrated in both O'Grady's and Russell's novels in civilisations that control flight. Both books feature unlikely flying argosies, patrolling the skies above subject peoples in a manner not dissimilar to Swift's *Gulliver's travels*. Russell had long been fascinated by aerial experiment. Invited on behalf of the *Irish Homestead* to an air show at Leopardstown, Dublin, in 1910, he joined thousands of other awestruck spectators and

> forgot all about agriculture when the first of these heavenly creatures got
> his bird to buzz and slide along the grass, and then, like a swimmer leav-
> ing the deep water and relinquishing the sand, it flung itself into the

---

1 The exact number of civil war fatalities is uncertain, although the intimacy of its combatants meant that each death or injury marked Irish life for the following decades. J.J. Lee reckons a 'probably exaggerated estimate of 4000 casualties'. *Ireland 1912–1985*. 69.   **2** O'Grady published *The queen of the world* under the pseudonym Luke Netterville. A fascinating book, O'Grady's text is supposed to be the account of the occult philosopher Gerald Pierce de Lacy's time travel to 2179 by the magic of a Bohemian mage. Once there, Lacy inspires the subjects of the Tyranny to rebellion. Exotic in detail and bizarre in conception, *The queen of the world* reveres the heroism of noble character that marks as individual O'Grady's inspirational two-volume *History of Ireland*.

bosom of the air, which bore it up, and it soared higher and higher in a long circle, and then, turning its huge yellow wings, it seemed to dash into the white sun fire and the silver sunlight. About two thousand years ago an old Irish legend says that at the fair of Tailtean there appeared airships of the Tuatha de Danaan, 'a great marvel in Erin', their last appearance. Now the world's great age begins anew. The flying years return. There was an aerial flyer in the fair at Ballymoney, in Antrim, in June, and another in the south this year, and unbelievable Dublin has now seen with its myriad eyes men 'scaling the blue air', not in poetry, as poor Mangan did, but in actual fact. It was the lordliest thing in the way of human achievement Ireland has seen since the days of the Tuatha de Danaan.[3]

Russell first suggested the idea of *The interpreters* in a letter to H.G. Wells in 1909 in advance of a trip by the English author to Ireland to meet Horace Plunkett and Lord Dunsany; Russell wondered if his correspondent had ever thought 'of writing a symposium upon science like the *Banquet* of Plato'.[4] This symposium would consist of debate between characters 'imprisoned in a revolution' that are 'to be executed the next day' and 'spend the night in hope and prophecy'.[5] Wells' novel of 1914, *The world set free*, is the closest of his contemporary works to Russell's suggestion.[6] The novel predicts the destruction of traditional society by atomic bombs, a cataclysm that inspires a French ambassador to gather likeminded individuals to resolve the conflict by the formation of world government.[7] Wells' novel was reissued in 1921, the year before *The interpreters* was published, Wells' preface noting that 'The dream of The World Set Free, a dream of highly educated and highly favoured leading and ruling men, voluntarily setting themselves to the task of reshaping the world, has thus far remained a dream'.[8]

The interpreters develops Wells' vision of enlightened leadership at a critical point in Irish history. For just as the Free State formed, Russell published a text that described how six revolutionary characters could act as catalyst to a new Ireland. An echo of Russell's admonition to Wells to write a Platonic medita-

---

3 G. Russell, 'NOTW', *IH*, 3 Sept 1910. 731.   4 A. Denson, ed., *Letters from AE*. 68.   5 Ibid.   6 It is possible that *The interpreters*' title was suggested to Russell by the character of Lieutenant Kurt in *The war in the air*. Kurt, half German and half English, interprets the events of the novel to Bert Smallways, the cockney everyman. Russell was aware of Wells' book: 'We love all talk in Ireland, deny it how we may, and as duelling and highway robbery are dead and the war in the air is not yet come, in default of earthquakes and volcanoes we accept changes of government or alterations in the constitution.' 'NOTW', *IH*, 8 Jan 1910. 22. He also wrote an appreciation of Wells the same year in the *Irish Homestead*, 'The dialogue of Mr. Wells', *IH*, 28 May 1910. 442.   7 Wells specifically mentions a 'big atomic bomb' in *The world set free*, 70. His prediction of the destructive power of such a weapon is unnerving when one considers that the discovery of nuclear fission was not announced to the public until 1939. The Manhattan project followed with the outbreak of the Second World War and the first self-sustaining nuclear reaction was achieved in 1942. Nagasaki and Hiroshima were the first victims of the new weaponry in 1945.   8 H.G. Wells, *The world set free*.

tion can be detected in *The interpreters*' preface where Russell describes his work as a symposium, a debate over a general principle by a group of characters, such as might be found in his stylistic model, Plato's *Symposium*. A further classical allusion can be read in the dedication of *The interpreters* to Stephen MacKenna, the translator of Plotinus and good friend of Russell's early discovery James Stephens.[9] MacKenna was a republican antipathetic to the use of violence by those against the Treaty. MacKenna and Russell knew each other well and both men remained friends despite their political differences, a considerable achievement for this fractious time.[10] Russell's dedication is an early signal of *The interpreters*' political dimension. For, notwithstanding the text's philosophical pretensions, *The interpreters* is primarily a symposium on Ireland's post-revolutionary status.

Russell found *The interpreters* a difficult book to write.[11] Neither did his first readers detect any clear authorial intention. Reviewers especially were confused, unsure of whether to read *The interpreters* as a contemporary political allegory, as a statement of Russell's own spiritual beliefs or as an uneasy merger of the two.[12] Their puzzlement was similar to the bewilderment that Yeats thought might accompany the first publication of *A vision* in 1925.[13] Unlike Yeats, who published *A vision* in a strictly limited number of copies, Russell risked his work on the general public, a gamble that resulted in the most disappointing sales of his mature career.[14] *The interpreters* is a symposium but, in con-

---

6. **9** E.R. Dodds compiled a memoir, complete with letters and journal extracts, of MacKenna after his death in 1934. MacKenna led a various life, as a journalist in Russia who reported on the insurrection on the *Potemkin* in Odessa in 1905 and as a volunteer for the Greeks in their war against the Turks. The man that emerges from this account is melancholic, his moods tempered by great gifts of speech and compassion. Russell attended MacKenna's evenings with, among others, James Stephens and Padraic Colum. See E. R. Dodds, ed., *Journal and letters of Stephen MacKenna*. **10** Dodds notes, 'To the surprise of many of his friends, MacKenna declared himself unhesitatingly for repudiation of the Treaty.' Dodds further remembers that MacKenna's 'friendship with men like Curtis and myself continued unbroken, and Æ remained for him "a noble gentleman despite his utter inability to see our republican point of view"'. Edmund Curtis was to become Professor of History at TCD. He later wrote historical reviews for the *Irish Statesman*. *Journal and letters of Stephen MacKenna*. 60–2. **11** Russell wrote to the Macmillan company in a letter received 17 May 1922 that 'I am doing my best under great difficulties to get on with "The Interpreters" but the atmosphere here at the moment is not helpful to the kind of thinking I am trying to do. I have completed sixteen chapters out of twenty & I hope after a holiday I will be able to finish the work quickly.' Macmillan Archive, BL ms 55002/ 71. **12** The *Irish Times* for example felt that Russell's 'theorisings follow so hard on the heels of fact that the most philosophically minded reader will be unable to keep the two divorced'. *Irish Times*, 29 Dec. 1922. 2. **13** In his 'Dedication' to the 1925 edition of *A vision*, Yeats wrote 'I have moments of exaltation like that in which I wrote "All Soul's Night", but I have other moments when remembering my ignorance of philosophy I doubt if I can make another share my excitement ... I most fear to disappoint those who come to this book through some interest in my poetry and in that alone'. xii. **14** Russell sent the manuscript of *The interpreters* to Macmillan in a letter received 17 Aug. 1922 with a message any publisher dreads: 'I do not expect any great popularity for it but I think as with other books of mine it will finally pay

text of Russell's political and literary work in the 1920s, it is also a manifesto. *The interpreters*, despite its narrative fictions of spiritual discovery and political revolution, is a proposal for Irish cultural nationalism to evolve in response to the advent of Irish statehood in 1922. It appeared just two months before the first publication of Yeats' 'Meditations in time of civil war' in the *Dial*.[15] Both works are closely informed by their immediate context, the Irish civil war, a conflict precipitated by the June 1922 Free State attack on the republican garrison in occupation of the Four Courts since April that year.[16] Yeats' poetry comes to a very different conclusion from *The interpreters* however, his speaker considering the death of civilisation, with the civil war symbolic of a wider collapse. The retreat that Yeats' speaker offers as an alternative to violence is claustrophobic, the refrain of the poem's sixth section to 'Come build in the empty house of the stare'[17] an invocation to nature for the reconstruction of a disturbed order:

> We are closed in, and the key is turned
> On our uncertainty; somewhere
> A man is killed, or a house burned,
> Yet no clear fact to be discerned:
> Come build in the empty house of the stare.[18]

There is little suggestion of uncertainty in *The interpreters*. The post-revolutionary period is as much a motivation to Russell's text as it is here for Yeats, but the two writers emerge with radically different responses to it in their work. If you did not know the date of *The interpreters*' publication you might not guess that a civil war raged at all, a simple fact inescapable from Yeats' title. But where Yeats takes the aftermath of revolution as his subject, with the 'dead young soldier in his blood',[19] *The interpreters* starts with problems pre-revolution. It is set on the very cusp of rebellion; it opens with one of its six main characters, the poet Lavelle, crossing an unnamed city to witness the outbreak of an uprising. Entranced, the poet was 'but dimly aware of his fellow citizens' and felt 'raised above himself by the adventure on which he was bent'.[20] This opening passage sets the tone for much of what follows. Unlike the squalor through which the protagonist moves in the opening passage of Liam O'Flaherty's 1925 novel of the civil war, *The informer*,[21] Russell's character is bent on adventure. This

its publication'. It is not clear it ever did. Macmillan archive, BL ms 75. **15** 'Meditations in time of civil war' was published as seven individual poems, rather than as one poem in seven sections (as it was in *The tower* in 1928), in the *Dial*, 74: 1, Jan. 1923. 50–6. Also in the *London Mercury*, 8:39, Jan. 1923. 232–8. For ease of reference, page numbers given here refer to the version published in *Yeats's poems*. **16** For an account of this see M. Hopkinson, *Green against green*. 115–22. **17** *Yeats's poems*. 312. **18** Ibid. **19** Ibid. **20** G. Russell, *The interpreters*. 1. **21** *The informer*'s main character, Francis Joseph McPhillip, is on the run after an assassination. He enters a Dublin hostel-

romantic sensibility suggests that an examination of the grisly mechanics of revolution will not be *The interpreters*' concern. The need to avoid base reality further explains Russell's choice of a symposium as the medium for his narrative. Masquerading as a philosophic discourse, *The interpreters* debates the fundamentals of political revolution without soiling itself with violence.

The interpreters is set in a prison cell, a focus to each character's development; as Russell wrote to Shaw in June 1921, 'All thinking comes at last to the self. Having divorced as much of the universe as is available the mind at last begins to gnaw itself in hunger, and that is the beginning of mysticism, magic, religion, & all the science of consciousness'.[22] He was all the while trying to write *The interpreters*, 'a futurist book' that would 'go out of present controversies in discussing what solution the politics of time have to the politics of eternity'.[23] The cell also evokes the aftermath of the Easter Rising, the general population unaware of the significance of the rebels' initial assembly to fight against superior force. The peaceful demeanour of the characters in the night before their death has something of the resigned quality of Pearse's last poem, 'The wayfarer', written just before his own execution.[24] But each moment the prisoners wait, like the condemned volunteers of 1916, for death, allows *The interpreters* time to rewrite the scene of Irish revolutionary nationalism's most revered moment. By 1922, Irish nationalism traced the stations of Pearse's life from his proclamation of the republic to his execution at Kilmainham. The reality of Pearse's sacrifice was an unchallenged tenet of Irish nationalism, even during the civil war. *The interpreters* in effect creates a new myth of origin for post-revolutionary Ireland from a tradition of martyrdom that was crowned by the sacrifice of Pearse and company in 1916. Tellingly however, Russell replaces the sixteen dead of the Easter Rising with six standards of his own, each of whom has a chapter of *The interpreters* devoted to an exposition of his individual ideal. Lavelle, the first character to whom the reader is introduced, is a poet. Leroy, Lavelle's first companion in the cell, is an anarchist, accompanied by Culain, the labour leader, Brehon, the historian, Rian, the architect and Heyt, an imperial businessman wrongly arrested by state security. Each character has limited individual presence and speaks in a voice often indistinguishable from that of the narrator. 'The Interpreters', we are told, 'may be taken as a symposium between scattered portions of one nature dramatically sundered as the soul is in dream'.[25]

ry at the start of the text to see 'Men sat at all the tables. Some read. Others played games. The majority, however, sat in silence, their eyes staring vacantly in front of them, contemplating the horror of their lives'. 11. **22** G. Russell to G.B. Shaw, 30 June 1921, Shaw papers, BL ms 50548/192. **23** Ibid. **24** 'The wayfarer' regrets that 'The beauty of this world hath made me sad,/ This beauty that will pass'. After a vision of pastoral tranquillity, the speaker's 'heart hath told me:/ These will pass,/ Will pass and change, will die and be no/ More,/ Things bright and green, things young and/ happy;/ And I have gone upon my way/ Sorrowful'. P. Pearse, *Poems*. 31. **25** G. Russell, *The inter-*

The resulting similarity of each character's voice is a problem for the reader. It minimises debate between rival ideas and makes long passages of dialogue difficult to follow as the reader forgets which character is speaking. Russell could not write dialogue. John Eglinton reacted so badly to this that he labelled the whole work pointless.[26]

But to perceive *The interpreters* as a political myth consciously created helps the reader negotiate Eglinton's dismissal of the text: the foundation of Russell's post-Treaty doctrine inevitably involved a repetition of much of what the writer had considered in the previous decade. Myths are motivated by heroism. Accordingly each character in *The interpreters* exhibits some special aptitude. Culain's name is an obvious derivative of the Irish legendary hero Cuchulain and the historian Brehon is reminiscent of Standish O'Grady. Russell thought O'Grady inspired the Irish literary revival with his publication of the *History of Ireland*, an imaginative account of the heroic legend of the red branch. Neither are the main characters the only focus of Russell's epic attention. With Lavelle's arrest the reader is briefly made aware of the prison's other inhabitants. These rebels become heroic in death, just as Terence MacSwiney gained transcendence by hunger strike in Brixton prison. One prisoner shouts 'All here for Valhalla!' as Lavelle enters the cell; the poet replies 'I also am a traveller'.[27] Reference to Norse epic is odd but for heroic action to be universal the narrator can make no direct reference to Ireland, wracked in schism by 1922. In epic terms each character presents himself to his audience in the cell with an account of his lineage, a feature common to heroic literature. The architect Rian asserts that 'We artists built first for the gods and we did our best work for them'.[28] After years of service to individuals the architect promises art to the multitude; 'To work for the world will be like working for the gods again'.[29] The narrator provides a lineage for Brehon and Lavelle as 'The historian had been followed by creative writers like Lavelle, in whom the submerged river of nationality again welled up shining and life-giving'.[30] It is relevant to note Russell's use of water as a metaphor for rejuvenation; Yeats uses the fountain as a symbol of life's abundance in his later poetry, an image of continual imaginative replenishment.[31]

---

preters. viii. **26** Eglinton wrote that 'True seriousness, above all in philosophical dialogue, should be debonair, sympathetic, ironic, and so more convincing than when it is declamatory and hierophantic; and in reading Æ, one has the feeling – for want, no doubt, of some preliminary and shining Socratic examination of the meaning of the terms employed – that it is an attempt to grapple with problems which do not exist'. 'Dublin letter: January, 1923', *Dial*, 74: 2, Feb. 1923. 189. **27** G. Russell, *The interpreters*. 10. **28** Ibid. 38. **29** Ibid. **30** Ibid. 41. **31** See for example the female figure who 'can seem youth's very fountain,/ Being all brimmed with life' in 'The gift of Harun Al-Rashid' and the first section of 'Meditations in time of civil war' in which the 'abounding glittering jet' of 'a fountain' is in contrast to the 'empty sea-shell flung/ Out of the obscure dark

Russell replicates Yeats' interest in permanency in his creation of a heroic mode in *The interpreters*. It is part of his attempt to ensure the survival, in the Bakhtinian sense, of epic, or closed, time.[32] To allow the nation of his narrative to achieve statehood would be for Russell, as David Lloyd argues, to allow the death of heroic time by the fulfilment of national destiny.[33] To keep the nation forever without a state is to provide the writer with an environment in which a fiction of unity might be maintained. Statehood is the text's pivotal concern and haunts each character. It marks the end of a heroic mode of national struggle and hails the start of new forms of state power consolidated in a material structure. This possibility emerges in debate; in *The interpreters* each revolutionary faces his own redundancy, a fact with which the logic of each individual's discourse must struggle. The fitness of an individual to survive the transition between nation and state is the determining criterion for success in the philosophical debates of *The interpreters*. Such transition is charted in each of the six main individual's contributions to the text. Each character is introduced in sequence and their narrative order of appearance provides the reader with an initial key to understanding their final importance. There is a similarity between this schematic aspect of *The interpreters*' composition and the twenty-eight embodiments and one non-human phase of *A vision*, each being representative in Yeats' work of a stage of human development. Russell was listed in phase twenty-six, alongside Calvin, Luther, Cardinal Newman and George Herbert. Despite Russell's puzzlement at *A vision*, Yeats' placement of intellectual and psychic development within a schema relative to human endeavour and esoteric influence is not far in inspiration from Russell's creation in *The interpreters*. For each character's speech in Russell's work is presented to the reader in an order as rigorous as that preserved in *A vision*. The substance of each writer's opinion on the relation of the eternal to the immediate differs greatly but their basic impulse is similar, to trace a spiritual history of human achievement. Russell's dedication to this task in *The interpreters* symbolises his belief that, with the construction of a system that related vision to actuality, the future of Irish civilisation could be anticipated. In *The interpreters*' immediate context this future charts the evolution of Irish cultural nationalism's accommodation with Irish statehood.

The primary political struggle in the text occurs between capitalism and what Russell describes as state socialism. Heyt, the autocratic industrialist, is a

---

of the rich streams'. *Yeats's Poems*. 338, 308.   **32** In 'Epic and novel', Bakhtin argues that in epic 'the respected world of the heroes stands on an utterly different time-and-value plane, separated by epic distance. The space between them [*the singer and listener*] is filled with national tradition'. *Dialogic imagination*. 14. By use of such epic context, Russell places his characters in a safe, because inaccessible, place.   **33** Lloyd writes that 'The foundation of the state puts an end to the epic of its historical destiny in a performative act that abolishes history at the same time as it allows the epic to be fulfilled'. *Anomalous states*. 73.

symbol of individual character grown dominant over weaker, less conscious individuals. Heyt's political attitudes evidence Russell's belief in the *Irish Homestead* that 'The old aristocratic idea has reincarnated as capitalism'.[34] The labour leader Culain is in contrast a modern character, whose existence depends on industrial, rather than feudal, organisation. He represents a reaction against aristocracy and is the centre from which 'the workers of the nation had been brought to take part in the revolt'.[35] Considering Russell's dialogue with radical labour since 1913 we might expect Culain to be a cipher for James Connolly or Cathal O'Shannon. But in the epic terms deployed by *The interpreters*, Culain is compared instead to Cuchulain. From his first description Culain is attributed with having the same concentration of energy about his character that caused Cuchulain to change form in the midst of battle.[36] Cuchulain is the hero of O'Grady's *History of Ireland* and was the definite symbol, to Russell, of Irish identity. To associate Culain with Cuchulain is to associate labour with nationalism. Culain is a composite of the revolutionary energy that redefined Ireland in the nine years from 1913 to 1922. He loses his identity in the process. Culain is an archetype, the mould into which a future national consciousness can be poured. Accordingly, his power over the working class derives from his being 'an almost superhuman type of themselves, a clear utterer of what in them was inarticulate'.[37] The labour leader is gifted with a powerful voice but is left in an imaginative limbo. He can speak for, but not with, the working class. Accordingly, Culain describes his political inspiration in terms that defy rhetoric: 'As between myself and Heaven it was the intuition of the unity of humanity which led me to become communist'.[38] His ideological antecedents are religious rather than political and he relates his faith in humanity to 'Christ' and 'Buddha'.[39] The narrator as utopian and impractical finally undermines the labour leader's ideas; the first response by a prisoner to Culain's speech is 'I do not understand'.[40] Culain's vulnerability is apparent from this intrusion. He is 'almost superhuman' but his weakness derives from an inability to traverse fully the distance between individual and mass life.

John Eglinton was irritated by *The interpreters'* presentation of political argument in such abstract fashion, feeling that the conduct of debate between labour and capitalism was irrelevant to a state enduring civil war. Eglinton's impatience is understandable; *The interpreters* debates theory at a time when the new state was in danger of collapse, with the possibility of renewed British occupation in

---

34 G. Russell, 'Shaping the future', *IH*, 6 Jan. 1923. 2.   35 G. Russell, *The interpreters*. 34.   36 When Cuchulain first met the kings of Erin they 'were astonished … for smooth and pleasant was his countenance, and his stature not great'. When he later dueled with Ferdia at the ford, 'straightaway there arose a spray and a mist from the trampling of the heroes, and through the mist their forms moved hugely, like two giants of the Fomoroh contending in a storm'. S. O'Grady, *History of Ireland*. 165, 236.   37 G. Russell, *The interpreters*. 35.   38 Ibid. 95.   39 Ibid.   40 Ibid. 99.

the event of republican victory.[41] What Eglinton misses in his reading of the book is that in 1922, under cover of philosophical abstraction, Russell changes sides. Russell, an anarchist and one time confidant of James Connolly, had been faithfully sympathetic to Irish labour in the previous decade of his editorship of the *Irish Homestead*. *The interpreters* marks Russell's farewell to radical labour activism. Distrustful of the common mass of the revolutionary army whose fate its narrator determines, *The interpreters* is deeply sceptical of what Russell, just six years before in *The national being*, perceived to be a 'general will' that 'always intends the good'.[42] The fact that Culain's socialism fails Russell's test of political relevance to the new order is apparent from the end of his speech:

> A silence followed during which Rian watched that prisoner of puzzled countenance who could not understand Culain, and whose expression indicated that now less than ever could he relate the politics of time to the politics of eternity. The sullen eyes, knit brow, and impatient feet grinding on the floor, betrayed the anger of one at home in practical action who finds himself trapped in a web of incomprehensible abstractions.[43]

The working class is relegated to inferior status by its inability to perceive a complex reality. The rebels in the cell, other than the six main characters, assume the status of the general population after a revolution – important as the basic fabric of society but with little actual power. Appropriately Culain's only vocal supporter is Rian, the architect, an artist whose skill depends on the ordering of raw material into functional edifice. The reader is left with the impression that the working class will be simply the human material in the post-*The interpreters* state project. In contrast, Heyt, Culain's antagonist, is representative of all that Russell was previously against. He is anti-democratic, capitalist and denies the importance of national identity. But Heyt is capable of engendering a sense of social cohesion that the revolutionary characters cannot. Heyt is in essence representative of the deep aversion to popular democracy that Russell developed during the civil war.[44] The capitalist is Russell's alternative to the

41 The British government nearly attacked the Four Courts. It put the Free State government under enormous pressure to act against republican forces with the suggestion that it would enforce the Treaty in Ireland if the independent government could not. See M. Hopkinson, *Green against green*. 115–22.   **42** G. Russell, *The national being*. 107.   **43** G. Russell, *The interpreters*. 119.   **44** Russell's mistrust of democratic society's ability to legislate safely for itself was pronounced during this period. Russell had elsewhere argued that he would rather have 'one autocrat with good intentions than several millions who don't know what is wise and what is foolish'. 'NOTW', *IH*, 1 Oct. 1921. 669. This was not an isolated remark: 'one can only pray that Heaven will send us a powerful autocrat with ability to govern and a real desire to lead and educate the people so that they will be able to govern themselves'. 'Democracy on trial', *IH*, 10 June 1922. 362.

anarchy he associated with mass agitation, the pivotal figure around which Russell's post-revolutionary state can be arranged in an orderly, efficient corporatism. We find that Heyt can converse with the poet and the other prisoners on their own terms and in their own language. The narrator reckons that

> Everyone in this age sought for the source and justification for their own activities in that divine element in which matter, energy, and consciousness when analysed disappeared. It was an era of arcane speculation, for science and philosophy had become esoteric after the visible universe had been ransacked and the secret of its being had eluded the thinkers.[45]

So can capitalism, in the form of Heyt, be made amenable to culture as Heyt's autocratic vision responds to intellectual stimulus. Such interaction depends on the acquisition of a spiritual dimension by capitalism. Heyt duly insists that he is not a materialist: 'The power I spoke of does not lie in the generation of mechanical force but in the minds which organise control.'[46] *The interpreters* is a primer for state-sponsored action, with the intellectual class the unlikely new master of capital development. *The interpreters* exhibits a similar obsession with order in its debate on cultural imperatives, conducted mainly by Lavelle and Brehon. The narrator describes Brehon as the inspiration of a cultural revival identical to Ireland's in the late nineteenth and early twentieth centuries. Brehon, like Standish O'Grady, is brought the nation 'forth young and living from its grave'.[47] The historian's achievements were 'followed by creative writers like Lavelle, in whom the submerged river of nationality again welled up shining and life-giving'.[48] This river was 'bathed' in by the 'youth of the nation' who, once cleansed, rebelled against the 'empire, its mechanical ideals, and the characterless culture it imposed upon them'.[49] This is an impressive, if thinly veiled, attempt to record a definitive impression of the history of Irish literature in English and its political effect from 1870 to independence. Russell uses his narrative voice to codify this interpretation of the past as the dominant context for the ensuing monologues, rather than have such a context established by dialogue between characters. The narrator's sense of history is definitive as it sets the parameters by which characters can judge their own respective motives for becoming involved in rebellion. This idea makes the reader further aware of how deeply all the main speakers' ideas are connected to the narrative's foundational fictions. There is no room in *The interpreters* for deviation from the history that it represents.

Appropriately, Brehon presents the relationship between himself and Lavelle, the historian and poet, as natural, combining between them two of the

---

45 G. Russell, *The interpreters*. 70. **46** Ibid. 67. **47** Ibid. 41. **48** Ibid. **49** Ibid.

main functions of the epic, the exercise of memory and its articulation in the imagination. Brehon does not rehearse the details of their relationship in a manner in which any reader of Russell's prose over the previous decade and more would be familiar. He does not reiterate the fact that Lavelle's cultural revival was inspired by Brehon's retrieval of the epic. Brehon rather details what he achieved after the publication of his history. He became disenchanted with culture and turned his imagination to a discovery of 'that vast life which is normally subconscious in us'.[50] Brehon's occult interest parallels his growing belief in a universal organisation of human society as 'the lure of national ideals began to be superseded by imaginations of a world state'.[51] The expression of human consciousness and the organisation of human political association become one, as a definition of the subconscious leads to a mechanism capable of satisfying human desire. The expression of Brehon's ideas is arcane but it contains a disturbing political subtext. The historian acted in concert with a number of other mystics and

> the will of many in unison was powerful enough to transcend the bodily life so that in meditation together consciousness rose like a tower into heaven, and we were able to bring back some knowledge of the higher law.[52]

Meditation precedes the perception of a new order. As Brehon admits elsewhere, 'The apprehension of law is but the growth in ourselves of a profounder self-consciousness.'[53] His concept of law binds together the concepts of self-regulation and self-perception in a potentially authoritarian manner. But Brehon's idea of order would remain secret without the creative power of Lavelle, the poet. The historian's discussion with Lavelle is Brehon's preparation of the artist for a commitment to a new revival, this time based on science and international association rather than literature and nationalism. Lavelle questions Brehon's intentions, aware that the historian's ideas will result in the death of 'our nation, its culture and ideals' with its replacement by 'an unresisted materialism'.[54] As the poet convinces himself of the historian's logic, *The interpreters* resolves itself into a programme for a new revival. All the pre-revolutionary elements of Irish nationalism, political, cultural and literary, are refined down to the basics of Russell's post-civil war doctrine of intellectual and Free State authority. This is the remarkable point of *The interpreters*. It marks Russell's accommodation with forces felt necessary to the survival of the new Irish state, with industry, share options and the attraction of foreign capital. This is a change of substantial cultural importance to post-Treaty Ireland as Russell jet-

---

50 Ibid. 138.   **51** Ibid.   **52** Ibid. 139.   **53** Ibid. 131.   **54** Ibid. 134.

tisons his revival rhetoric of national inclusion to create a critical vocabulary partisan in its vision of social order. The civil war was the definite impetus to the reactionary nature of much of Russell's political theory post-1922. But its lessons mapped a new territory for Russell in the latter phase of his literary career, with an increasingly authoritarian cultural polemic expressed in support of European corporatism and a conservative, even reactionary, Irish polity.

The interpreters would be dull if its two artists were engaged together in a struggle for supremacy over the capitalist Heyt, victim of a dialogue determined by the familiar poles of the spiritual and material, the heroic and pragmatic, rehearsed so regularly since the start of the Revival. Equally, Irish nationalism was, since 1916 at least, obsessed over the defeat of superior force by sacrifice. The interest of *The interpreters* lies in the change that occurs in the relationship between Lavelle and Brehon, a change of substantial cultural importance to post-Treaty Ireland. Russell establishes his terms carefully, stressing the relative inadequacy of his words to offer any suitable explanation as to the nature of national identity. Brehon did not think that 'words' could 'ever represent, to one who has no direct vision or intuition of his own, what the words signify'.[55] Brehon suggests that he will be speaking to an audience already clairvoyantly aware of his ideas. Words only complicate matters further:

> Speech is not like a mirror which reflects fully the form before it; but in speech things, which by their nature are innumerable and endless, are indicated by brief symbols. For speech to convey true meanings there must be clairaudience in the hearing.[56]

Brehon offers a partial insight into structural linguistics. But instead of suggesting that symbols (or signifiers) can only hold a contingent relationship to that which they represent (the signified), Brehon instead argues that the true value of what he says exists at an intuitive level, beyond the sign. Meaning and understanding already pre-exist within an adequately evolved consciousness. So Brehon can speak only to the converted, a fact that promotes all those characters that listen and understand in *The interpreters* to a privileged, even elite, discourse. As Brehon continues to speak, the full implications of this point become clear. The historian remarks that, of the four speeches that have preceded his, only three had their basis in spirituality. Rian asks if it is 'Leroy's anarchic ideals that have no spiritual foundation?'.[57] To Brehon they do not because anarchists will not 'attain their full stature until they comprehend the spiritual foundations on which other political theories rest, and can build on them as do the devotees of beauty or love or power'.[58] This is fundamental to *The interpreters*. Beauty,

---

55 Ibid. 121.   56 Ibid. 122.   57 Ibid. 124.   58 Ibid. 125.

love and power are represented each in its turn by Lavelle, Culain and Heyt. They correspond in number to the three 'fundamentals' of the universe that Brehon has already described, 'matter, energy and spirit': 'We can surmise beyond these nothing except that transcendental state where all raised above themselves exist in the mystic unity we call Deity.'[59] The reader is left with a political theory that relies for success on the creation of three elements within it, beauty, love and power. The definitive factor in this equation is the belief put forward in *The interpreters* that humanity is in the Iron Age, that part of *Theo*-sophical time frame that signifies materialism and a supreme distance from the deity. Since all characters inhabit this Iron Age, the central most important fig-ure must be Heyt, already himself a successful adherent to its laws. In this one sense the interpreters are the characters around Heyt, specifically Lavelle and Culain, who pass on knowledge of beauty and love to the iron agent who remains mute for the rest of the text. Here *The interpreters* is highly determin-istic, intent on the amelioration rather than the redefinition of the material con-ditions in which it imagines itself to exist.

As the conversation changes to discuss the morality of physical force, Bre-hon is further privileged to interpret events for Heyt. The historian remarks that if a state is won by force then so must it be sustained. Then 'there is no real freedom'.[60] If on the other hand there is a 'reliance on spiritual law' then 'we draw others naturally to seek for a like fullness of their own being'.[61] This is similar to Culain's earlier statement, which was undermined, that spiritual change must precede material revolution. It is acceptable from Brehon because it is framed against the perception of a spiritual agency that Culain did not share. Brehon redefines Culain's ideals to introduce to them an element of con-trol, an element that did not exist previously. 'Others', in Brehon's words, main-tain their anonymity while 'we', the privileged readers, comprehend the arche-types in whose image those following us to consciousness will be cast. Beyond the discussion of culture and politics between Culain, Heyt, Lavelle and Bre-hon, there are two characters excluded from the main current of debate. The first is Rian, the architect, already dismissed by Brehon because of his sympa-thy with Culain, the labour leader relegated below Heyt. The second is Leroy, the anarchist. To Brehon, Leroy's anarchism 'is heroic to defy the universe. I admire but I cannot follow.'[62] Leroy never defines anarchy as a coherent strat-egy despite the fact that we know Russell was committed to the subject in his first decade of editorship of the *Irish Homestead*. But Leroy's dismissal is evi-dence, in context, of Russell's subtle discrimination against the anti-Treaty side in the civil war. Under direction of William Cosgrave, successor to Michael Collins as chairman of the Free State Executive Council, republican forces were

59 Ibid. 122–3.   60 Ibid. 141.   61 Ibid.   62 Ibid. 115.

designated as 'Irregulars' by the Irish press.[63] 'Irregulars' of course lack the order and authority of the state, a condition also shared by anarchists. The fact that Leroy has no place in the post-revolutionary terrain mapped out in *The interpreters* is an early indication of the antagonism that Russell maintained against republicans for the near decade of the *Irish Statesman*'s publication.

The main body of the symposium ends with a consideration of the qualities of other prisoners in the cell. As Brehon finishes his speech, Leroy asks of the others 'What [they] think of all this?'[64] Notably, the prisoner Rudd's answer is not in direct speech but is mediated by the narrator. He 'broke out with much profanity that he had never heard so much folly'.[65] It is plain that the psychological change for which Brehon had called for has not taken place, as Rudd remains 'baffled in his efforts to understand things remote from his mentality'.[66] The prisoner continues his polemic: 'one world was enough for him; one small county all he could think about'.[67] Rudd's tirade ends with a retreat to the far corner of the room, followed by Rian's sympathy that his 'emotions'[68] have overcome him. This word is important because it relates Rudd's character to that of the young men whom Russell thought kept the civil war going by joining political clubs and having 'their emotions … whipped up like cream'.[69] There is a constant tension in Russell's journalism post-1922 between the new generation used to the violence of the First World War and the generations that preceded it. Much of Russell's then contemporary work stresses in contrast the foundational work of movements or organisations formed from the turn of the century. In a speech to the Sociological Society in London at the start of 1922 Russell was keen to point out the influence of co-operatives, labour, Sinn Féin and the Literary Revival on his contemporary Ireland.[70] All of these were in place before 1914.

In *The interpreters* it seems as if the new, tainted generation is to be summarily dismissed. Since Rian cannot think of Rudd's being 'influenced by beauty or any of the other divinities' he decides that this prisoner 'belongs to your household, Leroy'.[71] Leroy replies, 'I accept him.'[72] Ignoring for the moment the pretence that Leroy, or indeed any of the other main speakers in *The interpreters*, is in a position to accept anyone into their ranks, since all but one are due for execution, it is important to realise the full political significance of this gesture.

---

63 Hopkinson notes that 'Cosgrave's Government put a heavy stress on authority – circulars to the Press ordered that the Government should be referred to as "The National Government" and not "The Provisional Government", and that the Republican opposition, of all shades, should be known as "Irregulars"'. *Green against green.* 180. 64 G. Russell, *The interpreters.* 156. 65 Ibid. 66 Ibid. 67 Ibid. 68 Ibid. 157. 69 G. Russell, 'NOTW', *IH*, 4 Aug. 1923. 494. 70 Russell claimed 'These movements in their spiritual blending and interaction represent the stage of self-realisation the national Absolute has reached in Ireland to-day. If the leaders were dead the movements would continue.' *Ireland, past and future.* 9. 71 G. Russell, *The interpreters.* 157. 72 Ibid.

Leroy is an anarchist and Free State government propaganda during the civil war consistently referred to the anti-Treaty forces as such. It is instructive to read the press censorship guide issued by the pro-Treaty forces during 1922 to see just how political such labelling was. The directive ordered that 'The Army must always be referred to as the "Irish Army", the "National Army", "National Troops", or simply "troops" '.[73] On the other hand 'The Irregulars must not be referred to as the "Executive Forces", nor described as "forces" or "troops". They are to be called "bands", or "bodies" of men.'[74] Placing the youth Rudd with the anarchist Leroy held a great deal of contemporary political significance, one which is partially obscured by the formal register of the text's language, supposed as it was to represent a degree of objectivity. Rian now asks a prisoner called Brugha (obvious related to Cathal Brugha, the anti-Treaty leader shot outside the Hammam Hotel, O'Connell Street) why he joined the rebellion. Brugha answers Rian by saying that 'I heard rebellion talked since I was a child. It was so with my family for generations. They were in every insurrection. It was a tradition with us.'[75] These words are taken directly from the Treaty debate and are based on comments made by Austin Stack, the former associate of Michael Collins and anti-Treaty leader who was also killed in the civil war. In Dáil discussion at the end of 1921, Stack rose to speak in support of de Valera because

> this question of the oath has an extraordinary significance for me, for, so far as I can trace, no member of my family has ever taken an oath of allegiance to England's king … I was nurtured in the traditions of Fenianism.[76]

The similarity between Stack's words and those of Brugha in *The interpreters* is striking. Stack's reference to the oath, the symbolic central issue over which the two sides fought, adds another level of meaning to Brugha's remarks. It suggests that Russell is attempting to disable the foundations of anti-Treaty doctrine in *The interpreters*; Rian dismisses Brugha for 'ancestor worship. I could not place you in any of our categories unless I knew the mood of the first ancestor. He may have been another Leroy'.[77] At this point the symposium closes with Brugha and the ideology that he implicitly represents redundant, sidelined even by Leroy, a character who is himself outside the mainstream of *The interpreters'* defining moments.

---

73 The directive from which the preceding quotation is taken was published for propaganda use against the pro-Treaty government in the *Republican War Bulletin*, 1: 3, 12 August 1922. 2. The two quotations that I give are the first two points of twelve in the directive, apparently issued by the publicity department of the pro-Treaty army at Beggars Bush Barracks.   **74** Ibid.   **75** G. Russell, *The interpreters*. 158.   **76** *Official report: debate on the Treaty between Great Britain and Ireland signed in London on the 6th December 1921. Session Dec. 1921–Jan. 1922*. 28.   **77** G. Russell, *The interpreters*.

The end of the symposium is not however the end of *The interpreters* as the work finishes with a poem, 'Michael', the previous debates brought to closure in verse. Since the text as a whole is concerned with the necessity of intellectual direction of the post-revolutionary state, it is important to read 'Michael' as Russell's evidence of Irish literature's ability to speak for the new polity. This is a massive gesture and, ironically, to realise it Russell relates his work to an English poet. John Butler Yeats compared the style of Russell's poem to Coleridge but it is to Wordsworth, who published 'Michael' in his *Lyrical ballads* of 1800, that Russell looks.[78] Wordsworth's 'Michael' is a pastoral that dramatises the decline of traditional, rural English capital relations. Michael is a shepherd who works a hill farm in old age with help from his son Luke. His happiness is disturbed by a financial crisis that forces Luke to leave their smallholding. Corrupted by the 'dissolute city'[79] in which he works, Luke forsakes his father: 'ignominy and shame/ Fell on him, so that he was driven at last/ To seek a hiding-place beyond the seas'.[80] Michael and his wife Isabel die and the farm is levelled. Russell's 'Michael' follows a similar trajectory. Michael is now the son of a fisherman on the west coast of Ireland but leaves his village for the city and becomes lost, like Wordsworth's Luke, in urban anonymity.

Crucially, Russell's Michael is, we see, the son, rather than the father of Wordsworth's poem. Richard Bourke has suggested that Wordsworth's poem represents the failure of patrimony in face of political change.[81] If so, Russell's recasting of 'Michael' as a filial voyage of discovery is an attempt, perhaps like *The interpreters* itself, to create a stable connection through poetry between past and present. The political contingencies of such an enterprise lie in Russell's redefinition of the society that the later Michael inhabits. Bourke contends of Wordsworth's 'Michael' that the poem represents Wordsworth's inability to resolve a late-eighteenth-century idea of individuality with English political reality.[82] The ideal of self-hood that Wordsworth proposed had no correlative social status. Russell too tries to create an identity, of the intellectual as state director, before social ratification. He tries to resolve this difficulty by reversing

---

158.   **78** In a letter to John Quinn, dated 19 January 1920, the elder Yeats wrote that 'There is not a word in the poem which is not common sense of the sort which Coleridge called the substance of poetry'. Denson typescript. 354.   **79** W. Wordsworth, *Poems.* 466.   **80** Ibid. 467.   **81** Bourke suggests 'the unnerving aspects of subjectivity come to haunt the poet's agrarian scheme in *Michael.* Subjectivity, or consciousness, asserts itself in this poem as an unwelcome intruder. It appears with the apparently intolerable characteristics of foresight and anticipation. As we shall see, this intrusion discredits the integrity of the law of patrimonial succession upon which Wordsworth's ideal commonwealth is premised'. *Romantic discourse and political modernity.* 78–9.   **82** Bourke, again, finds that, in 'Michael', 'we come up against the central tension operating in Wordsworth's political speculations between action and thought, the *vita activa* and the *vita contempliva*, politics and philosophy: between, on the one hand, a political order and, on the other, a preoccupation with its normative basis; between the republic and an estimation of its legal foundation'. Ibid. 105.

the terms of Wordsworth's dilemma. Russell uses his symposium to articulate a vision of society able to accommodate an ideal of cultural activism before poetry, introduced at the end of the text, stakes its political claim. In *The interpreters* Lavelle, who claims to have had a 'dream about one who died in an old insurrection of our people hundreds of years ago', recites Russell's poem.[83] But 'Michael' was previously printed privately in 1919 and was published both in the first, aborted, edition of the *Irish Statesman* in 1919 and in the *Dial* in 1920. It starts as a pastoral, far removed from the urban cell that is setting for *The interpreters*. The speaker describes a collection of 'fisher folk' who shelter from a storm 'snug under thatch and sheltering wall'.[84] Michael leaves this communal idyll for the city; Wordsworth's poem contains a similar departure scene before Luke leaves for London. Russell also had Tennyson in mind when he wrote 'Michael's opening section. He wrote as early as 1909 that

> To a child its first glimpse of the big city is as intoxicating as a visionary's glimpse of the Heavenly City, the New Jerusalem. It seems a wonderful city of palaces, and the child goes back to the lonely farm with an intense longing and hope that some time it may live altogether in these luminous streets. It is a feeling so common that Tennyson used it to illustrate the inspiration of the hero of Locksley Hall:
>
> > Eager-hearted as a boy when first he leaves his
> > father's field,
> > And at night along the dusky highway near and
> > nearer drawn,
> > Sees in heaven the light of London flaring like a
> > dreary dawn,
> > And his spirit leaps within him to be gone before him
> > then,
> > Underneath the light he looks at, in among the
> > the throngs of men.[85]

Russell's Michael too has a vision, the strength of which lies in the quality of his character's intuition. Michael is drawn to 'some deep being' that is hidden to even the most sensitive reader: 'Some mystery to the wise ... clouded o'er by Paradise'.[86] Michael can never afterwards recall his vision with clarity; as he tried to remember it his 'Imagination still would fail'.[87] But he has been charged, like the other characters of *The interpreters*, with a spiritual inspiration. Michael has met in this heavenly world a series of beings with 'countenance divine'; in turn 'lofty things to him were said/ As to one risen from the dead'.[88]

83 G. Russell, *The interpreters*. 159.   84 Ibid. 161.   85 G. Russell, 'A missionary island', *IH*, 11 Sept. 1909. 737.   86 Ibid. 165.   87 Ibid.   88 Ibid.

Reference to resurrection is a gesture towards Pearse and evidence of the poem's wider attempt to wrest symbolic force from the dead revolutionary.[89] Russell did this to take Pearse's presence from the generation that he immediately inspired and place the dead rebel, through the medium of 'Michael', safely into the care of a new canon. The sense of containment this implies is reflected in Michael's experience of the city, itself the antithesis of nature in Romantic poetry. Michael inhales

> the city's dingy air,
> By the black reek of chimneys smudged
> O'er the dark warehouse where he drudged,
> Where for dull life men pay in toll
> Toil and the shining of the soul.
> Within his attic he would fret
> Like a wild creature in a net.[90]

Michael is distanced from his origins as memory fades. Like Luke in Wordsworth's 'Michael', he is in danger of losing his identity by forgetting his roots. But where Luke was destroyed by materialism, Michael is saved by a chance encounter with 'one of that eager kind,/ The army of the Gaelic mind'.[91] It is ironic that Michael should come to the city to be made aware of his folk traditions but his education symbolises a fusion between the ancient and modern, the rural and the urban that troubled Wordsworth's 'Michael'. Russell immediately encounters a problem with his poetic synthesis as Michael is exposed to new knowledge by a 'story of the famous dead'.[92] The pressure of Irish nationalist martyrology intrudes upon his new poetic freedom. Since *The interpreters* was published at the end of 1922, one might reasonably expect that the list of the dead would include Connolly, MacDonagh or Pearse. Russell avoids their presence by casting back to the heroic tradition uncovered by O'Grady in the *History of Ireland*. His speaker looks to Cuchulain and 'the wanderers who set sail/ And found a lordlier Innisfail',[93] a reference to O'Grady's account of the Milesians' arrival in pre-historic Ireland.[94] He further accommodates the Irish language with a reference to 'the vagrant poets, those who gave their hearts to the Dark Rose'.[95] The main concern is how history exerts influence on the present: 'How may the past, if it be dead, its light upon the living shed?'[96] The answer is that the past exists to be remade in a series of con-

---

89 In Pearse's poem 'The fool', the speaker is certain of afterlife: 'Lord, I have staked my soul, I have staked/ the lives of my kin/ On the truth of thy dreadful word ... I speak to my people and say ... Ye shall call for a miracle, taking Christ at/ his word'. *Poems*. 336. **90** G. Russell, *The interpreters*. 166. **91** Ibid. 168. **92** Ibid. **93** Ibid. **94** O'Grady's record of the Milesians can be found in his *History of Ireland: the heroic period*. 60–5. **95** G. Russell, *The interpreters*. 168. **96** Ibid.

temporary productions, to connect those who 'wrought ... the legend of the Gael' with the 'warriors of Eternal Mind,/ Still holding in a world gone blind'.[97] Russell resolves his anxiety over the inability of culture to affect the new state by endowing the qualities of heroic characterisation described in 'Michael' upon the intellectual himself. This is a novel development, as epic rests with the pen and not the hero.

'Michael' next moves forward three years in time to 'the season of the risen Lord', and once more the reader is reminded of the dead of that recent Easter. To the speaker rebellion is the ascension of 'the Lord in man', freed from the 'dark sepulchre of fear'.[98] In language reminiscent of Russell's earlier poem 'Apocalyptic', the fighters in 'Michael' stand 'wilful, laughing, undismayed,/ Though on a fragile barricade'.[99] *The interpreters* is again exposed in its aim to incorporate the heroic tradition of Irish revolutionary nationalism to Russell's own programme of intellectual activism. The immediate effect of such accommodation also serves the need of *The interpreters'* myth to be universal as it occludes the reality of civil war. This sense of distance is inferred in lines that describe Michael's death: 'he was far away .../ Afloat upon the heavenly seas'.[100] The poem ends. Lavelle now claims to have added a new gloss to 'Michael' which comprises a further two stanzas. He has been moved 'by what was said in this room'[101] and leaves it to Rian to decide whether or not this new ending suggests any change in his ideals. The addition of a final two stanzas is a fiction of *The interpreters*. Both are included in the 1919 text and neither contains any new material. Russell's intention then is to draw specific attention to Lavelle's transformation. The poet is moved in these stanzas to question the impulse behind self-sacrifice. We may 'choose this cause or that, but still/ The Everlasting works its will'.[102] The reasons for individual sacrifice are various:

> Some for a gentle dream will die:
> Some for an empire's majesty:
> Some for a loftier mankind,
> Some to be free as cloud or wind.[103]

'To the memory of some I knew' had already, we know, tried to synthesise such various impulses in a unified national force. Russell failed in 1917 because of his affection for Connolly. 'Michael' has a parallel lapse as it admits to the importance of state power in the redefined national project. From *The interpreters'* earliest pages Lavelle, the poem's speaker, has been ambivalent about the creations of empire around him; he is described as a potential traitor because of

97 Ibid. 168–9.   **98** Ibid. 169.   **99** Ibid. In 'Apocalyptic', 'only those can laugh who are/ The strong Initiates of Pain'. *The gods of war*. np.   **100** Ibid. 170.   **101** Ibid.   **102** Ibid. 171.   **103** Ibid.

his admiration for a fleet of airships outside the cell window.[104] These airships are perfect examples of the union between 'power' and 'beauty' that underpins Lavelle's attraction to imperial order and, by extension, to Heyt. Lavelle's aesthetic displaces his poem's nationalist sentiments to initiate a new politics ordered by occult divination. Lavelle suggests that Michael died for an abstract notion other

> Than that grey island he had known.
> Yet on his dream of it was thrown
> Some light from that consuming power
> Which is the end of all desire.
> If men adore it as the power,
> Empires and cities, tower on tower,
> Are built in worship by the way,
> High Babylon or Nineveh.
> Seek it as love and there may be
> A Golden Age or Arcady.
> All shadows are they of one thing
>   To which all life is journeying.[105]

As 'Michael' ends, *The interpreters* draws to a close. Only Heyt is freed. Leroy, 'always generous',[106] points out his enemy's real identity to his captors. Thus the anarchist, whose politics remain profane because they are not based in divinity, recognises his better in Heyt and motions him to leave. Lavelle too 'would have intervened on behalf of the old historian,'[107] Brehon, but could not because his elder signalled that he would stay. This is a heroic gesture but in a formal sense at least Brehon's escape was impossible, as it would confuse the significance of Heyt's exit. The interpreters, anarchist, architect, historian, labour leader and poet have taught the capitalist the virtue of national culture. Trained to the occult control of the national will, Heyt can re-order an entire world by his respect of its general principles, the particulars of which have been made clear to him in *The interpreters*. Heyt is Russell's symbol of the world beyond the Irish nation as imagined in the literary revival, scion of capital and imperial order. He is Russell's contract with the material world beyond the Free State,

---

104 On seeing the airships 'One of the prisoners cursed bitterly. But with Lavelle, the poet in him made him for an instant almost traitor to the nation, stirred as he was by that vision of the culmination of human power soaring above the planet.' G. Russell, *The interpreters*. 30. Interestingly the central character of H.G. Wells' *The war in the air*, Bert Smallways, on board a German airship, wondered if 'Indeed, wasn't he a sort of traitor? He wondered how the aerial fleet must look from down there. Tremendous, no doubt, and dwarfing all the buildings.' 65.   **105** G. Russell, *The interpreters*. 172.   **106** Ibid. 179.   **107** Ibid.

Russell's recognition that idealism must adapt to a reality more prosaic than that allowed in the early days of national evangelism. The reader alone is privileged to witness Heyt's exit through the words of the narrator; 'moved by what he had heard', he was 'understanding' that 'these men were different from all he had imagined of them'.[108] All the arguments to which Heyt has been exposed act internally and require no articulation. Heyt 'hesitated for a moment as if he would have said or urged something' but instead shook his head, as if he realised how impossible it now was to effect anything, and he left them without a word and went out to make the world in his own image'.[109] We are left not with a speech but an archetype to shape the world's future.

After publication, promotion of *The interpreters* was carefully managed. It was reviewed in the *Irish Times* on the same day that the paper published Russell's 'Open letter to Irish republicans' with an approving editorial. Significantly, criticism of *The interpreters* was most severe with regard to its literary deficiencies; the *Irish Times* reviewer thought it lacked characterization and drama, debating philosophy in abstract terms to deter the casual reader.[110] *The interpreters* was an instrumental, and not aesthetic, achievement. The *Irish Times'* editor observed that 'Mr. Russell is an Irish philosopher who unites an intense patriotism with an almost unique aloofness from the passions of politics'.[111] In his book, '"The Interpreters" (which we review to-day), he speaks as one holding no form of political creed, but contemplating all'.[112] He urges the extremists, for Ireland's sake and the sake of their own hearts and consciences and ideals, to lay down the weapons of strife'.[113] The *Irish Times* saw Russell's work as a support to Irish civility.

> Paris is about to spend four million pounds on civic improvements. To-day, at the dawn of a new era, a neglected and bedraggled Dublin is the capital of a land of woe. Our countryside is bare and broken. A wage dispute threatens to close our railways. These things could not be if our boasted love of Ireland really deserved the title of patriotism. The teaching of Mr Russell's letter is needed, in some part, by many others than those to whom it is addressed.[114]

Russell's open letter follows on the next page. Violence, he suggests, turned the public against republicans, tired as they were of six years and more of conflict at home and abroad. Republicans, he wrote, should respect the majority that accepted the Treaty because conflict was a fever that could disable the body politic, the result being complete material and moral collapse. Russell admitted

---

108 Ibid.   **109** Ibid. 179–80.   **110** 'Books of the week', *Irish Times*, 29 Dec. 1922. 2.   **111** 'The way of peace', *Irish Times*, 29 Dec. 1922. 4.   **112** Ibid.   **113** Ibid.   **114** Ibid.

the harshness of Free State security policy but thought of republicans that 'the majority regard you, not the Government of the Free State, as the cause of their suffering; and, while they may be turned from it because they think some of its acts harsh or unwise, they are not therefore moved to support of your policy'.[115] He urged a return to constructive work, the ideal of pure nationality in practice; 'Can you not', he asked, 'find simple work in those fields were too little has been done, and with respect for your political ideals, by the genius, wisdom and energy you exhibit?'[116] Republicans must, wrote Russell, transfer their grievance to intellectual debate. Like Heyt at the end of *The interpreters*, Russell felt he understood the rebel mind:

> Most of you have to come to prominence as activists only during recent years. A man who is now dead, a man who was dear to me, Erskine Childers, had great ability – greater, I think, for peace than war – but can you tell me those who, if you were all killed, would have left behind, as Pearse or Connolly or MacDonagh or Childers did, evidence of constructive thought or imagination? Which of you are architects, mastercraftsmen in the art of nation-building?[117]

The preoccupation with building, with the construction of a national psyche to support the state, increased as collapse edged closer; Russell's 'Open letter to Irish republicans' was published the same day as a Free State soldier was reported dead in the village of Ring, Co. Kerry. There were other, more unlikely victims. A mine destroyed Mr Denis McCullough's piano warehouse on Dawson Street the night previous. As the year turned, the security situation improved and the republican threat to the new state decreased. Russell was now confident enough to cast questions of national reorganization in terms of retrospect. His 'Lessons of revolution' was published by the Jesuit quarterly review *Studies* in March 1923. First issued by University College Dublin academics in March 1912, *Studies* is still in press today. Its two predecessors were the *Lyceum*, published between 1887 and 1894, and the *New Ireland Review*, published between 1894 and 1911. *Studies* was an intellectual review whose pages were little relieved by either illustration or advertisement. Early issues contained poetry by Katherine Tynan and Padraic Colum and prose by Patrick Pearse. The journal's strong links with the revolutionary generation surfaced in articles published on Thomas MacDonagh, Joseph Plunkett and Pearse in the months after their 1916 executions. *Studies* constantly strove to come to terms with the Ireland that appeared in the second decade of the twentieth century with articles on trade unionism, civil disorder, European nationalism and new forms of Irish

---

115 'Open letter to Irish republicans', *Irish Times*, 29 Dec. 1922. 5. **116** Ibid. 6. **117** Ibid.

writing. In this it was ably assisted by the Jesuit priest Stephen Brown, whose *Ireland in fiction* of 1916 is a neglected critical classic. *Studies*, unlike its co-religious rival the *Catholic Bulletin*, supported the Treaty and dedicated its pages to discussion of future state policy in education and economics. Thomas Finlay, editor, Jesuit priest and Professor of Political Economy at UCD, and first editor of the *Irish Homestead*, was a main reason for the journal's broad capacity. He was also one of three principal officers of the IAOS; the other two were R.A. Anderson and George Russell.

The personal and professional connections between the now editors of the *Irish Homestead* and *Studies* opened new readerships to each. We noticed how the *Irish Homestead*, in its early years, published positive reports of parish priests' support of Irish co-operatives. We can see that Russell used *Studies* to speak to the new Irish elite, the young men, mostly, educated in the national university and now in power. In 'Lessons of revolution', Russell first discussed Russian failures since 1917. Lenin and Bukharin now agreed that their greatest mistake was to precipitate an uprising before social conditions could sustain it. Critical attributes like 'Intellect, science, administrative ability could not be improvised, being evolutionary products'.[118] The moral for Irish revolutionaries was clear. Easter week

> triumphed solely in externals. Our spiritual, cultural, and intellectual life has not changed for the better. If anything, it has retrograded. Nothing beautiful in the mind has found freer development. In so far as anything is done efficiently, it is done by administrators, educationists, officials and guiders of industry, who maintain, so far as permitted by circumstances, the habits engendered before the war for independence.[119]

A republic would not change this. The only possible strategy was to adapt to current conditions before national evolution threatened extinction. New attributes, of civil and practical intelligence, must be engendered in the Irish people:

> Earth is dense with traditions of perished nationalities. If a nation is like a dissolute youth who impairs his vitality by excesses, it will perish as surely and by as inexorable a law of life as the debauchee. There comes a point where recovery is impossible. Something – a skeleton or larva – may survive, but not the nation with confident genius. There will always be herdsmen to look after the bullocks; but the genius of the Gael, if this conflict continues for much longer, will have vanished from its place of birth. The

---

118 G. Russell, 'Lessons of revolution', *Studies*, March 1923. 2.   **119** Ibid.

curious in psychology may seek to trace a flash of character here and there in some state of the new world to a possible Gaelic ancestry –

'a phrase,
As in wild earth a Grecian vase'.[120]

Russell seals his argument with lines from Padraic Colum's 'A poor scholar of the forties', from Colum's first collection, *Wild earth*, a poem that suggests that intimate connection between the life of the land and culture that Russell had promoted throughout a career in co-operative organization.[121] The *Irish Homestead* had been Russell's mouthpiece in this endeavour for nearly two decades. Horace Plunkett, as proprietor, felt that the new state demanded a new journal. He had published a short-lived weekly under the title the *Irish Statesman* from June 1919 to June 1920 to support his Irish Dominion League. Edited by Warre B. Wells, it intended to secure the 'immediate establishment of self-government for Ireland within the Empire'.[122] Despite poetry and prose contributions from Yeats, Shaw and, indeed, Russell, the journal failed for lack of financial support.[123] Its last issue promised afterlife.

> It is our hope … that when the coming Irish State enters upon its national and international career, a new series of THE IRISH STATESMAN will be forthcoming to fulfil its mission by offering the same counsel and advice in the building up of the new Ireland that it has submitted to those who are striving to lay its foundations. Should this hope come to fruition, those who may then say that we sowed better than we knew will have underrated our estimate of Ireland's human and material resources.[124]

Plunkett, as usual, did not rest long with a good idea. He began to attract potentially sympathetic Irish-American donors to the revival of the *Irish States-*

---

120 Ibid. 6.   **121** Russell was long fond of the poem. He quoted the same line in praise of Colum in 'NOTW', *IH*, 17 Feb. 1912. 135.   **122** H. Plunkett, 'The Irish Dominion League', *Irish Statesman* (first series), 28 June 1919. 13.   **123** The production cost of any journal is difficult to estimate but the following letter from H.F. Norman to Horace Plunkett of 23 February 1915 does give some idea of the margins that the *Irish Homestead* operated on: 'Herewith statement of accounts for the "Homestead" for the years 1912, '13 and '14 as requested. This is made out in half years because of the two advertising seasons. A summary of yearly losses is appended. 1912 and 1913 are typical years. Taking the history of the "Homestead" from the start there have been only a few years in which profits have been made and the normal losses for some years are somewhere from two to three per cent of the cost of running the paper. You will notice that the loss for 1914 is therefore abnormal being about 14% of the cost of production. Had the second half year of 1914 been normal the paper should have come out about square or, at the worst, the loss should not have been above the average in view of the fact that the expenditure showed a decrease as compared with the two preceding years'. H.F. Norman papers, Plunkett Foundation (citied subsequently as PF) ms NOR 2.   **124** H. Plunkett, 'Vale atque ave', *Irish Statesman*, 19 June 1920. 577.

man, under new editorship to support the Free State, in late summer 1922. Plunkett corresponded with J.S. Cullinan of New York over the prospects of the new review.[125] He proposed a draft constitution for the journal that allowed for the registration of the Irish Statesman Publishing Company Limited in Dublin with capital of $150,000. The paper would

> stand for the faithful observance of the Treaty (with such amendments as may be agreed to by the parties thereto) and a Constitution framed in accordance with its terms. It will promote the principles of justice and liberty, will advocate a persistent endeavour by the State to improve the condition of every section of the Irish people, will seek to maintain in the national economy a just balance between the several interests – more particularly between those of the rural and the urban communities – and uphold the belief that these objects can best be attained by constitutional means and not by violence, no man being deprived of his property otherwise than by due process of law and on fair compensation.[126]

The result was a meeting of potential donors at the Bankers' Club, New York, on the evening of 16 October 1922. Diners formed an organising committee comprised of Cullinan, James Byrne, Richard Campbell, Edward Doheny, Lawrence Godkin, George MacDonald, Morgan J. O'Brien, John A. Poynton and John Quinn. James Healy was appointed assistant secretary to Campbell.[127] All agreed to secure one hundred people to underwrite a dollar total equivalent to £30,000. Government sanction was also sought and received; President William Cosgrave thought highly of the project.[128] There was trouble over the appointment of an editor. Robert Lynd was considered, as were P.S. O'Hegarty and Lennox Robinson. None was suitable. Plunkett then

---

125 J.S. Cullinan (1860–1937), was an American corporate official. See A. Denson, *Printed writings by George W. Russell (Æ)*. 36–7. Cullinan first met Plunkett in the United States in 1920. He was in turn a correspondent of Charles MacCarthy, an American political theorist who also wrote to Plunkett. M. Digby, *Horace Plunkett*. 261. Also F. Carroll, *American opinion and the Irish question 1910–23*. 23, 252.   **126** H. Plunkett to J.S. Cullinan, letter dated 8 September 1922.   **127** They were James Byrne (1857–1942), Richard Campbell (1872–1935), Edward Doheny (1856–1935), Lawrence Godkin (1860–1929), George Macdonald (nd), Morgan O'Brien (1852–1937), John Poynton (d. 1934) and the great patron of all Irish literary causes, lost or otherwise, John Quinn (1870–1924). Of these, Campbell, a Larne-born New York judge, was closest to Russell, and broadcast a eulogy for the Irish writer on American radio months before his own death in 1935. M. Digby, *Horace Plunkett*. 261. As regards the financial agreement, 'Each of the American supporters received securities to the extent of his participation unless such securities were sold to finance wider distribution; in which case he would be refunded his proportionate amount of sales.' A. Denson, *Printed writings by George W. Russell (Æ)*. 37.   **128** Horace Plunkett wrote to J.S. Cullinan on 17 October 1922 that 'Through a friend both of myself and of President Cosgrave, I learned yesterday that the latter was wholly in favour of the Irish Statesman project'. PF ms IRS6.

approached Russell. His old friend was not, at first, keen. Russell expressed his doubts in a letter to Yeats that exhibits the detached, artistic pose that Russell always tried to cultivate with his contemporary.

> Plunkett offered me the position of Editor. As I am situated at present I have some spare time I can devote to writing books like 'The National Being', 'The Candle of Vision' & 'The Interpreters'. If I edited the Irish Statesman on Plunkett's lines I would have to give up this literary work which is the best I can do and likely to be of some permanence. The Irish Statesman would absorb all my thought & I would waste myself on ephemeral weekly journalism. I do not feel I have wasted my time on the Irish Homestead because I have made some fundamental ideas part of the Irish mentality and that in the countryside. A sixpenny weekly might do good work but it would not affect the common mind only the fairly well-to-do who will not have the power here they have in England & the USA. I do not mind poverty for a good cause. I do object to wasting my life on transient articles week by week if the ideas do not percolate into the mass whose opinion passions & prejudices are the foundation on which our social order must be built. I would prefer the few hundreds I receive for editing the Homestead to three times the amount for editing a paper which would take all my thought, prevent me doing any literary work for myself and which would not leave me the consolation of thinking I was creating a tradition of decent life among the mass of the people. I have explained this to Plunkett & I explain it to you.[129]

Expressions of Russell's disinterest can be taken invariably as evidence of intrigue.[130] A compromise was found the coming week. Russell agreed to edit the *Irish Statesman* if the *Irish Homestead* could be incorporated into it and sold at a cheaper rate than Plunkett suggested.[131] The weekly *Irish Statesman*, now

---

129 G. Russell to W.B. Yeats, letter dated 10 May 1923, Richard Finneran et al, eds., *Letters to W. B. Yeats*. Vol. 2. 438.   **130** See for example Russell's plea of innocence to James Stephens the week after he denounced the Irish establishment from the stage of the Albert Hall in defence of James Larkin in November 1913. 'I believe now', he wrote, 'I could fill a hall in any labour centre in England & be hailed as a labour leader if I wanted. But I only want peace to go on writing and I don't seem able to get it.' Richard Finneran and Mary Fitzgerald, eds., *Some unpublished letters from AE to James Stephens*. 2   **131** H. Plunkett wrote excitedly to J.S. Cullinan on 18 May 1923 that Russell, 'this phenomenally independent courageous and lucid Irish thinker has reconsidered his refusal to edit the Irish Statesman. He will do so on a condition which I fully approve. It is that the revived organ should acquire his Irish Homestead which would be a sort of appendix to the Statesman – an amalgamation similar to that of two well known British weeklies, the Nation and the Athenaeum.' Russell 'by the way, should be a persona grata with Catholics. He does not subscribe to their faith but he never offends it. The enclosed noble utterance was published in a Catholic journal.' (Plunkett refers to 'Lessons of revolution', *Studies*, March 1923. 1–6.) PF ms IRS 19.

priced three pence, had found its editor. The *Irish Statesman* Publishing Company was duly incorporated under the Companies (Consolidation) Act of 1908 on 13 September 1923.[132] Its directors were Horace Plunkett, Senator James Douglas, George O'Brien, Lennox Robinson and Lionel Smith-Gordon. It had nominal capital of £35,000, made up of shares valued at £1 each. The final purchase of the *Irish Homestead* was made from its liquidator on 23 October 1923 for £1746 fully paid shares in the *Irish Statesman*. The first list of *Irish Statesman* shareholders is further revealing. Besides Horace Plunkett, the majority individual responsible with 200 shares, George Bernard Shaw held 100 shares, Lord Monteagle ten shares, Sir John Keane, the Irish Decorative Art Association, Belfast, and Robert Fitzhenry, parish priest of Our Lady's Island, Wexford, all held five shares each. The ITGWU held twenty-five shares, with twenty-nine co-operative societies also investing. The Revd John Ryan of the Catholic University, Washington D.C., also held an interest. The *Irish Statesman* was, from the start, well connected and well supported, its shareholders, like the readers it hoped to attract, ranging across class, creed and country. It had impeccable establishment and financial credentials. With Percy Gillespie appointed business manager at premises at 16–18 South Frederick Street, Dublin, the new journal entered the world in circumstances entirely favourable, promised as it was three instalments of $25,000 each from its American supporters, to be paid in total by December 1924.[133] Russell planned for the *Irish Statesman*'s first issue from mid-August. It appeared on 15 September 1923 while Plunkett was in England. Percy Gillespie remembered his difficulty in securing printing paper in the middle of a dock strike. Mission achieved, he 'motor-cycled like hell out to Baldonnel that evening with the "first-off", No. 1 copy to put it on a plane so that Sir Horace could have the earliest possible sight of it whilst staying in Weybridge, Surrey'.[134] The *Irish Statesman* enjoyed a suitable entry to the world. By essays on road and air, industry, science and culture, it would, for the next seven years, explore the range of Irish modernity. It managed, under Russell's editorship, to sustain an evolving relationship between the Irish intellectual and political elites. In doing so it lost the democratic impulse that sustained the *Irish Homestead*, which quickly became the *Irish Statesman*'s silent partner. Its passing removed a vibrant forum from Irish rural and urban life alike, a weekly

---

132 All details of capitalisation and shareholdings given here can be found in the Irish Statesman Publishing Co. Dissolved Company File NA ms COMP 1/ D7206, National Archives.   **133** The balance sheets of the *Irish Statesman*, audited by Albert Swain of O'Connell Street, Dublin, survive. In 1924 there was a balance of £12,364, the journal having spent the large sum of £3195 on organizing and publicity, leaving a meagre £34 cash in hand. In 1925 the balance was £18,407. In 1926, £21,699. In 1927, £22,415. In 1928, £22,587. See Irish Statesman Publishing Co. Dissolved Company File NA MS COMP 1/ D7206.   **134** Percy Gillespie, 'I remember', *Sir Horace Plunkett centenary handbook*. 12.

that had sustained an interest in anarchism, labour and Sinn Féin through sub-
jects various as the poetry of Padraic Colum and butter preservation. Through
Ireland, Europe and America, thousands of readers waited to see could the *Irish
Statesman* match it.

5 / Irish statesman: 1923–4

The first issue of the second edition of the *Irish Statesman* was published on 15 September 1923. The last issue of the *Irish Homestead* had promised the previous week that its successor would be a 'fresh enterprise in Irish journalism'.[1] This was true, in the sense that no other Irish journal of the period managed to combine political commentary and cultural analysis over such a sustained period of time as the *Irish Statesman*. Published once a week for seven years, the *Irish Statesman* was edited by Russell and his two assistants, James Good and Susan Mitchell, until her death in 1926. Each had between them a long publication record in journalism, literature and politics. Mitchell had been assistant editor of the *Irish Homestead* for the previous two decades and was primarily responsible for the journal's literary reviews.[2] Mitchell is perhaps most famous for her 1916 study of George Moore but her association with Russell began as early as 1904 with the publication of six of her poems in his *New songs* collection.

Good was a journalist of international reputation[3] and was leader writer for the *Freeman's Journal* and the *Irish Independent*. Furthermore, his publication of two books on unionism qualified him to help the *Irish Statesman* in its desire to treat 'all living in Ireland, North or South, as one people'.[4] Good was also the Irish correspondent of the *New Statesman* and a main contributor to the *Manchester Guardian*'s 1923 supplements on the Free State.[5] His publication in the *Manchester Guardian* is signal of his support for the Treaty as the supplement was prefaced by Cosgrave and contained articles by other leading members of

---

1 G. Russell, 'The end of an old and the start of a new enterprise', *IH*, 8 Sept. 1923. 570.   2 There is some debate as to the exact nature of Mitchell's relationship with Russell. Hilary Pyle, in *Redheaded rebel*, her biography of Mitchell, maintains that there was no love affair between the two. Adrian Frazier's life of *George Moore* suggests otherwise but admits a lack of evidence to prove the point. Certainly there was uncommon tenderness in Russell's lament for Mitchell in the *Irish Statesman* after her death in March 1926. See 'In Tirnanogue. *A dream*', *Irish Statesman* (Second series. Cited subsequently as *IS*), 8 May 1926. 232.   3 H.W. Nevinson, war correspondent for the *Manchester Guardian*, recalled of the 1918 conscription crisis that 'I found all my conspicuous friends in Dublin united in opposition to the English Parliament's decree – Mrs. Green, Æ' and 'James Good, wisest of journalists'. *Fire of life*. 346.   4 G. Russell, 'A confession of faith', *IS*, 15 Sept. 1923. 3.   5 The *Manchester Guardian* published a three-volume supplement on the Free State under the general title, *Manchester Guardian commercial European reconstruction series. Ireland.* The publication dates for each were 15 Mar. 1923, 10 May 1923 and 26 July 1923. Good published in all three, on subjects diverse as 'Political parties in the Free State' and 'Modern Irish art'.

the government such as Kevin O'Higgins, Vice President and Minister for Home Affairs. Connections such as this were of value to the *Irish Statesman*, a journal that intended to provide the 'best opportunity' for its readers to conduct 'free and frank discussion of the political, social and economic problems now clamant for solution'.[6]

Before publication of the *Irish Statesman*, political or cultural publications in Ireland tended to be conservative in their design. Within the Free State newspapers generally conformed to the same format with headlines followed by pages of advertising, news articles and sport. A cursory glance at any 1923 issue of the *Irish Times*, the *Irish Independent* or the *Freeman's Journal* will bear this point out. Contemporary literary magazines were either short-lived (like *To-morrow*) or lacked political commentary (like the *Dublin Magazine*). The *Irish Statesman* differed from its competitors by taking its model from outside the Free State. It looked to the English journal the *New Statesman*, similar both in title and appearance. Visually both journals are almost identical, with the same type face making up an average of four pages of editorial comment followed by columns of opinion, reviews and letters, all interspersed by advertising. Furthermore, the editorial commentary of the *Irish Homestead* had its name changed from 'Notes of the week' to 'Notes and comments' in the *Irish Statesman*, in a gesture to the *New Statesman's* 'Comments'. These weekly 'Comments' themselves contained James Good's reports on Ireland throughout the 1920s. Neither did the *New Statesman's* Irish connections end there. One of its longest serving columnists was Robert Lynd, a native of Belfast and a close friend of Good.[7] The largest individual investor in the *New Statesman* in 1913 was George Bernard Shaw.[8] Shaw published in the first issue of the *Irish Statesman* in 1923. He also provided, along with Horace Plunkett, the impetus to the first appearance of a journal under the title of *Irish Statesman* in 1919 under the editorship of Warre B. Wells. Understanding why Shaw and his associates were interested in the publication of independent (in the sense of non-party) journals in England in 1913 and in Ireland in 1919 is fundamental to any reading of the *Irish Statesman* in 1923.

The *New Statesman* was founded in 1913 as Sidney and Beatrice Webb's attempt to support and direct the Labour Party's growth in Great Britain. The journal was to remain independent of and yet allied to parliamentary labour. The difficulty of maintaining such a policy became apparent in the 1920s as the *New*

---

6 H. Plunkett, 'The revival of the Irish Statesman', *IS*, 15 Sept. 1923. 6.   7 Lynd published a weekly column in the *New Statesman* under the title 'YY'. He was also literary editor of the *Daily News*. Good and Lynd were educated at the Royal Belfast Academical Institution and remained friends with him until Good's sudden death in 1930.   8 'The Statesman Publishing Co. Ltd.' was established in October 1912. The first issue appeared in 1913 under the editorship of Clifford Sharp; the poet J.C. Squire was literary editor. For details of Shaw's involvement see A. Smith, *The New States-*

Statesman drifted towards the Liberal Party even as Sidney Webb became in 1923 a front bench spokesman for the British Labour Party.[9] In 1923, the *Irish Statesman* similarly declared itself to be 'informative, independent' and 'non-partisan'[10] in its interest in Irish politics. It did at the same time support the Treaty, declaring the agreement to be, in the words of Horace Plunkett, 'the best settlement obtainable in the conditions'.[11] Such support sided the journal with Cumann na nGaedheal as the practice of politics in the Free State in 1923 still proceeded in nearly every instance from one's support for or antagonism to the Treaty. That the *Irish Statesman*'s founder should state his journal's support of the Treaty so readily is an early indication of the limits imposed on the journal's independence. The *Irish Statesman* was never an official organ of Cumann na nGaedheal policy but its advocacy of strategies that sustained the Treaty sided the journal with the ruling party. The *Irish Statesman* was not intended to be 'a party journal in any sense in which such a description could be fittingly applied'[12] but the implicit suggestion remains that the term 'party journal' applies to some degree.

The *Irish Statesman* further had the luxury of financial support from wealthy investors. The *Freeman's Journal* noted the success of Plunkett's negotiations with his 'Americans of Irish blood'[13] in its review of the *Irish Statesman*'s first issue. The paper noted that 'The format and price are altogether attractive' and that the price of '3d weekly ... seems but little short of philanthropy'.[14] If true charity is given without thought, one is entitled to ask questions as to its real nature when money is directed towards the publication of a political review. This point was not lost upon the republican journal *Éire*, a publication that appeared in January 1923 to commemorate the fourth anniversary of the foundation of the first Dáil in January 1919. *Éire* remained stubbornly opposed to the Free State until it ceased publication in October 1924. Its anonymous editor remarked caustically, and no doubt jealously, of the *Irish Statesman* in September 1923 that it had 'been raised from the dead by the sort of miracle which British Imperialists can always work. It's done with money.'[15]

The 'British Imperialist' to whom *Éire* refers is Horace Plunkett. The paper ignores, or is unaware of, the fact that American investors had bought an interest in the political life of the Free State, specifically with reference to the maintenance of the Treaty, this being one of the first issue's main declared aims. Russell demanded full editorial independence for the *Irish Statesman*[16] but there is

man. 40–42.   **9** Webb eventually sold his interest in the *New Statesman* and it merged with the *Nation* in 1931, its task to revive 'democratic socialism in Britain'. A. Smith, *The New Statesman*. 245. **10** H. Plunkett, 'The revival of the Irish Statesman', *IS*, 15 Sept. 1923. 6.   **11** Ibid.   **12** G. Russell, 'A confession of faith', *IS*, 15 Sept. 1923. 5.   **13** H. Plunkett, 'The revival of the Irish Statesman', *IS*, 15 Sept. 1923. 6.   **14** 'The Irish Statesman', *Freeman's Journal* (cited subsequently as *FJ*), 15 Sept. 1923. 7.   **15** 'The Irish Statesman – the new Imperial push – and Mr. Shaw!' *Éire*, 6 Oct. 1923. 2.   **16** Plunkett promised that 'the independence of the Irish management' was 'of the very essence of the scheme'. 'The revival of The Irish Statesman', *IS*, 15 Sept. 1923. 6.

little doubt that he felt the weight of his donors' conservative tastes.[17] Further-more, the journal was published with the specific intent of influencing and adjusting Free State government policy. The *Irish Statesman*'s 'independence' was conditional upon the fact that its editor did not stray too far from the con-sensus opinion of the leaders to whom he appealed. It is in this respect relevant to note that the *Irish Statesman*'s main controversy with Cumann na nGaedheal was over censorship at a time when, as Denis Gwynn suggests, 'the main work of consolidating the new regime was done'.[18]

Shaw had already put forward the idea in 1919 that if a political journal was to be a success, its editorial policy and political attitude must be consistent from the start.[19] Shaw was definite in his demands for the programme to which the first *Irish Statesman* should accede, arguing that with the advocacy of a federal solution for Ireland's independence the country would gain access to 'a share in the higher statesmanship'[20] that Shaw felt only Westminster could provide. Four years later an independent Dáil existed and circumstances had changed greatly. But there is no reason to assume that Shaw's belief in the necessity to affect policy at the highest level had also changed. Likewise Horace Plunkett was careful to make both himself and his ideas known to the most senior mem-bers of the Executive over the intervening period. He took 'pains to interest Cosgrave, then President, and Kevin O'Higgins, the best mind in the Irish Cabinet, in his agricultural policy'.[21] Plunkett 'believed, as always, in educating, imperceptibly if possible, the governing mind'.[22] As a close reading of the first issues of the *Irish Statesman* will show, the exercise of such influence was exact-ly the point of the new journal's existence.

The first and most obvious point to note about the publication of the *Irish Statesman* is the date of its first issue. It appeared on 15 September, just three weeks after a Free State general election and four days before a new Dáil com-menced sitting. The journal's appearance can be interpreted as a kind of open-ing gambit. Russell pitched the *Irish Statesman* towards an educated readership that might in turn be able to act upon the new deputies in the Dáil, fresh as the large majority of them were to the practice of elected representation. Russell's interest in these new members was predicated on the fact that he felt many of them to be dangerously inexperienced. He made great play of this problem in

17 Russell wrote to Ernest Boyd in New York in 1925: 'I thought of you long ago as an American correspondent. I had suggested it to Plunkett and between ourselves he was alarmed lest your radi-calism might upset the Americans who contributed the funds to start the *Irish Statesman* and from whom he hopes to get more. You see they promised to pay in three yearly instalments quite a big sum and they are very touchy.' A. Denson, ed., *Letters from Æ.* 168.   **18** D. Gwynn, *The Irish Free State.* 191.   **19** Shaw wrote to Horace Plunkett, *c.*15 June 1919, that 'the line to be taken by the paper in its first number will decide our fate: we cannot consider it too carefully'. D.H. Lawrence, ed., *Bernard Shaw: collected letters.* 618.   **20** Ibid.   **21** M. Digby, *Horace Plunkett.* 260.   **22** Ibid.

the final issues of the *Irish Homestead*, suggesting that many of the new representatives had no opinions on policy beyond that which referred directly to the Treaty.[23] James Good repeated Russell's misgivings in the *New Statesman*. Good quoted Russell to the effect that 'we shall have a considerable body of deputies who will get into the Dail, and do their thinking afterwards. But how, if from long disuse, the mind will refuse to function?'[24]

The answer to Russell's question was provided in the pages of the *Irish Statesman* itself. It was to be the forum to provide both deputies and the educated classes of Ireland and abroad with guidance on problems of politics and culture. This intention can be gauged from the powerful group that Russell assembled to write for the journal, 'the most famous living Irishmen and Irishwomen'[25] whose number included Yeats, Stephens, Shaw, Gogarty and Lady Gregory. The relative strength of these institutional literary figures was bolstered by the fact that Cumann na nGaedheal did not fare particularly well at the August polls, taking only an extra five seats in a Dáil enlarged by 25 seats to 153. Disquietingly for supporters of the treaty, Sinn Féin, the republican party, took 44 seats when predicted to take only 30. With the pro-Treaty Labour Party taking 15 seats it was true that Sinn Féin could not disrupt the business of the Dáil, not least because its deputies refused to take their seats. But the close result did mean that Cumann na nGaedheal needed all the support it could muster in order to give the impression of a nation united behind the Treaty.

At such a time the *Irish Statesman* promised to reach a crucial, educated audience in the Free State with a guaranteed circulation of 10,000 copies for at least the first six issues.[26] The journal appealed to an 'interested clientele, including the wealthiest and most influential Irish citizens, farmers, merchants, professional men, clergy, civil-servants – co-operative officials supplying farm and household requirements to over 150,000 homesteads'.[27] This last group is especially interesting as their mention illustrates how the management of the *Irish Homestead* was prepared to hand over its readership in the co-operative movement to a journal that actively supported the Treaty. The co-operative movement was itself avowedly non-political and had protested its innocence from intrigue throughout the previous five years of unrest. That the *Irish Statesman* could now openly pledge its co-operative readers to the support of the Treaty illustrates the degree to which the journal's management shifted their indepen-

---

23 Russell recorded his impressions before the election after reading 'a bundle of about twenty country papers which report at greater length than the daily papers the speeches made locally by candidates. We cannot say that we were greatly illuminated. In the majority of cases the great asset of the candidates, the main facts on which they relied, were the ill-deeds of their opponents.' 'Mean economics', *IH*, 18 Aug. 1923. 521. **24** J. Good, 'The Free State elections', *NS*, 25 Aug. 1923. 562. **25** G. Russell, 'The end of an old and the start of a new enterprise', *IH*, 8 Sept. 1923. 570. **26** See advert placed in the *Freeman's Journal* on behalf of the *Irish Statesman*. *FJ*, 11 Sept. 1923. 1. **27** Ibid.

dence towards Cumann na nGaedheal. This in turn promised a potentially huge inroad into the rural communities for the supporters of the Treaty, communities where republican forces had often found support.[28] Again the republican paper *Éire* reacted angrily to this development: it felt that the 'members of the co-operative societies throughout Ireland have grave cause to quarrel with Plunkett House if it allows its purely non-political organ to be merged in a Free State Imperial propaganda weekly'.[29] *Éire*'s attempt to create dissent within the co-operative movement failed but its anonymous editor was right to point out the inconsistency of its independent position.

Russell's first editorial in the *Irish Statesman* was entitled 'A confession of faith'. Its three pages detail Russell's hopes for and demands of the Free State. His first main point is to reassert the value to his contemporary Ireland of the movements with which he was involved in the period before the First World War. In doing so, Russell sets the intellectual and geographical bounds of the *Irish Statesman*. For

> Up to 1914 … In Europe and America a fresh interest had been quickened with regard to the country because of its literary movements, its poetry and drama, the renaissance of the Gaelic mind, the organisation of its agriculture and industry, and the increasing hope of a national government under which unhampered by any external power, these cultural and economic forces might have full play.[30]

Russell repackages the sequence of Irish history to make his point. In the first place, 1914 and not 1916 is the crucial year in the foundation of the Irish state. Russell does this to avoid conflict over the true nature of the revolutionary tradition, a conflict still current in the civil war with both pro- and anti-Treaty forces claiming in their propaganda that each represented the genius of men like Pearse.[31] Russell also sublimates conflict over the nature of a distinct-

---

28 Calton Younger quotes the opinion of General Michael Brennan that it is not 'fully appreciated, even now, that outside Dublin "the whole Civil War really turned on Limerick". He puts it that "the Shannon was the barricade and whoever held Limerick held the south and the west" … Liam Lynch believed that by isolating the South, where Republicans were already well entrenched, he could frustrate the setting up of the Free State.' *Ireland's civil war.* 370–1. **29** *Éire* further re-christened Russell's journal the 'Free Statesman'. In 'The "Irish Statesman" – the new Imperial push – and Mr. Shaw!' *Éire*, 6 Oct. 1923. 2. **30** G. Russell, 'A confession of faith', *IS*, 15 Sept. 1923. 3. **31** By 1923 Republican propaganda on 1916 was generally emotive: 'The Stupid British. If the British Government had the sense to give Cosgrave and Mulcahy the job in 1916. What short work they would have made of Padraig Pearse and the other irregulars'(n.p: n.d.). Free State propaganda took the form of rebuttal: 'MEANS TO AN END! The Anti-Treatyites are fond of voting the dead who died for Ireland! And invariably they vote them against the Treaty! If Collins, Mulcahy, etc., had died they would be voted "Anti" also!! Listen to Padraig Pearse himself … "Home Rule to US would have been a means to an end". ("The Spiritual Nation"- P.H. Pearse). VOTE FOR THE

ly Irish identity into broader questions of European association. The First World War was symbolic to Russell of a rupture in the growth of continental thought. It was the impetus to a development of what he described as militarism, a state of mind that prevailed not only in Ireland but also in Germany, Russia and Italy.[32] Russell's insistence on the value of the Literary Revival and the co-operative movement is rooted in his wish to stress their distance from such problems and highlight their potentially remedial significance for the Free State. At a time when the protocols of the new state were still to be codified, Russell wanted to make sure that his own interests were appreciated to the degree that they were ingrained in the state's apparatus. This is the crucial point to make about the first issue of the *Irish Statesman*. It is the platform from which Russell and his associates assert their claim to authority within the Free State. An analysis of the contributors to the first issues is the key to understanding the type of influence sought by Russell and the nature of the political and cultural alliances he created to do this.

The cover of the first *Irish Statesman* advertised two articles other than the editor's 'A confession of faith'. These were George Bernard Shaw's 'On throwing out dirty water' and James Douglas' letter entitled 'The Executive Council and the Dail'. Shaw's essay is a supplement to Russell's implicit criticism in his editorial of the post-1916 revolutionary tradition of Irish nationalism. Shaw believed that the war for independence had fostered

> a common opinion in Ireland that the Cabinet in London, untroubled by English problems, and indifferent to the adventures of M. Poincare, Signor Mussolini, and the fall of the mark, occupies itself solely with sending orders to President Cosgrave to arrest and torture that devoted local patriot, Padraig (çi devant Patrick) Soandso, of Ballysuchandsuch.[33]

Shaw's satire is sharp. By reducing the heroes of Irish revolutionary nationalism to figures of stereotype he attempts to minimise their general importance to the practice of European politics as a whole. Yet Shaw's attack on Irish nationalism is not indiscriminate. President Cosgrave had arrived in Dublin from Switzerland only the day previous to this article's publication, to great applause from the *Freeman's Journal*. The paper noted that 'Dublin witnessed one of the greatest demonstrations in its history in the reception given to President Cosgrave on his return to Ireland from Geneva, where he gained the Irish Free State

TREATY!'(n.p.: n.d.). O'Brien Collection, NLI LOP 117/26.   **32** To Russell 'What took place here was an infection from the high fever in which Europe existed, that our militarism was as definitely of epidemic character as that black influenza which a couple of years before swept over the world.' 'The return to the normal', *IS*, 22 Dec. 1923. 454.   **33** G. Shaw, 'On throwing out dirty water', *IS*, 15 Sept. 1923. 8.

entry into the League of Nations'.[34] By its support of Cosgrave in a broadly European context, Shaw's polemic is guided at republicans who criticised the validity of the Free State's entry to the League.[35] The Free State did not, in their view, have the independence of action necessary to make international alliance worthwhile. Shaw's argument therefore that 'Nationalism must now be added to the refuse pile of superstitions'[36] is tactical and aimed at one specific instance of Irish nationalist thought in 1923.

The proof of this can be found in a publication of Shaw's ten years earlier in an Irish supplement to the *New Statesman*. In this essay Shaw used nearly the exact same words that he did in 1923 but to prove a different point. In 1913 Shaw derided the 'old-fashioned romantic nationalism of which the South is so deadly tired'.[37] This line appears in context of Shaw's argument that the Ulster problem could only be solved by nationalism's acceptance of northern union-ism as a legitimate expression of cultural association. In 1913 the Orangeman is portrayed as the irreconcilable whose opinions must be assimilated if there is to be peace. Shaw strikes a recurrent note in 1923 in support of a Free State gov-ernment that might not have existed at all without 'romantic nationalism.' Shaw's assertion that 'we are now citizens of the world'[38] in the *Irish Statesman* is less a credo of internationalism than a marginalisation of republicanism. The Sinn Féin deputies were after all keenest in their insistence on a Gaelic Ireland independent of an outside influence made tangible to them by the Treaty.

Shaw ends both essays by referring to Moore's 'Let Erin remember the days of old'.[39] In 1913 Shaw declared that the 'hackneyed fisherman who saw the round towers of other days in the waves beneath him stirring, pursued his lucra-tive occupation on the banks of Lough Neagh, and was no doubt an Orange-man'.[40] In 1923, Irish republicanism is Shaw's target. He associates those who are against the Treaty with isolation and regression. Shaw uses Moore's roman-ticism to criticise the apparent unreality of republican politics. The solution for Ireland's problems is to 'Let the fisherman who strays on Lough Neagh's bank

34 'Nation's hearty greeting', *FJ*, 15 Sept. 1923. 5. **35** A republican booklet of 1928 expresses this antagonism to international association: 'In a moment of weakness, war-weary leaders yielded to the enemy. The nation for whose honour men had given their blood and gladly died … was again betrayed to her despoiler … The dishonour to cleanse which Irishmen had poured out their blood from 1916 to 1923, still stains the fair fame of Ireland. Twelve years after Easter Week Ireland remains, unfree and unredeemed, still bound to the British Empire.' 'Seacranaide'. *Easter Week and after*. 11. **36** G. Shaw, 'On throwing out dirty water', *IS*, 15 Sept. 1923. 9. **37** G. Shaw, 'A note on Irish nationalism', *New Statesman* (cited subsequently as *NS*) *supplement on the awakening of Ire-land*, 12 July 1913. 2. **38** G. Shaw, 'On throwing out dirty water', *IS*, 15 Sept. 1923. 9. **39** Shaw alludes to the second and third verses of Moore's poem: 'On Lough Neagh's bank, as the fisher -/ man strays,/ When the clear cold eve's declining,/ He sees the round towers of other days/ In the wave beneath him shining; Thus shall memory often, in dreams/ sublime, Catch a glimpse of the days that are over;/ Thus, sighing, look through the waves of time/ For the long faded glories they cover'. *The poetical works of Thomas Moore*. 187–8. **40** G. Shaw, 'A note on Irish nationalism', *NS*:

when the clear cold eve's declining be thrown into it. And then Ireland will have a chance at last.'[41] Both the fisherman in 1923 and the Orangeman ten years earlier serve as representative types. The image of the fisherman locks into notions of the west of Ireland and the islands off its coast, a landscape of which Shaw is contemptuously aware as he writes. He offers the idea that any 'man who divides the race into elect Irishmen and reprobate foreign devils (especially Englishmen) had better live on the Blaskets, where he can admire himself without much disturbance'.[42] Again the stereotypical fisherman brings to mind literary representations of isolation and, by implication, separation.

Such symbolic separation is directly analogous to Sinn Féin's popular appeal to the Irish electorate that the Free State withdraw from the League of Nations, the Imperial Conference and the British Commonwealth.[43] All of these international bodies were in contrast significant to supporters of the Treaty such as Shaw and Russell of the place to which Ireland could aspire if its international obligations were met. As Russell remarked, 'When we think of the great figures' of Irish history, we think of those who 'have affected powerfully the thought of the world, from the remote missionaries who from Ireland invaded Europe with the Gospel of Christ, down to the era of Swift, Berkeley, Goldsmith, Sheridan and Burke'.[44] At points like this it is easy to see how Russell's support of the Free State and his interpretation (and indeed creation) of Irish history are co-dependent. The Free State's international obligations, with its accession to the League of Nations and its participation in the Imperial Conference at the end of 1923 become bound in Russell's rhetoric to cultural imperatives that are held to have existed from pre-Norman times. Since the Normans were typically held to be the first invaders of native Ireland an appeal to the missionaries' faith lays a forcefully indigenous claim to all subsequent cultural activity. This means that once again the divisions of religion and culture that are usually thought to have affected the course (if one can accept that there is such a thing) of Irish history are marginalised by Russell's invocation of a very specific past that perfectly suits his political present.

A further gesture towards the political situation of the Free State can be found in the third article that receives front-page advertisement in the *Irish Statesman*. James Douglas' 'The Executive Council and the third Dáil' differs from both the essays of Shaw and Russell as a technical article that concerns the Dáil's apparatus. Douglas was himself a Free State Senator and a prosperous

supplement on the awakening of Ireland, 12 July 1913. 2.   **41** G. Shaw, 'On throwing out dirty water', *IS*, 15 Sept. 1923. 9.   **42** Ibid.   **43** Mary MacSwiney expressed Sinn Féin's policy in this area: 'the Sinn Fein policy has been defined. It is that all authority in Ireland is derived exclusively from the people of Ireland: that we do not, and will not, recognise any authority of the King of England or any other alien – direct or indirect, real or nominal, in our country'. M. MacSwiney, 'Sinn Fein and the Future', *IS*, 22 Dec. 1923. 464.   **44** G. Russell, 'A confession of faith', *IS*, 15 Sept. 1923. 5.

Dublin businessman. He was well acquainted with Russell, the two men having visited Lloyd George in 1917 to impress upon the British prime minister the suitability of full dominion status for Ireland.[45] Douglas continued his involvement in Irish politics and was close to Michael Collins, sitting on the committee that drafted the first, rejected, constitution of the Free State.[46] He was summoned in 1923 by de Valera to mediate between Sinn Féin and the government in order to create a cease-fire.[47] Unsuccessful as these talks were, they indicate the high regard in which both pro- and anti-Treaty groups held the Senator.

Douglas' article in the *Irish Statesman* argued that if a motion were to come before the Dáil that concerned the affairs of a ministry that did not sit on the Executive Council then deputies should have a free vote on that motion.[48] Here lies the importance to the *Irish Statesman* (incorporating as it did the *Irish Homestead*) of Douglas's letter. Patrick Hogan, the Minister for Agriculture, did not sit on the Executive Council. Douglas was in effect suggesting that agricultural matters should be voted on in the Dáil without government interference. Of course, were the government not to exercise its influence in this matter then deputies might be more open to outside persuasion. Douglas was at the same time being forward as a member of the Senate in proposing changes to the lower, and more powerful, chamber's protocol. The Vice President of the Free State, Kevin O'Higgins, soon made clear that he did not appreciate the Senate's interest in matters pertaining to the Dáil.[49] Cleverly, Russell published Douglas' piece as a letter to avoid the threat of a clash with the government. The first issue of the first edition of the *Irish Statesman* in 1919 had similarly used its correspondence columns to publish a letter from Horace Plunkett that outlined the aims and policies of the newly formed Dominion Home Rule Party.[50] That Plunkett founded the journal is not mentioned. Plunkett's letter was published in the correspondence column as if on merit, the editor simultaneously acknowledging his patron's influence while trying to assert a semblance of independence.

45 B. Sexton, *Ireland and the crown*. 24.   **46** The first Free State constitution drafted by this committee at the start of 1922 was rejected by the British government, partly because 'Collins informed James C. Douglas, a member of the committee very close to him, that the constitution should be that of an independent state and that a reference to the King or British Commonwealth "should be left to be inserted by the Provisional Government in so far as it might be considered necessary"'. B. Sexton, *Ireland and the crown*. 56.   **47** D. O'Sullivan, *The Irish Free State and its Senate*. 112.   **48** O'Sullivan explains that 'Three Extern Ministers were appointed during Mr. Cosgrave's first administration (December 1922), and all three – Messrs. Patrick Hogan, J.J. Walsh and Finian Lynch – were members of the Dail, holding respectively the portfolios of Agriculture, Posts and Telegraphs, and Fisheries'. All three portfolios were subsequently added to the Executive Council in May 1927. *The Irish Free State and its Senate*. 89.   **49** In 1926 O'Higgins vetoed Douglas' proposal that Senators be nominated to sit on the Executive Council. See D. Gwynn, *The Irish Free State*. 213.   **50** See H. Plunkett, 'The Irish Dominion League', *Irish Statesman* (first series), 28 June 1919. 13–14.

The correspondence column of the first issue of the *Irish Statesman* in 1923 was thus used as a vehicle for members of the Senate close to Russell to air their opinions. This explains the publication of Alice Stopford Green's 'Ireland and the League of Nations' beside Douglas's letter. In this Green simply states that as a member of an international community 'we may learn much to give in service to Ireland – the generosity which comes of free brotherhood, the high courage of such association, and the sense of common duty'.[51] Green's rhetoric is high-flown but her proximity to Douglas in the *Irish Statesman* betrays a political reality of the Senate. Both Green and Douglas were associated with an independent group of Senators who met under the chairmanship of Andrew Jameson.[52] They 'habitually consulted together in regard to the measures which were to come before the House; but they were not bound by any pledge, and they frequently voted on opposite sides in divisions'.[53]

This lack of formal cohesion has been interpreted to be signal of a fundamental weakness of the Senate's Anglo-Irish members: 'unorganised and unsupported by a formal party, the range of political manoeuvre of the individuals was severely limited'.[54] The eventual outcome of this lack of institutional support was that the independents 'were forced to identify themselves completely with the pro-Treaty party'.[55] But when we consider the antagonism of central government figures like O'Higgins to organised Senate interference with the Dáil, it might rather be suggested that Douglas and Green's 'disorganised' method of working might have been the most effective, no matter how difficult its effect is to trace. Their publication in the *Irish Statesman* might even suggest that they themselves realised this, as each preferred to have their ideas presented in a journal that itself played to the ear of the elected elite. In this sense at least the observation that the Senate was 'chiefly a gathering of distinguished public opinion whose opinions cannot fail to carry weight and whose influence is much greater than their actual legislative powers'[56] is rather astute than critical.

Russell's adoption of important senate members such as Douglas and Green was part of his wider strategy for the *Irish Statesman*. The journal was designed to be a vehicle by which Russell's ideas could be translated into actual policy. The transfer between ideas and actions was not however a simple one. Nothing illustrates this point better than Russell's interest in Odon Por's 1923 book *Fascism*, the English-language introduction to which Russell had written. Russell reviewed the text in the first issue of the *Irish Statesman*. In its general content the review simply describes Italian fascism in 1923 as a further example of the unrest caused across Europe by the First World War. It was a reaction against the 'chaos'[57] that destabilised Italian politics and industry after the

51 A. Green, 'Ireland and the League of Nations', *IS*, 15 Sept. 1923. 23–4.   52 D. O'Sullivan, *The Irish Free State and its Senate*. 266–7.   53 Ibid. 266.   54 P. Buckland, *The Anglo-Irish and the new Ireland*. 298–9.   55 Ibid. 299.   56 D. Gwynn, *The Irish Free State*. 206.   57 G. Russell, 'Review

armistice. The fascists' success lay in their co-option of labour into their movement's autocratic structure. To Russell, fascist 'leaders were not really reactionary. Mussolini had been a socialist, and for all we know may still have deep
socialist sympathies'.[58] Russell's sympathy for the fascists is conditional on his
ability to use their achievement to instruct his own Irish readership. For 'If the
guild movement and the co-operatives had a leader of powerful character who
could have harmonised their activities the Fascist movement would never have
come to power'.[59] Russell's interest in guild socialism had been outlined in *The
national being* but his qualified criticism of the co-operatives is telling.[60] Co-
operation is still to Russell the ideal mode of social organisation but in this 1923
review co-operation means economic organisation independent of political representation. If 'We might say of fascism that it is now using force to bring about
an efficient organisation of the Italian democracy and Italian political institutions'[61], then we might also say of the Free State in 1923 that force was also used
to challenge traditional authority.

This is not to suggest that Russell supported either government or republican violence. But he was not averse to suggesting that violence would certainly
occur if economic problems in the state were not addressed. As prophet of this
destruction Russell takes the threat of violence from its immediate Irish context
and relates it to a European framework. He does this in order to intimidate the
Free State legislature with the possibility that a group similar to the Italian fascists might threaten its authority in Ireland. The government would in turn
have been well aware that a number of the same newspapers that gave it Irish
support regularly reported favourably on the fascists' activity in Italy.[62] In a
future period of popular discontent it might be difficult to guess which side the
media would support. It is important then to note how the *Irish Statesman* did
react to the first major crisis of the third Dáil in October 1923. The first Sinn
Féin ard-fheis after the August elections was held at the end of September. The
Irish Statesman recorded that:

> The country desires to have done with the internment camps … (But)
> the Government requires more authoritative assurances than it has yet
> received that the liberation of the prisoners will not be a prelude to a

of *Fascism* by Odon Por', *IS*, 15 Sept. 1923. 18. **58** Ibid. **59** Ibid. **60** Russell believed that
'there never can be any progress in rural districts or any real prosperity without such farmers' orga-
nizations or guilds'. *The national being.* 39. **61** G. Russell, 'Review of *Fascism* by Odon Por', *IS*,
15 Sept. 1923. 20. **62** The *Irish Times* steadfastly supported the Free State government. It also
reported favourably on Mussolini's seizure of power by his march on Rome on 27 October 1922.
It welcomed the success of the 'Forty thousand Fascisti … up in arms'. 'Fascismo triumphs', *Irish
Times*, 30 Oct. 1922. 4. The *Irish Independent* was initially less enthusiastic. It wondered if 'responsibility may have the effect of curbing the wildness of [Mussolini's] party. But it is a big venture, and
Italy to-day stands trembling on the edge of a precipice.' 'Fascismo', *Irish Independent*, 30 Oct. 1922.

revival of the war-makers of the campaign of violence. We trust that the Sinn Fein Ard-Fheis will have the political insight and the moral courage to give these assurances, and the whole nation will be behind them.[63]

The journal's hope for reconciliation with Sinn Féin was short-lived. James Good, the *Irish Statesman*'s assistant editor, reported three weeks later in the *New Statesman* that the 'war-makers, who kept in the background during the elections, have recovered their ascendancy'.[64] At the same time, 'some 500 political prisoners in Mountjoy started a hunger strike to secure their unconditional release',[65] a radical tactic, Good suggests, used to marginalise Sinn Féin moderates within the ard-fheis. Good continued to inform British opinion on the hunger-strike over the coming weeks in the *New Statesman*, pointing out to his readers that the continuation of the hunger strikes lay in Sinn Féin's prolonged struggle for moral authority in the Free State:

> The greatest obstacle to a general amnesty is that Sinn Fein still insists that this is its right as the legitimate government of Ireland, whose powers have been usurped by an unauthorised junta of politicians. So long as every modification of martial law is twisted into a recognition of the sovereignty of the Republic, Mr. Cosgrave and his officials cannot be harshly criticised for their reluctance to stake everything on a policy of conciliation.[66]

Good continued to report on the hunger strike until its demise. By the first December 1923 he welcomed its total collapse as the 'reward of the Government's stubborn refusal to be bullied into surrender by people who, as Æ said in the Irish Statesman, "do not think and have only an abnormal and inherited capacity for suffering"'.[67] This is a harsh statement that suggests where Russell's sympathies lay in the crisis. For all Russell's prophecy of a revolution in his review of Por's *Fascism*, the hunger strike only resulted in a reiteration of Russell's support for the Cumann na nGaedheal government. But throughout the hunger strike the only factual observations of the crisis by a member of the *Irish Statesman*'s staff were made by Good and were published not in the Irish paper but in the *New Statesman*.[68] The *Irish Statesman* reported the problem in abstract terms, if at all. The hunger-strike is represented to be a symbolic action, significant of the fact that 'if the majority of the population are individualists carrying on petty and personal enterprise, group egomania arises in more

4.   **63** 'The prisoners', *IS*, 29 Sept. 1923. 73.   **64** J. Good in 'Comments', *NS*, 20 Oct. 1923. 35. **65** Ibid.   **66** J. Good in 'Comments', *NS*, 6 Oct. 1923. 727–8.   **67** J. Good in 'Comments', *NS*, 1 Dec. 1923. 231.   **68** Good's reports on Ireland throughout 1923 can be found in the last page of 'Comments' in the *New Statesman* under the title 'An Irish correspondent writes'.

violent and ignorant forms'.[69] The hunger-strike was therefore a passing phenomena, a crisis due not to a 'flaw in national character' but to the possibility
that the Free State was in a certain stage of 'social evolution'.[70] Russell pro-
gresses from this assertion to defend, not to criticise, the government's martial
action to protect itself for even 'The more highly evolved nations exhibited in
their earlier stages all the ferocity of uncontrolled interests which they condemn
in nations like our own'.[71]

Russell's use of the metaphor of evolution to describe growth in the state is
similar to his earlier comparison of Ireland to a child in *The national being*.[72] The
change in his thinking between 1916 and 1923 concerns the state's ability to
challenge 'uncontrolled interests'.[73] Whereas in *The national being* Russell imagined the state to be a unified being, or a single identity, he is confronted in 1923
with the fact of a major schism in Irish political society. Russell's blueprint for
national growth cannot deal with this problem democratically. For all of Russell's insistence on the need for 'understanding' and 'reconciliation' between
pro- and anti-Treaty organisations,[74] Russell's rhetoric is bounded by its insis-
tent use of metaphors of growth and evolution. Both concepts suggest the existence of a certain end to be achieved. By their supposed relation to the cycles of
natural existence they also predicate the future of that which they are supposed
to represent.

Only in moments of rupture or chaos does this plan become endangered.
The civil war was to Russell exactly such a break. Thus the meaning for Russell
of the apparent paradox that 'Dictatorships spring up all over Europe as the
direct consequence of a war to make the world safe for democracy; in Italy,
Spain, Germany, Russia and in other countries'.[75] The relevance of this to the
Free State's experience is that 'The muddle in political and economic affairs in
Ireland if continued lends itself to the creation of a mood in which dictatorships
become possible'.[76] At a time when the Free State had just joined the League of
Nations, Russell uses the very idea of Europe as a warning to the government.
Political unrest on the continent is described in terms of contagion, the pallia-
tive offered being the influence of the cultured classes:

---

69 'Notes and comments' (cited subsequently as 'N&C'), *IS*, 27 Oct. 1923. 195.   **70** Ibid.   **71**
Ibid.   **72** *The national being* begins: 'In the year Nineteen Hundred and Fourteen Anno Domini,
amid a world conflict, the birth of the infant State of Ireland was announced'. 1. The conceit is
developed over the following pages: 'so, as the incidents of life reveal the innate affinities of a child
to itself, do the adventures of a nation gradually reveal to it its own character and the will which is
in it'. 3.   **73** 'N&C', *IS*, 27 Oct. 1923. 195.   **74** By the end of 1923 Russell desired to 'find rec-
onciliations or unities' between republicans and Free Staters instead of 'mere animal conflict'. His
plea was for a return to 'the decencies of normal life'. 'The return to the normal', *IS*, 22 Dec. 1923.
454.   **75** 'N&C', *IS*, 20 Oct. 1923. 163   **76** Ibid.

No doubt there are injustices and wrongs at the root of the conflict between labour and capital. But if reason does not supersede passion in these conflicts the tendency in Ireland will be towards a Fascism which may not be as intellectual as the Italian, and may be much more reactionary'.[77]

That Russell can 'utter this warning in the interests of Irish democracy'[78] suggests the extent to which he has realised the need for authority (symbolised in this case by Italian fascism) in his own political program. Russell's creation of a fascist threat is opportunistic and made to satisfy the *Irish Statesman*'s establishment of its own authoritative voice. It seems perverse, but Russell's use of a fascist motif is equally a sign of his support of the Treaty as his intellectual access to the movements and effects of European politics shadows the Free State's entry into the League of Nations. Russell asserts his independence from the government by reference to Italy while simultaneously suggesting his support for it by accepting as valid the international framework into which the Free State entered. Thus he can state some six issues later that Ireland is 'becoming Fascist. We are one of the least sentimental of people … We are democrats when democracy works. If democracy does not work efficiently, the Irish will give bureaucracy or autocracy its chance'.[79] In October Russell had described fascism as a danger to Irish democracy. By December, fascism was but a logical alternative to it.

On the same date, the first of December, Good reported in the *New Statesman* that the hunger-strike was over and which Russell was able to consign the 'hunger-strike', the 'rifle, the cudgel' and the 'yell at meetings'[80] to past history. With the crisis over, Russell changes his claim to authority. For just at the moment the government can claim victory over the hunger-strikers so now does Russell claim that 'At least two Ministers' have 'kicked Irish middlemen publicly for being too many, grasping and inefficient'.[81] It will be remembered that fascism was, in Russell's mind at least, a reaction against exactly such corruption. Complementary to Russell's praise for the Irish Ministers is one further remark: the 'whole of the speech of the Minister for Agriculture was practically an incitement to Irish farmers to bestir themselves and carry out the second part of Sir Horace Plunkett's formula: Better farming: Better Business: Better Living'.[82] It is true that Plunkett was able to exert some degree of influence on the Minister for Agriculture, Niall Hogan: a bill framed by the Minister was later placed before the Dáil and would have passed into law were it not for the collapse of Cosgrave's Government.[83] But in 1923, Russell's appropriation of the Minister's words is telling.

---

77 Ibid. **78** Ibid. 163–4. **79** 'N&C', *IS*, 1 Dec. 1923. 356. **80** Ibid. 355. **81** Ibid. 356. **82** Ibid.
83 Denis Gwynn wrote in 1928 that 'To assist the Co-operative schemes, the Government had decided, before the end of the fourth Dail in April 1927, to introduce a Co-operative Act and also to estab-

Throughout the hunger strike Russell rarely, if ever, allowed direct reference to the crisis in the pages of the *Irish Statesman*. If referred to at all the hunger strikes appeared only as an example in an argument made to support the idea of a wider malaise in Irish society. The *Irish Statesman* had the potential to publish some of the most informative articles possible on the crisis, as Good's contributions to the *New Statesman* show. For Good, despite his obvious pro-Treaty sympathies, was conscious of republican suffering. Interpreting the hunger strikes to be a ploy to influence the proceedings of the Sinn Féin ard-fheis of October 1923, Good was objective enough to also decry the killing of an 'active Irregular'.[84] Good hoped that 'This was the last of the ghastly series of murders which disgraced the final stage of the civil war, murders in which both sets of combatants are equally involved'.[85] That Russell did not let the *Irish Statesman* benefit from his assistant editor's rational insight suggests something of Russell's instrumental approach to the practice of journalism in the *Irish Statesman*. Russell's silence over the hunger-strike and his manipulation of the terms by which fascism might be understood by his Irish readership are indicative of the political intrigue in which he was involved. But in order for the *Irish Statesman* to maintain its 'independent' status, Russell had to cloak his opinions in abstract terms. This was a drawback in times of crisis as the editor's opinion was not often directly expressed. But Russell's silence was a tactical form of self-censorship because as soon as his general interests were secure, then his own authority was reasserted.

This explains the silence over the hunger strikes, followed by the welcome offered to fascism on their collapse. As soon as the Treaty party was once more secure, Russell's dialogue with it could start again.[86] The irony is of course that Russell's very immediate and very partisan interjections into Irish cultural and political life were veiled in a rhetoric of permanence and objectivity. Indeed, as the 'Notes and comments' of October 1923 show, the more pressing the problem was, the more abstract did Russell's theorisings in the *Irish Statesman* become.[87] The conditional nature of Russell's support for the government after

---

lish an Agricultural Credit Organisation. Political disturbances have delayed both measures for a time; but Mr. Hogan has succeeded in obtaining sanction from the Dail for an extremely bold stroke of policy which he decided on his own responsibility'. *The Irish Free State*. 297–8. Whatever the truth of this last assertion Hogan was about to fulfil two of Plunkett's main co-operative objectives.   **84** J. Good, in 'Comments', *NS*, 20 Oct. 1923. 35.   **85** Ibid.   **86** It is no coincidence that Mary Mac-Swiney's exasperation with the *Irish Statesman* came to a head at the end of December 1923: 'some of us hoped that it would at least be a helpful – a fairly impartial journal' she wrote. But 'Republicans have been woefully disappointed. Week by week the paper gets worse.' M. MacSwiney, 'Sinn Fein and the future', *IS*, 22 Dec. 1923. 463.   **87** Russell's abstractions did have their political use. Despite *Éire*'s criticism of the *Irish Statesman*, the republican paper 'hesitates to believe that Mr. George Russell is deliberately and willingly stage-managing this new anti-Irish campaign. His own contributions to the paper he edits are usually free from unpatriotic utterances and the senseless, carping criticism

the hunger strike is symptomatic of his understanding of the nature of political growth in 1923. To Russell, 'Political freedom is not, as so many of us in Ireland imagine, an end in itself'.[88] It is rather a process whereby the state cannot function without the intervention of a cultured elite to bring harmony to its actions. The need for this elite to have influence within the Irish state explains the need for the *Irish Statesman*. This point became so imperative to Russell that it informed his very understanding of what the function of art was in general. Russell came to understand culture as the channel by which

> the natural will is always acting on the individual, drawing him out of himself, enlarging his mind, making him a better citizen, civilising him in fact, so that he becomes incapable of joining with others to loot on a large scale, because world opinion is ever present to him, and world opinion of what is proper conduct for civilised people becomes his own opinion.[89]

Russell's concept of culture as put forward here stresses its normalising effect. Culture has the ability, Russell argues, to sedate the citizen. His reference to looting shows the degree to which the civil war had affected his perception of Irish society, with the widespread destruction of property anathema to his need for a settled society in which culture could act with due process. The association that Russell makes between culture (or, as he calls it, civilisation) and the regulation of anti-social behaviour is important in context of the *Irish Statesman*'s response to the hunger strike. The authority that Russell desires to have is regulatory. But in order to assume this kind of power, Russell created a theory of history that justified his contemporary interventions in Ireland by placing his actions within a scientific framework. History and science act in this formula as the two definitely observable precedents from which culture could work its moral force. Russell had an important precedent for this theory of action in Shaw's *Back to Methuselah*, a book that he read with great interest as he wrote sections of *The interpreters* in 1921.[90]

which characterises most of the remaining articles'. 'Current comments', *Éire*, 19 Jan. 1924. 7.   **88** 'N&C', *IS*, 22 Sept. 1923. 37.   **89** G. Russell, 'Our barbarians', *IS*, 8 Mar. 1924. 806.   **90** Russell wrote to Shaw on 30 June 1921 that 'I have just returned from a holiday and was delighted to have your book. I have spent the last two evenings with it, and it interests me more than anything of yours. For I think you are coming at last on your meditation on life to consider the nature & power of the soul. All thinking comes at last to the self. Having divorced as much of the universe as is available the mind at last begins to gnaw itself in hunger, and that is the beginning of mysticism, magic, religion, & all the science of consciousness'. G. Bernard Shaw papers, BL ms 192. Shaw's theory of the relation of culture, history and science to each other in the preface to *Back to Methuselah* fore-shadowed a general interest in what Oswald Spengler was to call the 'logic of history' in the *Dial* in 1924. Two passages from Spengler's *Downfall of the west* were published in the *Dial* in November

In his preface to *Back to Methuselah* Shaw argued that the accepted interpretation of Darwinian evolution was misguided. Shaw proposes the validity of what he terms to be creative evolution in contrast to the more popular theory of Darwin's circumstantial evolution. To follow the argument more closely is to understand the impact that Shaw's alternative understanding of evolution was to have on Russell's belief in the growth of a cultured elite. Shaw's first point in the preface is that the idea of evolution was current in Europe for at least fifty years before Charles Darwin published his *On the origin of species*. Darwin's grandfather Erasmus was aware of such a mechanism in the history of species. So indeed was Goethe. Shaw develops this point by suggesting that the younger Darwin's evolutionary writings were more widely accepted simply because they were so deterministic and thus more easily understood. Shaw asks, 'Why did not Erasmus Darwin popularize the word Evolution as effectively as Charles?'[91] The answer for Shaw is, as I have already suggested, that the younger Darwin's 'Circumstantial selection is easier to understand' being 'more visible and concrete'[92] than the concept of creative evolution as put forward by scientists such as Erasmus Darwin or Lamarck. Their theory of 'Evolution as a philosophy and physiology of the will is a mystical process, which can be apprehended only by a trained, apt, and comprehensive thinker'.[93] Already one can see the beginnings of the attraction of such a philosophy of progression for Russell. Shaw's ideas complement Russell's own belief in a cultured elite perfectly. Shaw continues to delineate further the potential of this theory of creative evolution. He argues that

> Though the phenomena of use and disuse, of wanting and trying, of the manufacture of weight lifters from men of ordinary strength, are familiar enough as facts, they are extremely puzzling as subjects of thought, and lead you into metaphysics the moment you try to account for them.[94]

The answer to Shaw's question as to the reasons behind the relative unpopularity of Erasmus Darwin's theory of evolution is that an understanding of it requires an element of creative thought not available to the majority of the citizenry. In a manner similar to Russell's expression of the growth of a world con-

and December that year. Spengler wrote 'In this book for the first time an attempt is hazarded at determining history in advance. Its purpose is to pursue, through its still unrun stages, the destiny of a culture, and precisely the one culture on the earth at this time that is nearing completion: that of Western Europe.' 'The downfall of western civilisation', *Dial*, Nov. 1924. 361. By their interest in the effect of culture upon the future history of society Russell, Shaw and Spengler were addressing a very current concern.   **91** G. Shaw, 'Preface', *Back to Methuselah*. 401.   **92** Ibid.   **93** Ibid. **94** Ibid.

sciousness there is an element of prophecy in all of this. For Shaw, the doctrine that he describes is 'Lamarckian evolution, formerly called Functional Adaptation and now Creative Evolution'.[95] In the movement from function to creation there exists an act of the imagination, which changes the defining features of that which is being described. This in turn underpins the theory of conflict that accompanies Shaw's definitions of creative evolution. In doing so his vocabulary lapses into the rhetoric of evolutionists who rather subscribed to Malthus' theory of the struggle for survival.[96] For Shaw, 'Self-control' becomes 'the quality that distinguishes the fittest to survive'.[97]

In the end nothing changes much between Shaw's theory of evolution and Charles Darwin's except for the fact that survival will be predicated in Shaw's mind by the quality of the individual's will rather than his or her ability to adapt to a new physical environment. Accordingly, Shaw pronounces that in the future 'The real Class War will be of intellectual classes; and its conquest will be the souls of the children'.[98] Whether consciously or not, Shaw provides Russell with a model by which to relate the growth of consciousness in the select individual to the need for that consciousness to be expressed institutionally by means of an elite. By understanding Shaw's theory of creative evolution (for it is really Shaw's rather than Lamarck's or Erasmus Darwin's), Russell admits himself to a cult-like understanding of the world around him. The similarities of the attractions of this admission to the earlier attractions of Theosophy are great. To Shaw

> Creative Evolution is already a religion, and is indeed now unmistakably the religion of the XX century … It will be seen then that the revival of religion on a scientific basis does not mean the death of art, but a glorious rebirth of it. Indeed art has never been great when it was not providing an iconography for a live religion. And it has never been quite contemptible except when imitating the iconography after the religion had become a superstition.[99]

Two years later Shaw defined Irish nationalism to be exactly such a superstition.[100] Russell's belief was based, like Shaw's in this preface, partly on the understanding that twentieth-century advances in science reinforced rather than challenged their respective beliefs in the ability of the intellect to order the

---

95 Ibid. 405.   **96** Thomas Robert Malthus published the first edition of *An essay on the principle of population* in 1798. Gillian Beer writes of Malthus' understanding that 'the reproductive energies of man, if not curtailed, must always outstrip the means of providing him with food. To Malthus fecundity was a danger to be suppressed – particularly by draconian measures among the human poor.' *Darwin's plots*. 33–4.   **97** G. Shaw, 'Preface', *Back to Methuselah*, 409.   **98** Ibid. 422.   **99** Ibid. 425–6.   **100** G. Shaw, 'On throwing out dirty water', *IS*, 15 Sept. 1923. 8.

world around it. Shaw's challenge to Darwinian evolution as it is commonly perceived is in this context a repudiation of the influence of the animal or unconscious in human affairs. For Shaw, science becomes only another path to a destination that both literature and religion approach. Russell similarly perceived a connection between science and a mystic appreciation of material phenomena, a fact that suggested the final sanction of spirituality in both. That poetry was for Russell the ultimate approach to these secrets of the universe is suggestive of his perception of his own place in this scheme of things. For Russell the refutation of such an important scientific figure as Charles Darwin by Shaw heralded a significant change in the fabric of society in general:

> The doctrine that might is right received scientific sanction for a generation, until the psychologists began to investigate states of consciousness that were not provided for in the Darwinian philosophy, and the scientists themselves began to push their explorations of the atom to a point where it seemed miraculous as spirit, and the reaction from matter to spirit began … The poets may once more sing about the soul without being told on scientific authority that consciousness is only an affectation or imitation of matter.[101]

Once again we can see the relation of this kind of pronouncement to Russell's interest in the translation of the poet's abstract singing into material power. The whole question of science's journey to mysticism is predicated by the perception that science had become in the preceding century valued above the arts. By merging the two Russell hopes to gain something of science's ability to influence society's perception of itself. With the translation of the hard facts of science into the language of philosophical enquiry, there lies the possibility that other modes of pragmatic expression may be brought under the artist's sphere of influence. By extension the state itself becomes 'a being with power over life and death, thought and bodily existence'.[102] The state is in this case the bridge between observable fact and metaphysical suggestion, a unity that can only be maintained by the influence of the artist who perceives the influence of both worlds. The artist's vision acts as a stimulus to the state's growth. Accordingly, as the Free State 'comes to self-consciousness it must develop within it all the functions, capacities and desires that the greatest of States have developed'.[103]

---

101 'Querist', 'Literature and life: art, science and civilisation' (cited subsequently as 'L&L'), *IS*, 15 Mar. 1924. 15.   **102** G. Russell, 'The growth of national self-consciousness', *IS*, 23 Feb. 1924. 742.   **103** Russell most admired the early Greek republics, 'We may be able to make another Attica out of Ireland.' 'Rural clubs and national life', *IS*, 13 Sept. 1924. 7. In *The republic* Plato argued that 'there would never be a perfect state or society or individual until some chance compelled this minority of uncorrupted philosophers, now called useless, to take a hand in politics … and compelled society to listen to them; or else until providence inspired some of our present rulers and

To come to such self-consciousness the Free State must forget itself. This is partially because the history to which Russell refers relies for its meaning on psychological suggestion rather than established fact. It is the history of a certain section of an intellectual elite rather than the record of a people. In order to do this Russell appropriates a nationalist rhetoric that supports the belief in a chosen people to confer legitimacy on his own preferred cultural elite. One can see that history is for Russell a means by which the artistic imagination can be proved to have material power. To Russell, the

> true history of Ireland would attach as much importance to the creation of bodiless moods as to material events, and be as concerned with literature as with laws, conflicts, warriors, or statesman. What is a nation but an imagination common to millions of people. Is there anything else to it? I doubt it.[104]

Typically, Russell hides his contemporary concerns under a veil of archaism. The designation of conflict in Ireland in the period after 1916 to a domain of 'warriors' and 'statesmen' softens the criticism that Russell has for their modern equivalents. It also illustrates by its deployment of language infused with literary reference Russell's instrumental use of literature to create identity and power.[105] This can be seen clearly in Russell's response to Sean O'Casey's *Juno and the paycock*, a play that becomes 'history in the making, rather than history dramatised'.[106] To Russell, history is a process that can be affected by, and indeed is predicated upon, culture. He can then ask, 'What will come out of *Juno and the Paycock?*'[107] Furthermore, Russell senses that he is behind the productions of writers such as O'Casey. He thinks of himself as the controlling voice that dictates, quite literally, what will or will not be effective in society at large. This leads Russell to predict that

> Yeats, no doubt, will incline the next generation to gravity and beauty, while James Stephens, who is so full of humour and understanding, will save them from being prigs. They will act through many men and women, and the birth of their imaginations will be as important in the evolution of Irish character and nationality as the fight in easter week.[108]

kings, or their sons, with a genuine love of true philosophy'. 235. **104** 'Querist', 'L&L: the antecedents of history', *IS*, 10 May 1924. 271. **105** Russell regularly used literary characters to make political points: 'If we did not cut a very heroic figure as the shillelagh-waving playboy of the nations, is it an improvement to change motley for the yellow stockings, cross-gartered with green and white, of Malvolio sick with self love?' 'Methods of controversy', *IS*, 10 Nov. 1923. 265. Malvolio is Olivia's humourless steward in Shakespeare's *Twelfth night*. **106** 'Querist', 'L&L: the antecedents of history', *IS*, 10 May 1924. 272. **107** Ibid. **108** Ibid.

The comparison of the literature of Yeats and Stephens to the direct action of the Easter Rising seems far-fetched until one considers that the rebellion itself did not function symbolically in the minds of the majority of the Irish population until after the executions. It might also be pointed out that, in retrospective terms at least, there has been no greater argument for an understanding of the Rising as an attempt at blood sacrifice than the poetry of Patrick Pearse. What might also be noted in the context of Russell's argument is the powerfully exclusive nature of his sense of cultural history. To promote Yeats and Stephens, Russell must pitch their work against the competing attraction of the Rising and those who lay claim to its revolutionary heritage. Russell proudly asserts of Yeats that the poet 'has made the name of his country shine in imagination to the rest of the world a hundred times more than any of the political notorieties whose names are on every lip here'.[109]

These 'notorieties' are exactly the individuals that republican propaganda celebrated to be the true heirs to Ireland's past. One contemporary pamphlet includes among its list of 'Famous Irregulars … Owen Roe, Red Hugh, Tone, Emmet, Lord Edward, Mitchel, Smith O'Brien, O'Donovan Rossa, Pearse, Tom Clarke, MacSwiney, Cathal Brugha'.[110] All are dead but their silence is their strength. Each individual stands as a silent rebuke to the contemporary order of the Free State, incorruptible in his martyrdom. It is no coincidence that the pamphlet contrasts these 'irregulars' to the government: for 'They all fought in the same cause. None of them were respectable Colonial Ministers drawing £33 a week.'[111] The reference to government salaries is significant as it contrasts further the sacrifice of the dead to the greed of the living, a common theme in republican criticism of the Free State. To combat this caricature of government relations Russell makes the still living Yeats an iconic figure in order to stand as a symbol of his own ideal order.

Russell's use of Yeats as a cultural icon complements his belief in the power of a controlling perception in society. Yeats is designed by Russell to function as an archetype to which the rest of society might aspire. Russell's observation that 'A false Irish character has been created, and we have yet to find ourselves nationally'[112] was predicated on his belief that he, and those he created, could provide the basis for a true character. The point of Russell's polemic on Irish identity rests in the subsequent assertion that 'We shall never find our true genius until we can shepherd all those lost sheep of our nationality back to the ancient Irish love of culture and respect for the aristocracy of character and intelligence'.[113] Russell provides his audience with a mission, to bring the Irish people back to their true home. To do this he argues consistently for a 'respect

109 G. Russell, 'Literature and civilisation', *IS*, 24 Nov. 1923. 325. **110** O'Brien collection, NLI LOP117/3. **111** Ibid. **112** 'N&C', *IS*, 22 Dec. 1923. 451. **113** Ibid.

for the aristocracy of character and intelligence'. The terms of this reference are necessarily vague and the means of accession to membership of this elite are not made immediately clear. On a first reading, these lines can be read paradoxically as the expression of a meritocratic faith. With character and intelligence, all can aspire to the aristocracy.

That Russell already imagines certain types of character and intelligence as being most fit for his feudal paradigm is only made explicit when he refers to the specific precedents that he imagines such a system as having. He draws the reader's attention to the 'precedent of Denmark', which like Ireland 'lost a province' and was subsequently 'demoralised as we are to-day'.[114] Russell identifies the three main elements behind a national regeneration. Denmark's salvation came as its 'intellectuals, its writers, its professors united in a crusade to educate and reanimate their despairing countrymen'.[115] Neither is salvation too strong a word as the intelligentsia are invested with what amounts to a sacred mission: 'they went over Denmark kindling courage, the facing up of their financial difficulties by work and their ignorance by education'.[116]

Work and education are offered to the general population as the subaltern cultural currency of inspiration and knowledge. This sense of Russell's tailoring the possibilities of high culture for the needs of general society is reinforced elsewhere in the *Irish Statesman* when Russell writes that 'The purpose of civilisation' is itself to 'put a moral skin upon ... passions and subdue them to law'.[117] The concept of education is further delineated from that of the wisdom of the elite by the argument made that 'It is the lesson of long centuries to put such a skin on society'.[118] Education becomes merely an instrument for the regulation of society by culture. It has no real effect on the beings exposed to it for 'if the skin is broken by law, or civil conflict, if the moral compact lose power and prestige, it is at once seen how much of human nature is still savage'.[119] Education then is part of an ongoing process that can be fashioned to suit the requirements of a national ideal.[120]

That culture can be so amorphous so as to be changed according to expediency serves to underline its instrumental nature for Russell. By stressing its expedient nature however, Russell exposes the distance that he holds to exist between the mass of the people upon whom culture will act and the tiny minority who will control its actions upon them. Once more, in stressing literature's ability to adapt Russell suggests how it represents to him the expression of a

---

114 G. Russell, 'N&C', *IS*, 29 Sept. 1923. 68.   **115** Ibid.   **116** Ibid. 68–9.   **117** G. Russell, 'N&C', *IS*, 19 Jan. 1924. 579.   **118** Ibid.   **119** Ibid.   **120** Interestingly, Macmillan reissued Russell's *Deirdre*, first published in book form by Maunsel in 1907, in 1922 in a school's edition. Produced cheaply with a soft back, *Deirdre* was one of a range of texts produced in this year for use in Irish education. The Free State Minister for Education was Eoin MacNeill, an authority on Gaelic literature.

higher guiding consciousness, the sign in effect of an aristocracy of character and intelligence. The definition of literature that he gives is accordingly that 'The literature a nation needs is a literature the people can live with, which adds beauty and delight to life and interest to character, and which reveals and interprets the nature by which they live'.[121] This begs the question of to whom Russell refers when he writes that 'Such a literature we have begun to create'.[122] His audience are in contrast part of an 'ignorant people' who 'do not know of the transfiguration of life and nature which takes place when we have absorbed into our own the spirit of great writers, or how much we lose when we are empty of these nobilities'.[123]

In this context it is the iconic figure of Yeats that becomes central to Russell's pronouncements on culture in the *Irish Statesman*. The first requirement Russell had of Yeats was the latter's assertion that 'Mr. Yeats has confessed that he would hardly have thought it worthwhile writing his lyrics if he had not been influenced by imagination of a national literature'.[124] Once again, Russell describes the quality of the poet's imagination in mystical, religious terms. This is a quality not shared by the rest of the population. As Russell remarked of Yeats' character, the 'majority are not so self-conscious'.[125] Russell's assistant editor in the *Irish Statesman* was even more explicit on this point in her review of Yeats' Noh play *At the hawk's well*. Mitchell declared herself to be 'still doused by my experience and incapable of criticism'.[126] Her profession of semi-consciousness fits well with Russell's association of poetry with an entrance into a mystical state. The conclusion to this insight follows as Mitchell seeks to assuage the poet's worries: 'Mr. Yeats need not fear that the Noh play will ever be mixed with commercialism. Its beauty is for the few and the chosen.'[127]

Yeats is declared to be the poetic champion, a feeling only reinforced by Russell with the award of the Nobel Prize to Yeats at the end of 1923. Russell welcomed the honour as significant of something more tangible than the acknowledgment of wide literary appeal. For Russell, the Nobel Prize was a symbol of the world's realisation that in Yeats 'there was restored to Ireland a spirit which had not existed since the Book of Kells. After a thousand years the spirit of the artist was re-born upon a far higher plane.'[128] The millenarian undertones to this comment are not difficult to hear. The suggestion of reincarnation that Russell makes further suggests the messianic quality that he attributes to Yeats'

---

121 G. Russell, 'Literature and civilisation', *IS*, 24 Nov. 1923. 326. **122** Ibid. **123** Ibid. **124** 'Querist', 'L&L: the future development of Gaelic', *IS*, 29 Sept. 1923. 82. **125** Ibid. **126** 'S. L. M.', 'At the hawk's well: an appreciation', *IS*, 12 April 1924. 142. Mitchell's review was of a private production of the play that had been 'performed recently' in Yeats' own drawing room. Incidentally, the first production of *At the hawk's well* was performed on 2 April 1916 in the drawing room of Lady Cunard. See A.N. Jeffares and A.S. Knowland, *A commentary on the collected plays of W.B. Yeats*. 83. **127** Ibid. **128** G. Russell, 'Literature and civilisation', *IS*, 24 Nov. 1923. 325.

arrival (while also working as a sly corrective to any personal pride on Yeats' part).

Russell goes on to stress the greatness of Yeats' achievement by contrasting it to the 'arid' Ireland of the previous century, alive only to the 'animal vitality in Lever, Lover and Carleton'.[129] Such caustic remarks are served only on prose as any attack on the 'patriotic poetry'[130] to which he then refers might be construed as an anti-national expression, thus weakening Russell's broader argument for unity among the people under their poetic superiors. Russell continues by placing Yeats definitely within the Revival, as he came from a movement in which 'the thoughts of young Irishmen of genius began to turn inward and backward to Gaelic Ireland',[131] the touchstone since Russell's early reading of Standish O'Grady of all Irish literary inspiration.

Within this movement 'Yeats was undoubtedly the greatest artist'.[132] The definition of this greatness is further remarkable. To Russell, Yeats 'may be regarded as the pivot around which Irish literature began to take on quality ... Through it, as through a transparency, the world received its first revelation of what was beautiful in Irish tradition.'[133] The great artist acts as a pivot. He facilitates the legitimate expression of the race in a manner similar to those 'great figures ... of heroic legend', the stories of whom Russell elsewhere described as the reflection of 'the imagination of the people'.[134] According to this argument Yeats, as the heroic pivot that Russell creates, becomes himself voiceless as an individual, existing for Russell rather as a symbol of what he admires and, more importantly, what he seeks to promote in Ireland.

Russell consolidated the *Irish Statesman*'s reputation in 1924. Keen to avoid too immediate controversy, Russell's main energies were channelled into the promotion of the journal as a suitable forum for the new generation of Irish writers who had begun to publish in the decade previous. Austin Clarke, F.R. Higgins, Liam O'Flaherty and, less regularly, Francis Stuart all contributed to the *Irish Statesman* in 1924.[135] But Russell's journal did not enjoy unchallenged access to the works of young Irish writers in the period. A young Con Leventhal, later lecturer in French literature in Trinity College Dublin and friend of Samuel Beckett, had his article 'The *Ulysses* of Mr. James Joyce', excised by printers on grounds of propriety from the *Dublin Magazine*, even after he had

129 Ibid. 326. **130** Ibid. **131** Ibid. **132** Ibid. **133** Ibid. **134** G. Russell, 'A confession of faith', *IS*, 15 Sept. 1923. 5. **135** Perhaps the best contribution of all was Austin Clarke's poem 'The lost heifer (a Jacobite song)', *IS*, 11 Oct. 1924, 138. It was collected, like many of Clarke's 1924 submissions to the *Irish Statesman*, in the next year's *The cattle drive in Connaught*. The 'heifer' was a Jacobite symbol for Ireland. The poem's second stanza is exceptional: 'Brightness was drenching through the branches/ When she wandered again,/ Turning the silver out of dark grass/ Where the skylark had lain,/ And her voice coming softly over the meadow/ Was the mist becoming rain'. 138. See also F.R. Higgins, 'Shavaun Lavelle', *IS*, 17 May 1924. 296. L. O'Flaherty, 'The salted goat', *IS*, 26 Jan. 1924. 616–17. H. Stuart, 'Art and energy', *IS*, 8 Nov. 1924. 270.

gone so far as to correct galley sheets. In a rage, Leventhal, writing under the pseudonym of L.K. Emery, joined with the poet F.R. Higgins to publish the *Klaxon*, a journal that lasted for one issue only between the winter and spring of 1923 to 1924.[136] Notwithstanding its extreme fugitive status, the *Klaxon* is the most innovative, inventive and radical journal of the Free State period. Besides contributions from Francis Stuart and Thomas MacGreevy, Leventhal's spiky editorial announced the arrival of a new generation of Irish artists in language that would have graced any continental modernist manifesto.

> We are the offspring of a gin and vermouth in a local public-house. We swore that we were young and would assert our youth with all its follies. We railed against the psychopedantic parlours of our elders and their old maidenly consorts, hoping the while with an excess of Picabia and banter, a whiff of Dadaist Europe to kick Ireland into artistic wakefulness.[137]

The *Klaxon* favoured dada for its iconoclastic vitality and its title page featured a reproduction of what is there described as a 'Negro sculpture in wood'. A simple figure without adornment, this work is an example of the 'primitive' style favoured in the early twentieth century as an alternative to the received traditions of Western art.[138] Interestingly, it is acknowledged to be the property of Grace Henry, the wife until 1930 of Paul Henry, the Irish landscape painter and friend of James Good, the *Irish Statesman*'s assistant editor.[139] Ethnic art objects represented pure experience, unspoilt by effete European culture. As Leventhal put it,

> We are no more dreamers, but drunkards, standing on the remote spaces of Ireland with our eyes to ends of the earth. These last years have mel-

---

136 Leventhal recalled his controversial assessment of Joyce, the author's response to it and the *Klaxon*, in his essay on 'Seumas O'Sullivan' in Liam Miller, ed., *Retrospect: the work of Seumas O'Sullivan and Estella F. Solomons*. 7–20. **137** L.K.E., 'Confessional', *Klaxon*, winter 1923–24. 1. **138** Harrison notes in *English art and modernism* that 'Interest in "primitive" sculpture flourished in England immediately after the [First World] war'. 218. Harrison quotes the English art critic Roger Fry's response to such objects in Fry's essay 'Negro sculpture': 'So far from clinging to two dimensions, as we tend to do, he actually, underlines, as it were, the three-dimensionalness of his forms. It is in some such way, I suspect, that he manages to give his forms their disconcerting vitality, the suggestion that they make of being not mere echoes of actual figures, but of possessing an inner life of their own.' 218. Fry's occult sense of African sculpture is typical of a Western criticism that interprets non-European phenomena to be 'other' and strange. The *Klaxon*'s reproduction of an African image may be understood in this context as an attempt to shock the journal's readership with a disturbing, because alien, object. **139** S.B. Kennedy suggests that 'with the exception of the Belfast painter Colin Middleton in about 1936, Irish artists during the twenties and thirties ignored both Dadaism and Surrealism despite the fact that these movements, and Surrealism in particular, then dominated practically all forms of European intellectual expression'. *Irish art and modernism*. 34. The *Klaxon* contradicts this.

lowed our youth: we are tasting life, as athletes desiring the vitality of those Greeks before the squabbling days of Socrates.[140]

True to its intentions, the *Klaxon*'s first article was Percy Ussher's part translation of Brian Merriman's bawdy *Midnight court*. The journal's highlight is the source of Leventhal's original difficulty with the *Dublin Magazine*, 'The *Ulysses* of Mr. James Joyce', a critique so perceptive as to be later rewarded with an admiring letter from the self-exiled author himself. Leventhal identifies Joyce as a modernist and places *Ulysses* among its contemporary European art movements. For, he remarks,

> Mr Joyce is essentially the product of his age, or perhaps, as with all genius, a little ahead of it. In him we find collected all the strivings of the modern world. This year's pictures at the Salon d'Automne have precisely the same affect as *Ulysses* on the conventional mind. It calls the true ugly, because truth comes in the shape of a squatting lady with an abundance of fat.[141]

The two great successes of the 1923 Paris Salon d'automne were the Russian painter Pavel Tchelitchew and the Spanish Pedro Pruna, both of whom were influenced deeply by Picasso's then interest in dada. Dada originated in Zurich and one of its founders, Hans Arp, could 'affirm that Tristan Tzara [a Romanian artist] discovered the word Dada on the 8th of February 1916 at 6 o'clock in the evening ... This took place at the Café de la Terrasse in Zurich and I had a roll of bread up my left nostril.'[142] Whatever Arp's culinary tastes we can easily see that dada meant to shock and was a challenge to available forms of aesthetic and political order. Adherents like Picabia introduced scientific or geometric elements to their painting and dada journals like *291*, *Der Ventilator* and *Wrong-Wrong* experimented with type-face, lettering and fragmented design.[143] Leventhal identified *Ulysses* explicitly as 'a point of contact with the writings of some young Frenchmen known as dadaists' whose 'current ... weeklies swarm with ... gigantic hyperbole'.[144]

Leventhal's interest in the extreme prepared him well for his next periodical appearance in the pages of *To-morrow*, edited for two issues in August and Sep-

---

140 L.K. Emery, 'Confessional', *Klaxon*, winter 1923–4. 2.   141 L.K. Emery, 'The *Ulysses* of Mr. James Joyce', *Klaxon*, winter 1923–4. 16.   142 R.H. Wilenski, *Modern French painters*. 261.   143 Francis Picabia lived from 1879 to 1953 and was a French exponent of dada. His images 'have their origins in scientific illustration rather than art'. R. Brettell, *Modern art 1851–1929: capitalism and representation*. 42. Brettell observes that 'If there is an anti-movement in the history of modern art, it is Dada. Its name is nonsensical; its membership was shifting and unpredictable; and its aims had more to do with randomness, total freedom of expression, absurdity, and abandon than with the construction of a new aesthetic system for replication by others'. 42. Dada was in context of the *Klaxon* the perfect symbol of a new generation unwilling to be lead by its predecessors.   144 L.K. Emery, 'The *Ulysses* of Mr. James Joyce', *Klaxon*, winter 1923–4. 17–18.

tember 1924 by Frances Stuart and Cecil Salkeld. The journal probably took its title from a play of the same name written by Henry O'Hanlon and performed by the Irish Theatre, Hardwicke Street, of which Cecil Salkeld's mother Blanaid was a member, for six nights from 18 December 1916. This work, set in a morgue, was described in *New Ireland* as 'a type of play we rarely see in Ireland, but which is common enough on the Continent'.[145] It was a 'gruesome', if 'fascinating'[146] meditation on life and death. The periodical *To-morrow* was printed as a broadsheet newspaper with eight pages of three columns of type, and contained contributions from, among others, F.R. Higgins, Liam O'Flaherty and Iseult Gonne. It raised the controversy of Yeats' poem 'Leda and the swan', which made its first Irish periodical publication here after earlier inclusion in the *Dial* in June 1924. Reviled by the *Catholic Bulletin* as Yeats' 'stinking sonnet', the poem's complex of erotic mythology was calculated to offend majority opinion. Lennox Robinson's short story 'The Madonna of Slieve Dun' was no less of a challenge; it suggested the rape of a country girl called Mary Creedon by a vagrant and her subsequent delusion that she was mother of a new Christ. The story ends with her death and the boasts of the drunken tramp. The *Irish Statesman* refused to publish Yeats' poem because it was too disturbing. To publish Yeats and Robinson in one issue of *To-morrow* was to so effectively employ modernist shock tactics that the journal had to be sent to England for publication. *To-morrow* did not survive its second issue. Con Leventhal's first contribution to *To-morrow* was 'A primitive', a review of Liam O'Flaherty's second novel, *The black soul*. Leventhal found in it 'an intense background in the wild Atlantic roaring around the shores of Inverara'.[147]

> Mr O'Flaherty has rid himself of the 'malaise' of the century. He is not afraid of passion or instinct. He is not conscious of complexes or inhibitions, and finds in the Aran Islanders characters that contain the ferocity and bravery of Aboriginals.[148]

Leventhal casts the west of Ireland as unspoilt Europe, still intact with its primitive sensibility. The wild stretches of its seaboard do not allow for modern weakness and the brutal facts of its peasant economy reduce material striving to survival. Leventhal embraced this natural state as the antidote to mass participation in movements that obliterated individual perspective. But his anti-authoritarian perception placed him in direct opposition to those Irish writers intent to sustain order in the new state. The older generation's power to direct thought was evident even in the pages of *To-morrow*, whose editorial manifesto, 'To all artists and writers', Yeats wrote but attributed, falsely, to Stuart and

145 Robert Hogan and Richard Burnham, *The modern Irish drama: the art of the amateur 1916–1920*. 52–3. **146** Ibid. 53. **147** L.K. Emery, 'A primitive', *To-morrow*, 1:1, August 1924. 7. **148** Ibid.

Salkeld. The conflict between radical selfhood and civic order is evident in Yeats' qualified polemic of modernity. For,

> We condemn, but not without sympathy, those who would escape from banal mechanism through technical investigation and experiment. We proclaim that these bring no escape, for new form comes from new subject matter, and new subject matter must flow from the human soul restored to all its courage, to all its audacity. We dismiss all demagogues and call back the soul to its ancient sovereignty, and declare that it can do whatever it please, being made, as antiquity affirmed, from the imperishable substance of the stars.[149]

Russell was unmoved. 'Here', he wrote of the *Klaxon*, 'Irish youth is desperately trying to be wild and wicked without the capacity to be anything but young'.[150] Russell saw no point to the modernists' iconoclasm, ending that 'The Younger Generation ... full of talent' is 'not quite sure whether it should be wide awake like its military contemporaries or dreamy like its literary predecessors'.[151] Russell shows a lamentable lack of imagination in this response, ignoring the potential of the European avant-garde to Irish culture when its rebellious tendencies threatened his own cultural authority. It was unfortunate too that Russell's consolidation of the *Irish Statesman* in 1924 coincided with his increasing conservatism in verse. The stilted formalism of Russell's occasional poem, 'Ireland, 1924' bears the most serious evidence of this decline.

> A nation is whate'er it loves.
> If love be dead it too must die.
> Go, give an offering of doves
> To win its immortality.[152]

Russell's one concession to the editors of the *Klaxon* was to adapt the *Irish Statesman* to the instruction of the new generation. Feeling perhaps that new Irish writers were in danger of misdirection, Russell decided to channel their energies.[153] James Stephens was summoned to instruct readers on how best to create character in novels in the 'Literature and life' columns.[154] Yeats published a rewritten version of a poem first written in 1890 and even Lady Gregory made a rare

---

149 H. Stuart and Cecil Salkeld, 'To all artists and writers', *To-morrow*, 1:1, August 1924. 4.   **150** G. Russell, 'The younger generation', *IS*, 19 Jan. 1924. 594.   **151** Ibid.   **152** G. Russell, 'Ireland, 1924', *IS*, 15 Mar. 1924. 9.   **153** Russell held great influence over young Irish writers. He claimed in a letter of January 1919 to Charles Weekes that 'I get lots of things to vet from all kinds of folk and I try to help them if they show talent. I have discovered in this way, and edited most of the new Irish writers, Stephens, Colum, Seumas O'Sullivan, Austin Clarke, among others'. Denson typescript. 345. **154** See for example, J. Stephens, 'The novelist and final utterance', *IS*, 22 Mar. 1924. 140–1. Also, 'Growth in fiction', *IS*, 17 May 1924. 301–2.

contribution to the journal.[155] Charmingly, Yeats declared in the short preface to his poem that 'Even in its rewritten form it is still a sheaf of wild oats'.[156] The literary authority of Yeats and Russell was restated in the late summer of 1924 with the announcement of the Aonach Tailteann literary awards. The Tailteann games, as they were popularly known, were first held in the second millennium before Christ under the aegis of King Lughaidh Lamhfada in honour of his foster mother Tailte. They were resumed after an eight-century break by the Irish Free State to celebrate independence. In an Ireland just recovering from civil war the establishment of a national games was also a welcome tonic for a tired people. Besides athletic competitions the games included literary sections whose most prestigious judge was Yeats. Russell felt that the games were an excellent instrument 'to educate Irishmen generally to know what is highest'[157] in literature. The *Irish Statesman* welcomed the 'awards announced by Senator Yeats'[158] to Stephen MacKenna, James Stephens and Oliver Gogarty perhaps because, of these three, only MacKenna was not a contributor to Russell's journal. The awards were a vindication of Russell's literary editorship of the *Irish Statesman*, now implicitly recognised to be a cultural journal of national importance.

The year ended with Russell optimistic of the *Irish Statesman*'s continued success. With Yeats sympathetic to his cause of Irish literary rejuvenation and the correspondence pages of the journal brightened with the occasional controversy conducted by ambitious new writers,[159] Russell predicted a bright future for Irish life and letters. 'Unless', Russell predicted, 'something unforeseen recharges the Irish soul with hatred we may expect relations between Irishmen of all parties to become fairly normal in a year's time'.[160] After a long career of prophecy, Russell was confident enough to welcome in late 1924 a new period of intellectual prosperity. The *Irish Statesman*, its first stage successfully completed, now faced the challenge of development with the new state.

---

155 W.B. Yeats, 'An old poem re-written', *IS*, 3:9, 8 Nov. 1924. 266. The poem is a version of 'The dedication to a book of stories selected from the Irish novelists', collected in 1892's *The countess Kathleen and other legends*. The version in the *Irish Statesman* substantially varies in incidentals from that published in *Yeats's poems*. 80–1. **156** Ibid. **157** G. Russell, 'The Aonach Tailteann literary awards', *IS*, 16 Aug. 1924. 719. **158** Ibid. **159** Austin Clarke, F.R. Higgins, Liam O'Flaherty and Francis Stuart enjoyed the indulgence of the correspondence columns of the *Irish Statesman* in early 1924 to debate the nature of national energy. O'Flaherty's contribution was the most pointed: 'the human race has not advanced from savagery to culture on the feeble crutches of philosophy. What epics have there been written about the disputations of scholars? Did Homer write of philosophy or the hunting of wild boars and the savage wars waged around stone-walled cities? Did Shakespeare live in the days of twenty per cent. (*sic*) interest on oil stocks and the loathsome mouthings of Ramsay MacDonalds at Geneva about Leagues of Nations that are based on fraud, corruption, and the usury of slim-fingered, cultured bankers?' *IS*, 18 Oct. 1924. 171. O'Flaherty's rage would be a welcome addition to any literature. **160** G. Russell, 'N&C', *IS*, 27 Dec. 1924. 487.

6 / Intellectual engineer: 1925–7

The years 1925 to 1927 were crucial to the *Irish Statesman*'s consolidation as a journal conversant with all critical areas of Irish political and cultural activity. The masses of journals, pamphlets and newspapers produced in the period attest to the vigorous debate contested over the Irish language, industry and identity.[1] Conversely, this was a short period of electoral security for the Free State, as Ireland settled into its new order and the Dáil functioned efficiently as a legislature. The *Irish Statesman* responded to this political stability by producing a parallel claim to cultural authority. Russell made the *Irish Statesman* a publication that based its reputation on its ability to present specialist views on any subject relevant to Ireland's independence. In an attempt to maintain the consistency of the *Irish Statesman*'s opinion, Russell cultivated the range of writers available to him, adding new recruits such as Sean O'Faolain when necessary. Each contributor to the journal was an expert in his or her own chosen field; political analysis, for example, was shared between Russell, Good, the assistant editor, and P.S. O'Hegarty. O'Hegarty was a prominent nationalist author and Secretary from 1922 of the Department of Posts and Telegraphs. His writing complemented the *Irish Statesman*'s support for the Free State by its often vicious polemic against republicanism. O'Hegarty's 1924 book, *The victory of Sinn Féin*, had excoriated Mary MacSwiney and de Valera for their incompetence and had alleged their personal responsibility for the civil war. Although his contributions to the *Irish Statesman* were rarely as pointed, his very presence in the journal was a significant register of Russell's opinion of republicanism. For economic analysis, Russell relied upon George O'Brien, Professor of National Economics at University College Dublin, and author, between 1918 and 1921, of three innovative economic histories of Ireland from the seventeenth to the nineteenth centuries.[2]

1 The O'Brien collection of journals and pamphlets in the National Library of Ireland is good evidence of the immense activity of the period. Among the journals collected there are *Banba* (1912–22), *Éire–the Irish Nation* (1923–4), *Forward* (1924–43), *Irish Worker* (1923–32), *Labour Opposition* (1925–6), *Nation* (1927–30), *New Leader* (1923–32), *Voice of Labour* (1921–5), *Workers' Republic* (1921–3) and *Young Ireland* (1919–23). There are hundreds of pamphlets, the reproduction of articles from journals and newspapers by interested political organisations a common practice of the period. 2 O'Brien wrote *The Economic history of Ireland in the eighteenth century* (1918), *The Economic history of Ireland in the seventeenth century* (1919) and *The Economic history of Ireland from the union to the famine* (1921). This last was dedicated to Horace Plunkett, an indication of O'Brien's

Edmund Curtis, Professor of History at Trinity College, reviewed Irish historical publications. Curtis further found time to review novels and, strangely perhaps for a Trinity fellow in this decade, drama productions in the Irish language at the Abbey theatre. Unfortunately for him, he also lost his wife, Margaret Barrington, to another member of the journal's set, Liam O'Flaherty. The *Irish Statesman* also counted on the positive support of Alice Stopford Green, a historian of early Ireland respected by political opinion.[3] Green was a prolific author and a long time friend of the editor, an association continued until her death in 1929. As regards the Irish language, Russell supplemented his own writings on the subject with the opinions of the young Sean O'Faolain. The editor's friendship with Osborn Bergin, Professor of Irish at University College Dublin, also encouraged this respected linguist to contribute an occasional article, lending an associated status to Russell's own writing on the subject. Art reviews were shared between Russell and Thomas Bodkin, a barrister and a Director of the National Gallery from 1927, who contributed occasionally to the journal.

Irish literature enjoyed the attentions of the most varied panel of writers available to the *Irish Statesman*, a source of occasional irritation to Russell.[4] The editor generally restricted himself to a codification of the terms by which Irish literature might be understood in the 'Notes and comments' and 'Literature and life' columns. Russell's direct appreciation of the literature restricted itself to his reviews of favoured Irish writers. Before her death in 1926, Susan Mitchell's main task as editorial assistant was her provision of regular and astute reviews of fiction. Younger writers such as Frank O'Connor, Monk Gibbon and F.R. Higgins contributed original work and, excepting Higgins, occasional critical analysis. The *Irish Statesman* also profited from the submission of essays by James Stephens, Forrest Reid and Lennox Robinson. Yeats joined these more established writers even more rarely in the journal's pages. His contributions to the *Irish Statesman* were predominantly political.[5]

Appreciation of developments in English literature in the journal was limited to occasional controversy between the English poet Herbert Palmer and Frank O'Connor's early associate, Geoffrey Phibbs.[6] Russell contributed appre-

sympathy with co-operation, a sympathy that extended to O'Brien's contributions to the *Irish Statesman*. **3** The Minister for Education, Eoin MacNeill, recommended Green's *Irish national tradition* to schoolchildren in 'Irish educational policy', *IS*, 17 Oct. 1925. 168–9. Green is most remembered for *The making of Ireland and its undoing* (1908) and *Irish nationality* (1911). **4** Russell complained of his contributors to the *Irish Statesman* that 'They all want to write poetry and nothing else, and I who can write poetry as well as any of them have to write political and economic articles which few other people seem practical enough to do'. Denson typescript. 415. **5** The sum of Yeats' contributions to the *Irish Statesman* in 1925–6 were 'An undelivered speech', *IS*, 14 March, 1925, 8–10, and 'The child and the state (speech made to the Irish literary society on November 30)', *IS*, 5 Dec. 1925, 393–4, concluded in the next issue. The first article concerned divorce and the second state education. **6** Palmer is now almost entirely forgotten even though he was the author of several collections in his

ciations of Milton and Keats to the 'Literature and life' columns but there was little acknowledgement, beyond occasional positive notice in the brief 'Magazines' section, of the achievements of contemporary English literary reviews such as the *Criterion*.[7] An intellectual appreciation of the matters that concerned these publications is more often to be found in the pages of the *Dublin Magazine*, edited by Seumas O'Sullivan. Finally, Walter Starkie, a Professor in Spanish and lecturer in Italian literature from 1926 at Trinity College, conducted music and drama reviews. Starkie's infatuation with Italian culture was important to Russell's appreciation of changes in European politics in the later 1920s. It was, for example, Starkie who interviewed Mussolini for the *Irish Statesman* and Starkie's wife, an Italian fascist herself, who helped organise it.[8]

All these writers were at the centre of the *Irish Statesman*'s output in the middle years of the 1920s. No other Irish journal of the period could rely on such a distinguished list of contributors. Together they made the *Irish Statesman* a powerful instrument of authoritative opinion through which Russell published expert analysis on any subject. Discussions of language, literature, economic regeneration and political association were all concerns of the journal. The *Irish Statesman* seems to have had an opinion on everything, from the American involvement in Panama to the provision of milk for schoolchildren in the Free State. But, as the select nature of the *Irish Statesman*'s contributors might suggest, the journal's opinions were, to a great degree, uniform, a result perhaps of the fact that Russell's authority as a cultural commentator was completely vested in it. It is the subtle exercise of this authority that marks the passage of the *Irish Statesman* through the middle of the 1920s.

Russell used the new year edition of 1925 to make a definitive statement of his understanding of post-independence Irish culture. Both the article and the reactions it elicited from the *Irish Statesman*'s readership are important registers of the condition of cultural debate in the Free State at this time. In 'Old tradi-

lifetime. His *Vampire and other poems* (1936) contains a poem, 'Through curtains of darkness', first published in the *Dublin Magazine*, and 'The celestial country', a meditation on one of Russell's paintings given to Palmer by the artist as a present. Geoffrey Phibbs is better known by the name he later adopted, Geoffrey Taylor. Born in England, Phibbs was of a Sligo ascendancy family. As Geoffrey Taylor he later became poetry editor of the *Bell* and published, in 1944, *Irish poems of today: chosen from the first seven vols. of 'The Bell'*. For Palmer's dispute with the then Phibbs and O'Connor (mostly a pedantic distraction over poetic form) see his 'Anglo-Irish literature', *IS*, 5 Dec. 1925. 397.   **7** See G. Russell, 'L&L: Keats and his circle', *IS*, 14 March 1925. 15–16. Also his 'L&L: the anatomy of a poet', *IS*, 23 May 1925. 338, 340. This last is an extended review of Denis Saurat's *Milton, man and thinker*.   **8** Starkie's personal account of his meeting with Mussolini is fascinating in its suggestion of Mussolini's awareness of then-contemporary Ireland. At the time of his interview, Kevin O'Higgins, the Vice President of the Executive Council and Free State Minister for Justice, had just been murdered (it will be noted that O'Higgins was styled 'Minister for Home Affairs' until April 1924 and 'Minister for Justice' thereafter). Mussolini remarked simply of O'Higgins that 'I admired him'. *The waveless plain*. 392.

tions and the new era', Russell reiterates the importance of racial blending to Ireland's success as a nation, both in the past and the future, an opinion offered since Russell's first *Irish Statesman* editorial in September, 1923. The tone of Russell's article in 1925 is however more discernibly militant, asserting that 'We cannot exorcise what is blended biologically and culturally beyond recall in the make-up of nine tenths of the people. The pure Celt does not exist'.[9] Russell uses the terms 'Celtic' and 'Gaelic' interchangeably to suggest that the concepts of racial and linguistic purity make for a dangerous combination. Russell does this to argue the weakness of a pure Irish state, adrift from the modernising tendencies of contemporary European thought. For Ireland

> has given birth, if it accepts all its children, to many men who have influenced European culture and science, Berkeley, Swift, Goldsmith, Burke, Sheridan, Moore, Hamilton, Kelvin, Tyndall, Shaw, Yeats, Synge and many others of international repute. If we repudiate the Anglo-Irish tradition, if we say they are aliens, how poor does our national life become. We have simply nothing to show since the remote days when Gaelic was dominant. There is nothing in our literature, in our science, in our culture, to make Europe take the least interest in us. We become a perfectly undistinguished people.[10]

The sentiments expressed in this passage are crucial to an understanding of Russell's cultural polemic. It contains all the elements that marked Russell's concern over the increasing attention given in the Free State to nativist linguistic projects. With the foundation of the Gaeltacht commission and the drive to have Irish taught in all levels of state schooling there was a definite possibility that Irish would be institutionalised as the state language.[11] To countermand this, Russell argues that the Irish language is unable to adapt to modern conditions. Thus we find Russell, the apparent mystic, celebrating the empirical achievements of Kelvin and Tyndall.[12]

Russell in effect conceived of Anglo-Ireland as the central modernising tendency in Irish culture, despite its having its roots in the relatively pre-industrial eighteenth century. The high achievement of Russell's Anglo-Ireland was its contribution to nineteenth-century science. The Anglo-Irish are educated in a practical discipline critical to the success of the Free State's modern develop-

---

9 G. Russell, 'Old traditions and the new era', *IS*, 3 Jan. 1925. 522. **10** Ibid. **11** The commission was appointed by order of the Executive Council on 27 Jan. 1925. General Richard Mulcahy was chair. **12** William Thomson, Lord Kelvin, was born in Belfast. The Chair of Natural Philosophy at the University of Glasgow for fifty-three years, his principal achievement was the discovery of the second law of thermodynamics. John Tyndall too held a Chair of Natural Philosophy, but at the Royal Institution. He investigated the properties of radiant heat.

ment, a caste capable of endowing independent Ireland with the fruits of their specialist knowledge. Russell's construction of this version of Anglo-Ireland was bound to offend. It is indeed relevant that Daniel Corkery defended Gaelic Ireland from the charge of redundancy in *The hidden Ireland*, first published in January 1925. Ostensibly a study of Irish-language Munster poets of the eighteenth century, *The hidden Ireland* was, to its author, a reclamation and recovery of the lost history of a once-dominant caste.[13] Implicit in Corkery's literary history was the assumption that the continued revival of Irish was critical to the spiritual integrity of the Free State. Corkery's opponents were those who argued that Irish was a language unsuitable to the requirements of efficient statehood:

> To revive Irish cry the Progressives – Progressives! – is to stay the wheels, to put the hands of the clock back. They are filled with a vision of whirring wheels, glistening belts, flying argosies – a mechanical world, its speed ever accelerating, its speed ever increasing! ... If those whose very dreams have become mechanical still see any use for the arts, it can only be that they pay lip-service to old saws. How anyone who cares for literature can bear to see a language, any language, die is a thought beyond us.[14]

Corkery's insight was to realise that independence was the greatest danger to the Irish language. The demands of an international capitalist economy whose transactions were conducted in English threatened the revival of a separate national language. Russell's own vision of a scientific, rational Anglo-Ireland is in this context part of a post-Treaty doctrine that, since *The interpreters*, accommodated itself with a free, capitalist, Irish state. Russell argued in the *Irish Statesman* for a 'rich tolerance and acceptance'[15] of both Anglo and Irish cultures but, as I have already suggested, he equally felt that Irish-speaking, or as he would have it, Gaelic, culture was unsuited to the modern world. The reality of Russell's multicultural ethic is betrayed by the biological metaphor that he employs to describe it. He wrote:

> Nothing could be worse for a country than a dull uniformity of culture. It is the conflict of cultures and ideas which bring about intellectual vital-

13 Edmund Curtis reviewed *The hidden Ireland* in the *Irish Statesman* in January 1925. Curtis described Corkery's book as 'one of the most convincing arguments yet made for the perpetuation of a speech which up to 1600 stood high among the cultivated languages of Europe'. Curtis leaves open the question of the development of Irish after 1600. E. Curtis, 'The twilight stars of Gaelic poetry', *IS*, 31 Jan. 1925. 660.   14 D. Corkery, *The hidden Ireland*. xii-xiii. It is possible that Corkery has Russell in mind as one of the 'progressives' of this passage. His 'flying argosies' strongly remind of Russell's description of airships in *The interpreters*. *The interpreters* was, as we discussed, the expression of Russell's acceptance of the new, scientific, Irish state.   15 'Old traditions and the new era', *IS*, 3 Jan. 1925. 522.

ity. They wed together and beget new and vigorous children and prevent that anaemia which comes when ideas of the same kind are inbred and inbred until a kind of imbecility in the progeny results.[16]

Flinders Petrie's *The revolutions of civilisation* suggested to Russell the correlation between biology and culture that he outlines above. Russell establishes such a link in the *Irish Statesman* to give scientific validity to his claim that the Free State was in absolute need of Anglo-Ireland's service. Petrie's work is mentioned frequently in the journal as a source of Russell's analysis.[17] *The revolutions of civilisation* was Petrie's attempt to systematise his analysis of the growth and decline, as he saw it, of human culture from prehistory to the present. Petrie's idea was to separate periods of advanced human civilisation from those of retrograde achievement by tracing periods of flux between the two standards in disparate individual cultures. His investigation led Petrie to ask under what conditions civilisations flourish, a question whose answer was vital to Russell's hopes for the *Irish Statesman* as a catalyst to Irish achievement in the 1920s. Petrie's basic finding was that 'In every case in which we can examine the history sufficiently, we find that there was a fresh race coming into the country when the wave was at its lowest',[18] the wave in this case being an image of the culture's rise or fall. Petrie's belief is important to Russell's interpretation of the course of Irish history as put forward in the *Irish Statesman*. The periods that Russell attends to are those of cross-pollination, with his repeated references to Danes, Saxons and, more recently, the Anglo-Irish.

Implicit in both Petrie's and Russell's theories of cultural contact is the idea that one of the two cultures involved must assume a weakened position to allow the newer, more vigorous race to refresh it. Thus Russell creates a vision of Gaelic Ireland feeble in power and lost to communication from the outside world. The Anglo-Irish arrive and are stimulated to new achievement by contact with a previously alien culture. The actual dynamics of this relationship are factually untenable. Pressingly, there was the obvious problem of the Anglo-Irish in 1920s Ireland, defeated by the Land Acts and deserting the country in ever-greater numbers.[19] But to point this out is to ignore the contingent fact that Russell's history of the Anglo-Irish is a conscious fabrication. It is a myth of the past intended to fortify a future position. It is the expression of a hope that a resurgent Irish culture in the 1920s can be regulated, not just by a political or religious minority, such as the Anglo-Irish were, but by a cultural one,

16 Ibid. 523.   **17** See for example 'The Gaelic and Anglo-Irish cultures', *IS*, 17 Jan. 1925. 587. See also Russell's reply to a letter called 'Mixed races' by 'Medicus' in which he mentions his support for Petrie, *IS*, 27 Mar. 1927. 71. Also 'N&C', *IS*, 11 Dec. 1926. 316.   **18** F. Petrie, *The revolutions of civilisation*. 114.   **19** For a discussion of this, see Brown's chapter 'The fate of the Irish left and of the Protestant minority', in *Ireland*. 102–37.

for which Russell will speak. Petrie's final caveat to *The revolutions of civilisation* suggests how Russell's rhetoric of cultural integration is but a holding pattern for power. To Petrie, it was obvious that

> if the view becomes really grasped, that the source of every civilisation has lain in race mixture, it may be that eugenics will, in some future civilisation, carefully segregate fine races, and prohibit continual mixture, until they have a distinct type, which will start a new civilisation when transplanted. The future progress of man may depend as much on isolation to establish a type, as a fusion of types when established.[20]

Russell was influenced strongly by Petrie's belief that racial evolution might lead finally to the creation of a superior breed. In terms of this idea, the Irish-speaking natives were, to Russell, far down the order of progress. Russell believed that the Anglo-Irish were one of the superior strains, transnational, and thus somehow more universally human, in their achievement. Ingratiatingly, Russell called the Anglo-Irish a race 'of which any country might be proud'.[21] Only the 'ignorant' would deny their value, just 'as savages might throw away precious ores of which they were unable to discern the uses'.[22] The association of primitivism with the opponents of Russell's version of Anglo-Ireland is significant in context of Petrie's eugenicist commitments. Petrie predicts the arrival of a culture superior to those previously existing. In Irish terms, Russell attaches the achievements of Anglo-Ireland to a scheme whereby their acceptance into Free State culture will provide the basis for a new and vigorous civilisation. This constitutes the subtlest part of Russell's polemic and the site of his partial divergence from Petrie. For Russell's arguments on behalf of the Anglo-Irish are finally concerned less with the practice of eugenics, than with the creation of a viable myth whereby the Anglo-Irish can be posited as the nucleus of a new, post-Treaty Ireland. Anglo-Ireland does not provide Russell, as it did Yeats, with noble symbols in decline, a death of culture. It meant instead future resurgence.

The Anglo-Irish become the basis of myth and Russell uses their image in a manner similar to the way in which O'Grady created a new legend of the Red Branch in his *History of Ireland*. Tyndall, Kelvin, Yeats and Synge rarely, if ever, figure as the authors of individual work in the lineage presented by Russell in the *Irish Statesman*. Their personal philosophies are, in this context, of little interest, for their collective value was their iconic silence. This value was most difficult to maintain contra Yeats and his stubborn resistance to Russell's attentions can be registered most strongly at exactly those times when Yeats might

---

20 F. Petrie, *The revolutions of civilisation*. 131. **21** 'The Gaelic and the Anglo-Irish cultures', *IS*, 17 Jan. 1925. 586. **22** Ibid.

have been expected to speak responsibly and publicly. Yeats' submission to the *Irish Statesman* of the notes to his undelivered Senate speech of February 1925 on divorce is a strong case in point.[23] For Russell the Anglo-Irish existed as a mythical presence that sustained the *Irish Statesman's* right to intervene in Free State political debate. But the myth he recounted was the means whereby English and Irish speakers, Protestant and Catholic, Saxon and Gael, could be bound by an orthodoxy amenable to artistic intervention. The myth was valuable because it was indeterminate and emotive. The scientific improbability of Russell's theory of race is, simply, unimportant. The myth's primary function was to act as an assimilative, living legend.

But the decline of Anglo-Irish political authority in the Free State also suggested a weakness in Russell's project. For it ensured that a newly resurgent Irish-speaking culture might successfully resist its claims, especially since individuals prominent in movements such as the Gaelic League staffed many of the institutions of the Free State.[24] In an attempt to circumvent this problem, Russell published the opinions of writers critical of Irish-language teaching. First among these was Sean O'Casey. O'Casey was independent from institutional nationalism but retained a general respect for his continued support for the Dublin working classes. O'Casey spoke for an almost subterranean constituency and his anger over the poor's disenfranchisement from the new state fed his resentment at the time wasted in debating abstract subjects like the Irish language.[25] O'Casey's angry advocacy was supplemented in 1925 with the more balanced polemic of Sean O'Faolain. What connected both writers to the *Irish Statesman* was their ability to play the role of internal dissident, of the Irish speaker disaffected with the demands made on the Free State population by the Irish language movement. O'Faolain was a writer of impeccable nationalist pedigree who had taken the republican side in the civil war. He was also a native of Cork and a former close friend of Daniel Corkery. O'Faolain satisfied the criteria of linguistic ability and political association demanded of any advocate of

23 Yeats' 'Unpublished notes' were in fact an attack on Cosgrave's introduction of a Divorce Bill into the Dáil, with subsequent referral to the Senate. Yeats accused Cosgrave of committing 'an act of aggression' against the Protestant minority. Russell published the article but was uncomfortable with Yeats' combative stance. Russell depreciated 'a discussion on lines which would involve religious controversy'. Both writers' opinions from *IS*, 4:1, 14 March 1925. 4, 8.   **24** The most obvious example being Eoin MacNeill, Minister for Education. Russell accommodated MacNeill within the *Irish Statesman* by publishing an unprecedented four-article series of MacNeill's 'Irish educational policy' in October and November 1925. Russell's manoeuvring was rendered useless by MacNeill's resignation over the boundary agreement with Northern Ireland.   **25** See for example O'Casey's letter 'The innocents at home' in which he alleged that 'the attachment to Irish on behalf of the elders of the nation is a fancy fraud and a gigantic sham. They know it to be a sham, and consequently, want to give it the appearance of reality by forcing it down the throats of the defenceless children.' *IS*, 10 Jan. 1925. 560. For an account of a child's death in the tenements see O'Casey's short story, 'Mollser', *IS*, 25 April 1925. 200–2.

Irish Ireland. But Russell was intelligent enough to provide the *Irish Statesman* as a forum for a writer eager to expand his intellectual horizons beyond Cork.

O'Faolain's first contribution to Russell's journal was a letter published in September 1925. In it he questioned the relation of his contemporary Irish literary tradition to the eighteenth century, a connection that Corkery made in *The hidden Ireland*.[26] He disagreed with 'those who would like to project the eighteenth century into the twentieth under the impression that they were thereby reviving the real Ireland'.[27] To O'Faolain, Irish literature in the eighteenth century was merely the record of the final words of an already defeated people. Unfortunately for him this was exactly the tradition promoted by the 'Irish revival ... of to-day'.[28] O'Faolain desired to promote an invigorated Irish language tradition. Accordingly,

> Those who go digging in the Gaeltacht to-day will only get a tradition about a fag-end of a fag-end of a culture, and if they are there seeking culture they will waste much time. But, it is another matter if the educationalists and the revivalists should attempt to force this uneducated tradition on a country like ours, which is already in the European current, and whose literature, in Irish, as in English, will be part and parcel of Europe's gift to the world.[29]

O'Faolain dismisses the Gaeltacht at the same time that an important governmental commission was collecting evidence from around Ireland to secure a policy that would benefit areas designated as Irish speaking. O'Faolain's commitment to the Irish language is not in doubt, but his criticism of the teaching of Irish was succour to the *Irish Statesman* in its effort to secure English as the medium of technical literacy. More importantly, O'Faolain's recognition of the English-language literary tradition in Ireland was a public sign of accommodation with Anglo-Irish literature from a writer previously associated with Corkery.

Another of Corkery's early discoveries was Frank O'Connor, who began to publish regularly in the *Irish Statesman* in 1925 and 1926. O'Connor's contributions to the journal were mostly English translations from original Irish poetry. His 'Sever me not from thy sweetness!' is part of an excellent sequence of variations on the Mad Sweeney legend that Seamus Heaney was later to adapt.[30] Russell's interest in O'Connor's poetry coincided with the *Irish Statesman*'s promotion of Austin Clarke in 1925. The two writers' poems were high points of the journal's literary output. It is surprising now to read how much the two

---

26 The full title of Corkery's book is for example *The hidden Ireland: a study of Gaelic Munster in the eighteenth century*. 27 S. O'Faolain, 'The best Irish literature', *IS*, 5 Sept. 1925. 816. 28 Ibid. 29 Ibid. 30 F. O'Connor, 'Sever me not from thy sweetness! (The mad king's song from Suighne Geilt)', *IS*, 21 Nov. 1925. 330.

complemented each other, especially since O'Connor is presently most associated with O'Faolain as a fellow short-story writer and Cork realist. Clarke was at this time heavily immersed in his readings of Irish legend, as his submissions to both the *Irish Statesman* and *Dublin Magazine* show. The finest of these is perhaps 'The son of Lir', published by Russell in July 1925.[31] This poem is playful in the manner of James Stephens' Irish translations, a quality in English that Russell appreciated.[32] Clarke wrote in a manner similar to O'Connor, in that both translated from Irish into English while retaining a respect for the original forms of the poetry they translated. Russell felt that their writing was exactly the kind of work that had inspired the first wave of the Revival, as Anglo-Irish literature was infused with what he referred to as the Gaelic spirit.[33] Thus, Russell, in his review of Clarke's *The cattle drive in Connaught*, declared himself

> inclined to rate the poetry in this book ... higher than that in any since The Vengeance of Fionn had made us aware that a new poet with authentic vision had come to carry on the tradition of Anglo-Irish literature and enrich it.[34]

Russell responds to Clarke with a view that Anglo-Irish literature exhibits an essential quality. Its authenticity derives from its attachment to the legends of Gaelic Ireland. Russell's appreciation of Clarke is heavily coloured by his desire to read the younger poet in context of Russell's own concept of Anglo-Ireland. To Russell, Clarke is the voice of a culture constantly enriched by its Irish literary antecedents. The vision, for example, that Russell ascribes to Clarke is reminiscent of that of the aisling poets. The complexities of cultural debate in the decade are realised in an awareness that the aisling, according to Corkery's *The hidden Ireland*, was no longer a viable medium for national literature.[35] Russell contradicts Corkery in order to brand Clarke with a Gaelic influence, the authentic mark of Russell's Anglo-Irish culture.

Russell's own poetry was almost paralysed by its need for authenticity. Russell published only one new poetry collection in the 1920s, *Voices of the stones*, in

---

31 A. Clarke, 'The son of Lir', *IS*, 11 July 1925. 555.   **32** Stephens' skill as a translator is apparent in his renderings of O'Bruadair and Raftery, collected in Lennox Robinson's 1925 *Golden treasury of Irish verse*. Robinson's introduction credits Russell and Yeats with helping the editor select his book.   **33** Russell created a template for his appreciation of such an achievement in his review of James Stephens' *Collected poems*. He wrote that in the book 'Perhaps the most perfect poetry judged merely as art are the reincarnations from Gaelic, in which he rarely sets himself the almost impossible task of translating poetry into poetry, but takes an idea, an emotion and gives it a new body'. G. Russell, 'L&L: The poetry of James Stephens', *IS*, 6 Nov. 1926. 206.   **34** G. Russell, 'Review of *The cattle drive of Connaught and other poems*', *IS*, 28 Nov. 1925. 370.   **35** Corkery wrote 'After the terror of 1798 the *aisling* poem is heard no more; though the genre may still survive, it is used now to comfort some lover's heart, and not the heart of the nation.' *The hidden Ireland*. 144.

1925. Blake is a dominant influence throughout much of *Voices of the stones* and Russell was keenly aware of the relative absence of his own voice in the collection. He felt a sense of underachievement with its publication and wrote to James Stephens that he was 'a little sad' and thought there were only 'half a dozen lyrics of quality'[36] in it. The collection is prefaced by a quotation from *The voyage of Bran*, an early indication of its mythic preoccupations. It reads, 'The shining rock/ From which arise a hundred strains', the conceit being that poetry finds its inspiration in permanence. The prose-poem dedication to Padraic Colum confirms this suggestion as Russell writes 'I made these verses in a rocky land'.[37] The remainder of the dedication outlines the dual interest in the relationship between imagination and immutability that marks most of the poems in *Voices of the stones*. Only the stones have kept their 'purity'[38] since the Fall. This collection is an attempt to give voice to that essence:

> with my cheek
> Pressed to their roughness I had part regained
> My morning starriness, and made these songs
> Half from the hidden world and half from this.[39]

This double vision is, unfortunately, more than half the problem. The poems are generally confused in their choice of imagery and rarely communicate any sense of wonder to the reader. Too often they are given over to a romantic poetic language that makes the reader question the individual authenticity of the poet's vision. Even a successful poem like 'Magnificence' is haunted by the presence of Blake. The *Dublin Magazine* noted the decline, its reviewer reading in the collection indications of 'a triviality, of a lessening sympathy with human weakness, of a despair that is not real, of a wavering in essentials, not to be found in his previous work'.[40]

But the obvious and sometimes laboured artifice of Russell's poetry confirms more than his artistic fall. It is also indicative of the poet's attempt to give his work validity in the Anglo-Irish context that he has created. The references to Bran and the mystic permanency of the stones are evidence of a perception that links nature with spiritual purity. This connection was a common theme in literary descriptions of the west of Ireland during and after the Revival. The west was the symbolic stronghold of the native Irish; Russell's evocation of imagery associated with it is an indication of a calculated failure in his poetry. He sacrifices individual diction to his desire for verse to fit into his own version of Anglo-Irish literature: epic in timeframe, romantic in sensibility and Gaelic in inspiration.

---

36 G. Russell to J. Stephens, letter dated August 1925. J. Finneran (ed.), *Some unpublished letters from Æ to James Stephens*. 32. **37** G. Russell, *Voices of the stones*. vii. **38** Ibid. viii. **39** Ibid. **40** 'Voices of the stones. By Æ', *Dublin Magazine* (cited subsequently as *DM*), Aug. 1925. 62.

A similar sense of calculation can be read in two of the final three poems of the collection. These poems, 'A prisoner: Brixton prison, September 1920' and 'Michael', form a coherent political epilogue to the mythic synthesis attempted in the rest of the text. Together they share some common themes with other poems in the collection – the death of spiritual innocence being explored in both 'A holy hill' and 'Michael' for example. The difference between the two final poems and the rest is that their explicit subject is political revolution. In 'Michael' the revolutionary moment is the 1916 Easter Rising. In 'A prisoner', it is Terence MacSwiney's death by hunger-strike in 1920. Russell's renewed interest in this second poem is evidence of his attempt to annex MacSwiney's legacy for his own vision of Ireland. MacSwiney represented for Russell an element of republicanism acceptable to his Anglo-Irish synthesis. Russell wrote to James Stephens in 1925 that 'Republicanism is dust and ashes' while predicting that 'a few glimmering sparks … will be kept alive to be blown into flame in some future when the fire is needed'.[41] It is suggestive to think that Russell, with his description of MacSweeney as a 'light-bringer',[42] imagines his subject to be one of those 'glimmering sparks'. In effect, MacSwiney's reputation in poetry will provide an inspirational narrative to orthodox post-Treaty Irish culture.

In contrast to Russell's poem of the rising, 'Michael', the full title of 'A Prisoner: Brixton, September 1920' is exact as a record of place and time, though MacSwiney is himself strangely absent from the text. He is sacrificed a second time, on this occasion to symbolism instead of the republic. MacSwiney is the icon designed to focus the energy that Russell associated with republicanism into a new Ireland. When the poem was first published in 1920, the speaker imagined a unified and independent nation. The Ireland of 1925 had experienced a fracture of the consensus briefly held before the Treaty. Or, as the speaker has it in 'Waste', another poem in *Voices of the stones*, the civil war had 'spoilt the sacrifice' of the dead for 'words hollow as wind'.[43] It is ironic to read the Treaty represented as an empty formula in Russell's poetry since this option was used by de Valera to justify his taking the oath of allegiance to enter into the Dáil in 1927. The point however is that by MacSwiney's sacrifice in 1920, the individual acquired a corporate importance. The speaker urges MacSwiney to 'Burn on, shine here, thou immortality, until/ We too can light our lamps at the funeral pyre'.[44] The immediate result of this sacrifice will be the reward of an ability to 'conquer the dragon pain'.[45] Finally, the poem admits the fact of MacSwiney's death as 'the candles of God already are burning/ row on row:/ Farewell, light-bringer; Fly to thy fountain again'.[46] In death MacSwiney returns to a source of inspiration common to all humanity.

41 G. Russell to J. Stephens, letter dated August 1925. J. Finneran, ed., *Some unpublished letters from Æ to James Stephens*. 33–4.   **42** G. Russell, *Voices of the stones*. 47.   **43** Ibid. 44.   **44** Ibid. 46.   **45** Ibid.   **46** Ibid. 47.

Such ritual purification was, in 1920, part of the preparation for MacSwiney's nationalist martyrdom. In 1925 however the poem takes on new meanings as it is subject to different contexts for reading. MacSwiney's sister Mary was prominent in Sinn Féin, an irridentist who continued with the party to its electoral eclipse in 1927. Mary MacSwiney's vitriol was often directed at Russell in the correspondence columns of the *Irish Statesman*. The dismissive answers he afforded her complaints are indicative of the weak position Russell felt she occupied.[47] Russell's appropriation of the image of her dead brother in 1925 is ghoulish but it is also evidence of his belief that Irish republicanism was finished as a political force. Its martyrs could be safely sequestered in preparation for the evolution of a new era. Terence MacSwiney had the perfect credentials to be subject to such an act of poetic coercion as republican propaganda celebrated his life as a lesson in purity. Daniel Corkery, a long-time friend of MacSwiney, found comfort in the civil war, remembering

> Among all these whisperings, jobbings, hypocrisies, we move with Terence MacSwiney's name on our lips, his words in our ears, his image in our eyes. And we are unperturbed. For we are sure that, did he see all this, he would do as we have done – only more strongly, more wisely, more purely, more religiously, being possessed of so much greater powers of soul and will.[48]

The intensity of feeling that Corkery describes was evidence of the energy that Russell desired to see unleashed in the new state. The revolutionary fervour of the Anglo-Irish and civil wars was to be conducted into new channels, away from divisive splits over the Treaty.

The major split left unresolved by the end of 1925 was the physical partition of Northern Ireland from the rest of the island. The first election to the northern parliament in May 1921 saw forty Unionist candidates returned to six each of the Irish Party and Sinn Féin.[49] James Craig was Prime Minister of an administration that was allowed, by Article Twelve of the Anglo-Irish Treaty, to remain an integral part of the United Kingdom even as the Free State assumed Dominion status. The same article stated that a commission be formed, from the two Irish and one British governments, to determine definitely a border most compatible with the aspirations of local inhabitants in consideration also

---

47 Russell's replies were often brutal. He wrote in September 1925 that he was sure 'one thing' he never did. He had 'never in his life encouraged Irishmen to kill each other. We wonder if Miss Mac-Swiney's conscience is as clear.' 'Clairvoyance', *IS*, 19 Sept. 1925. 48.   48 D. Corkery, 'The light-bringer', *Poblacht na h-Eireann* (southern edition), 25 Oct. 1922. 2. This was a Terence MacSwiney memorial number.   49 For a lucid account see Thomas Hennessey, *A history of Northern Ireland 1920–1996*, 20–54.

of geography and economics. The Boundary Commission did not in the end sit until June 1924. Its findings, of a border shortened by fifty-one miles, were leaked to the London *Morning Post* on 7 November 1925, resulting in the resignation from the Commission of the Free State representative, Eoin MacNeill. Russell tried to find a solution to the crisis the following week, proposing federal settlement to a national problem.

> We desire unity between the two bodies as much as anybody, but we do not believe that the way to that unity lies in obliterating differences, in insisting that either the people on the Free State must give up their nationalism or that the people in the six-county area must learn Gaelic whether they like it or not. No progress can be made on this line. The advocates of unity must not seek out differences and insist on extinguishing them, but find out possible points of unity and accentuate these. That is, the solution of the problem which most affords hope is a Federal solution which would leave each area free to preserve the cultural traditions it clings to and will not in this generation give up; and bring about unity of administration where a common policy was obviously economically sound. This is the only line of approach to the problem which seems to us at all hopeful. We may by degrees bring transport, post, agriculture, even customs and excise under an Irish Federal Government, no question of national tradition, no cultural prejudice would embarrass negotiations over such matters. It would be pure business, a saving of money to both communities.[50]

Russell remained supportive of the Free State government throughout the winter of 1925, maintaining the position that the problem of partition could not be solved by legal sanction. Resolution lay with the coming generations, separation to be overcome by mutual aid and interest. But a section of northern nationalists were dismayed at a compromise absolving the Free State from financial debt to the British exchequer (a legacy of the Anglo-Irish Treaty) in return for recognition of the northern state and negation of the cross-border Council of Ireland. Others accepted the new situation. The *Irish News* was 'glad this Settlement has been made and signed'.[51] 'The Nationalists of the Six Counties must look ahead, examine their political resources and resolve to utilise them', to 'realise, once and for all, that their fate in Ulster rests with themselves'.[52] The *Irish Statesman* followed much the same argument.

---

50 G. Russell, 'N&C', *IS*, 14 Nov. 1925. 291–2.   51 T. Hennessey, *A history of Northern Ireland 1920–1996*. 40.   52 Ibid.

We think that the Agreement *is* a great event, the greatest Irish event since the signing of the Treaty. Our Northern Government can no longer be suspicious about the policy of the Free State in regard to it, and we believe that with the abandonment of Free State claims on Northern territory and population a change of attitude of the majority in the North to its own minorities will soon be obvious. It was not in human nature to be altogether just to a powerful minority inside a State when it was allied in sentiment with the peoples of another State, and the object of the alliance appeared to be the overthrow or weakening of the Northern Government. With that danger past we have no doubt the Northern Government will do all in its power to make the minority contented citizens, and we hope that any advances it may make will be well met. We recommend to our Nationalist countrymen in the Northern area the example set by the vast majority of ex-Southern Unionists who have frankly accepted the Treaty settlement, and are more and more becoming sincere and loyal citizens of the Free State, and the change is so marked with many that we doubt whether a majority of these would, if they had it in their power to revert to the Union, not prefer to remain under the Treaty settlement.[53]

The obvious difference between the Protestant and Catholic minorities, north and south, was one of economics and residual privilege, in neither of which northern Catholics enjoyed an advantage. But Russell's main concern, whatever his northern roots, was the security of the southern state. He was pleased that Irish republicans could no longer gain votes by propaganda over Free State payments to the British Treasury. But he also considered that any minority, religious or political, must accept some discomfort as a price of citizenship. Besides,

It is impossible to imagine settlements between States where there will not be loose ends, injustices to groups and individuals and real grievances. But nations and their problems are not like problems in geometry or Euclid which can be solved with mathematical exactitude. The infinite complexity of human life forbids the hope of such mathematical finality. Even those who live under a State which they accept are always groaning about something or other which hurts them spiritually or economically on the civilisation they live in. These diversities of sentiment will probably never be harmonised until the universe is withdrawn into God.[54]

53 G. Russell, 'N&C', *IS*, 12 December 1925. 419.   54 G. Russell, 'An honourable agreement', *IS*, 12 December 1925. 422.

The heavenly state is mathematical exactitude, the resolution of contradictions in one unity. It was a place impossible to find in legislature or representative assembly. But the cold lines of futurity did emerge in Ireland with the construction of a massive hydro-electric scheme on the river Shannon. It was symbol to Russell of a new phase of post-Treaty Ireland, a first step to a higher order. The Shannon scheme was to provide the Free State with an indigenous source of energy to power industrial development. Built between 1925 and 1929, the project consisted of a dam and power station at Ardnacrusha in Co. Limerick. Construction photographs of the scheme, with a head and tail race excavated by a huge array of mechanical plant, show a massive landscape of upturned rock and soil.[55] The dam itself sits before the river with its concrete facing and spiral iron turbine casings. The whole edifice is completely functional, indeed almost brutalist, in architectural style. When officially opened by President Cosgrave in 1929 the dam was a formidable presence in the Limerick countryside, its anomalous presence in rural Ireland stressed by the literature that advertised tours of this new wonder of state progress.[56]

As the prime industrial project of the Free State, the Shannon scheme was the subject of a concerted government publicity drive.[57] Seán Keating, the former pupil of William Orpen, was commissioned to record the construction of the power station and produced a number of paintings on the subject, the most famous of these 'Night's candles are burnt out', first exhibited at the Royal Academy in London in 1929.[58] Suitably, the theme of Keating's commission was 'The dawn of a new Ireland'.[59] Denis Johnston echoed Keating's interest in the birth of an industrial Ireland in his 1931 play, *The moon on the yellow river*. Set

55 Thirty thousand tonnes of large and small plant were imported to Ireland for the scheme. Construction photographs are reproduced in M. Manning and M. McDowell, *Electricity supply in Ireland: the history of the ESB*. The head race and tail race were the excavations needed to increase the degree by which water approached the turbines to provide a higher energy yield.   **56** Great Southern Railways offered half-price excursions to the Shannon development, advertised by a Titan figure holding rods of lightning above the dam with the legend 'VISIT THE SHANNON WORKS'. This image combines the industrial with the epic in a manner that can best be described as futurist. Models of the dam were also exhibited at the Dublin spring show in Ballsbridge. See M. Manning and M. McDowell, *Electricity supply in Ireland: the history of the ESB*. 42.   **57** The Cumann na nGaedheal government was still so proud of its achievement in 1932 that it dedicated a chapter of the *Saorstát Eireann official handbook*, entitled 'Power supply in the Irish Free State', to it. 157–62. **58** Fintan Cullen discusses 'Night's candles are burnt out' in context of Russell's art reviews in the *Irish Statesman*. The painting itself details a number of figures set before the dam at Ardnacrusha. Cullen suggests that 'Progress is the theme of Keating's allegory. The mechanical digger (seen on the horizon) has replaced the armoured car (seen behind the group to the left); the eager young family on the right look towards the new source of power, while the corresponding three men on the left either sit immobile on a wheelbarrow, drink buttermilk or use an old-fashioned oil lamp to examine a skeleton ... Keating's Ireland is, to use O'Faolain's phrase, "an unshaped society", but it is a representation of Ireland facing up to its contemporary condition.' F. Cullen, *Visual politics: the representation of Ireland 1750–1930*. 168–9.   **59** S.B. Kennedy, *Irish art and modernism*. 171.

in the shadow of a completed power station, Johnston's play examines the tensions that the hydro-electric plant introduces to rural Irish life.[60] The *Irish Statesman* too saw the Shannon scheme as the point of departure between the old Ireland and the new. It would inspire

> the mass of the people into the attitude of mind proper to a self-governing nation, and that can be done by concentrating on constructive policies and paying much less attention to those who still believe they are slaves.[61]

The reference to slavery is a repudiation of the republican maxim that the Free State was in thrall to the British Empire by virtue of its use of the English language and its adherence to the economic terms of the Treaty. The Shannon scheme thus assumed added symbolic prestige as it represented an attempt to create exactly that kind of economic independence that republicans cited as the main criterion of independence. The scheme's construction also fostered ultranational commercial associations as a German company helped Ireland take its place among the industrialised nations of the modern world. The *Irish Statesman* was sure that the 'Irish people' would appreciate the attempt to have 'one of their great economic problems' solved

> in the big modern way. They will feel the engineering genius and knowledge which has gone into its making, the kind of thoroughness which had made Germany one of the greatest economic forces in the modern world, and they will be less inclined to listen with patience to the schoolboy economics of the Sceiligs.[62]

'Sceilig' was the pseudonym of Sean Ua Ceallaigh, an Irish language writer, former President of the Gaelic League and President of Sinn Féin from 1926 to 1930.[63] Russell in this context refers to Ua Ceallaigh's status as contributor to

---

60 A brief plot of the play details the attempt by a local force of republicans under the command of Darrell Blake to destroy a hydro-electric power station in the west of Ireland. Amid much digression, the republican bid fails with the execution of Blake by the Free State officer Lanigan. The German engineer responsible for the plant is accused of responsibility for Blake's death by the other characters, as the defence of his power station has interrupted the accepted rules of conduct previously held between the play's antagonists. A subtle reflection on the effect of modernity on rural Ireland, *The moon in the yellow river* is uncompromising in its examination of the violence that created independent Ireland. As the Free State office Lanigan says to the German engineer Tausch after the death of Blake, 'I suppose you think I enjoy that, when it means a bullet in my own back sooner or later. But enjoy it or not, I've always been taught that it's not words but deeds the country needs, and I'll go on doing what I can, no matter.' 138. **61** 'N&C', *IS*, 21 Mar. 1925. 38–9. **62** 'The Shannon scheme', *IS*, 28 Mar. 1925. 67–70. **63** The *Catholic Bulletin* was published monthly. Nearly every editorial of its 1925 series contains criticism of Russell or Yeats. It labelled

the *Catholic Bulletin*, a journal pathological in its dislike of the *Irish Statesman*. The hope that readers of the *Catholic Bulletin* would repudiate it after exposure to the glories of the Shannon scheme mimics the enthusiasm of Irish language activists to infuse their culture with more 'national' characteristics. The Shannon scheme becomes a very definite symbol of cohesion made possible by a post-Treaty, rather than an Irish-speaking or republican, nation. Russell's concept of a post-Treaty Ireland envisaged a nation where these last two movements were marginalised. Thus, by implication, the creation of a newly industrialised Ireland threatened an entire previous understanding of what being Irish was. The *Irish Statesman* fully recognised this. In response to the Shannon scheme, its own belief was that

> the average Irishman is bored stiff with being primitive, and centuries behind other States with science, culture, and organisation, and once he tastes the fascination of being modern and up to date he will tend to become a perfect glutton for modernity. The Abbey dramatists of the next generation will lose their material, and the living dramatists had better make hay while the sun shines, for the supply of primaeval rustics will tend to diminish, and in the peasant play of ten years hence the farmers will be talking about units of horse-power instead of the mist on the bog or the wind on high lonely hills.[64]

The side-effects of industrial modernity are surprising. The peasant will disappear from drama because his inefficiency makes him uninteresting and archaic. The farmer, in contrast, adapts to modern circumstance and discusses horsepower. The problem for Russell in Ireland however was that in 1925 agriculture still dominated the economy. Even a journal recommended by the *Irish Statesman* to its readership for the accuracy of its economic analysis recognised this:

Russell and his contemporaries as the 'associated Æsthetes' who 'consider themselves a *Super-Race*', a criticism that would suggest the *Catholic Bulletin* paid close attention to Russell's defence of the Anglo-Irish. Interestingly, the journal offered 'G.W. Russell and his clique … Daniel Corkery's new book. They will there see how the Gael, the one Irish nation with the one Irish literature and culture, regards, and dealt with, and will deal with, this mongrel upstart called Anglo-Irish tradition and culture. But the power of the Æsthetes to even understand the plain lesson of "*The hidden Ireland*" is what must be doubted. Good judges say that it would be more reasonable to expect a turnip to do thinking than to expect the Æsthetes to realise the silly, sordid, and aggregated thing that they are'. *Catholic Bulletin*, Feb. 1925. 102–3. The relationship between the *Catholic Bulletin* and the *Irish Statesman* is further discussed in M. O'Callaghan, 'Language, nationality and cultural identity in the Irish Free State, 1922–27: the *Irish Statesman* and the *Catholic Bulletin* reappraised', *Irish Historical Studies*, Nov. 1984. 226–45. O'Callaghan argues particularly that the *Catholic Bulletin* was atypical in its cultural extremism. O'Callaghan sees both journals as involved in 'a post-colonial search for a satisfactory "national character"'. 244.   **64** 'N&C', *IS*, 30 May 1925. 356.

'In Ireland agriculture is the dog and manufacture a very diminutive tail.'[65] To the *Round Table* this observation was elementary and any government that did not recognise it would be in for a 'rude awakening'.[66]

But to recognise this is only to recognise the obvious fact that Russell's version of Anglo-Ireland did not depend for its success on social or economic conditions. It might even be argued that his myth of Anglo-Ireland became more potent the further it was divorced from such reality. Thus we find Russell celebrating his belief in a scientific, mechanical society in a journal incorporating the *Irish Homestead* and edited from Plunkett House in Merrion Square. Similarly, Russell's vision of Anglo-Ireland was, as I have already suggested, a mirage. It was, in its silence over areas of discourse that it could not integrate, calculatingly dismissive. This in part explains Russell's hesitancy to address the problem of religious difference in the *Irish Statesman*. Religion has long served as a symbol of cultural and political association in Irish life. The reason for the *Irish Statesman*'s ignorance of so fundamental a problem is simple. The journal's political myth could not accommodate it.[67] Russell's silence is less due to personal ignorance than to an awareness that, of all the different registers of opinion and ideology in the Free State, religion was the most dangerous because the churches already had their own myths of association. Established eligion represented an area in which Russell had absolutely no authority and his weakness in this area is reflected in the vicious caricature he was subject to in denominational publications such as the *Irish Rosary* and *Dublin Review*.[68] In face of such entrenched opposition, Russell's vision of Anglo-Ireland represented a formidable risk for the *Irish Statesman*. It was after all the articulation of the vision of a state that had not yet come into being. Russell could afford to take this chance because, unlike the government, the *Irish Statesman* was able to idealise without suffering at the polls (unfortunately any evidence of a detrimental effect on the journal's sales no longer seems to exist). The journal's silence on questions of religion ensured its editor received only personal opprobrium. But in promot-

65 'Ireland: events in the Free State', *Round Table* (cited subsequently as *RT*), Dec. 1926. 136. The *Round Table* was an English review of international affairs. Its Irish correspondent was J.J. Horgan, a unionist with great respect for Horace Plunkett. Horgan wrote a memoir of his pre-1918 experiences in *Parnell to Pearse*. **66** Ibid. **67** Reflecting on the absence of religious discussion in the *Irish Statesman*, Brown suggests that Russell 'largely ignored how religion was often regarded as a badge of social, economic and national identity and this may account for his inability to influence the country in any profound way'. *Ireland*. 129. **68** The *Irish Rosary* cast Russell as a low-church demagogue: 'George Russell, who might have been a statesman and a leader of the people' was instead 'a sort of ponderous, dissenting preacher'. 'Those Irish pagans', *Irish Rosary*, Dec. 1925. 953. The *Dublin Review* was equally dismissive: 'Let Yeats believe in his fairies, Æ in his Buddha, with the Irish trade-mark, and James Stephens in his *Uberseele*. It is their affair not ours. We have theological tenets of our own'. 'Those Irish pagans!' *Dublin Review*, Oct-Dec. 1925. 192. The *Irish Review* was published by Dominicans in Dublin and the *Dublin Review* by the Catholic publishing house Burns, Oates and Washbourne of London.

ing concrete projects like the Shannon scheme the *Irish Statesman* ran the risk of antagonising in fact the very people who would, it hoped, eventually benefit from industrial development. Russell, as with *The interpreters* in 1922, tried to envision change before its definite arrival. This was a strategy easier to sustain in a fictive form. Its promulgation as the policy of a journal that relied in large part for its continued existence on sales could, by miscalculation, alienate the *Irish Statesman* from its readership.

The contract for the scheme was signed with the German engineering firm of Siemens-Schuckert in August 1925. The total cost of the project was to be £5.2 million, a massive sum when one considers that the entire government expenditure for the year 1926 to 1927 was only £24 million.[69] Initially even the radical *Voice of Labour* welcomed the project. Its construction would alleviate the conditions of the unemployed who, 'in common with the Labour Party, are prepared to give the Shannon Electricity Bill a chance, provided that the rights and privileges of their class are safe-guarded'.[70] Trouble soon developed when Siemens offered its Irish labourers a wage of 8*d.* per hour, an offer improved to £1.12*s.* per week with free lodging for a fifty-hour week. The company argued that this wage was reasonable when compared to that of the average rural labourer, then around 25*s.* for a 60-hour week. The unions however pressed for a higher, urban industrial wage to be paid to the workers. The two sides remained in deadlock until December, with the union cause substantially weakened by Siemens' success in the recruitment of strike-breaking labour from Limerick city. Defeated in a motion on behalf of a wage increase in the Senate in December 1925 the struggle failed and normal relations were resumed by early 1926.[71]

Despite the ITUC labelling the scheme 'useless and untouchable',[72] Russell was unafraid to show where his sympathies lay. In response to claims that wages were too low in Limerick the *Irish Statesman* replied that 'We must have the mechanical foundations laid for the efficient modern State, antecedent to raising the standard of living here to what it is in other countries'.[73] The *Irish Statesman* reiterated its support for the government's stance on the matter two weeks later when it praised a speech critical of the unions made by the Vice President, Kevin O'Higgins.[74] In doing so Russell alienated those sections of labour, from the parliamentary to the radical, previously well disposed towards him. It will be remembered that the *Voice of Labour*, under the editorship of Cathal O'Shannon, vigorously supported Russell's defence of the co-operatives in the war of independence. Now it condemned him. For 'Nowhere in Ireland – except per-

69 J.J. Lee, *Ireland*. 109. **70** *VoL*, 16 May 1925. 4 **71** Details of the disturbance and figures for wages are taken from M. Manning and M. McDowell, *Electricity supply in Ireland: the history of the ESB*. 41–3. **72** The ITUC's opinion is recorded in 'Comments', *NS*, 9 Oct. 1926. 727. **73** 'N&C', *IS*, 10 Oct. 1925. 132. **74** 'N&C', *IS*, 24 Oct. 1925. 195–8.

haps in the columns of "Irish Truth" and "The Irish Statesman" – are voices to be lifted up publicly in opposition to Labour's welcomed stand'.[75]

The Labour Party fully supported the boycott in the Dáil. Indeed, the assistant secretary of the special TUC meeting convened to discuss the boycott in the autumn of 1925 was R.J.P. Mortished, a Labour intellectual who contributed several articles to the *Irish Statesman* in 1923. After the controversy over the Shannon project he saw fit only to submit a letter critical of Russell to the journal and diverted his other writing to a rival of the *Irish Statesman* set up in Cork in 1926, the *Irish Tribune*. The *Irish Statesman*'s support for the Shannon scheme as an agent of modernisation meant that its editorial policy became even more associated with what the *Voice of Labour* decried as an 'anti-Labour Ministry'.[76] But just as Russell's project of industrial modernity, with all its concomitant cultural change, seemed secure as its potential was realised in the defeat of the Shannon boycott, changes within republicanism posed a further problem. De Valera split from Sinn Féin in 1926 to form Fianna Fáil. While doing so de Valera continued an overture to Labour that had started the previous year. The journal *Sinn Féin* noted as early as January 1925 that its party's president had 'twice stated the permanent attitude of the party, namely by repeating its adhesion to the Democratic Programme of Dail Eireann and by stating definitely that unemployment must be ended'.[77] Fianna Fáil courted Labour, so marginalizing Russell.

This did not concern the *Irish Statesman* in the period before the 1927 election. The journal gave the impression that it believed republicanism to be a political relic of the civil war. Such confidence irked republicans. A stream of bitterness rankles throughout *Sinn Féin*'s responses to the *Irish Statesman*. It complained of 'incessant misrepresentation' by its rival, a journal composed by 'publicists who think they have a divine mission to distort, confuse, and misinterpret the policy and principles of the independence movement, and to call the result Irish statesmanship'.[78] The *Irish Statesman* had interests other than the decline of *Sinn Féin*. But *Sinn Féin* was prescient in its criticism of Russell's misrepresentation of its ideas. For the republican journal conceived of itself as the voice of a relevant political movement with a future. Russell was convinced that it only mouthed an echo of the past. More galling for *Sinn Féin*, the *Irish Statesman* desired to appropriate the energy Russell associated with the revolutionary movement that *Sinn Féin* alone felt it represented. Russell agreed with the consensus opinion in 1926 that republicans would disappear at the polls. But, as the

75 'The Shannon boycott', *VoL*, 28 Nov. 1925. 1.   **76** *VoL*, 16 May 1925. 4.   **77** 'Unemployment as great a threat as conscription', *Sinn Féin*, 17 Jan. 1925. 5.   **78** 'Events of the week', *Sinn Féin*, 11 April 1925. 3.   **79** 'Ireland: events in the Free State', *RT*, June 1926. 587.

Round Table suggests, this did not mean that Cumann na nGaedheal would assume sole control of the state.

> With a general election approaching next year and the Government by no means popular, any national leader with a considered policy and a clear record should have little trouble in creating a formidable Opposition, but we doubt if a majority, or even a considerable minority, of the electors will be foolhardy enough to present Mr. De Valera with another blank cheque, having regard to the figure for which he filled in the last.[79]

De Valera and, by association, Fianna Fáil, are summarily dismissed. Neither was Russell convinced that the Labour Party could achieve power. Labour's R.J.P. Mortished wrote to the *Irish Statesman* to criticise its 'bewailing lugubriously the lack of an Opposition in the Dail'.[80] He could not 'refrain from pointing out … that what the Dail lacks is not an Opposition but a Ministerial Party'.[81] Russell's reply reveals where he thought the future might lie. He doubted, 'considering the vocations of our population, if it will return a majority of labour deputies'.[82] But he did 'think it possible the country might give a majority to an ably led Radical Party'.[83] Russell does not elaborate on a definition of what a radical party might be. But his interest in Mussolini throughout this period suggests that he associated radical politics with fascist Italy. There are compelling reasons for this suggestion, to be found in Russell's celebration of a united national being ten years earlier, a belief that the nation should be united under one leader, to act as one entity. To promote this radical corporatism, he framed his thoughts in the same words used to express the *Irish Statesman*'s support for the Shannon scheme in 1925. To Russell,

> A young state derives its best vitality from the quality of the futurist imagination in it … In Italy, under the leadership of that political Kaiser, Mussolini, a new organisation of state and nation is taking place … An equally unfettered governing power has been set up in Russia, calling itself a dictatorship of the proletariat, bent on the creation of the socialist state … They have all in common … an organic unity capable of equally swift and powerful action whether at home or in international affairs … A wise autocracy is not unbecoming in a young state.[84]

In effect, Russell is agitating for the creation of a similar movement in Ireland. He provides any potentially radical, as he has it, Irish movement with a rationale

---

80 R. Mortished, 'Irish labour and the ranch system', *IS*, 6 Feb. 1926. 684.   **81** Ibid.   **82** Ibid. 685.   **83** Ibid.   **84** G. Russell, 'Futurist policies', *IS*, 9 Jan. 1926. 550.

that incorporates nationalist rhetoric in an international outlook. It was a flamboyant move and one not entirely appreciated in the offices of the *Irish Statesman* itself. Just the next week Good was quick to publish his view that the

> disease of such communities would be better met by the frankest and most conciliatory acceptance of the democratic ideals, drawing the heterogeneous elements into a unity by fair play and recognition as may be of group sentiments rather than by repression and dictatorships.[85]

Good's unease was due to his association of Italian political violence with republican agitation in Ireland. Good felt that Ireland had 'plenty of would-be Mussolinis' who mercifully 'lack both brains and imagination, and their simple minds cannot soar above the idea of holding the nation up with a gun'.[86] With Good's association clear between fascism and republicanism it must have been difficult for him to support, let alone understand, his editor's increasing belief that the future rested in a political model that Good felt to be repressive and inadequate. Good was not alone in his disquiet over his contemporaries' appreciation of Italian fascism. The *Irish Tribune*, the first journal to be set up in direct competition with the *Irish Statesman*, worried over a Free State run by a 'small coherent group of Mussolinis allied to a set of powerful Civil servants'.[87] The *Irish Tribune* was established in Cork in 1926 'by an alliance of Cork republicans and dissatisfied Free Staters led by Alfred O'Rahilly'.[88] O'Rahilly was a TD and Professor in Economics at University College Cork; the *Irish Statesman* was immediately familiar to him. His brother Thomas O'Rahilly, Professor of Irish at Trinity College Dublin before his return to Cork in 1929, clashed with Russell in the *Irish Statesman*'s correspondence columns in 1925.[89] Alfred O'Rahilly's colleague in the Cork Economics department was Professor John Busteed, author of articles contributed to Russell's journal on the subject of national finance in 1926.[90]

The *Irish Tribune* was so intimate with the *Irish Statesman* that the Cork journal's appearance was practically identical to that of its rival, with weekly

85 'N&C', *IS*, 16 Jan. 1926. 581. **86** J. Good, in 'Comments', *NS*, 3 Jan. 1925. 351. **87** 'Is Cumann na nGaedheal dead?' *Irish Tribune*, 10 Sept. 1926. 5. **88** Ibid. **89** See for example T.O'R's letter 'Gaelic and Irish nationality', *IS*, 14 Jan. 1925. 591–2. Notice that O'Rahilly, like his then fellow Trinity professor, Edmund Curtis, signs only his initials. The Trinity College board prohibited the university's address from being attached to any controversial or public articles in the press. This prohibition must have stretched informally to stop individuals signing copy, an indication of the vulnerable state, both political and financial, that Trinity felt it was in. See R.B. McDowell and D.A. Webb, *Trinity College Dublin, 1592–1952*. **90** The *Round Table* recorded that 'Professor Busteed of Cork University College has recently published some illuminating articles in the Irish Statesman in our national economic statistics'. 'Ireland: events in the Free State', *RT*, June 1926. 596.

commentaries preceding columns of opinion and literary review. The *Irish Tribune* further copied the *Irish Statesman's* policy of creating a core of experts upon whom its analysis depended. The first of these was Andrew Malone, who was appointed editor of the *Irish Tribune* by O'Rahilly. Malone's real name was L.P. Byrne, but he is more commonly remembered for pseudonymous publications such as the 1929 history of the Abbey theatre. Malone's political credentials were labour and nationalist. He was also the author of a series of articles on dramatic criticism in the *Dublin Magazine* in 1925.[91] Political analysis was generally shared between the editor, Corkery and Alfred O'Rahilly himself. The *Irish Tribune's* economist was John Busteed. He was a contemporary of George O'Brien, the *Irish Statesman's* economist, and contributed a reply to an O'Brien article in *Studies* in 1930.[92] Alfred O'Rahilly and his brother Thomas were the publication's Irish-language experts. Literary reviews were shared between Malone, Daniel Corkery and, more infrequently and less sensibly, by Alfred O'Rahilly. F.R. Higgins and Frank O'Connor occasionally contributed poetry to the journal.

The *Irish Tribune* competed with the *Irish Statesman* from its first issue. Malone's first editorial was in direct imitation of Russell, the only major difference between the two being Malone's populism. He did not intend the *Irish Tribune* 'to cater for an exclusive literary set or indulge in high-brow pedantry for the benefit of a select metropolitan coterie'.[93] The *Irish Tribune's* central concern was Malone's 'belief and hope that the ultimate and proper vehicle of Irish culture is the Irish language'.[94] This was hardly a novel suggestion. Any number of Irish journals, from the *Leader* to *Sinn Féin*, supported the language revival. What is interesting about the *Irish Tribune* is its attempt, before Malone's dismissal, to create an independent nationalist journal sympathetic to republicanism while 'Accepting the Treaty position as a fact'.[95] This last point captures the true potential of the journal. For if the *Irish Tribune* could reconcile these two political opposites to each other on an equal basis it would threaten Russell's assimilative project in the *Irish Statesman*. Its revival of a moribund republicanism into a new alliance with the Free State would put paid to Russell's nostrums for a post-Treaty Ireland.

In order to create such an alliance the *Irish Tribune* had to present itself as an impartial platform where the views of rival parties could be expressed. It had great difficulty doing this. Dialogue was too often substituted by the publication from issue to issue of columns of party commentary from either Free State

91 See for example Malone's 'The conservatism of J.M. Barrie', *DM*, Feb. 1925. 470–9. Also 'From the stalls: the triumph of Juno', *DM*, March 1925. 535–8.   **92** See G. O'Brien, 'Agriculture and employment in the Free State', *Studies*, June 1930. 177–85. Busteed's good-natured response covers the following five pages.   **93** 'Foreword', *Irish Tribune*, 12 March 1926. 4.   **94** Ibid.   **95** Ibid.

or republican spokespeople.[96] The journal's editorial latitude extended to the publication of essays on Irish figures as diverse as Tim Healy and Patrick Pearse.[97] The latter features on Patrick Pearse by Desmond Ryan still make for interesting reading but personal reminiscences rarely prove to be the cement upon which new political alliances are made. Russell realised this in his poetry, recasting Terence MacSwiney into a post-republican hero. The *Irish Tribune* did not have such insight and, as such, the memoirs of Healy and Pearse were notable politically only because of the identity of their authors, William O'Brien and Desmond Ryan. Both men were heavily involved in the Irish labour movement and their publication in the *Irish Tribune* suggests the sympathy that Malone had for a working-class perspective.[98] Malone's editorship of the *Irish Tribune* is in this respect an indication of the direction the *Irish Statesman* might have taken had Russell maintained his interest in the Irish left after the war of independence.

As a literary journal the *Irish Tribune* suffered from the capability of its rivals. The *Dublin Magazine* published high-quality verse and prose throughout the mid to late 1920s. The *Irish Statesman* too offered writers an educated and established audience. Abroad there was a host of literary reviews, the *Dial*, the *Criterion* and the *Calendar* among them. From its first issue, the *Irish Tribune* failed to rely on creative writing. The simple reason for this seems to have been that few writers submitted their work to the journal. F.R. Higgins' first poem in the journal, 'The grief', was not published in the *Irish Tribune* until 30 April and Frank O'Connor's first appearance was even later; his short story 'Sion' was published on 6 August. Sean O'Faolain's first contribution was in fact a letter, titled 'The national programme',[99] and followed by a short story on 14 May. Whatever the reasons for the *Irish Tribune*'s relative lack of literary success, the delay in O'Connor and O'Faolain's appearances in its pages is still surprising. Their slowness to publish in a journal whose literary editor was their old tutor Daniel Corkery can only be explained by the growing rift between them and

96 A good example is P.D.'s rejection of de Valera, 'When the election comes', *Irish Tribune*, 16 July 1926, 18–19. See also Frank Gallagher's response, 'An appeal from republicans', *Irish Tribune*, 13 Aug. 1926. 9–11.   **97** D. Ryan, 'The Pearse I knew', *Irish Tribune*, 16 April 1926, concluding the issue of 30 April. W. O'Brien, 'Tim', *Irish Tribune*, 12 March 1926, concluding the following issue. **98** Ryan and O'Brien were to combine later in Ryan's 1949 edition of James Connolly's writings, *Labour and Easter Week*, to which O'Brien appended an introduction. In the 1920s, O'Brien won a Dáil seat for Tipperary in the June general election of 1927 but lost it almost immediately in the subsequent contest in August. He was president of the ITUC in 1925. Sean MacLysaght recorded O'Brien's memoirs in *Forth the banners go*, a useful insight to the dedication of this lifelong trade unionist. Desmond Ryan remained active as a historian of the Irish labour movement and of the Easter Rising. Malone had previously published in O'Shannon's paper, the *Voice of Labour*, and was supportive of O'Casey's labour roots. The first issue of the *Irish Tribune* included an essay by Malone on 'Synge and O'Casey'.   **99** S. O'Faolain, 'The national programme', *Irish Tribune*, 30 April 1926. 16–17.

their mentor. O'Faolain did not publish in the *Irish Tribune* after an argument with Aodh de Blacam about Corkery's *The hidden Ireland*, occasioned by a letter critical of the book by Frank O'Connor sent to the *Irish Tribune*.[100] O'Connor himself did not publish in the journal again until the end of November, just five issues before the *Irish Tribune* ceased production.[101]

The *Irish Tribune*'s treatment of economics was perhaps less controversial. It recognised immediately that the Free State was 'struggling for its economic existence; we are faced with urgent problems of education, unemployment, housing, agriculture, industry'.[102] It approached these problems constructively and intelligently. It promoted co-operation within its pages, a movement that Russell had neglected since the incorporation of the *Irish Homestead* into the *Irish Statesman* in September 1923. The *Irish Tribune* felt that in the Free State there was 'a wide sphere for the co-operative credit society. We think that the members of the Cork Agricultural and Economic Society are doing a service to the nation'.[103] Furthermore, the journal advertised the example of 'America and other countries' where 'great headway has been made in a very brief period where co-operative effort has been aided largely by legislation'.[104] The *Irish Tribune*'s support for the co-operative movement was almost singular in the Irish press. The *Irish Tribune*'s stance was due no doubt to Malone, a writer with a long-standing respect for Horace Plunkett and the author of a history of the Irish Agricultural Wholesale Society in 1919.[105]

The journal's development was however stunted by Malone's dismissal from the *Irish Tribune* at the beginning of June. His departure signalled a further decline in the *Irish Tribune*'s editorial standard, despite the promotion of capable writers such as Corkery to the board. No definite editor seems to have replaced Malone but there is a strong impression that Alfred O'Rahilly was the main concern behind the journal. The reason given for Malone's dismissal was negligent conduct of the *Irish Tribune*'s business accounts. But it is hard not to infer from the journal's editorials after Malone's departure that the other mem-

---

100 O'Connor wrote that 'Mr. Corkery would have us believe that until … man makes his peace with The Spirit of the Nation that work will go for nothing. I do not believe it. I do not believe that the spirit of the nation … is a permanent and unchanging thing. I say that if his people did not accept this man and his work, whatever his beliefs, whatever his tradition, his people did not prove themselves worthy of him.' F. O'Connor, 'The heart has reasons', *Irish Tribune*, 25 June 1926. 18. Corkery replied that O'Connor had 'a very immature mind' to suggest such a thing. D. Corkery, 'A landscape in the west', *Irish Tribune*, 2 July 1926. 22. O'Faolain defended O'Connor in 'The spirit of the nation', *Irish Tribune*, July 23 1926. 23. In the interest of fairness, de Blacam defended Corkery from O'Faolain by asking 'Have we a literature?' *Irish Tribune*, 30 July 1926. 16–18. **101** O'Connor wrote reviews for the issues of 26 Nov. and 3 Dec. 1926, and contributed a poem, 'Lullaby of adventurous love', *Irish Tribune*, 3 Dec. 1926. 20–1. **102** 'The oath', *Irish Tribune*, 19 Mar. 1926. 4. **103** 'Agricultural credit', *Irish Tribune*, 2 July 1926. 4. **104** M. Murphy, 'The farmer and co-operation', *Irish Tribune*, 20 Aug. 1926. 12. **105** See L.P. Byrne, *Twenty-one years of the IAWS: 1897–1918*.

bers of the editorial board were unhappy with his free-thinking independence. Malone attempted to create in the *Irish Tribune* an inclusive sense of Irish identity relevant to his readership. Evidence of this can be read in Malone's brave attempt to collapse the distinction between Gaelic and Anglo-Irish literature in an effort to answer the question 'What is an Irishman?'[106] He suggested that 'the Anglo-Irish will claim everyone born in Ireland who attained distinction anywhere as Irish. Those of the Gaelic stream will not.'[107] To Malone, that was 'the great dividing line'.[108] The *Irish Tribune* offered its own answer to the conundrum:

> It is not sufficient in order to be an Irishman (for purposes of inclusion in school books) to have been born in Ireland. It is also very important that something outstanding should have been done in Ireland and for Ireland ... Those whose 'spiritual home' is England are English – nothing can gainsay that. But it may be neither a good nor a generous policy to keep harping on that string.[109]

This passage was Malone's final contribution to the journal. But his writing is evidence of the *Irish Tribune*'s general effort to redefine a national identity separate from racial purity. Malone's redefinition would allow an alternative, civic identity to grow. His editorial opinion was not typical of the Irish weekly press in the late 1920s, a press that tended to be either dismissive of its opponents, as in the case of the *Irish Statesman*, or abusive, like the *Leader*.[110]

The journal became more polemical in the months afterwards, exhibiting a tendency for personal slander that Malone had restricted. In one bitter attack on the *Irish Statesman*, that 'organ of Protestant opinion',[111] a label that would never have surfaced under Malone's editorship, the *Irish Tribune* criticised its competitor's support of the American President Coolidge's non-intervention in Mexico.[112] The *Irish Tribune* found the Dublin journal's support curious, especially coming 'from those who are accorded such a full measure of freedom by the Irish Catholic majority'.[113] The *Irish Tribune*'s resort to sectarianism rose perhaps from its sense of frustration at being disenfranchised from the cultural and political centre of Dublin, a centre that partly expressed itself in the *Irish Statesman*. As the voice of a second city, the Cork journal complained that 'As

---

106 'Week by week', *Irish Tribune*, 28 May 1926. 7. **107** Ibid. **108** Ibid. **109** Ibid. **110** The *Leader* was the most entertainingly direct of the three journals. It had no time for 'Mr. W. British Yeats, a most superior person since he won the prize for poetry'. It saw its duty to defend the Irish press from 'English dirties and cheap jack poets, be they English by birth or by blood'. 'Current topics', *Leader*, 21 Mar. 1925. 152. **111** 'Week by week', *Irish Tribune*, 20 Aug. 1926. 5. **112** The Catholic church was persecuted sporadically in Mexico after the revolution of 1910. From July 1926, there were no church services for three years as the clergy refused to comply with anti-clerical ordinances in the constitution. **113** 'Week by week', *Irish Tribune*, 20 Aug. 1926. 6.

things are Dublin has the monopoly'.[114] Culturally it felt marginalised and could 'see no reason why selected sections from the Museum and Art Gallery should not be loaned to provincial cities for long or short periods'.[115]

Politically, the *Irish Tribune* was alienated. It predicted a collapse of the republican vote in the coming 1927 elections and in compensation attempted to cultivate the attention of J.J. Walsh, Free State Minister for Posts and Telegraphs, who came from Cork. But he withdrew from Cumann na nGaedheal in the election year over a party dispute about free trade.[116] In cultural terms too the journal was disappointed. Part of its impetus derived from the promotion within its pages of the Irish-language movement, a commitment made stronger by Corkery's promotion to literary editor after Malone's dismissal. But Cumann na nGaedheal disappointed the *Irish Tribune* by its response to the Gaeltacht commission's report, made public in 1926. It found 'the comments of President Cosgrave on the report of the Gaeltacht commission cruelly disappointing'.[117] The *Irish Tribune* focussed its disappointment in a polemic of the state of the government machine in general:

> This shading and skirting of Free State problems, on the Commission system, will no longer cut ice. An effort should be made to give effect to the recommendations of the Commission, or the State should not be called upon to acquiesce in such useless and costly machinery.[118]

The signal tone of the *Irish Tribune* was disillusion. It folded in December 1926, after appearing weekly since 12 March of that year, without any notice to its readership that its publication would cease. The *Irish Tribune* had faltered in its attempt to create a viable alternative to the *Irish Statesman* after Byrne's dismissal. But the *Irish Statesman* held all the advantages that the *Irish Tribune* was denied: a base in Dublin and intimate contact with a range of Free State Ministers, TDs and Senators.[119] The *Irish Statesman* was edited by an internationally recognised writer and supported by an excellent assistant editor in James Good. Its one weakness was the continuation of funding from its American donors. Literary journals never pay their way. The American committee members of the *Irish Statesman* were ever more reluctant to fund a journal that ran constant losses.[120] An increase in sales required increase in advertisement, the cost of which could not be borne lightly. As it was, areas peripheral to the cap-

---

114 'Week by week', *Irish Tribune*, 14 May 1926. 5.   **115** Ibid.   **116** J.J. Lee, *Ireland*. 119.   **117** 'Week by week', *Irish Tribune*, 22 Oct. 1926. 7.   **118** Ibid.   **119** Apart from Eoin MacNeill's contributions to the *Irish Statesman* in October 1925, the journal also received letters from the independent unionist deputy Bryan Cooper (see *IS*, 12 Dec. 1925), of whom Lennox Robinson later wrote a biography. See too the periodic articles from Senator James Douglas (for example his 'Notes on proceedings in dominion parliaments', *IS*, 16 Jan. 1926. 586–7.)   **120** The *Irish Statesman* suffered a trading loss of £3,366 in its first year and £2,844 in its second. The journal had

ital sold few copies, partly due to poor distribution. Percy Gillespie reported that the *Irish Statesman*'s northern canvasser found 'only one copy per week is sold in the town of Letterkenny, only two in Buncrana, in Strabane not a single copy, though Eason's stall at the railway there sells three per week!'[121]

The years that followed offered new challenges to the *Irish Statesman* and its editor as the Free State evolved beyond the immediate post-revolutionary period. Fianna Fáil took their seats in the Dáil for the first time on 11 August 1927 to face a Cumann na nGaedheal administration on the defensive and shocked by the July assassination of Kevin O'Higgins. After a second election in September 1927 the Dáil was near evenly split between the two main parties.[122] Coincident with this radical change in the political landscape, the debate over literary censorship erupted into bitter controversy. Censorship then became the motion over which the *Irish Statesman* redefined its agenda a last time before it ceased publication in 1930.

£5,300 capital in its account at the Bank of Ireland at the end of its second year of publication. Correspondence between Horace Plunkett and Judge Campbell shows the tensions between the two parties. The American contributors were prepared to fulfil their initial syndicate agreement of £10,000 in the third year of the *Irish Statesman*'s publication, but no further. See Horace Plunkett to Judge Campbell, 13 Oct. 1925, IRS 35/1, Percy Gillespie to Horace Plunkett, 15 Oct. 1925, IRS 41/1, and Horace Plunkett to Percy Gillespie, 26 Mar. 1926, IRS 50, PF. **121** Percy Gillespie to Horace Plunkett, 15 Oct. 1925, PF ms IRS 41/1. **122** Richard Dunphy notes of the September 1927 election that both parties 'had secured substantial increases in their vote, eating into the middle ground'. But this fact 'should not lead us to conceive wrongly that the balance of forces was potentially favourable to both; Fianna Fáil was on the offensive, conquering new ground, Cumann na nGaedheal was on the defensive, absorbing its old allies'. *The making of Fianna Fáil power in Ireland*. 133.

7 / The enemy: 1927–30

The final three years of the 1920s saw Cumann na nGaedheal come under increasing political pressure. With the foundation of Fianna Fáil and the entrance of republican deputies into the Dáil, the pro-Treaty parties for the first time faced an organised and capable parliamentary opponent. Used to a degree of latitude in their legislative actions due to the numerical weakness of their previous opposition, Cumann na nGaedheal reacted to Fianna Fáil with panic.[1] The republican party's strength was perceived to be its popular idealism, and the Censorship Bill can be understood at least in part as a government attempt to introduce radical legislation to recover political momentum. By introducing the Bill, however, the government risked alienating part of its previous constituency. The government's courtship of a rural, Catholic populace was anathema to the *Irish Statesman*, a journal whose readership was more likely to be middle class, liberal-minded and urban. As the bishops preached self-abnegation, the *Irish Statesman* advertised golf equipment and foreign travel, hardly the stuff of nationalist orthodoxy.

Russell believed that official acknowledgement of the Literary Revival's national importance was key to the state's foundation. The government's introduction of the Censorship Bill in 1928 upset Russell's assumption of official sympathy as legislative regulation of literature threatened his coterie's critical authority. Russell attacked censorship on the grounds that his Irish literary project alone was responsible for the cultivation of moral order in the post-nation state. That the republicans' return coincided nearly exactly with the murder of Kevin O'Higgins, a close friend of Horace Plunkett, only increased his anxiety.[2] James Good, assistant editor of the *Irish Statesman* and columnist in the *New*

1 To his credit, Percy Gillespie, business manager for the *Irish Statesman*, saw his chance. In a 15 June 1927 appeal to H.F. Norman for more IAOS advertisement in the journal, he 'remarked that the present Election was fought in the advertising columns of the newspapers, and who doubts that Fianna Fail were in this respect the more clever propagandists? The point however that I wish to make is that a propagandist and advertising body is taking a <u>big risk</u> as to success if it <u>completely ignores</u> press propaganda.' H.F. Norman papers, PF ms NOR 13. 2 Plunkett recorded regular, and familiar contact with O'Higgins, the Vice President of the Executive Council and Minister for Justice, in his diary throughout the mid 1920s. After dinner on 31 August 1925, Plunkett praised O'Higgins' 'high order of intelligence'. They met again for conversation at the Plunkett Foundation on 1 November 1926. Plunkett diaries.

Statesman, sensed that the Censorship Bill was a government attempt to out-manoeuvre Fianna Fáil.[3] Such a Bill offered the Free State government an opportunity to reclaim the radical political tradition that Fianna Fáil threatened to appropriate.[4] The slight to the *Irish Statesman* that this departure involved was not lost upon its editors. Ever perceptive, Good noted in the *New Statesman* that the Bill's first draft was published on the day that the recipients of the literary awards were announced at the 1928 Tailteann games.[5]

In these, Yeats was recognised for his achievement in *The tower*, Shaw for *St Joan* and Father Dineen for his Irish language dictionary. That Yeats and Shaw were two of the most prominent Irish writers to voice their opposition to the censorship in the *Irish Statesman* is further evidence of the intimate nature of the controversy. Good interpreted the simultaneous publication of government and Tailteann proclamations to be significant of a shift in Cumann na nGaedheal thinking. He wrote of the Tailteann games that

> Most of the Irish writers have worked hard to achieve its success, and some of them flattered themselves that it might serve as the nucleus of an Irish Academy of Letters. This project, which had advanced so far that negotiations were in progress to induce the Free State Government to accord recognition to a representative body of creative literary artists, had been blown sky-high by the Censorship of Publications Bill.[6]

The loss of administrative support for a proposed literary academy was of course significant of more than a lack of government imagination. A split between political and aesthetic considerations in the practice of independent statehood was, to Russell, disastrous. By robbing his voice of authority, the state left a void to be filled by the clamour of an under-educated mob. His detractors' general lack of cultivation made them amenable to subversion and the

3 Good suggested that 'The fear of the Government is not that they have gone too far, but that when the Bill comes before the Dail next month Fianna Fail may strive to score at their expense by insisting that the screw has not been tightened sufficiently'. 'The Free State censorship', *NS*, 1 September 1928. 132.   4 Good, again, caught the wider mood in his record in the *New Statesman* of a popular air: 'One widely circulated ballad thus describes the Cumann na nGaedheal candidates: Once I pictured John Bull as a knave and a liar./ But never, no never will do so again;/ Garryowen is a tune that I used to admire,/ But 'God Save the King' has a greater refrain!/ I will pull down the structure by Griffith erected,/ Uproot the foundations and alter the plan;/ Nor rub shoulders with those with foul treason infected,/ Live rich and respected – a practical man'. 'Free State elections', *NS*, 28 May 1927. 206–7.   5 The Tailteann games were first held in the second millennium before Christ. They were resumed, in 1924, 1928 and 1932, after an eight-century break by the Irish Free State to celebrate independence. Besides athletic competitions the games included literary sections whose most prestigious judge was Yeats. Stephen MacKenna, James Stephens and Oliver Gogarty were the first recipients of the Aonach Tailteann literary awards in the late summer of 1924.   6 J.W. Good, 'The Free State censorship', *NS*, 1 September 1928. 632.

effects of political manipulation. In rhetoric reminiscent of that used against republicans during the civil war, Russell asserted his authority by stressing that the study of literature was a professional practice, open only to its initiates. His opponents were accordingly a 'group of fanatics incapable of exercising a critical spirit about literature and shouting vociferously about books whose purpose they are incapable of understanding'.[7]

Russell's ability to use the *Irish Statesman* as a forum in which to criticise government policy is symbolic of the institutional influence at his command. Far from being the isolated and unread voice of intellectual opinion, the *Irish Statesman* was an instrument of cultivated judgement, enjoying an educated and well-connected readership. Even if there were doubts as to the devotion of the journal's readers, the list of benefactors to the *Irish Statesman* in 1929 is a formidable collection of Free State luminaries.[8] Russell's political orthodoxy rested on his belief that cultural institutions could influence state development. Intellectuals were guardians of the national faith and any attack made on their integrity was equally an attack on the state tradition. To Russell the equation was simple, if arcane:

> Let beauty fade, and in some mysterious way, public spirit, sacrifice, enthusiasm, also vanish from society. Its foundations of its morale have been obstructed. If we destroyed in Ireland our National Gallery, our Abbey Theatre, our Feis Ceoil, and our poetic and imaginative literature, the agencies by which the mysterious element of beauty filters into national consciousness, we are certain that in fifty years the nation would be corrupt or dead.[9]

Russell's appeal was made to a government well aware of the propaganda value of Ireland's literature to the state's international status. The institutions that Russell lists in the above passage are 'agencies'[10] able to popularise concepts of Irish political identity. Indeed organisations like the Abbey Theatre were important enough to the function of the Free State to receive official financial patronage. Furthermore, a Cumann na nGaedheal government that included such able media manipulators as Desmond Fitzgerald could not be slow to realise the damage that a rebellion by Irish writers might cause.[11] The government's pre-

7 G. Russell, 'A censorship over literature', *IS*, 12 February 1927. 543. 8 The *Irish Statesman* encountered severe financial difficulties in its defence of a libel action in 1928 arising from a November 1927 review of a collection of Irish songs by Seamus Clandillon. Contributors to a defence fund for the journal included Osborn Bergin, Thomas Bodkin, Lady Gregory, Senator S.L. Brown, K.C., the marquis of Landsdowne and Senator Jameson. See *IS*, 19 January 1929. 398. 9 G. Russell, 'Art and national life', *IS*, 21 May 1928. 227. 10 Ibid. 11 George Morrison's afterword to *The Irish civil war*, a collection of photographs and text, notes of 1922 that 'The Sinn Fein Party's Director of Publicity, Desmond Fitzgerald ... was one of Ireland's earliest media men with

dicament in 1928 can be recognised by the fact that ministers were willing to take this risk regardless of the consequences. What Cumann na nGaedheal did not appreciate was the degree to which Russell imagined the executive powers of the state to be coterminous with the operations of the nation's creative intellects. The collapse of negotiations over the funding of a proposed academy of letters is typical of the misunderstanding between the government and the intellectual coterie surrounding Russell that resulted in the bitterness of debate over the Censorship Bill.

In 1922 the Irish Free State adopted the entire body of British common law.[12] There was no difference between Irish and British legislation on the control of obscene literature in the immediate post-Treaty phase. The first divergence was the Censorship of Films Act in 1923. The censorship of printed matter was in one sense the next logical step for the Free State government to make, but it should be noted that such legislation was aimed specifically at popular entertainment, rather than literature or art. Neither was censorship simply a subject for debate in the Dáil. A number of religious organisations involved themselves in the agitation for stricter moral control of newspapers and books, among them the Irish Vigilance Association and the Catholic Truth Society. Determined to regularise the state's approach to the censorship of printed matter, the government instituted a Committee of Enquiry on Evil Literature in 1926. Its report was delivered to the government in December of that year and its details published in the spring following. This document formed the basis of the Censorship Bill first published on 13 August 1928.

The Bill was first referred to in the *Irish Statesman* on the eighteenth of that month, leaving the journal six weeks to respond to deputies and public opinion before the Dáil resumed sitting in October. In his first report Russell was moved to admit of the Bill 'that we do not like it, that there are provisions in it that by obscurity of wording may lead to grave interference with liberty of thought'.[13] The *Irish Statesman* further questioned 'the wisdom of these "recognised associations"'[14] referred to in the Bill. Such associations were a legacy of the report of the 1926 Committee on Evil Literature and described organised groups of concerned citizens. Each association was able under the terms of the draft Bill to refer offensive or indecent publications to the Minister for Justice. Such publi-

a real appreciation of the importance of photographs in communications'. 782. Fitzgerald was a Cumann na nGaedheal minister in 1928. Furthermore, the government was so anxious about Fianna Fáil's efforts to raise funds for a party paper, the *Nation*, in America that it despatched Cosgrave to publicise the Free State. Conveniently, Cosgrave attended a joint reception for himself and, ironically, Russell. Russell then spoke on the President's behalf to this meeting of the Foreign Policy Association. For a brief account see H. Summerfield, *That myriad-minded man*. 243. **12** A record of the Free State censorship's legislative genesis can be read in M. Adams, *Censorship: the Irish experience*. **13** 'N&C', *IS*, 18 August 1928. 464. **14** Ibid.

cations could then be censored if necessary. Russell had by this early stage identified his two main objections to the Censorship Bill. The first was against its
imprecise wording, with the possibility that censorship might become more
indiscriminately applied by a subsequent administration than its then contemporary supporters envisaged. The second was that the recognition of associations
of concerned citizens, unlicensed except by virtue of their collective morality,
threatened individual liberty.

It will be noticed however that both these objections revolve around the
same preoccupation, that of control. For Russell was not an advocate of unfet-
tered free speech. During the civil war Russell made little mention of the regular suppression of the republican press.[15] Equally, the *Irish Statesman* was itself
susceptible to a form of censorship from its American investors, the critic
Ernest Boyd himself unable to become the journal's American correspondent
because of their influence.[16] What Russell is concerned with in his criticism of
the Free State censorship is less the freedom of speech than with the method of
its control. Russell refers to the criminal law as the appropriate method of censorship as its authority rests in a system that, if not impartial, is at least accessible. Legality affords Russell a critical ally in his attack on the Censorship Bill as
its rulings are based on precise renderings of the written word. In this area
above all Russell could function at an advantage to his adversaries. It is no coincidence that the phrase the *Irish Statesman* most often uses to refer to recognised associations is 'semi-literates'. To label these groups with such a tag is to
associate them with the mob and identify them as enemies of a state dependant
on legal precedent and formal association for its very existence. One need only
think of the Anglo-Irish Treaty itself, and the battles fought over it, to realise
the implicit rhetorical power of Russell's legalistic strategy.

Russell invoked a fear of revolution throughout his articles on the
Censorship Bill in late August and September of 1928. The main text by which
he expressed his discontent was the leader of 25 August, 'The Censorship Bill'.
Russell asked of the recognised associations if they were 'associations of intelligent and cultivated men? Or are they associations of fanatics, the associations
which have been clamouring for a censorship and seizing and burning excellent
journals like the *Observer* and *Sunday Times*?'[17] Both these latter publications

---

15 The republican press was regularly suppressed during the civil war. The Free State registered
its antipathy towards republican propagandists in the execution of Erskine Childers, republican
director of publicity. It should be noted that Russell was one of many individuals to press for lenien-
cy for the unfortunate Childers. It should also be noted that Sean O'Faolain briefly succeeded
Childers in his post, a preparation of sorts for his submissions to the *Irish Statesman*. **16** Russell
wrote to Boyd in August 1925: 'I thought of you long ago as an American correspondent. I had suggested it to Plunkett and between ourselves he was alarmed lest your radicalism might upset the
Americans who contributed the funds to start the Irish Statesman and from whom he hopes to get
more'. A. Denson, ed., *Letters of Æ*. 168. **17** G. Russell, 'The Censorship Bill', *IS*, 25 August 1928.

were illegally destroyed because of their publication of information on birth control. Russell does not mention this qualification but rather concentrates on the fact that:

> We have to be very precise in our definitions. There are thousands of books we read without approving of the ideas. But a disapproval to lead to suppression – that would be revolutionary. Men would conspire against the orthodoxies of opinion the State would impose upon them.[18]

Russell's identification with the state through the prefix 'we' is significant. Russell, and by extension the *Irish Statesman*, is the voice of authority, responsible not only for the moral state of the general public but actively engaged in the moulding of its national consciousness. Russell's greatest fear since independence was the anarchy that might result from the separation of the creative intellect from state power. To Russell, both formations have a shared responsibility to act on behalf of a population that is incapable of self-regulation. The Censorship Bill is an intrusion into this shared nexus, an unwelcome revelation, and indeed repudiation, of the mutual understanding that was previously held to exist between the *Irish Statesman* and certain sections of Cumann na nGaedheal. Accordingly, Russell reserves his sharpest criticism for the functionaries who would replace him as official censors. He felt their situation would be 'very unhappy – their intelligence made transparent to the world'.[19] 'We wonder', he wrote, 'what kind of people will have courage to go upon the Board to supervise the reading of their betters?'[20] September ended in disillusion for Russell, as he feared that the Dáil would ratify the Censorship Bill with little opposition, with Fianna Fáil, the party that had pressed for a quick introduction of censorship throughout 1928, only worsening its terms. 'We confess', he wrote, that 'we have not much hope of modification, for the Opposition in the Dail, so far as we can judge by the utterance of their leaders, are upon this point more illiberal than Ministers who introduce the Bill'.[21]

Seeking to prevent a rout, Russell published an inflammatory article by Yeats in the *Irish Statesman*, fiercely critical of the censorship. Yeats' article was a clear attempt to destabilise the Bill before it reached the Dáil. The government was at pains throughout the entire debate to stress that the censorship was entirely non-sectarian in nature. This position was difficult to maintain, especially after the Lenten pastorals of 1928, vigorous in their dismissal of all immoral forms of public expression. The publication of the Censorship Bill also coincided with a Free State census that showed a huge decline in the Protestant population of the twenty-six southern counties since 1911.[22] While the government tried to

487.   **18** Ibid.   **19** 'N&C', *IS*, 1 September 1929. 505.   **20** Ibid.   **21** G. Russell, 'Freedom and coercion', *IS*, 8 September 1928. 6.   **22** The *Irish Statesman* reported that the third volume of the

present the censorship as the expression of a homogenous public morality, Russell published Yeats's article, 'The Censorship of Publications Bill', to embarrass the Government over the religious aspects of its legislation.

Yeats obliged Russell by referring initially to the definition of 'indecency' offered as the standard for censorship by the government. Yeats noted that the Bill declared 'in its introductory section that "the word 'indecent' shall be construed as including 'calculated to excite sexual passion'"'.[23] Yeats was further 'convinced that this definition ridiculous to a man of letters, must be sacrilegious to a Thomist. I cannot understand how Catholic lawyers, trained in precision of statement and ecclesiastics, could have committed such a blunder.'[24] Yeats' appreciation of the finer points of Catholic dogma is less the point than is his sly ability to introduce religious dissension into the debate. The Minister for Justice, Fitzgerald-Kenney, was himself a lawyer and Yeats' attack was personal enough for the minister to take sarcastic note of it in his introduction of the Bill to the Dáil on 18 October 1928:

> One gentleman of very high literary ability, whose only fault as a literary man is, I think, that he does not write enough, and who has a great store of personal information, has attacked this definition … on the grounds that the words 'calculated to excite sexual passion' are entirely heretical. I would point to venture out that I, personally, can hardly follow the criticism which has been passed upon the use of these three words in this definition, because I cannot understand the class of book which would excite some person just to proper love and might not excite others towards unlawful lust.[25]

Russell had in the meantime capitalised on Yeats' article by subsequently publishing Padraic Colum's religious criticisms of the Bill. Just five days before Fitzgerald-Kenney made his above remarks to the Dáil, Colum predicted that a censorship would expose the religious authorities to 'resentment and mockery'.[26] The censorship would result in the 'moment that countries predominantly Catholic have most to fear – an anti-clerical movement. This means a division of the people deeper than any division we know of.'[27] By publishing two separate criticisms of the Censorship Bill for its exercise of religious prerogative, Russell hoped to create as much controversy about the Bill as possible. But

Free State census of population showed that 'From 1911 to 1926 the Catholic population in the Free State declined by 2.2 per cent, the Jews by 3.1 per cent, while the various Protestant denominations … declined by 32.5 per cent. There were 103,000 fewer Protestants in the Free State than in 1911.' 'N&C', *IS*, 23 February 1929. 487. **23** W.B. Yeats, 'The censorship and Thomas Aquinas', *IS*, 22 September 1928. 47. **24** Ibid. **25** Dáil debates vol. 26, 18 Oct. 1928. 596–7. **26** M. Lyster, 'Padraic Colum on the censorship', *IS*, 13 October 1928. 107. **27** Ibid. **28** 'N&C',

behind this propaganda screen there was offered simultaneously to the government the possibility of the *Irish Statesman*'s adoption of a more moderate
approach to censorship. For in the very same issue that Colum predicted religious catastrophe, the journal noted that since 'a censorship in some form
seems inevitable, we think there should be concentration upon the amendments
of the most indefensible clauses'.[28] The editor's sanguine tone is in sharp contrast to Colum's depression at the thought of mass religious dissociation. The
ethics of utilising religious controversy to make one's political point are dubious but the publication of Yeats and Colum in debates on this matter were effective enough to ensure that the minister responsible for the Bill had personally
to reply to their criticisms in the Dáil.

The Minister for Justice was surprised at the anger that his Bill aroused. He
imagined perhaps that Russell and his associates would realise that they were,
by virtue of their status, practically immune to the effects of the proposed censorship's prohibitions.[29] The minister specifically remarked that the Bill 'has
been attacked ... by extremists, demonising it as an unwarrantable infringement
on the liberty of the subject and of the rights of free citizenship'.[30] The *Irish
Statesman* was quick to respond to the minister's criticism by replying the following week that:

> Our protest was made because of the kind of literature attacked by the
> fanatical reformers and the recognition given by the Bill to associations
> which were not content to attack the baser sort of journal, which
> destroyed books by great writers who had never been regarded as inde-
> cent, books which could only have been burned because of philosophi-
> cal or economic or religious ideas which were not those of the reform-
> ers. To permit this to go on would represent a grave danger to the intel-
> lectual life of the Free State.[31]

The conciliatory tone of the above passage is matched the following week by
the appearance of a new series of articles in the *Irish Statesman*, published under
the title 'As others see us'. Essentially a propaganda vehicle for the journal's

IS, 12 October 1928. 103.   **29** The minister made great effort in the Dáil to separate the functions
of the Bill from that of a draconian literary censorship. He cited a number of texts to make his case,
not altogether convincingly. Thackeray's *Vanity fair* would be ignored, despite the fact that the character Becky Sharp was not 'entirely a moral woman'. 598. *Othello* too was immune, despite some 'very
objectionable expressions'. 598. The Minister continued 'In a famous modern book of verse – "The
Shropshire Lad" – there is a poem which ... advocates suicide. It would not come under that definition of "contrary to public morality" because it would be entirely different from what this Bill is actually dealing with. This Bill deals solely with questions of sexual morality or sexual perversion.' 602.
Dáil debates vol. 26, 18 October 1928.   **30** Dáil debates, vol. 26, 18 October 1928. 594.   **31** 'The
debate on the censorship', *IS*, 27 October 1928. 146.

opposition to the Bill, the subject of the first instalment of 'As others see us', a series of interviews conducted by Russell's French confidant Simone Téry,[32] was the President himself, William Cosgrave. A blunt and none too subtle reminder of the public projection of the government that the *Irish Statesman* could make, the next interview was with the Minister for Agriculture and personal favourite of Horace Plunkett, Patrick Hogan.[33] This panegyric labelled the Minister as 'the hardest working member of the Cabinet'[34] and continued the praise that the *Irish Statesman* had reserved for Hogan since his appointment. As Minister for Agriculture, Hogan was often congratulated in the journal for his appreciation of Horace Plunkett's co-operative ideals. As Hogan's Agricultural Bill passed the Dáil without division in 1927, for example, the *Irish Statesman* noted with pleasure that 'It is by the proper co-ordination of State aid and voluntary organisation, as Sir Horace Plunkett said, that our agriculture would become prosperous. That co-operation he desired is now becoming a reality'.[35]

Russell's strategy was to split the Cumann na nGaedheal cabinet over the question of censorship. Hogan's interview with Téry was published the very week that Hogan resumed debate over the second stage of the Censorship Bill to the Dáil.[36] Russell's policy had some effect as the Minister stated to the assembly that the Bill should instate 'a censorship which is limited in the most stringent and specific way'.[37] Like Russell in the *Irish Statesman*, Hogan felt that it would be 'extremely difficult [in this country] to get anyone … fit to censor books'.[38] Having offered these provisions the Minister went on to deliver a witty and savage attack on the morality of the opposition Fianna Fáil party, questioning their ability to perceive the truth of an argument after their abandonment of principle to enter the Dáil.[39] Hogan's sally was a public attempt to obscure the divisions that Russell so clearly perceived to exist within the government party. As the *Irish Statesman* noted the next week, Hogan was one of

32 Téry's friendship with Russell dated from her experience as a journalist in the Irish civil war. She later authored *The island of poets* which contained a section on Russell. Russell can be found writing warmly of Téry in a letter to L.R. Bernstein of February 1929. See A. Denson, ed., *Letters of Æ*. 181.   **33** Plunkett met Hogan regularly throughout 1928. Plunkett discussed agriculture with Hogan the same day, 16 October 1928, that he lunched with John Healy to discuss 'the last flicker of the RC Church, Censorship Bill and compulsory Irish. I ought to be in the fight.' It seems hard to believe his enthusiasms were not transmitted to Hogan, the man whom Plunkett thought 'the best agricultural Minister in Europe'. Plunkett diaries.   **34** S. Téry, 'As others see us IV – Interview with Patrick Hogan and other Ministers', *IS*, 27 October 1928. 147.   **35** 'N&C', *IS*, 29 October 1928. 172.   **36** It is speculation to suggest that the government picked Hogan to introduce the resumed second reading of the Censorship Bill to the Dáil to appease its literary critics. What is certain is that Hogan had before this date taken no previous part in Dáil debates on censorship.   **37** Dáil debates vol. 26, 24 October 1928. 830.   **38** Ibid. 829.   **39** Hogan was possessed of a sharp wit: 'I listened to this debate very carefully. We were all very virtuous and anxious to make the other fellow virtuous … I suppose the next time we are taking an oath we will call it an empty formula and push the bible two feet away.' Dáil debates vol. 26, 24 October 1928. 830.

the ministers who listened to the Minister for Justice's ensuing speech in 'a scornful silence'.[40] Satisfied that he could embarrass the government by pursuing such tactics, Russell consistently vilified Fitzgerald-Kenney in the following months for his inability to construct a suitable censorship. The Minister for Justice was unfortunate in his enemy as Russell's derision marked Fitzgerald-Kenney off from the support more generally offered Cumann na nGaedheal by the *Irish Statesman*.

Russell was not foolish enough to imagine that his journal enjoyed a popular support strong enough to disable the censorship. What he managed to do was to identify individual elements within the government, isolate them, then reduce their personal authority. This tactic suited perfectly Russell's growing belief that ministers were themselves conduits for a new Irish identity, prompted by independence to an appreciation of state efficiency. Russell noted previously in 1927 that 'The tendency to bring about an organic unity in the national being has become the most noticeable thing in the Free State'.[41] Further to this, Russell observed that 'Atoms or cells seem to be modelled by some overwhelming instinct which imposes its law upon them. It operates primarily through Ministers.'[42] Russell reifies the function of elected representatives to a paradigm of general order. The *Irish Statesman*'s cultivation of Hogan, the Minister for Agriculture, is indicative of Russell's understanding that the government is the proper conduit for the dissemination of Russell's own ideals. This in turn modifies the understanding Russell had of democratic government, as electors choose only the means by which they will be ordered rather than the means by which order might be changed. In this complex, the Minister for Justice's recommendation in the Censorship Bill that certain associations of lay people be recognised as the first implements of a state censorship is anathema to Russell's belief that regulation should be the preserve of an enlightened elite. Russell's opposition to censorship once again reverts to his disagreement with the Minister for Justice over the means by which media control is to be exercised. Russell's concern over the Censorship Bill's deregulation of state authority to recognised associations was then symptomatic of his broad concern that cultural authority might pass from the directors of the Literary Revival.

As the Censorship Bill progressed through the Dáil, Russell kept pressure on the Minister for Justice by publishing a further attack on it by George Bernard Shaw on 19 November. This was the first major article that Shaw had contributed to the *Irish Statesman* since its first issue in September 1923. Shaw himself had followed a personal interest in the operation of state censorship since the first decade of the twentieth century. Called before a joint committee of the

40 'N&C', *IS*, 3 November 1928. 163.   **41** G. Russell, 'The dominating idea', *IS*, 9 April 1927. 107.   **42** Ibid. 107.

British parliament in 1909, Shaw, like Russell later in the *Irish Statesman*, argued that censorship must only be exercised under the due process of law. Censorship of drama was at the prerogative of the Lord Chancellor and Shaw found it unfair that this official had 'absolutely at his disposal my livelihood and my good name without any law to administer behind him'.[43]

One of Shaw's interrogators in this committee was Hugh Law, one time Lord Chancellor of Ireland. Law's son became a Free State deputy and spoke against the censorship in the Dáil in 1928. The younger Law was also a close associate of Russell, who wrote the preface to Law's 1926 study, *Anglo-Irish literature*. Speaking in the Dáil, this latter Hugh Law informed the Minister for Justice that he had made it his 'business' to consult about the censorship 'a great number of people … including writers, a body which I am myself a very modest, humble member'.[44] Since Law had often contributed to the *Irish Statesman*, the inference is that Law speaks with knowledge of Russell's opinion on the subject. More than that, his associations suggest the degree to which Russell, through figures like Hogan and Law, was able to exert pressure on the Dáil by virtue of having access to members sympathetic to his ideas.

Russell meanwhile pressured the government from the pages of the *Irish Statesman* by his publication, in November, of Shaw's essay. Shaw first appealed to the Catholic church to distance itself from the Bill, if only to reassure the Protestant north. Shaw, like Colum, predicted that if this did not happen, a clerical backlash would follow, because 'when all these monstrous follies are being perpetuated by way of purifying Ireland the Church will be blamed for it. Already it is said on all hands that the Censorship Bill is the Church's doing'.[45] Shaw finished by suggesting that if Ireland

> having broken England's grip on her … slips back into the Atlantic as a little grass patch in which a few million moral cowards are not allowed to call their souls their own by a handful of morbid Catholics, mad with heresyphobia, unnaturally combining with a handful of Calvinists mad with sexphobia (both being in a small and intensely disliked minority of their own co-religionists) then the world will let 'these Irish' go their own way into insignificance without the slightest concern. It will no longer even tell funny stories about them.[46]

This passage marks a critical point in the *Irish Statesman*'s response to censorship. Shaw's rhetorical geography consists of a world whose first boundary is England and whose mass is the civilisation of Europe beyond it. The image of

43 G.B. Shaw, *Shaw on censorship*. 4. This was a Fabian pamphlet produced to publicise Shaw's criticisms of British theatre censorship.   **44** H.A. Law, Dáil debates vol. 26, 18 October 1928. 621.   **45** G.B. Shaw, 'The censorship', *IS*, 17 November 1928. 207.   **46** Ibid. 208.

Ireland slipping back into the Atlantic, lost beneath a wave of religious dogma, is a powerful one. But it is also the product of a political sleight of hand, as Shaw takes onto himself the voice of arbiter between the Irish nation and the outside world. States operate by treaties and association, the Free State itself having taken an important role in the League of Nations by the time Shaw's article was written.[47] Furthermore, the *Irish Statesman* was aware of the influx of outside capital into the Free State, the journal peppered throughout this period by adverts from the American oil company Texaco.[48] Each advertisement celebrated the arrival of this multinational conglomerate in the Free State by angular diagrams of sophisticated machinery and reports of new flight records set by aeroplanes using Texaco fuel. The *Irish Statesman*'s readership was also well aware that Ireland was in no danger of economic isolationism under the administration of Cumann na nGaedheal, not least because of the favourable and regular reports that the Ford factory in Cork received in the journal's pages.[49]

Shaw proposes a myth of Free State regression. It is a myth created to empower Shaw, and writers like him, with a prophetic voice by which to influence the politics of a state within which writers had as yet found no formal place. Shaw derided a nation for its inadequacy, when in fact the nation's transition to statehood already made such criticism anachronistic. Shaw's article is a masterful piece of polemical writing but it fails on one critical point. It reads, in context of the adverts for Texaco petrol and Ford tractors, as out of date, an echo without substance.

The proof of Shaw's irrelevance is that Russell, after the publication of Shaw's article, committed his energy to lobbying for change to the Censorship Bill rather than to Shaw's demand for its complete dismissal. In this Russell was successful. To follow the progress of the Censorship Bill through the Dáil between October 1928 and March 1929 is to notice that the areas of the Bill which were most contested were those brought to public attention by the *Irish Statesman*. There were now three specific problem areas for Russell. The first was the definition of indecency. As Russell noted in the *Irish Statesman*, the

47 The Irish Free State was admitted to the League of Nations on 10 September 1923. Michael Kennedy discerns a development of Free State foreign policy in the following period. He suggests that from 1926, 'External affairs were beginning to signify more than Anglo-Irish affairs. The stance taken at the Assembly and the Council elections was European and international.' 91. Furthermore, 'the League's work drew Ireland's diplomats out of the Anglo-Irish core that represented Irish foreign policy since the 1921 Treaty. They were moving in the European as well as the Commonwealth mainstream'. 120. *Ireland and the League of Nations, 1919–1946*. **48** The banner headline 'Texaco is coming' appears above a map of Ireland connected to an oncoming ship by bolts of lightning in the *IS*, 8 December 1928, and *IS*, 15 December 1928. **49** Under the subtitle 'Advance Cork' the *Irish Statesman* noted that the Ford factory was due to increase its production from 40 to 150 units a day, making it 'the biggest single industry in the Saorstat'. 'N&C', *IS*, 3 August 1929. 425.

problem might arise from a broad definition of the term that a secular theory such as evolution might be banned from schools, as it had been in parts of the United States.[50] The second was the power of private associations to refer obscene literature to the Minister for Justice. Finally, Russell was concerned over the number of censors to be elected to the board, primarily because he felt, like Milton before him, that since so few would be qualified to judge, it would be difficult to appoint worthy candidates.[51] On the first point, Russell was reassured by the time the Bill passed through the Dáil. The *Irish Statesman* accepted the Minister's assurances that the Bill would be applied sparingly to literature. Its assistant editor, James Good, reported in the *New Statesman* that 'it is expected that books will be handled cautiously, with the exception of birth-control literature, which is to be automatically banned without reference to the Censorship Board'.[52]

Russell's support of this aspect of the Bill's most draconian provision is interesting, especially in context of Oliver St John Gogarty's submissions to the Senate on the matter. Russell had long favoured Gogarty, and Yeats made him a poetry award at the 1924 Tailteann games.[53] Gogarty published frequently in the *Irish Statesman* throughout the latter part of the 1920s, even going to the length of conducting personal exchanges with Russell through poetry.[54] Crucially for Russell, Gogarty had also been a Senator since 1922. Gogarty used his position in the Senate to support his associates' attacks on the censorship. Gogarty, like Russell, fiercely denounced aspects of the Censorship Bill that affected creative literature but was, again like Russell, more circumspect when the question of birth control arose:

> No one who has any care for a nation's welfare can for one moment countenance contraceptive practices, which are a contradiction of a nation's life. In England the condition of the miners and the unemployed

50 The schoolteacher John Stopes was convicted in Tennessee in 1925 of teaching evolution in what was sometimes referred to as the 'monkey trial'. The state law that banned the teaching of evolution was not revoked until 1968.　**51** Milton's *Areopagitica* is a classic anti-censorship text. In it Milton argues that 'he who is made judge to sit upon the birth or death of books, whether they may be wafted into the world or not, had need to be a man above the common measure, both studious, learned, and judicious; there may be else no mean mistakes in the censure of what is passible or not, which is also no mean injury'. 27–8. In the Free State, the Senate revised the Dáil's proposed membership of the censorship board from nine to five. The *Irish Statesman* responded to this in 'N&C', *IS*, 4 May 1929. 163–6.　**52** J.W. Good, 'Comments', *NS*, 30 March 1929. 783.　**53** Ulick O'Connor notes that Gogarty won 'the Tailteann gold medal for poetry, for his book *An Offering of Swans*. The week following, Yeats crowned Gogarty with a wreath of bay leaves at a meeting of the Royal Irish Academy, in recognition of his feat.' *Oliver St. John Gogarty*. 214.　**54** For evidence of this mutual indulgence see Russell's 'To G.R. and O.G.', *IS*, 13 August 1927, and Gogarty's 'To Æ going to America', *IS*, 21 January 1928. 457. The 'G.R.' of Russell's poem is Graeme Roberts, the contributor of a poem called 'Mountain' to the same issue.

is as it is because England has allowed its capital to go into yellow, brown and black labour, so that the Government tolerates clinics for education in the practice of contraception.[55]

A diagnosis of Gogarty's racism is suggestive of the dubious assumptions that underpin his subsequent opposition to a literary censorship. Gogarty, Russell and Yeats all shared the idea that the cultivated could be trusted to read even the most morally doubtful texts. What is interesting in Gogarty's speech is the way in which the shared assumption of national purification is made explicit by his discussion of birth control, an illiberality that is concealed by the rhetoric of detached criticism when he refers to literature. It is hard not to draw the conclusion that many of the opponents to the Censorship Bill were, like Gogarty, motivated to their defence of free speech by a reactionary desire to retain control of the outlets for critical debate from the power of the state.

Russell was himself most satisfied with the Dáil's rejection of the recognised associations. The 'number of Deputies, Fianna Fail, Cumann na nGaedheal and Labour', he observed, 'who resisted these proposals and defeated them was a pleasant surprise'.[56] The *Irish Statesman* now found that the 'Bill is much more reasonable in its post-Dail form than most expected who saw it in its first monstrous infancy'.[57] Russell was especially pleased about 'the amendment which swept out of the Bill the Minister's preposterous "recognised associations". This was absolutely the worst aspect of the Bill.'[58] It should be noted from Russell's praise of the Dáil as an effective democratic body able to amend the Censorship Bill, that many of the deputies who spoke most cuttingly of its weaknesses were friends of the *Irish Statesman* or associates of its editor. In the Dáil, the Bill's chief critic was William Thrift, Professor of Physics at Trinity College Dublin, and former member of the Committee on Evil Literature.[59] One of the *Irish Statesman*'s main contributors on the matter was Edmund Curtis, Professor of History at the same university. Russell was himself awarded an honorary doctorate at Trinity in July 1929, proof, if it were needed, of the private circles that represented public interest in the Free State. Furthermore, Hugh Law, as previously mentioned, spoke against the Bill, as did Bryan Cooper, an independent member of the Dáil whose unionist background did not hinder his desire to serve the new state efficiently. Cooper's letters were occasionally published in the *Irish Statesman*, and Lennox Robinson, one of the journal's directors, wrote his biography.[60]

---

55 O.St J. Gogarty, Senate debates vol. 12, 11 April 1929. 87.   56 G. Russell, 'Unrecognised associations', *IS*, 2 March 1929. 510.   57 'N&C', *IS*, 30 March 1929. 64.   58 G. Russell, 'Unrecognised associations', *IS*, 2 March 1929. 510.   59 Thrift held a University of Dublin seat in the Dáil. Unionist in politics, he was also a friend of the father of *Irish Statesman* contributor and Trinity fellow Walter Starkie. Thrift was provost of Trinity from 1937 until his death in 1942. 60 Cooper died prematurely. Robinson published his affectionate study, *Bryan Cooper*, in 1931. For

In the Senate were Gogarty, Sir James Douglas, a former speaker of the house and a director of the *Irish Statesman*, and Sir John Keane, who tried to make up for Yeats' loss to the debate by aping the poet's controversial tone from the *Irish Statesman*.[61] Russell was equally acerbic, but in private. Writing to Shaw to thank him for financial contribution to the *Irish Statesman*, he thought of the journal as a

> form of insurance which will exercise free thinking in Ireland as the une-ducated Catholic (*sic*) are becoming rather tyrannous. I have plenty of educated Catholic friends who were in terror lest the paper should stop and they worked very hard to keep it alive. They hate the censorships and the secret sectarian societies & Catholic masonry – and like me to fight their battles for them. I have been astonished to find the fierce anti-clerical spirit growing up here among the Educated Catholics. I think there will be an explosion of this within the next few years. There are so few Protestants in the State that by the nature of things an internal fis-sure in the predominant religion is necessitated.[62]

Time proved Russell wrong. But in the immediate context, Russell felt the Bill was an acceptable compromise between the state and its intellectuals. It proved to be nothing of the sort. As early as 1932, the letter of invitation to join a prospective Irish Academy of Letters stressed the need for writers to combine in opposition to it: 'our sole defence' wrote Shaw and Yeats is 'the authority of our utterance'.[63] Sean O'Faolain found his *Bird alone* banned from 1935 to 1947 and Kate O'Brien *The land of spices* banned from 1941. Other writers prescribed included James Baldwin, Ernest Hemingway, Christopher Isherwood, Marcel Proust, H.G. Wells and Emile Zola. Considering the list, it is surprising that more people did not volunteer to read for the Censorship Board. The situation improved in 1967 with Brian Lenihan's Censorship of Publications Bill. As Minister for Justice, Lenihan limited the period of prohibition for books to twelve years. Thousands of banned books came back into circulation. Today, the proliferation of electronic media offers state control a new problem.

---

examples of Cooper's letters to the *Irish Statesman* see 12 December 1925 and 10 April 1926. Cooper spoke as an independent member of the Dáil in the censorship debate of 18 October 1928, advising caution in the wording of the Bill. **61** Keane felt that 'If ex-Senator Yeats, whom we miss so much, was here to-day he would put this case more forcibly than I could'. 71. Keane saw the Censorship Bill as evidence of 'despair' on behalf of a Catholic church that did 'not have confidence in its power to control its members'. 714. It resorted to legal coercion rather than an appeal to faith. The Minister for Justice was 'sorry that questions of religion were brought into this matter'. 128. Senate debates vol. 12, April 11 1929. **62** G. Russell to G.B. Shaw, 21 February 1929. Shaw papers, BL ms 198. **63** J. Carlson, ed., *Banned in Ireland*. 7.

Russell meanwhile concentrated on developing his own vision of the future. It must be remembered in this context that the controversy over the Censorship Bill, important as it was as a test of Russell's ability to challenge an institutional threat to his own power, was in itself but part of Russell's wider programme of cultural rejuvenation. The Censorship Bill was no more than a threat to the means of production of Russell's new cultural fabric. The actual material to supply it, both textual and rhetorical, was something that Russell continued to ponder throughout this period. The editor of the *Irish Statesman* found renewed inspiration for his literary project in his review of Wyndham Lewis's polemical journal, the *Enemy*, published intermittently from 1927 to 1929. Lewis, an English intellectual and painter, had been the editor of *Blast*, the seminal modernist review and response to the Italian futurists. Russell, whose own *Irish Statesman* was intoxicated with the mechanical success of the Shannon scheme in the Free State, responded enthusiastically to Lewis' call for cultural rejuvenation in the *Enemy*. To Russell

> Those only are alive who are Futurist, who belong to that nationality of ours that is still unborn, but who see images of it lit up by the light which never yet was on sea or land ... The man who is truly alive will be original. He will invent new art forms, imagine a new psychology, a new nationality, a new social order, a new civilisation, all glittering from the mint of the living soul. It will all be shocking to the pack, but if the solitary and original have the courage to persist they will bestow beauty even on the mob.[64]

Russell's distrust of what he imagines to be an average mentality and his valorisation of the individual perspective are typical of a modernist aesthetic that is proto-fascist. Russell's criticism of the 'recognised associations' during the passage of the Censorship Bill through the Dáil can also be seen to reflect his aversion to what he terms here as the 'mob'. But the invention of an entirely new civilisation is the rhetorical flourish of a writer who hopes to achieve authority by osmosis. Instead of revolution, Russell advocates a controlled reaction to democracy. Politically, the energy of the modern artist's radical spirit is channelled through individual members of the state.

Russell's appreciation of Free State genesis is accordingly cast in terms that might be unfamiliar to more conventional students of the Anglo-Irish and civil wars. For 'Cold hard intelligence such as four or five of the Executive Council are gifted with, was needed to shape the Free State and give it its hard bony structure, its political character'.[65] Russell's insistence on terms such as 'hard'

---

64 G. Russell, 'L&L: enemies of society', *IS*, 26 March 1927. 66.   65 'N&C', *IS*, 23 April 1927.

and 'bony' reflects the influence of Lewis' rhetoric on his own perception of Irish history. The angular aesthetic of the *Enemy*, with its allusions to the remorseless progress of modernity through the development of science and art, finds a corollary in Russell's own appreciation of Free State industrial projects.[66] To Russell, the relentless pressure of the modern experience could only find its voice in turn in the engagement of Free State writers with the techniques of realism. In his review of Liam O'Flaherty's 1929 novel, *The house of gold*, Russell found

> a terrible vision of life in rural Ireland, with lust, greed and fear, supersti-
> tion instead of a soul of the people. It will enrage many who cannot bear
> to have Ireland or its people depicted for them in any other way than by
> the flattering of idealism and dream. Even to those who have more
> courage it will appear almost a nightmare of furious or ferocious emo-
> tions ... Our writers are becoming as passionate in their realism as Yeats
> and his early contemporaries were with their idealism and mysticism.[67]

Since Russell held Yeats to have been the primary voice in the successful cre-ation of a separate Irish cultural identity, his assignation to O'Flaherty of the power to divine a new perspective is significant. Russell believed that an age of realism had followed an era of idealism. O'Flaherty's insight is credited with the unveiling of this new perception of Irish life. O'Flaherty's emotions are intem-perate but Russell perceives that O'Flaherty registers through them the birth of a new order. Russell, from his reading of Flinders Petrie and, more recently, Oswald Spengler, was consumed by the idea that Europe was in decline, its cul-ture derivative and its politics emasculated.[68] O'Flaherty's wild style in *The house of gold* is alternative evidence to Russell that Ireland might still possess a pre-modern, radical culture. Writing of the Irish interest in folklore, Russell was

---

152.   **66** The *Enemy* was a collage of drawings, journalism and imaginative prose, predominantly attributed to Lewis. The first issue of the journal is prefaced by a passage from Plutarch's *Moralia* that explains its title: 'A man of understanding is to benefit by his enemies ... He that knoweth that he hath an enemy will look circumspectly about him to all matters, ordering his life and behaviour in better sort ... But forasmuch as amity and friendship nowadays speaketh with a small and low voice, and is very audible and is full of words in flattery, what remaineth but that we should hear the truth from the mouth of our enemies?' *Enemy*, 1:1, Jan. 1927. iv. Much of the journal contin-ues in this serious, portentous tone. The first issue is further remarkable for T.S. Eliot's 'A note on poetry and belief' and Lewis' illustrations. His 'Magellan' is especially striking. A black ink draw-ing of a sail ship amid a series of horizontal lines, 'Magellan' is reminiscent to a degree of the flu-idity of Umberto Boccioni's 1911 'States of mind II: those who go'. Boccioni's painting is repro-duced in C. Butler, *Early modernism: literature, music and painting in Europe 1900–1916*.   **67** G. Russell, 'Review', *IS*, 28 Sept. 1929. 76.   **68** The German language edition of Oswald Spengler's *Downfall of the west* was discussed in the *Irish Statesman* in 1926, an early recognition in the English-speaking world of its importance. See 'M.J.', 'L&L: the downfall of western civilisation', *IS*, 24 April

Quite certain that the spirit of the modern world and modern education will very soon put an end to the folk imagination and the folk memory. There is perhaps twenty-five years in which the collectors may get their harvest. After that the farmer's boy will be thinking of scientific farming and his literature will be the modern novel and the daily newspaper.[69]

To negotiate this transition, Russell directed the *Irish Statesman*'s review pages to investigate literary developments outside the Free State. December 1928 saw the journal review both Ezra Pound's *Selected poems* and Ernest Hemingway's *A farewell to arms*. Russell found Pound's writing improved from his previous work and suspected the influence of Pound's editor, T.S. Eliot, on the poet. Despite his reservation that Pound was a 'man of talent' who had only with effort approached the 'work of genius', Russell did concede that 'Free verse has never with Pound meant easy verse. I am sure he sweats over six or eight lines of verse like as (*sic*) other poets might over a long narrative.'[70] *A farewell to arms* left the *Irish Statesman* confused as to the nature of Hemingway's gift. 'I imagine', its reviewer noted, 'Mr. Hemingway with his power of writing dialogue in such short and vital sentences, which by their very inadequacy suggest so much, could write an extraordinarily interesting play.'[71] The *Irish Statesman* responded warmly to Virginia Woolf's *Orlando*.

> Dryden, Pope, Addison, Dr. Johnson and Boswell – the two latter only shadows, it is true – wander across the pages in company with courtiers and kings. We trace the slow flowering of our modern age and of the ages which have gone before, while the person of a young man or a young woman forms the single stems supporting these blooms ... *Orlando* is a book of which any writer might be proud.[72]

The representation of historical and cultural change through the perspective of a marginalised individual consciousness is typical of early-twentieth-century literature. That the *Irish Statesman* should recognise this in *Orlando* is a reflection of the attempt by some of its reviewers to come to terms with the 'modern novel'. What Russell understood to be modern was prophetic and realist. Prophecy was modern in the sense that, like O'Flaherty's *The house of gold*, it

1926. 183–4. Russell was never entirely convinced of the complexity of Spengler's thought but the German's prediction of European decline conformed to Flinders Petrie's conclusions drawn from research into the decay and development of ancient human cultures. **69** G. Russell, 'Magazines', *IS*, 8 Feb. 1929. 463. **70** G. Russell, 'Selected poems. By Ezra Pound', *IS*, 8 Dec. 1928. 280. **71** IH, 'Fiction', *IS*, 21 Dec. 1928. 323. IH can be identified as Irene Haugh. **72** RMF, 'Orlando: a biography. By Virginia Woolf', *IS*, 8 June 1929. 275.

sensed the birth of a new, virile western consciousness. It was realist because authors like Joyce, writing in a transition period between the folk and modern cultures, recorded the subjective turmoil of their subjects as they adapted to new conditions.[73] To do this is to invest modernity in writing with a considerable political significance. If Joyce's detractors, the state censors and literary critics, succeeded in silencing his texts, they would hinder the necessary expression of a new Europe. Russell countered this possibility by compulsion, always a strong, if under-acknowledged, element in his doctrine of co-operation. The political equivalent of the culturally restorative modern novel became the application of a vigorous corporatism. The national being was for Russell a body that required discipline, organisation and education. Accordingly, Russell welcomed the Italian fascist adoption of a charter of labour in 1927 with 'admiration and wonder':[74]

> Here is a Government which will stand no nonsense and which issued a communiqué to the industrialists warning them that the cost of living must come down … Only the strongest and sincerest government could act in this way. If the Fascists pull through and make a success of their policy the other ancient, mouldy moth-eaten governments will sit up and act also. Dear Heaven, how the world will be drilled in another quarter of a century![75]

A pseudonymous letter immediately objected to this section of the *Irish Statesman*, the correspondent pointing out that the Italian charter was transparently a document whereby labour could more easily be manipulated by the state.[76] Another letter immediately followed from the Italian embassy at the court of St James in support of the *Irish Statesman*.[77] That the *Irish Statesman* should receive such notice from the Italian elite is indication of the regard held for the *Irish Statesman*'s support of the Italian project.

---

73 Russell reviewed a series of Joyce's works in progress throughout the late 1920s. See for example his response to *Anna Livia Plurabelle* in the *IS*, 29 Dec. 1928 and of *Tales told of Shem and Shaun: three fragments from work in progress* in the *IS*, 6 July 1929. Russell recognised Joyce's talent but declared himself in both these reviews to be confused about the author's intentions. The reason for Russell's inclusion of these texts in the *Irish Statesman* was in part due perhaps to the editor's friendship with Padraic Colum who also wrote the foreword to *Anna Livia Plurabelle*. Colum of course supported Russell in his attack on the censorship, as discussed above. Thomas MacGreevy argued for Joyce's importance to Irish literature in a letter, 'Anna Livia Plurabelle', to the *IS*, 16 Feb. 1929. 475–6. Perhaps the most striking of MacGreevy's observations is not about Joyce at all: 'an essay', MacGreevy noted, 'by a Dublin student of Italian literature, Mr. Samuel Beckett, on the influence of Vico (who may be regarded in some ways as the Dante of the Counter-Reformation) on the construction and verbal technique of Mr. Joyce's work is shortly to be published in Paris'. 476. **74** 'N&C', *IS*, 28 May 1927. 272. **75** Ibid. **76** 'Politicus', 'The fascist state', *IS*, 25 June 1927. 375. **77** L. Villari, 'Fascism and labour', *IS*, 9 July 1927. 422.

There is no doubt that Russell sustained an interest throughout the latter years of the 1920s in the possible use of state power to regulate internal dissidence. His patience with any form of public opinion that he found objectionable was dangerously diminished. Russell thought, with no apparent sense of irony, that 'If we do not discourage our coercionists it will be a country only fit for tenth-rate human beings who have no mind, no spirit, and who are only fit to be herded like our cattle'.[78] The idea of a humanity lacking in spirit or intelligence, the two attributes that most make for an individual presence, is, in retrospect, disturbing but in context of Russell's previous writings this passage is but a more blunt extension of his belief in the primacy of elite regulation. It is fitting that Russell found a political form so sympathetic to his own preferences in the form of Italian fascism in the late 1920s. The radical brand of co-operation that he had developed over the previous twenty years helped to make him open to the corporatism of the then modern Italian state. Russell was aware of the shortcomings of the Italian administration. Able to admit 'The Fascists may have been destructive' he still felt that 'the intellectual aspect of the movement should be of interest to us in Ireland, who have by no means come to our ideal state, to marry it and live happily ever after'.[79] The bridal rites of such a union between intellectuals and the nation promised Russell the authority to speak for the Free State, the product, in his mind, of their marriage.

As the Irish state consolidated its independence towards the end of the 1920s, Russell embarked on a new and final phase of his career in the *Irish Statesman*. In these last two years of the journal's publication Russell developed an obsession with the possibility of Ireland's becoming a flight centre for the developing aviation industry. Flights were made between America and Europe for the first time in 1927, one of which was assisted by a pilot of the Irish army.[80] Russell saw in the development of these flights a means by which even the remotest parts of the Free State might be exposed to global influence. It is ironic that after a bitter battle over censorship and the regulation of information for Free State citizens that the *Irish Statesman* should further be urging the government to develop a global trade that might have a similar, culturally contaminating, effect, as those pro-censorship would have had it. The *Irish Statesman's* promotion of flight did however predate the censorship debate as it published an article on the subject in May 1928. Signed 'Viator' the author of the piece was possibly Gogarty, committed as he was throughout this period to the development of Irish aviation.[81] Typically, the article suggested that the provision of

---

78 G. Russell, 'The bull in Irish politics', *IS*, 22 June 1929. 307.   **79** G. Russell, 'L&L: the making of a fascist state', *IS*, 20 April 1929. 133.   **80** An officer of the Irish army, as reported in the quarterly of that organisation, *An t-Oglac*, April 1928, accompanied the 1928 flight of the German crew of the *Bremen* across the Atlantic.   **81** See for example Gogarty's humorous account of his first flying lesson in 'I pick up flying', *An t-Oglac*, 3:1, 1930 and 'Mid air' in the *IS*, 22 Oct. 1927.

a 'North-Atlantic air port' would 'give great assurance to the public mind and, we may forecast, would rank beside the Shannon scheme in securing for the Irish Administration a reputation for courageous foresight'.[82] This was wise advice, especially in context of the massive growth that European state airlines, Lufthansa predominant among them, had up to then experienced.[83]

One year later the *Irish Statesman* reiterated that 'Ireland is geographically a natural centre for the establishment of Atlantic air-ports'.[84] It further noted that the Irish pilot of the most recent flight to America, a Colonel Fitzmaurice, 'implored his countrymen to be less backward gazing and become more futurist'.[85] The date of this article suggests the degree to which Russell was prepared to reassert his drive to Free State modernity after the distraction of censorship. Russell followed this piece by publishing a poem by W.H. Hurley, simply titled 'Aviation'. Hurley himself is probably a pseudonymous creation of either Russell or Gogarty, as an author of the same name does not appear elsewhere in the *Irish Statesman* or any other Irish publications of the period, a fact too fortunate to be coincident. 'Aviation' celebrates flight:

> They fly with swift wings across the waste
> To spread the pulse of life, and bind
> The nations close in need and mind,
> Till earth be one, and war outpaced
> Where their sane spirit, scorning fears,
> Shall reach with newer strength to span the spheres.[86]

There is a dual awareness in this poem of the spiritual impulse to mechanical speed. The two modes function together, science working to a higher end than mere mechanism by its creation of a medium whereby the world can, to paraphrase the poem, be bound. Russell had himself been fascinated with flight since before the publication of *The interpreters* in 1922. But he found, in the Cambridge astrophysicist, A.S. Eddington's *The nature of the physical world*, evidence of a scientific practice that allowed for the operations of the irrational. Eddington's theories dominated Russell's aesthetic perspective in the second half of 1929 as the editor of the *Irish Statesman* attempted to impel the Free State's futurist direction.[87] Eddington's book was published in 1929, being the

In view of Gogarty's cavalier attitude to air travel one would be surprised if any reader ever gained the impression that flight was either safe or convenient. **82** 'Viator', 'An Irish air port', *IS*, 5 May 1928. 167. **83** Robert Lloyd Praeger, the Irish natural scientist and occasional contributor to the *Irish Statesman*, noted that 'The 1928 programme issued by the Deutsche Luft-Hansa Company … shows more than six hundred daily passenger flights between European cities'. 'In praise of flying', *IS*, 30 Nov. 1929. 247. **84** 'Ireland and aviation', *IS*, 6 April 1929. 86. **85** Ibid. **86** W. Hurley, 'Aviation', *IS*, 28 April 1929. 149. **87** Details of Eddington's achievements can be read in J.G.

product of a series of lectures first delivered in 1927. The purpose of Eddington's text was to suggest that since all objects are made of single atoms, the appearance of an object as solid to human perception is an illusion, the agglomeration of molecules giving only 'the substance of reality. As Eddington himself put it: 'It is because the mind, the weaver of illusion, is also the generator of reality that reality is always to be sought as the base of illusion. Illusion is to reality as smoke is to the fire.'[88] Accordingly, 'it is reasonable to enquire whether in the mystical illusions of man there is not a reflection of an undying reality'.[89] Eddington developed this idea into a defence of art from the attacks of science:

> In the mystic sense of the creation around us, in the expression of art, in a yearning towards God, the soul grows upward and finds the fulfilment of something implanted in its nature. The sanction for this development within us, a striving born with our consciousness or an inner light proceeding from a greater power than ours. Science can scarcely question this sanction, for the pursuit of science springs from a striving which the mind is impelled to follow, a questing that will not be suppressed.[90]

In response to Eddington, Russell composed the poem 'Beauty and science (after reading A. S. Eddington's Science and the physical world)',[91] published in the *Irish Statesman* in October 1929. In this prose poem Russell reflects on the suggestion that 'The apparition of earth and we ourselves/ are builded' is 'From these frail, fiery infitesimals'[92] or atoms. The speaker denies this sole possibility, suggesting that 'we can prove their mathematic to have/ erred' as a light within the psyche consumes the atomic power:

> For, at the first thought of that loveliness
> Within the psyche, the image began to shine
> As if those delicate lights had ceased to circle
> Around their suns, and hurrying to the image
> They had grown still within it, lighting there
> Myriads and myriads of their fairy fires.[93]

Crowther, *British scientists of the twentieth century*. Eddington was, by the end of the 1920s, something of a popularising, scientist in the latter-day mould of Hawking or Gould. The Macmillan book lists in the *New Statesman* literary supplement for May 1927 lead with a description of Eddington's *Stars and atoms* as 'A book for the general reader'. *NS*, supplement to vol. 29, 21 May 1929. i. **88** A.S. Eddington, *The nature of the physical world*. 319. **89** Ibid. **90** Ibid. 327–8. **91** The careful reader will of course note that in his dedication Russell carelessly refers to Eddington's 'Science and the physical world' when he should refer to its actual title, *The nature of the physical world*. The mistake is perhaps significant of the impression Eddington's discourse on science and art made upon the poet. **92** G. Russell, 'Beauty and science', *IS*, 19 Oct. 1929. 128. **93** Ibid.

Bizarre as this rendering of atomic theory into the vaguest realms of mystical poetry is, one must still realise that Russell is engaged in a debate then current in the British periodical the *Realist*. Russell's line, for example, that 'we can prove their mathematic to have erred',[94] has its source in a May 1929 article in the *Realist* by Professor H. Levy, 'Is science credible?'[95] We can assume that Russell became aware of the *Realist* as its literary editor, Gerald Heard, reviewed H.G. Wells' *Meanwhile* in the *Irish Statesman* in August 1927. In his own article, Levy was less moved than Russell by Eddington's submission that since atoms are invisible to the human eye it must take faith to believe in them. Instead of insisting on the physical reality of these objects, Levy solved Eddington's problem by stating that the existence of atoms was, whether verifiable or not, a logical necessity of Einstein's theory of relativity. Complicated as this sounds, Levy's argument is simplicity itself. It is that, while trying to formulate a unified theory of the functions of the universe, the scientist must accept the inadequacies of both his senses and his equipment. These deficiencies noted, 'The object of science' was, as Levy quoted from Einstein, 'to coordinate experiences, and to bring them into a logical system'.[96] This article was critical to Russell's appreciation of Eddington as it provided the scientist and the intellectual with equal status, each equipped with inadequate tools by which to explore the eternal. In this mutual respect, Russell's description of Eddington as one of the great 'intellectual engineers'[97] is fitting both to Eddington and to Russell, since the course of the latter's career in the *Irish Statesman* was the careful exercise of a literary instrument in pursuit of a cultural construction.

In comparison, one of Patrick Kavanagh's earliest publications was placed beside Russell's 'Beauty and science' in the *Irish Statesman*. Russell, it seems, picked Kavanagh's poem 'The intangible' deliberately as a companion piece to his meditation on Eddington's work. Kavanagh invokes images of 'Indian/ Vision of thunder./ Splendours of Greek,/ Egypt's cloud-woven glory'.[98] The young poet reads like Russell's adept, the speaker's classical allusions not yet prepared for the irony of later poems like 'Epic'.[99] There is a suggestion of the speaker's distrust of the ancients' 'thread-worn story'[100] but the last two lines of 'The intangible' are those most relevant to Russell's response to Eddington in

94 Ibid. **95** Levy wrote that 'Mathematical reasoning is recognised as logic in one of its purest forms, for into the English language there has crept the custom of confusing the two words "mathematical" and "logical". It is, therefore, something of a shock to the outsider when he learns that even in pure mathematics there is a history of error.' 'Is science credible?', *Realist*, 1:2, May 1929. 133. **96** Ibid. 137. **97** G. Russell in reply to S. O'Casey, *IS*, 30 Nov. 1929. 251. **98** P. Kavanagh, 'The intangible', *IS*, 19 Oct. 1929. 128. **99** The speaker of Kavanagh's 'Epic' has 'lived in important places, times/ When great events were decided'. He compares the record of rural Irish squabble with Homer's Greece, a poet whose ghost remembers 'I made the Iliad from such/ A local row'. *Complete poems of Patrick Kavanagh*. 238. **100** P. Kavanagh, 'The intangible', *IS*, 19 Oct. 1929. 128.

'Beauty and science'. In these, 'Two and two are not four/ On every shore',[101] a simple, elegant declaration against the empirical. To read these lines in context of Russell's reference to Levy in the *Realist* is to recognise the fact that, unwitting or not, Kavanagh is, like O'Flaherty with the *The house of gold*, to be co-opted into Russell's great post-national project. The irony of Kavanagh's election to such elevated status is played out well in Kavanagh's memoir *The green fool*, as the country intellectual arrives half-starved in Russell's presence, the only sustenance offered a discussion of Whitman and Emerson.[102]

Added to Kavanagh and O'Flaherty in the vanguard of a new Irish consciousness were to be the twin characters of O'Casey and Yeats, each of whom posed a separate problem for the *Irish Statesman*. O'Casey was the first to split publicly with Russell, the seeds of their antagonism laid in Russell's siding with Yeats and the Abbey directors in their rejection of O'Casey's *The silver tassie*.[103] The slight to O'Casey was magnified by the *Irish Statesman*'s publication of a negative review by Sean O'Faolain of the eventual London production of O'Casey's play.[104] In response to the playwright's letters to the *Irish Statesman* on the subject Russell rather patronisingly suggested that O'Casey read Eddington's *The nature of the physical world*. This is significant, not least because it suggests the way in which Eddington's text was by late 1929 to serve a similar purpose to the work of O'Grady in the earlier stages of Russell's career. Russell's evangelism was spoilt by his offensive suggestion to O'Casey that a reading of the book 'may complete your education about the complexity of human nature'.[105] The clear implication was that O'Casey's earlier plays, with the Dublin tenements as their subject, dealt only with the simple facts of external life. O'Casey reacted bitterly. Referring to an art review by Russell in the

---

101 Ibid. **102** The limits of Russell's success in the enlistment of new Irish writers can be read in Kavanagh's account of their first meeting in 1932. Kavanagh remembered that 'I wasn't listening to Æ. I was worried over the poor impression I was making. I was hungry – for poetry? Yes, but I was also physically hungry, and an empty stomach is a great egoist, and a bad listener to anything save the fry of rashers in a pan'. *The Green fool*. 229. Russell's distraction was due in part to the terminal illness that afflicted his wife. Violet Russell died two months subsequent to his meeting Kavanagh. The junior poet's lack of consideration reflects badly on Kavanagh's own aspirations. **103** In their capacity as directors of the Abbey Theatre, Yeats and Lennox Robinson returned the typescript of Sean O'Casey's *The silver tassie* to the playwright for revision before they would consider it for production. O'Casey sent their entire correspondence, which also implicated Walter Starkie and Lady Gregory in the controversy, to the *Irish Statesman* with a demand that it be published. Russell submitted to O'Casey's will but not before warning Yeats privately of O'Casey's intention. O'Casey was outraged by the *Irish Statesman*'s refusal to condemn the Abbey's decision. This marks the start of O'Casey's deep antipathy to Russell, ungenerously expressed in his later autobiographies. See the correspondence columns of the *IS* from 9 June 1928. **104** O'Faolain disdainfully remarked of the first production of the *The silver tassie* in England that the play was not 'good theatre as we understand the term in these islands'. In 'The silver tassie staged', *IS*, 18 Oct. 1929. 135. **105** G. Russell in reply to S. O'Casey, *IS*, 30 Nov. 1929. 251.

Irish Statesman, O'Casey suggested that if Russell could 'get a connection between the discoveries of Eddington in protons and electrons, with your discoveries in Art, then, I'm afraid, you know as much about Science as you do about Painting'.[106] Cuttingly, O'Casey ended his correspondence with a mockery of Russell's pretensions to the recruitment of a new Irish literary school. 'Remember me', he wrote, 'to all the boys and girls'.[107]

Russell's understanding of Yeats' role in the new state matured in tandem with his response to Eddington's work.[108] Russell began to find in Yeats the evidence of a character sufficient to speak on behalf of the elite to the mass. By 1929 Yeats had become to Russell the embodiment of a modern Cuchulain, the conduit, like the earlier hero in O'Grady's histories, of forces summoned from the collective unconscious. Russell's review of the 1929 edition of Yeats' *Selected poems* is in this respect revealing. Generally avoiding specific reference to Yeats' actual work, Russell suggested that:

> There is in every work of genius not only what is consciously in the mind of the genius, but much of what is unknown to himself. Emerson speaks of the great architect as building better than he knew, and Socrates says that in the mind of the poet there is a daemon who speaks through him truths from a profounder life than the conscious.[109]

Yeats' gift is his ability to articulate the unconscious desire of the audience that he addresses. Russell in turn sees Yeats as the precursor, the voice of a new order not yet come into its full power. The daemon that speaks through the poet offers a higher sanction to the actions of his devotees than that of democratic election. Since there is no conscious choice in the poet's selection of his voice, there can be nothing but compulsion in the following of its dictates. The fulfilment of its promise was a new civilisation, the reward to its devotees engaged in a realignment of European politics. Russell was aware of the consequences of this vision. Writing in the *Irish Statesman* just two months before the journal's final edition he predicted that because

---

106 S. O'Casey, 'Contradictions', *IS*, 14 Dec. 1929. 298.   **107** Ibid.   **108** Yeats was also interested in Eddington. He discussed the scientist's merits with Sturge Moore in the late 1920s. 'Eddington', Yeats noted in January 1926, 'said lately that all we have a right to say of the external world is that it is a "shared experience".' Moore replied in March 1926 that Eddington's work 'entirely accords with the common-sense view that science is a description of those properties of reality which can be abstracted, but the remainder, which Eddington sums up under the head Actuality, remains intractable to scientific method and contains most of the values of experience'. U. Bridges, ed., *W.B. Yeats and Sturge Moore*. 63–4, 79.   **109** G. Russell, 'L&L: the reading of poetry', *IS*, 9 Nov. 1929. 191–2.

The nationalities in Europe are old and have got so fixed it is possible the only way in which the United States of Europe could be brought about would be by the emergence of some conqueror of the Napoleon or Caesar type who would bring them all by force under one Government. It would, doubtless, be very unpleasant for a century or so, but it is possible that the great-grand-children of those dragged into a European confederation might look back on the conqueror as the greatest European who ever existed. I have no doubt in the future we shall have the United States of the World.[110]

Russell finds in his confirmation of a world federation the promise of mass consciousness working to one end that he perceived in O'Grady's Cuchulain and in his own version of Yeats in the *Irish Statesman*. The dictatorship of the mind that Russell imagines is but another step in the evolution of consciousness that he traces from the primitive to the advanced, its progress measured through the state's own attempts at scientific development. The Shannon scheme, like flight, is the physical equivalent to Yeats' poetry, the impetus to a new cultural arrangement that will be vigorous in the application of its ethics. Russell is in this final sense himself an intellectual engineer, the term by which he described the physicist Eddington. The *Irish Statesman* was Russell's major construction. But it was in financial difficulty by the late 1920s, its cash reserves drained, despite victory in court, by the costs of a libel case brought against the journal by a disgruntled author, angry at the negative review he received in its pages.[111] The *Irish Statesman*'s American investors were also affected by the Wall Street crash. These were the practical reasons for the journal's extinction on 12 April 1930, after nearly seven years of weekly publication. An extraordinary general directors' meeting of 3 April 1930 passed Lennox Robinson's resolution that 'The Irish Statesman Publishing Co., Ltd., be wound up voluntarily, and that Percy Morrow, of 13 Ash Field Road, Ranelagh, Co. Dublin, be … hereby appointed Liquidator for the purpose of such winding up'.[112] The company was fully dissolved on 17 December 1930.

The *Irish Statesman* was instrumental in creating intellectual support for the new state; it had also influenced important policy areas, of agriculture, censor-

110 G. Russell, 'Review of Oscar Neufang's *The united states of the world*', *IS*, 22 Feb. 1930. 562. 111 Henry Summerfield notes that in November 1927, Russell had 'published the respected scholar Dr Donal O'Sullivan's scathing review of a collection of Irish songs, and the compilers, Mr and Mrs Seamus Clandillon, brought a libel action against the reviewer, the editor and the paper.' 245. The trial ran from 29 October to 13 November 1929 and the jury returned after seven and a half hours with no verdict. The case was dismissed and an appeal by the plaintiffs was dismissed before it reached court. The damage was done however, with costs of £2500. An emergency committee had to gather funds to save the journal in January 1929. *That myriad-minded man*. 246–7. 112 Irish Statesman Publishing Co. Dissolved Company File NA ms COMP 1/D7206.

ship and electrification. It was fundamental to the development of new Irish writers. The bridge between the Literary Revival and the new generation come to print with independence, the *Irish Statesman* was the last testament of a cultural movement that had first spoken with O'Grady, Russell and Yeats some forty years before. O'Grady was now dead. Russell and Yeats survived. But neither assumed the popular audience of their earlier writing. As Russell warned readers of his final prose work, *The avatars*,

> I have, I fear, delayed too long the writing of this, for as I grow old the moon of fantasy begins to set confusedly with me. The Avatars has not the spiritual gaiety I desired for it. The friends with whom I once spoke of such things are dead or gone far from me. If they were with me, out of dream, vision and intuition shared between us, I might have made the narrative to glow. As it is, I have only been able to light my way with my own flickering candle.[113]

The essence of Russell's apologia is the substance of his genius: his ability to gather thoughts around him made the *Irish Statesman* a triumph of co-operative intellect. Horace Plunkett took up the point in his final submission to a title that he invented eleven years previous. It was a sad moment for the *Irish Statesman's* founder. His farewell to the journal also signalled the end of an editorial association that had bound him to Russell since 1905. Plunkett knew that 'we owe it to Æ that there is hardly an Irish man or Irish woman of distinction in this generation who did not read the paper or contribute to its columns'.[114] He consoled himself that the influence of the *Irish Statesman* might survive: 'The project', he wrote, 'from first to last was an invitation from the older generation to the younger men with whom the responsibility lies for shaping the destiny of the new Ireland which came into being with the Anglo-Irish Treaty. My prayer is that the example THE IRISH STATESMAN has set may be taken to heart, and that before long the gap it has left will be adequately filled.'[115] Plunkett, like Russell, was dead before the *Bell* was published under the editorship of Sean O'Faolain, one-time contributor to the *Irish Statesman*, but Plunkett would have approved of his legacy. A monthly commentary on Irish life in the world, the *Bell* cultivated a new audience of readers made available by state progress in education that Russell could only dream of.

The final issue of the *Irish Statesman* further contained a letter in recognition of its achievement from the Free State Minister of Agriculture, Patrick Hogan, a politician much in Plunkett's regard. Considering Russell's promotion of scientific efficiency, Hogan considered 'The loss to agriculture … first. It must be

113 G. Russell, *The avatars*. vii.   114 H. Plunkett, 'The passing of "The Irish Statesman"', *IS*, 12 April 1930. 106.   115 Ibid.

almost unique to find that one of the most distinguished men in English letters should be also a thorough master of agricultural economics. That such a combination should be at our service is a greater good fortune than we have deserved.'[116] In consolation, 'It must be a real satisfaction to you to know that your teaching has triumphed'.[117] Hogan then outlined the value of Russell's work since 1923. The Minister was

> of course well aware that your services have not been confined to agriculture since the establishment of the State. THE IRISH STATESMAN has consistently held up before the people an image of what decent citizenship involves. It has done more than any other journal to dissipate the moral and mental confusion with which we have been struggling. I believe that the work you have done cannot be undone, and while I know that you do not value material rewards, I feel that you will yet be happy in the realization that during the most critical period of modern Irish history, you succeeded through THE IRISH STATESMAN in becoming the outstanding moral influence in Irish journalism.[118]

Such sentiment was general. James Good informed the *New Statesman* that 'In a country where, as one of the characters in the *Irish R.M.* says, "If it was only two cocks ye' seen fightin' on the road, yer heart'd take part with one of them,"' the *Irish Statesman* 'was a daring experiment to run a weekly which refused to take sides'.[119] But faction was not the cause of failure. Any periodical publication has limited life, its vitality secured in the main by the varied interests of its editor. Russell was, by 1930, tired. Drained from twenty-five years and more of commissions, editing and writing, he could no longer anticipate the changes that continued to occur with rapidity in the culture that engaged him. The last issue of the *Irish Statesman* does show evidence of a new emergence in Irish intellectual life, with interest in continental modernism, music and visual art. Frank O'Connor, Russell's favourite,[120] reviewed *Our exaymination round his factification of Work in progress*, a book of essays from the publishers of *Ulysses*, Paris' Shakespeare Company. O'Connor sensed a connection between Joyce's new work and that of his contemporaries at home: 'in *Ulysses* form had become for Joyce as it became for some of the Irish poets, ritual'.[121] A 'great artist who

---

116 P. Hogan, 'The Irish Statesman', *IS*, 12 April 1930. 111.   117 Ibid. 112.   118 Ibid. 112. 119 James Good, 'Comments', *NS*, 12 April 1930. 3   120 Russell wrote to the American Vachel Lindsay on 22 Oct. 1931 to recommend 'the young poets & writers here. There is one young man Michael O'Donovan who writes under the pseudonym of "Frank O'Connor" who is a story-teller of genius and a fine poet. There are also Fred Higgins & Austin Clarke both very good.' Seumas O'Sullivan papers, TCD ms 4634/1019.   121 Frank O'Connor, 'Joyce – the third period', *IS*, 12 April 1930. 115.

was also a pedant', Joyce 'attached to form a significance that it has seldom had outside ritual'.[122] O'Connor was not enthusiastic about all Joyce's works, having 'never been able to appreciate Mrs. Bloom's soliloquy',[123] but he was keen to promote his friends' point of view: 'Two or three of these essays – I am thinking in particular of Samuel Beckett's, Eugene Jolas' and Thomas MacGreevy's – are very interesting, and with a little more detachment would have been first rate criticism.'[124] O'Connor learnt well from his elders; Russell and Yeats' ability to boost their enthusiasts was a constant source of irritation to their antagonists in the *Catholic Bulletin* and *Leader*. But O'Connor's review is evidence of a new movement abroad in Irish literature, as the brutality of past conflict in Ireland and beyond receded. A new war would threaten in time; but for now Walter Starkie could lament a world drained of significance. In the last century

> Wagner like a wonderful impressionist was able to conjure up worlds of space out of strokes and patches of colour. With a few bars of music he could create a world of soul – colours of starry midnight, sweeping clouds, sunlit distances, impending doom, despair. After him Spengler says all is impotence and falsehood, for there are nothing but industrious cobblers and noisy fools about who produce something for the market that will 'catch on' with a public for whom art, music and drama have long ceased to be spiritual necessities.[125]

Russell had the last word. His final editorial is a model of economy, grateful for the support he received and hopeful for the new generation to follow. He surveyed the territory of his thoughts and found that many had taken root. Southern unionists were reconciled to the new state; science was applied to agriculture and manufacture; the Treaty settlement was stable; young writers had emerged. He gracefully thanked both his fellow staff, notably James Good, and the Irish-American donors who had funded the journal to allow Free State readers 'to live intellectually beyond our means'.[126] He had worries. The growth of religious societies and their influence over public life was a threat. But safety would come when 'a new generation better educated than the present comes from the primary, secondary and technical schools and the universities to manhood and brings better-equipped brains to bear upon the problems of their country'.[127] This was for the untold future. The *Irish Statesman* ended Russell's major influence on Irish culture. With its last issue went much of his energy, and that of the revival he had directed, George Russell ready to climb to his proper dark.

122 Ibid.   123 Ibid.   124 Ibid.   125 Walter Starkie, 'L&L: modern music', *IS*, 12 April 1930. 114.   126 G. Russell, 'N&C', *IS*, 12 April 1930. 103.   127 Ibid. 104.

For twenty-five years the Editor has been a weekly commentator in THE IRISH HOMESTEAD or in THE IRISH STATESMAN on politics, economics, literature and the arts, and he could not have continued much longer, nor would it have been right for him to have continued. He belongs to a movement which began at the latter end of last century and which has now almost spent its force. A new Ireland is growing up with its own ideals of a culture, a social order and a civilization. It is only right that those who belong to the new era should be its propagandists, and not elderly men whose minds have lost flexibility and who have come to a kind of spiritual deafness when they listen to the talk of young genius. Before that last infirmity weighs heavily upon the Editor, he feels it is best to cease criticism and comment. He can still, like George Herbert, 'relish versing' and on looking back he feels his greatest pleasure was the discovery of Irish talent. He hopes that his part in many controversies will be forgotten. But he would like to be remembered for this, that he was the friend of the Irish poets, those who make the soul of the nation. To those readers who have borne with him for so many years the Editor gives gratitude and thanks, and so – good-bye.[128]

128 Ibid. 105.

King of dreams

George Russell lived for five years after the last issue of the *Irish Statesman*, slowly weakened by the onset of cancer. His became an increasingly vagrant life spent between two continents and three countries, Ireland, England and the United States of America, Russell travelling to New York in September 1930 to lecture on economics and literature. There he met Henry Wallace, an acquaintance from Ireland in 1912 and later Vice President of Franklin Roosevelt's administration, and lectured from Washington to Alabama, Georgia, Illinois and California, to university students, businessmen and literary societies.[1] Russell visited Chicago, Seattle and Los Angeles on his journey, rapt by the Rocky Mountains and by the Arizona desert. He returned to London in May 1931, exhausted, to spend the summer in Donegal before returning to Dublin. 1932 was a more difficult year, with the death of his two long companions, his wife, Violet Russell, and his mentor, Horace Plunkett.[2] Ireland became less congenial as the memories of past association threatened to overwhelm. Russell sold his Rathgar home of thirty years in July 1933 and removed to London, returning to Sheephaven in Donegal for a holiday. His last voyage to the United States of America began in December 1934; his reputation in agriculture and the arts resulted in a meeting with President Roosevelt in January 1935. Returning to England exhausted in March that year, he soon retired, temporarily as he at first thought (intending apparently to return to Ireland) to a Bournemouth nursing home, Stagsden. George Russell died there on 17 July 1935 at the age of 68 in company of friends including Constantine Curran and Oliver St John Gogarty.

Vale and other poems was the first book Russell published after the *Irish Statesman*'s demise. Issued in 1931, *Vale*, as the title suggests, is a leave-taking, its recurrent theme the loss of power, mental and physical. Dedicated to Seumas O'Sullivan, the collection has a desperate quality, of marshalled strength against decay. We find 'The gay'

---

1 Details of the extent of Russell's visit to the United States of America, from coast to coast, can be read in H. Summerfield, *That myriad-minded man*. 253–8.   **2** Violet Russell died on 3 February and Horace Plunkett on 26 March 1932.

> Holding sorrow and joy
> Hugged to my heart as one,
> Lest they fly on those wild ways
>   And life be undone.[3]

The title poem, 'Vale', laments lost vitality, the speaker separate from an earth that revolves beyond his influence. It remembers

> ... the heavenly hiding-place
> Wherein the spirit laughed a day.
> All its proud ivories and fires
> Shrunk to a shovelful of clay.

> It must have love, this silent earth,
> To leap up at the King's desire,
> Moving in such a noble dance
> Of wreathed ivory and fire.

> It will not stir for me at all,
> Nor answer me with fire or gleam.
> Adieu, sweet-memoried dust, I go
> After the Master for His dream.[4]

But Russell was not quite ready for his last journey, entering into controversy over the Irish Academy of Letters, of which he was the secretary and author of the society's rules.[5] The Academy was founded by Yeats and Shaw in 1932 and came under immediate criticism from Irish religious authority, one Father Gannon delivering a scathing lecture, 'The Irish Academy of Letters, unwelcome and unauthorised'. Russell published a response full of all the old vigour in the *Irish Times* of 15 November in defence of the Academy. He wondered why Irish writers alone were not 'entitled to select their associates, just as men of science, men of healing, men of law form their own associations and fix the standard of competence which entitles men or women to membership?'[6] The Academy

---

3 G. Russell, 'The gay', *Vale*. 5.   4 G. Russell, 'Vale', *Vale*. 3.   5 Details of the rules and meetings of the Irish Academy of Letters can be read in the Irish Academy of Letters records, NLI ms list 39 and the Seumas O'Sullivan correspondence, TCD ms 4635/1113. The initial membership of the Academy was a virtual afterlife of the *Irish Statesman*, including former contributors George Bernard Shaw as President and W.B. Yeats as Vice President, Austin Clarke, Padraic Colum, Oliver St John Gogarty, F.R Higgins, Frank O'Connor, Sean O'Faolain, Seamus O'Sullivan, Forrest Reid, Lennox Robinson and James Stephens.   6 G. Russell, 'The new Irish Academy', *Irish Times*, 15 November 1932. 7.

aimed 'to discover original genius and encourage it by recognition, by the award, probably, of prizes; and how necessary this is where literature is judged almost solely by party, political or sectarian standard'.[7] This was a noble aim, undone somewhat by Russell's subsequent December letter to the *Irish Times* on the same subject. In this Russell went to 'the real reason for all the controversy. It has been stated in various forms that we do not faithfully reflect the mentality of the people – that we are Anglo-Irish rather than Irish. For myself – I cannot speak for others – I admit both charges and am content, even proud to be called Anglo-Irish rather than Irish.'[8] The Anglo-Irish were 'the most virile and intelligent people in Ireland', including over time 'Berkeley, Burke, Goldsmith, Swift, Davis, Ferguson, Shaw, Yeats, Lady Gregory, Synge, Stephens, or, in politics, Wolfe Tone, Fitzgerald, Parnell, Griffith, Pearse'.[9] This last was a calculated offence, reminding readers of Pearse's English heritage.

> If all those who had that foreign strain in their blood were exiled from Ireland, there would not be more than two or three thousand pure Gaels left, and they would be mostly half-wits – the kind of people we meet in the West, their minds a clotted mass of superstition and ignorance, animated by a half-crazy energy, admirable material for picturesque dramatists or story-tellers like Synge and O'Flaherty, but hardly the material out of which a new civilization could be made.[10]

Reconciliation was beyond Russell's power. 'It sickens me', he continued, 'this assumption that our people would be as pure as Adam in Eden only for the contact with foreign literature. Every doctor in Ireland knows it is cant. Every clergyman knows it is cant.'[11] 'We can, of course, with our talent for organisation, get a million people on their knees before an altar in the Park; but did there come out of all that piety a single vision, a song, a music, any visible sign that the sacrifice was accepted and the fiery tongues had descended?'[12] Such criticism rose from a well of bitterness over the direction Ireland took after 1930. Russell no longer had the *Irish Statesman* to support his views, the Irish Academy of Letters his last redoubt before the new orthodoxy of church and state. This failed, he left Dublin for Glengariff with Osborn Bergin and Frank O'Connor during the week long Eucharistic Congress in June 1932.[13]

Russell tried to maintain the link between his own vision of 'works' and 'sacred reason'[14] in *Song and its fountains*, published in 1932. Dedicated to his wife Violet and son Diarmuid Russell, *Song and its fountains* continues the self-meditation of *The candle of vision* fourteen years previous. The book reveals,

7 Ibid.   **8** G. Russell, 'The new Irish Academy', *Irish Times*, 13 December 1932. 8.   **9** Ibid.   **10** Ibid.   **11** Ibid.   **12** Ibid.   **13** H. Summerfield, *That myriad-minded man*. 265.   **14** G. Russell, *Song and its fountains*. np.

more than any other, the intensity of Russell's early visionary experiences, his capacity for waking dreams evident from his fifteenth year. Russell felt the growth of second sight was evidence of possession, of a higher being trying to incorporate in him. 'There grew up', he wrote, 'the vivid sense of a being within me seeking a foothold in the body, trying through intuition and vision to create wisdom there, through poetry to impose its own music upon speech, through action trying to create an ideal society'.[15] This sense of the individual as site for multiple selves resurfaces in his literary criticism. Russell had

> often thought the great masters, the Shakespeares and the Balzacs, endowed more generously with a rich humanity, may, without knowing it, have made their hearts a place where the secrets of many hearts could be told; and they wove into drama or fiction, thinking all the while that it was imagination or art of their own, characters they had never met in life, but which were real and which revealed more of themselves in that profundity of being than if they had met and spoken day by day where the truth of life hides under many disguises. When we sink within ourselves, when we seem most alone, in that solitude we may meet multitude. The psyche, when it has evolved a higher quality of that element which mirrors bring, and by which it becomes self-conscious, may become not only aware of its own spirit but of that relation with other spirits which Kant divined. Here we may find one of the great sources of drama, poetry and wisdom. The psyche may, by the evolution of this sensitiveness, through love and sympathy, come to know that the whole of life can be reflected in the individual and our thoughts may become throngs of living souls.[16]

Russell found the same impulse as inspiration to his previous works: 'Even in my economic studies which led me to write *The National Being* I was brought to think less of circumstance than of the spirit behind national movements.'[17] From 'that I was brought to the more completely mystical mood of *The Interpreters*, where the politic of the characters is traced back to motions in Anima Mundi'.[18] The belief in evolving world order never left Russell. It resurfaced in *The avatars* of 1933, a sequel to *The interpreters* that revives characters with which we are by now familiar, namely Brehon and Lavelle. *The avatars* was Russell's last major prose work, the end of a book that he had begun to write, but discarded, during the mid-1920s. Like *The interpreters*, the stimulus to *The avatars* is external event; in 1922 it was the civil war, in 1933 the entrance of the republican party, Fianna Fáil, the year previous to state power. Russell's anxiety

15 Ibid. 9. 16 Ibid. 42–3. 17 Ibid. 99. 18 Ibid.

throughout *The avatars* is that his legacy of art reconciled to the state through the medium of the *Irish Statesman* (and also his literary prose and poetry) will be lost. The entrance of new political elites to power threatened his doctrine of practical policy under influence of the abstract intellect. *The avatars* itself starts with a young man, Paul, fleeing a city to train with an old artist, Michael Conaire, in the countryside. Something of Russell's unease with his contemporary Ireland surfaces in the gothic city that Paul, converted on the road to the west, describes, a place of corruption where

> The larvae of the dead hung about the living with unsatiated passion, and a base desire was never solitary, for it summoned up legions of evil affinities to urge it to its consummation. As the lights of the soul became extinguished, its darkened halls and corridors were thronged by sinister inhabitants breathing animalism and corruption. They held revelry within and hence came frenzies, obsessions and unappeasable desires. The boy, possessed by the shades, was made meet for its inhabitants. The character of the goat, the hog and the rat began to appear in men's faces and to efface the divine signature.[19]

The city inhabitants are lost to history, none able to 'trace ancestry beyond a grandsire'.[20] But Russell's imagination too is lost, perhaps because of an illness the extent of which he was not yet aware. An obsessive sexuality, too, haunts much of Russell's later work. The avatars appear as Aodh and Aoife, two changling children who prompt a revolution of 'natural spirituality',[21] a bacchanal of modernity. The young poet Felim Carew, encountered by Paul and Michael, predicts a revolutionary end to all this energy:

> There are obscure mystics scattered about everywhere. I never met such adorable wild people. They all seem to have woven into them some tapestry of nature and their being is shot through and through with threads of light. They are the vast nucleus of an army in conflict with the vast mechanism of the world. They are mobilising the great silences, mountains, lakes, sun and wind; things that have no hands to smite, making ready for the last battle between light and darkness.[22]

The artist is the medium of change in a mechanical society:

> It is we, the spiritual anarchists, pagan poets and vagabond idealists, who have injected our own wildness into the social order. The slaves of the

19 G. Russell, *The avatars*. 22. **20** Ibid. 23. **21** Ibid. 70. **22** Ibid. 60.

machine are becoming restless. No, it is not a passion for a new sharing out of wealth. The machine is efficient. Nobody is hungry now though the spirit may be starved. Everyone now is clothed in body though there may not be a rag of coloured fire about the psyche. No one is insecure, no one is homeless, unless they close their eyes to be bleak and homeless in the inner dark. It is the beginning of a spiritual renaissance. The State has nothing more to promise humanity, and when that is realised allegiance begins to fall away.[23]

The cycle of intellect will move, by this prediction, from state support to antagonism. The anarchism of Russell's early career, of which we read earlier, resurfaces in *The avatars* as a critique of Ireland in the 1930s. But this final reinvention of Russell's career sounds hollow. The two avatars transport to the stars without leaving written record of their gospel. As after Christ, a new disciple must record their teachings. The book ends with Paul and his companion Olive standing at the crossroads from where Aodh and Aoife took their heavenly ascent.

> In that pause of quietness Paul became aware that the years had changed him, that he had come to be within that life which as a boy he had seen nodding at him through the transparency of air or earth. For many years he had peered through that veil, but he himself, except for moments which were so transient that he was hardly aware of them until they were gone, had been outside the heavenly circle. Now something was living and breathing within him, interpenetrating consciousness, a life which was an extension of the life that breathed through those dense infinitudes. He could not now conceive of himself apart from that great unity. He knew he was, however humbly, one of the heavenly household. In that new exaltation the lights above, the earth below, were but motions of a life that was endless. He almost felt the will that impelled the earth on which he stood on its eternal round. Through earth itself as through a dusky veil the lustre of its vitality glowed. It shimmered with ethereal colour. Space about him was dense with innumerable life. He felt an inexpressible desire to be molten into that, into all life. He thought of that great adventure he and his friends were beginning, and what transfigurations in life and nature it would mean.[24]

Russell himself underwent one final transformation. *The avatars* was dedicated to W.B. Yeats, the original manuscript inscribed to 'My oldest friend and

23 Ibid. 100–1.   24 Ibid. 187–8.

enemy'. Russell lacked the courage to include this in the printed book but his elision could not hide an increasing obsession with Yeats in his declining years, one character of *The avatars* even singing 'Down by the Sally gardens' in the night.[25] Russell's relationship with Yeats is often understood to be significant only in their youth, when both first met at art school. But Russell was, by 1933, broken from the old habits that had sustained him for three decades and more. He had relinquished domains of work and domesticity – his office at the Plunkett House, his Rathgar home – and had lost the three people who most bound him to each, Susan Mitchell, Horace Plunkett and Violet Russell. As if sensing imminent collapse, Frederick Macmillan inquired of Russell's desire to write an autobiography, a testament to formative experiences now far-off. Russell replied in May 1934 that

> I had thought of writing some reminiscences but had put it off as I kept no journals and would have to trust largely to memory. But at present I am working at some poems and I can only do one thing at a time. When I get the verses published, which I think will be the last, I will think seriously of writing the kind of book you suggest. I have met many people who were interesting, not only to me but to others, folk like W.B. Yeats, whom I knew when I was sixteen, George Moore, Horace Plunkett, and the whole tribe of such writers, and I could possibly give pen pictures which would interest others. I will think about it and jot down occasionally ideas for such a book, and am glad you suggested it as I was thinking dreary about empty hours after I had finished with poetry.[26]

Russell did not complete this autobiography but a fragment, 'The sunset of fantasy', was published in the *Dublin Magazine* in 1938. We know of Russell's antipathy to Yeats' version of personality in his *Autobiographies* of 1913, but Yeats now offered Russell a framework by which he might, near the end of life, judge himself. Yeats' idea of the mask, the historical identity rent from individual circumstance, allowed Russell assume a new authority diverse of his own failing world, of a life transitory between Ireland, England and the United States of America. Yeats' conception of personality was salvation for a man who needed a new self-image to protect himself against the private frailties of a wandering mind (and so Russell waited anxiously on his death bed for a final telegram from Yeats, the one message that might bring closure to a phase of late development Russell had borrowed from his old adversary). Yeats' influence is immediate to the introduction of 'The sunset of fantasy', Russell's identification

25 Ibid. 26.   **26** George Russell to Frederick Macmillan, 31 May 1934. Macmillan archive, BL ms 55002/161.

with Anglo-Ireland far removed from George Moore's past memory of Russell's social ancestry in *Hail and farewell*. Then, on 'one occasion when Yeats was crooning over Æ's fire he had said that if he had his rights he would be Duke of Ormond'.[27] Russell answered 'Willie, you are overlooking your father', 'a detestable remark to make to a poet in search of an ancestry'.[28] The 'addition, "Yeats, we both belong to the lower middle classes", was in equally bad taste'.[29] Now, in his old age, Russell looked to shore up the falling stare. In 'The sunset of fantasy',

> I will indeed try to conjure up a vivid image of what I remember; but in this will select as all artists must do out of their own character and out of that part of me which is Irish and therefore fantastic. We of the Anglo-Irish have a dual character partly quickened by the aged thought of the world and partly inherited from an Irish ancestry. Ireland was never part of the ancient Roman Empire, and the imagination of the people has never been disciplined by philosophy or dialectic or science as other European peoples had been in whose minds something of the thought of Plato or Aristotle had incarnated.[30]

This, like all autobiography, is reinvention, Russell now member of a race he had himself recast at the height of his intellectual power in the 1920s, the Anglo-Irish then scions of a scientific development in the Free State, but now symbol, after Yeats, of a link to the pre-renaissance. Yeats, it seems, was always clear to Russell's mind. The first time the two met, 'as it seemed accidentally', Russell was, of Yeats, 'enchanted by that magic which only then half incarnated in him yet glowed all about him' and 'felt at once all he was to be'.[31] Few could have predicted Yeats' development as a poet from first to last, though Padraic Fallon found occult logic in the progress Yeats took to *The winding stair and other poems* in the *Dublin Magazine* of April 1934. Fallon wondered

> who could have foretold that *The Wanderings of Ossian* would lead at length to *The Tower*, to this – *The Winding Stair*; that the enchanted sleeper under the summer hill would awaken in this midnight, the coldness of the moon about him, his mind, once a disc reflecting a land of sun, now a very moon-metal turning in dark and light. So it is; and yet no *volte-face* but natural change; a progression – if one may change a figure – that, now reading backwards, seems to have tacked as erratically but as surely as the year to its seasonal ending, Spring and Summer melt-

27 G. Moore, *Vale*. 161.   28 Ibid.   29 Ibid.   30 G. Russell, 'The sunset of fantasy (a fragment of an unpublished book)', *Dublin Magazine*, January–March 1938. 6.   31 Ibid. 9.

ing into this Indian Autumn where all the passions and savours and colours of the year, refined to essences, to ghosts, are gathered in a brief, pale tumult, a sort of airy dance before the final fall into the Great Memory. The period of *The Tower, The Winding Stair* is important – more important, I have come to think in spite of myself – than any of the earlier periods, drunken though they were with vision of the golden lands, because in it he has come to realize intellectually an attitude that was once romantically sensuous. Himself now, unclothed, is his theme. He projects it in no blue wandering among islands, but in an unflattering, hard light.[32]

Russell made a different journey to his last collection, *The house of the Titans*, of 1934. These poems mimic Yeats as Russell assumed a voice that confused distance with security. Yeats was justified by the great portraits of the Municipal Gallery but Russell was lost in the 'Museum':

> Why sit I here communing
> With shapes of the dead mind,
> The outworn perfect beauty,
> The gods we left behind?
>
> Though here all gods are gathered
> The wonder has not grown.
> The gods speak to us only
> From their own natural throne.
>
> Not here, but in wild places
> Where wind and water reel
> In ecstasy, light-stricken.
> The gods may there reveal
>
> The forms that hold the sceptre,
> Brows bright with more than gold;
> All that through lips of wonder
> The sibyls breathed of old.[33]

The wild place Russell favoured was Sheephaven in Donegal, a favourite place for holidays and painting since 1904. He found refuge here until near the end of his life, writing to the American poet Vachel Lindsay in June 1931 of an

32 Padraic Fallon, 'The winding stair and other poems', *Dublin Magazine*, April-June 1934. 58–9. **33** G. Russell, 'Museum', *The house of the Titans*. 73.

Ireland still 'beautiful but not so exciting as it was when it was a romantic sulky after freedom'.[34] He enclosed with his letter sketches of the mountain Muckish, of lakeside and riverbank, but apologised for the slowness of his mind. 'I am sorry', he wrote, 'my own letter is so stupid, but there it is. I am on holiday. I see nobody. I read nothing. I eat griddlebead, drink buttermilk, sit by a turf fire, and walk over hills & try to empty my mind so that mother earth may come into it & talk to me a little. She used to breathe in me and I have hopes that she will sing a little song through me again'.[35] Russell's peaceful solitude in Donegal was recalled a decade later by Denis Ireland in his 'Journal for July' of 1942. Escaped from Belfast and German air raids, Ireland found himself in Donegal as darkness fell on the 'pandemonium and crematorium that is modern civilisation'.[36] 'To-night', he continued, 'in the long twilight of the north, Sheephaven lies like a sheet of silvered glass, reflecting the black shape of Muckish as in a mirror. I think of Æ. If ever the soul of a man hovered over a landscape, surely the soul of Æ hovers to-night over the marbled strand, dreaming in the dusk, undisturbed by the sound of surf.'[37] Russell, Ireland felt, would not have appreciated the world as it then was, 'a world that had repudiated the visionaries, the candle-bearers, the light-bringers, a world where the rattle of tank-tracks and the clatter of Bren-gun carriers drowned the music of the spheres and man had begun to fashion himself in the Image of the Machine'.[38] But still, 'Beyond the silvered mirror of Sheephaven a wisp of cloud wreathes the head of Muckish; the ring of sentinel mountains, shutting us off from the south, grows blacker in the evening light. So long as any one loves this tender, subtle landscape, black and silver under a sky of haunting grey, so long will the lover encounter the soul of Æ.'[39]

Russell had apologised to Vachel Lindsay from his Donegal retreat that 'I am too old (sixty five) to go romping across the ocean again and lecturing and I shall never hear you unless you come over to this side of the world'.[40] But he did make one final journey to the United States of America in December 1934. He travelled the country again, but M.L. Wilson, the Under Secretary for Agriculture, had to curtail Russell's itinerary due to the Irishman's increasing ill health. Russell had one great pleasure, lunch in Washington with President Roosevelt, a meeting at which both discussed American government support for artists by employment to paint in schools.[41] Russell was impressed. He returned to London in March 1935, intending to make his way to Dublin but

34 George Russell to Vachel Lindsay, 30 June 1931. Seumas O'Sullivan correspondence, TCD ms 4634/1003. **35** Ibid. **36** Denis Ireland, 'Journal for July', *Lagan*, 1942. 79. **37** Ibid. 80. **38** Ibid. **39** Ibid. 81. **40** George Russell to Vachel Lindsay, 30 June 1931. Seumas O'Sullivan correspondence, TCD ms 4634/1003. **41** Russell wrote to Estelle Solomons, wife of Seumas O'Sullivan, that 'The artists have been looked after. The President told me that they had got some hundreds of stranded artists, paid them a weekly subsistence allowance, the cost of

retired instead to Bournemouth. Informed of his cancer on 9 July 1935, he died nine days later. His body was removed to London's Euston Station and was taken from there by train and steamer to Dun Laoghaire.[42] Fittingly for this man of future vision, three aeroplanes met the boat as friends stood on the pier, ready to follow the hearse to Merrion Square and the Plunkett House. This took one hour and the cortege grew to a mile long as it followed Russell's old route home from work, through Rathmines. The Church of Ireland Reverend C.C. Duggan conducted the funeral on Saturday 20 July at Mount Jerome Cemetery. Frank O'Connor gave an oration to mourners who included Jack and William Butler Yeats, William Cosgrave, Eamon de Valera, Elizabeth, Countess Fingal and Russell's old co-operative colleagues, R.A. Anderson and Thomas Finlay. O'Connor spoke of 'the gratitude of two generations of Irish writers who were indebted to Æ for his encouragement and his help'.[43] Russell was 'a forerunner, a man in love with the future':[44]

> He might, if he had devoted himself to one art only, have been amongst the very greatest figures in the world; but if he had done so, he would not have been Æ, and Ireland, and we, would have been poorer for that. Since his death, remembering what he stood for and what he stood against, I have thought frequently of the proud lines of the old Arab poet: 'He saw the lightning in the East and longed for the East; if it had been in the West, he would have longed for the West, but I, seeking only the lightning and the glory, care nothing for the quarters of the earth'.
> Here, then, we leave him, in the faith that all that we loved in him has been joined to the lightning and its glory forever.[45]

Lightning, like glory, fades and leaves us to wonder, after brief illumination, the lasting influence of Russell's work and thought on Ireland. Throughout this book, I have located the strength and effect of Russell's radical intellectual and social commitment in both the *Irish Homestead* and *Irish Statesman*. These journals took meaning in the immediate, weekly events of a culture that underwent massive change in its transformation from the late nineteenth to the mid-twentieth centuries. We have followed George Russell from the occult to the foun-

---

paints & canvas & sent them to decorate schools & public buildings. It was a wonderful achievement this'. 'I really want to get back to Ireland ... But I am glad I came as I have had all kind of experiences, meeting ministers & high officials and watching their minds at work. My old friend Henry Wallace is the most important figure in the Roosevelt administration ... He has loomed up suddenly before America a great man.' George Russell to Estelle Solomons, 28 January 1935. Seumas O'Sullivan correspondence, TCD ms 4635/1228. **42** Details of Russell's funeral arrangements can be read in the *Irish Times* and London *Times*, 18, 19 and 22 July 1935. **43** *Irish Times*, 22 July 1935. 8. **44** Ibid. **45** Ibid.

dation of co-operative self-help in Ireland, from anarchism to Sinn Féin, from the 1913 Lock-Out to the 1916 Rising. The First World War and Russian Revolution have haunted our own Irish disturbances, the war of independence and civil wars. We have watched Russell refuse his revolutionary past to provide intellectual buttress to a Free State in constant danger of collapse. We have, all the while, flowed with a current of ideas, from futurism to science, from Ireland to Continental Europe and beyond, in a number of journals, not only Russell's but also the *All Ireland Review*, the *Dublin Magazine*, the *Enemy*, the *Irish Theosophist*, the *New Statesman* and the *Realist*, among others. The question, then, seems less of Russell's influence and more of Russell's intellectual intervention. The practical aspect of Russell's legacy, sometimes equally important as the ideal of intellectual engagement in decades of straitened finance, was a memorial fund, a source of revenue for many critics, novelists and poets throughout the years.[46] For now, the scholar reads Russell in the *Irish Homestead* and the *Irish Statesman* but rarely. But his commitment to the moment, to the intervention of the mind in matters of immense practical importance, was an education to the generation that followed. Frank O'Connor and Sean O'Faolain were early, and regular, contributors to the *Irish Statesman*. The *Bell* was their intellectual defence of a liberal, open Ireland in the 1940s and its origin owed everything to the *Irish Statesman* (the second issue even contains an O'Connor pen portrait of Russell). O'Faolain's editorial style, ironic, factual, polemic, owes much to Russell, and many of the issues the *Bell* addressed education, poverty, and censorship – were all preserves of the *Irish Statesman*. Hubert Butler was inspired as a young man by Russell's vision of an Ireland where

> a real village community would grow round every creamery and ... the principle of sharing would extend into every branch of life, spiritual, economic, cultural. The communal marketing of eggs and butter would lead to more intimate and domestic forms of sharing. Æ saw the hedges planted with apple trees and gooseberry bushes, as in Germany, and gymnasiums and libraries, picture galleries and village halls, to which each man or woman made his contribution according to his powers, so that each village became a focus of activity and debate.[47]

Butler's faith in the possibility of Russell's project was shaken by his own experience 'at the end of a relatively humane and sensible era and at the begin-

---

46 Details of Russell's Memorial Fund for 1950 reveal a list of entries graded by committee. A.N. Jeffares' *W.B. Yeats* was awarded an 'A', as was Benedict Kiely's *Call for a miracle*. The fund had a balance of £101 in November 1950, rising to £779 by the end of the decade. Seumas O'Sullivan correspondence, TCD ms 4640/2485, 4640/2488, 4640/2508, 4642/3170. **47** Hubert Butler, 'Divided loyalties', *Escape from the anthill*. 95–6.

ning of a cruel and chaotic one'.[48] But Butler's disillusion was born of Irish conflict in the 1980s. Now that some attempt has been made to find the '*modus
vivendi* between Unionist and Nationalist, between Catholic and Protestant'[49]
that was beyond Butler's sight in 'Divided loyalties', perhaps Russell's own belief
in the necessity of local community might once more be recovered. For Russell
rescued Butler from faction:

> When I was growing up, there was the *Irish Statesman*, which led me and
> many others out of the Anglo-Irish ghetto in which we had been
> brought up and reminded us that we were Irishmen. For our parents of
> the ascendancy it was easy and obvious to live in Ireland, but we of the
> 'descendancy' were surrounded in the twenties by the burnt houses of
> our friends and relations.[50]

Russell was a great editor, able to concentrate his readers' minds on the
immediate demands of the future. In the north of Ireland, Russell proved inspiration to a new generation of authors, including John Boyd and John Hewitt,
who saw Russell as an Ulsterman capable of making an impression in the wide
world, possessed of a vision beyond the 'wee six'. At the time of greatest pressure, when the Second World War threatened first isolation, then destruction,
Boyd followed Russell's old example and edited a journal, *Lagan*, a river that led
to confluence with the world's great waters. Boyd, however, found Russell's
townsmen more reticent of Russell's achievement. During the Second World
War, Boyd gave an adult education class in Newry, Co. Down:

> I enjoyed this class so much that the following winter I repeated my lec-
> tures on Irish literature to a smaller class in Lurgan. In Newry my class
> of about thirty-five students had been enthusiastic: in Lurgan the class
> was much smaller, fifteen at most, and apathetic. I could not understand
> at first why the same course could prove to be popular in one town and
> fall so flat in another. Then, after I gave a lecture on Æ, light dawned.
> My Lurgan class clearly disliked everything that Æ stood for, regarded
> him as a traitor to the Protestant and Unionist cause, and were not in the
> least pleased to learn that such a rebel figure was associated by birth with
> their deeply loyalist community. My suggestion that a plaque should go
> on display somewhere in the town was received in silence. 'No Æ here'
> was the message I got, and I was glad when the course ended.[51]

John Hewitt found more to admire in Russell's thought than these northern
countrymen. 'The Municipal Gallery revisited October 1954' promenades

48 Ibid. 96–7.   **49** Ibid. 95.   **50** Hubert Butler, '*The Bell*: an Anglo-Irish view', *Escape from the
anthill*. 147.   **51** John Boyd, *The middle of my journey*. 8.

before portraits of John O'Leary, George Bernard Shaw and James Stephens to reach

> George Russell, then, my fellow countryman,
> a lad this, as of seventy years ago;
> you could not tell from this slight beardless one,
> that this was he who, in day's afterglow,
> saw timeless creatures on gay errands run,
> for there's no lettered label here to show
>   what scale or scope this stripling promised us.[52]

This book is some answer to Hewitt's rebuke, a lettered label to suggest the scale of Russell's contribution to the Irish intellectual revival. Russell's work has not, until now, received sustained treatment in context of then contemporary events that might bring it back to life, rescued from obscurity by virtue of the past immediate, by our sight of Russell's journey through the storm of progress to a vision of Ireland now. Russell was a radical Irish intellectual fully engaged with the changes, cultural, economic and national, that transformed his society in somewhat over four decades. He was an active agent in the revolution and an international propagandist of independence. Russell was a connection point between Ireland and the world, a conduit, through the *Irish Homestead* and *Irish Statesman*, for the new literary, political and social doctrines that grew from nineteenth-century enlightenment. Developments in science, in chemistry and physics, as well as in art, in futurism and dada, prompted Russell to enquiry into the nature of his environment in Ireland and the world beyond. For Russell was not simply receptive of trends in global thought; he actively developed new modes of discussion. We know, for a fact, that Gandhi read *Co-operation and nationality* and *The national being*.[53] Russell's belief in self-help, and the moral benefits that accrued from industrial, as psychological, decolonisation, contributed to his Indian contemporary's own programme of national reconstruction. Russell was, by the end of his career, a writer of international reputation, an authority on mutual aid and editor for four decades of two journals that were read across continents. Agent of economic and national revolution in his own country, painter and author of pamphlets, poetry and prose, Russell was an intellectual idealist of the first order. A polemicist to match George Bernard Shaw, Russell was a creative thinker capable of rigorous practicality.

That we have forgotten this tells us much of our misunderstanding of Russell's period. We have constructed, over generations, a view of an Irish Literary Revival

---

52 John Hewitt, 'The Municipal Gallery revisited October 1954', *Collected poems 1932–1967*. 100.   53 Gandhi invited Russell to meet him in London in October 1931 but Russell could not attend because of his wife's illness. See H. Summerfield, *That myriad-minded man*. 262.

that limits both our understanding of literature and of revival. Irish writing in the late nineteenth and twentieth centuries was, as I have argued throughout this book, a literature committed to the moment, part of a cultural fabric that held writing to be one expression of minds that could also be consumed with agriculture, art, co-operation, education and, sometimes, revolution. So we have Patrick Pearse, educationalist, poet and militant. So we have Horace Plunkett, peer, facilitator and economic reformer. So we have William Butler Yeats, theatre director, poet and socialite comfortable by turns between Ireland and England. So we have George William Russell, editor, author and radical, a voice for social change and national revolution, an anarchist turned to the state. Ireland from 1890 to 1930 was a society experiencing relentless change, of parallel revolution at variant pace across the spectrum of modernity. I have tried in this book to follow Russell's negotiation of this ever evolving, complex state through his writings. I leave you in the conviction that George Russell was centre of an Irish intellectual culture that faced every development of its day with honesty, courage and commitment:

> Now you are gone, you seem a vision –
>   Something that haunted for a little time
> The splendour of the evening, or astir
>   With bees in bloom of time:
>
> Or, at the hour when mothers tell old tales
>   To children, something passing through
>   The gleams
> Of cottage windows; or, on Western gales
>   Riding, a king of dreams.
>
> Or about hawthorns lingering to greet
>   The earliest May amongst the blazing
>   Green,
> Or through the heather travelling to meet
>   Spirits we have not seen –
>
> A lovely radiance of a passing star
>   Upon a sudden journey through the gloaming,
> Lighting low Irish hills, and then, afar,
>   To its own regions homing.[54]

---

54 Lord Dunsany, 'Æ', *Irish Times*, 19 July 1935. 6.

Bibliography

JOURNALS AND NEWSPAPERS

All Ireland Review
An t-Oglac
Athenaeum
Bealtaine
Bell
Calendar of Modern Letters
Catholic Bulletin and Book Review
Criterion
Dial
Dublin Magazine
Dublin Review
Éire
Enemy
Freeman's Journal
Internationalist
Irish Freedom
Irish Homestead
Irish Independent
Irish Opinion
Irish Peasant
Irish Rosary
Irish Statesman (1st Series)
Irish Statesman: with which is incorporat-ed the Irish Homestead (2nd Series)
Irish Theosophist
Irish Times
Irish Tribune
Klaxon
Lagan
Leader
London Mercury
Manchester Guardian
New Statesman
Pioneer
Poblacht na h-Eireann
Realist
Republican War Bulletin
Round Table
Samhain
Sinn Féin
Spectator
Studies
Theosophist
Times
To-morrow
Unionist
Voice of Labour
Watchword of Labour

MANUSCRIPT COLLECTIONS

Alan Denson, 'Typescript in three volumes of the collected letters of George Russell (Æ)', National Library of Ireland
Arthur Griffith papers, National Library of Ireland
Irish Convention papers, Trinity College Dublin
Irish Statesman Publishing Company dissolved company file, National Archives
Edward MacLysaght papers, National Library of Ireland

Macmillan archive, British Library
H.F. Norman papers, Plunkett Foundation
William O'Brien pamphlet collection. National Library of Ireland
Seumas O'Sullivan papers, Trinity College Dublin
Horace Plunkett diaries and papers, Plunkett Foundation
George Bernard Shaw papers, British Library
Talbot Press archive, National Archives

PUBLISHED WORKS

A. Acton, V. Chernaev and W. Rosenborg (eds.), *Critical companion to the Russian revolution 1914–1921*. London: Arnold, 1991.

Hazard Adams, *Blake and Yeats: the contrary vision*. NY: Cornell, 1955.

Michael Adams, *Censorship: the Irish experience*. Dublin: Scepter, 1968.

Kieran Allen, *Fianna Fáil and Irish labour: 1926 to the present*. London: Pluto, 1997.

M. Amory, *Biography of Lord Dunsany*. London: Collins, 1972.

W. Anderson, *James Connolly and the Irish left*. Dublin: Irish Academic Press, 1994.

Bruce Arnold, *Irish art: a concise history*. London: Thames and Hudson, 1991.

K.C. Bailey, *A history of Trinity College Dublin 1892–1945*. Dublin: Dublin University Press, 1947.

Mikhail Bakhtin, *The dialogic imagination: four essays*. London: University of Texas Press, 1981.

Clifford Bax, *Some I knew well*. London: Phoenix House, 1951.

Gillian Beer, *Darwin's plots: evolutionary narrative in Darwin, George Eliot and nineteenth-century fiction*. London: Routledge, 1983.

Laurence Binyon, 'From The fourth of August', Up the line to death: the war poets 1914–1918. London: Methuen, 1976.

William Blake, *Complete writings*. Ed. G. Keynes. Oxford: Oxford UP, 1991.

H.P. Blavatsky, *The secret doctrine: the synthesis of science, religion and philosophy*. 1888. 2 vols. Pasadena: Theosophical UP, 1970.

Patrick Bolger, *The Irish co-operative movement: its history and development*. Dublin: Institute of Public Administration, 1977.

R. Bourke, *Romantic discourse and political modernity: Wordsworth, the intellectual and cultural critique*. London: Harvester, 1993.

D. George Boyce, *The Irish question and British politics, 1868–1996*. London: Macmillan, 1996.

——, *Nationalism in Ireland*. 1982. London: Routledge, 1995.

Ernest Boyd, *Ireland's literary renaissance*. Dublin: Maunsel, 1916.

John Boyd, *The middle of my journey*. Belfast: Blackstaff, 1990.

A. Boyle, *The riddle of Erskine Childers*. London: Macmillan, 1977.

R. Brettell, *Modern art 1851–1929: capitalism and representation*. Oxford: Oxford UP, 1999.

U. Bridge (ed.), *W.B. Yeats and Sturge Moore: their correspondence 1901–1937*. London: Routledge, 1953.

Sydney Brooks, *The new Ireland*. 2nd ed. Dublin: Maunsel, 1907.

Terence Brown, *Ireland: a social and cultural history*. London: Fontana, 1981.

——, *Ireland's literature: selected essays*. Mullingar: Lilliput, 1988.

——, *The life of W.B. Yeats: a critical biography*. Dublin: Gill and Macmillan, 1999.

Patrick Buckland, *The Anglo-Irish and the new Ireland 1885–1922*. Dublin: Gill and Macmillan, 1972.

——, *Irish unionism: 1885–1923*. Belfast: HMSO, 1973.

C. Butler, *Early modernism: literature, music, and painting in Europe, 1900–1916*. Oxford: Clarendon, 1994.

Hubert Butler, *Escape from the anthill*. Mullingar: Lilliput, 1985.

L.P. Byrne, *Twenty-one years of the IAWS 1897–1918*. Dublin: IAWS, 1919.

Julia Carlson (ed.), *Banned in Ireland: censorship and the Irish experience*. London: Routledge, 1990.

Thomas Carlyle, *On heroes, hero-worship, & the heroic in history*. Notes and Introduction by H.K. Goldberg. Oxford: California UP, 1993.

Edward Carpenter, *My days and dreams: being autobiographical notes with portraits and illustrations*. London: Allen and Unwin, 1916.

F. Carroll, *American opinion and the Irish question 1920–23: a study in opinion and policy*. Dublin: Gill and Macmillan, 1978.

Erskine Childers, *A strike-breaking army at work*. London: Daily Herald, 1919.

Austin Clarke, *A penny in the clouds: more memories of Ireland and England*. London: Routledge, 1968.

——, *The cattledrive in Connaught and other poems*. London: Allen and Unwin, 1925.

——, *The vengeance of Fionn*. Dublin: Maunsel, 1918.

William Clyde, *Æ*. Edinburgh: Moray, 1935.

C. Coates, *Some less-known chapters in the life of Æ (George Russell): being the substance of a lecture delivered at Belfast, November, 1936*. Dublin: for the author, 1939.

Coimisiun na Gaeltachta: statement of government policy on recommendations of the commission. Dublin: Stationery Office, 1926.

G.D.H. Cole, *A history of the Labour party from 1914*. London: Routledge, 1948.

Stefan Collini, *Public moralists: political thought and intellectual life in Britain*. Oxford: Clarendon, 1991.

Mary Colum, *Life and the dream*. Dublin: Dolmen, 1966.

Padraic Colum, *Wild earth: a book of verse*. Dublin: Maunsel, 1907.

Padraic Colum and E.J. O'Brien (eds.), *Poems of the Irish Revolutionary Brotherhood: Thomas MacDonagh, P. H. Pearse (Padraic MacPiarais), Joseph Mary Plunkett, Sir Roger Casement*. Boston: Small, Maynard and Co., 1916.

James Connolly, *A socialist and war 1914–1916*. Ed. P. J. Musgrove. London: Lawrence and Wishart, 1941.

——, *Labour and Easter week: a selection from the writings of James Connolly*. Dublin: At the sign of the three candles, 1949.

——, *Labour in Ireland. Labour in Irish history. The re-conquest of Ireland*. Dublin: Maunsel, 1917.

P. Connolly, *No bland facility: selected writings on literature, religion and censorship*. Ed. J.H. Murphy. Gerrards Cross: Smythe, 1991.

Tim Pat Coogan, *De Valera: long fellow, long shadow*. London: Hutchinson, 1993.

Tim Pat Coogan and G. Morrison (eds.), *The Irish civil war*. London: Weidenfeld and Nicholson, 1998.

Daniel Corkery, *The hidden Ireland: a study of Gaelic Munster in the eighteenth century*. Dublin: Gill, 1925.

J.G. Crowther, *British scientists of the twentieth century*. London: Routledge, 1952.

Fintan Cullen, *Visual politics: the representation of Ireland 1750–1930*. Cork: Cork UP, 1997.

Louis Cullen, *An economic history of Ireland since 1660*. London: Batsford, 1972.

Elizabeth Cullingford, *Gender and history in Yeats's love poetry*. Cambridge: Cambridge UP, 1993.

——, *Yeats, Ireland and fascism*. London: Macmillan, 1981.

Constantine Curran, *James Joyce remembered*. Oxford: Oxford UP, 1968.

J. Curran, *The birth of the Irish Free State: 1921–1923*. Alabama: Alabama UP, 1980.

Dáil Éireann, *Democratic programme*. np: np, 1919.

——, *Minutes of proceedings of the first parliament of the Republic of Ireland 1919–1921*. Official Record. Dublin: Stationery Office, nd.

George Dangerfield, *The strange death of Liberal England*. London: Constable, 1936.

R.B. Davis, *George William Russell ('Æ')*. Boston: Twayne, 1977.

R. Dawson, *Red terror and green*. London: John Murray, 1920.

Seamus Deane et al. (eds.), *The Field Day anthology of Irish writing*. 3 Vols. Derry: Field Day, 1991.

Aodh de Blacam, *Towards the republic: a study of new Ireland's social and political aims*. Dublin: Kiersey, 1918.

——, *What Sinn Féin stands for: the Irish republican movement; its history, aims and ideals, examined as to their significance to the world*. Dublin: Mellipont, 1921.

Alan Denson, *G.W. Russell (Æ) 1867–1935: a centennial assessment*. Kendal: for the author, 1968.

——, *Letters from Æ*. NY: Abelard Schuman, 1961.

——, *Printed writings by George W. Russell (Æ): a bibliography*. Illinois: Northwestern UP, 1961.

P.L. Dickinson, *The Dublin of yesterday*. London: Methuen, 1929.

Margaret Digby, *Horace Plunkett: an Anglo-American Irishman*. Oxford: Blackwell, 1949.

J. Di Salvo, G. Rosso and C. Hobson (eds.), *Blake, politics and history*. London: Garland, 1998.

E.R. Dodds (ed.), *Journal and letters of Stephen MacKenna*. Preface by Padraic Colum. London: Constable, 1936.

——, *Missing persons: an autobiography*. Oxford: Clarendon, 1977.

A.V. Douglas, *The life of Arthur Shelley Eddington*. London: Nelson, 1956.

Edward Dowden, *The life of Percy Bysshe Shelley*. 2 vols. London: Kegan Paul, Trench & Co., 1886.

——, *Studies in literature: 1789–1877*. London: Kegan Paul, 1878.

Richard Dunphy, *The making of Fianna Fáil power in Ireland: 1923–1948*. Oxford: Clarendon, 1995.

A.S. Eddington, *The nature of the physical world*. Cambridge: Cambridge UP, 1929.

R.D. Edwards, *Patrick Pearse: the triumph of failure*. London: Gollancz, 1977.

John Eglinton, *A memoir of Æ: George William Russell*. London: Macmillan, 1937.

Richard Ellmann, *James Joyce*. 1959. Oxford: Oxford UP, 1982.

Ralph Waldo Emerson, *English traits*. NY: AMS Press, 1979.

——, 'The Poet', *Ralph Waldo Emerson*. Ed. R. Poirier. Oxford: Oxford UP, 1990. 197–215.

B. Erkilla, Whitman the political poet. Oxford: Oxford UP, 1989.

Darrell Figgis, *Æ (George W. Russell): a study of a man and a nation*. 1916. NY: Kennikat press, 1970.

——, *The Gaelic state in the past and future or 'The crown of a nation'*. Dublin: Maunsel, 1917.

——, *The paintings of William Blake*. London: Ernest Benn, 1925.

——, *Recollections of the Irish war*. London: Ernest Benn, 1927.

——, *Sinn Féin catechism*. Dublin: Kiersey, 1918.

Richard Finneran and M. Fitzgerald (eds.), *Some unpublished letters from Æ to James Stephens*. Dalkey: Cuala, 1979.

Richard Finneran, G. Harper and W. Murphy (eds.), *Letters to W.B. Yeats*. Vol. 2. London: Macmillan, 1977.

David Fitzpatrick, *Politics and Irish life 1913–1921: provincial experience of war and revolution*. London: Gill and Macmillan, 1977.

——, *The two Irelands 1912–1939*. Oxford: Oxford UP, 1998.

——, 'W.B. Yeats in Seanad Éireann', *Yeats and the theatre*. Eds. R. O'Driscoll and L. Edwards. London: Macmillan, 1975. 159–175.

W.J. Flynn, *Free State parliamentary companion for 1932*. Dublin: Talbot, 1932.

J.W. Foster, *Fictions of the Irish Literary Revival: a changeling art*. Syracuse: Syracuse UP, 1987.

R.F. Foster, *Modern Ireland, 1600–1972*. London: Penguin, 1988.

——, *W.B. Yeats: a life. Vol. I. The apprentice mage 1865–1914*. Oxford: Oxford UP, 1997.

R.M. Fox, *Labour in the national struggle*. Dublin: Liberty Hall, 1945.

——, *The co-operative reference library, Dublin: an explanation and an appeal*. Dublin: np, 1925.

——, *Years of freedom: the story of Ireland 1921–1948*. Cork: Trumpet Books, 1948.

Adrian Frazier, *George Moore, 1852–1933*. London: Yale UP, 2000.

Grattan Freyer, *W.B. Yeats and the anti-democratic tradition*. Dublin: Gill and Macmillan, 1981.

Tom Garvin, *The evolution of Irish nationalist politics*. Dublin: Gill and Macmillan, 1981.

——, *1922: the birth of Irish democracy*. Dublin: Gill and Macmillan, 1996.

D. Geary, *Labour and socialist movements in Europe before 1914*. Oxford: Berg, 1989.

D. Gerhardus and M. Gerhardus. *Cubism and futurism: the evolution of the self-sufficient picture*. Oxford: Phaidon, 1979.

Luke Gibbons, *Transformations in Irish Culture*. Cork: Cork UP, 1996.

Monk Gibbon (ed.), *The living torch, Æ*. London: Macmillan, 1937.

Percy Gillespie, 'I remember', *Sir Horace Plunkett centenary handbook*. Dublin: National Co-operative Council, 1954. 11–13.

——, *The masterpiece and the man: Yeats as I knew him*. London: Hart-Davis, 1959.

Oliver St John Gogarty, 'An angelic anarchist', *Colby Library Quarterly*, 4:2 (May 1955). 24–8.

——, *An offering of swans*. Dublin: Cuala, 1923.

James Winder Good, *Irish unionism*. Dublin: Talbot, 1920.

Stephen Jay Gould, *Bully for brontosaurus: reflections on natural history*. London: Hutchinson, 1991.

C.D. Greaves, *The Irish Transport and General Workers' Union: the formative years 1909–1923*. Dublin: Gill and Macmillan, 1982.

Alice Stopford Green, *The making of Ireland and its undoing 1200–1600*. London: Macmillan, 1908.

Lady Gregory (ed.), *Ideals in Ireland: written by 'Æ', D. P. Moran, George Moore, Douglas Hyde, Standish O'Grady, and W.B. Yeats*. London: At the Unicorn, 1901.

——, *Lady Gregory's journals 1916–1930*. Ed. L. Robinson. Dublin: Browne and Nolan, 1946.

G. Griffin, *Socialism and superior brains: the political thought of Bernard Shaw*. London: Routledge, 1993.

John Gross, *The rise and fall of the man of letters: English literary life since 1800*. London: Penguin, 1990.

Denis Gwynn, *The Irish Free State 1922–1927*. London: Macmillan, 1928.

Edward Hagan, *'High nonsensical words': a study of the works of Standish O'Grady*. NY: Whitston, 1986.

W. Hancock and J. Van Der Poel (eds.), *Selections from the Smuts papers*, vol. 3 June 1910–November 1918. London: Cambridge UP, 1966.

Maurice Harmon, *Sean O'Faolain*. London: Constable, 1994.

Frank Harris, *Latest contemporary portraits*. NY: Macaulay, 1927.

C. Harrison, *English art and modernism 1900–1939*. London: Allen Lane, 1981.

L. Harrison and G. Sapelli (eds.), *Strikes, social conflict and the First World War: an international perspective*. Milan: Fondazione Giangiacomo Feltrinelli, 1992.

Thomas Hennessey, *A history of Northern Ireland 1920–1996*. Dublin: Gill and Macmillan, 1997.

John Hewitt, *Collected poems 1932–1967*. London: MacGibbon and Kee, 1968.

T.W. Heyck, *The transformation of intellectual life in Victorian England*. London: Croom Helm, 1982.

F.R. Higgins, *The dark breed: a book of poems*. London: Macmillan, 1927.

——, *Salt air*. Dublin: Irish Bookshop, 1923.

M. Hilleges, *The future as nightmare: H.G. Wells and the anti-utopians*. Oxford: Oxford UP, 1967.

Robert Hogan and Daniel Poteet, *The modern Irish drama: the art of the amateur, 1916–20*. Gerrards Cross: Colin Smythe, 1984.

J. Holloway, *The Victorian sage: studies in argument*. 1953. London: Archon, 1962.

Michael Holroyd, *Bernard Shaw*. Vol. 2: *1898–1918, the pursuit of power*. London: Chatto and Windus, 1989.

Homer, *The Iliad*. Translated by R. Fagles. Introduction by B. Knox. London: Penguin, 1990.

M. Hopkinson, *Green against green: the Irish civil war*. Dublin: Gill and Macmillan, 1988.

J.J. Horgan, *Parnell to Pearse: some recollections and reflections*. Dublin: Browne and Nolan, 1948.

H. Howarth, *The Irish writers 1880–1940: literature under Parnell's star*. London: Rockliff, 1958.

Marjorie Howes, *Yeats's nations: gender, class and Irishness*. Cambridge: Cambridge UP, 1996.

J. Hutchinson, *The dynamics of cultural nationalism: the Gaelic revival and the creation of the Irish nation state*. London: Allen and Unwin, 1987.

Samuel Hynes, *The Edwardian turn of mind*. London: Pimlico, 1992.

Irish Unionist Alliance, *Ireland of to-day. Sinn Féin and bolshevism. A warning to England*. Dublin: IUA, 1919.

R. Iyer and N. Iyer, *The descent of the gods: comprising the mystical writings of G. W. Russell 'Æ'*. Gerrards Cross: Smythe, 1988.

Frederic Jameson, *Fables of aggression: Wyndham Lewis, the modernist as fascist*. London: University of California Press, 1979.

S. Jansen, *Censorship: the knot that binds power and knowledge*. Oxford: Oxford UP, 1991.

A.N. Jeffares and A.S. Knowland, *A commentary on the collected plays of W.B. Yeats*. London: Macmillan, 1975.

Thomas Johnson, *The future of labour in Ireland: being the chairman's address to the delegates attending the Irish Trades Union Congress at the town hall, Sligo, on August 7th, 8th, and 9th, 1916*. Dublin: National Executive of the Irish Trades Union Congress and Labour Party, 1916.

Denis Johnston, *The moon in the yellow river, and The old lady says no*, Foreword by Constantine Curran. London: Cape, 1932.

Thomas Johnstone, *Orange, green and khaki: the story of the Irish regiments in the great war, 1914–1918*. Dublin: Gill and Macmillan, 1992.

C. Jordan, *A terrible beauty: the Easter rebellion and Yeats's 'great tapestry'*. London: Associated UP, 1987.

James Joyce, *Dubliners*. London: Cape, 1988.

——, *Ulysses*. Paris: Shakespeare and Company, 1922.

Richard Kain, *Susan L. Mitchell*. Lewisburg: Bucknell UP, 1972.

Richard Kain and J. O'Brien, *George Russell (Æ)*. London: Associated UP, 1976.

Patrick Kavanagh, *The complete poems of Patrick Kavanagh*. Ed. P. Kavanagh. NY: Peter Kavanagh Hand Press, 1972.

——, *The green fool*. 1938. London: Penguin, 1975.

John Kelly (ed.), *The collected letters of W.B. Yeats*. Vol. 1, *1865–1895*. Oxford: Clarendon, 1986.

——, *The collected letters of W.B. Yeats*. Vol. 3, *1901–1904*. Oxford: Clarendon, 1994.

John Kelly, Warwick Gould and Deirdre Toomey (eds.), *The collected letters of W.B. Yeats*. Vol. 2, *1896–1900*. Oxford: Clarendon, 1997.

S.B. Kennedy, *Irish art and modernism: 1880–1950*. Belfast: Institute of Irish Studies, 1991.

C.T. Kindilein, 'George William Russell (Æ) and the Colby collection', *Colby Library Quarterly*, 4:2 (May 1955). 21–4.

Prince Peter Kropotkin, *Fields, factories and workshops: or, industry combined with agriculture and brain work with manual work.* London: Hutchinson, 1899.

——, *Mutual aid: a factor in evolution.* London: Heinemann, 1914.

Peter Kuch, *Yeats and Æ: 'The antagonism that unites dear friends'.* Gerrards Cross: Smythe, 1986.

The Labour Party and Ireland. London: Labour Party, 1921.

Emmet Larkin, *James Larkin: Irish labour leader 1876–1947.* London: Routledge, 1965.

Hugh Law, *Anglo-Irish literature.* Foreword by Æ. Dublin: Talbot, 1926.

J.J. Lee, *Ireland 1912–1985: politics and society.* Cambridge: Cambridge UP, 1989.

R. Lister, *Beulah to Byzantium: a study of parallels in the works of W.B. Yeats, William Blake, Samuel Palmer and Edward Calvert.* Mountrath: Dolmen Press, 1965.

David Lloyd, *Anomalous states: Irish writing and the post-colonial moment.* Dublin: Lilliput, 1993.

——, *Ireland after history.* Cork: Cork UP, 1999.

Kathryn Ludwigson, *Edward Dowden.* NY: Twayne, 1973.

Robert Lynd, *Galway of the races: selected essays.* Ed. S. MacMahon. Dublin: Lilliput, 1990.

F.S.L. Lyons, *Culture and anarchy in Ireland: 1890–1939.* Oxford: Oxford UP, 1982.

——, *Ireland since the famine.* London: Weidenfeld and Nicholson, 1971.

J. Lyons, *Oliver St. John Gogarty: the man of many talents.* Dublin: Blackwater, 1980.

Thomas MacGreevy, *Thomas Stearns Eliot: a study.* London: Chatto & Windus, 1931.

Stephen MacKenna (trans.), *Plotinus: the ethical treatises. Being the treatises of the first ennead with Porphyry's Life of Plotinus, and the Preller-Ritter extracts forming a conspectus of the Plotinian system.* London: Medici Society, 1917.

Charlotte Elizabeth MacManus, *White light and flame: memories of the Irish Literary Revival and the Anglo-Irish war.* Dublin: Talbot, 1929.

C. McCarthy, *Trade unions in Ireland 1894–1960.* Dublin: Institute of Public Administration, 1977.

W.J. McCormack, *Ascendancy and tradition in Anglo-Irish literary history from 1789 to 1939.* Oxford: Clarendon, 1985.

R.B. McDowell, *The Church of Ireland: 1869–1969.* London: Routledge, 1975.

——, *The Irish Convention 1917–1918.* London: Routledge, 1970.

R.B. McDowell and D. Webb, *Trinity College Dublin 1593–1952: an academic history.* Cambridge: Cambridge UP, 1982.

Patricia McFate, 'The Interpreters: Æ's symposium and roman à clef', *Éire-Ireland*, 11:3 (Autumn 1976). 82–92.

Andrew Malone, 'Party government in the Irish Free State', *Reprinted from Political Science Quarterly Vol. XLIV:3, Sept. 1929*, NY: Academy of Political Science, 1929.

M. Manning and M. McDowell, *Electricity supply in Ireland: the history of the ESB.* Dublin: Gill and Macmillan, 1984.

P. Marcus, *Standish O'Grady.* Lewisburg: Bucknell UP, 1970.

A. Martin, *James Stephens: a critical study.* Dublin: Gill and Macmillan, 1977.

Patrick Maume, *'Life that is exile': Daniel Corkery and the search for Irish Ireland.* Belfast: Institute of Irish Studies, 1993.

B. Maye, *Fine Gael 1923–1987: a general history with biographical sketches of leading members*. Dublin: Blackwater, 1993.

S. Metress, *The American Irish and Irish nationalism: a sociohistorical introduction*. Lanham: Scarecrow, 1995.

J. Meyers, *The enemy: a biography of Wyndham Lewis*. London: Routledge, 1980.

E. Mikhail, *J.M. Synge: interviews and recollections*. London: Macmillan, 1977.

John Milton, *Areopagitica and education: with autobiographical passages from other prose works*. Ed. G.H. Sabina. Illinois: Davidson, 1951.

Arthur Mitchell and P. Ó Snodaigh (eds.), *Irish political documents 1916–1949*. Dublin: Irish Academic Press, 1985.

Arthur Mitchell, *Labour in Irish politics 1890–1930: the Irish labour movement in an age of revolution*. Dublin: Irish UP, 1974.

——, *Revolutionary government in Ireland: Dáil Éireann 1919–22*. Dublin: Gill and Macmillan, 1995.

John Mitchel, *Jail journal*. 1854. Dublin: University Press of Ireland, 1982.

Susan Mitchell, *Aids to the immortality of certain persons in Ireland charitably administered: a new edition with poems added*. Dublin: Maunsel, 1913.

——, *George Moore*. Dublin: Maunsel, 1916.

——, *The living chalice and other poems: a new edition with poems added*. Dublin: Maunsel, 1913.

W. Mommsen and H. Husung (eds.), *The development of trade unionism in Great Britain and Germany 1880–1914*. London: Allen and Unwin, 1985.

George Moore, *Hail and farewell*, 3 vols (*Ave, Salve, Vale*). London: Heinemann, 1911–14.

Thomas Moore, *The poetical works of Thomas Moore*. Ed. A.D. Godley. London: Oxford UP, 1915.

D.P. Moran, *The philosophy of Irish Ireland*. Dublin: Duffy and Gill, 1905.

C. Mowat, *Britain between the wars: 1918–1940*. London: Methuen, 1983.

B.P. Murphy, *Patrick Pearse and the lost republican ideal*. Dublin: James Duffy, 1991.

R. Murray and H. Law, *Ireland*. London: Hodder and Stoughton, 1924.

J. Natterstad, *Francis Stuart*. London: Associated UP, 1974.

H.W. Nevinson, *Fire of life*. London: Nisbet, 1935.

——, *Running accompaniments*. London: Routledge, 1936.

D. Newton, *British labour, European socialism and the struggle for peace 1889–1914*. Oxford: Clarendon, 1985.

J. O'Brien, *Liam O'Flaherty*. Lewisburg: Bucknell UP, 1973.

Margaret O'Callaghan, 'Language, nationality and cultural identity in the Irish Free State, 1922–27: the *Irish Statesman* and the *Catholic Bulletin* reappraised', *Irish Historical Studies*, 24:94 (1984). 226–45.

Sean O'Casey, *Autobiographies*. London: Macmillan, 1963.

——, *Juno and the paycock*. London: Macmillan, 1925.

——, *The plough and the stars: a tragedy in four acts*. London: Macmillan, 1926.

——, *The silver tassie: a tragi-comedy in four acts*. London: Macmillan, 1928.

——, *The story of the Irish Citizen Army*. Dublin: Maunsel, 1919.

Emmet O'Connor, *A labour history of Ireland 1824–1960*. Dublin: Gill and Macmillan, 1992.

——, *Syndicalism in Ireland 1917–1923*. Cork: Cork UP, 1988.

Frank O'Connor, *My father's son*. Dublin: Gill and Macmillan, 1968.

Sean O'Faolain, *Vive moi!* Boston: Brown, 1964.

Liam O'Flaherty, *The informer*. London: Guild, 1949.

——, *The letters of Liam O'Flaherty*. Ed. A. O'Kelly. Dublin: Wolfhound, 1996.

——, *Shame the devil*. London: Grayson, 1934.

Hugh Art O'Grady, *Standish James O'Grady: the man and the writer*. Foreword by Alfred Perceval Graves. Dublin: Talbot, 1929.

Standish James O'Grady, *The chain of gold: a tale of adventure on the wild west coast of Ireland*. Dublin: Talbot, 1921.

——, *The flight of the eagle*. London: Lawrence and Bullen, 1897.

——, *History of Ireland*: Vol. 2. *Cuculain and his contemporaries*. Dublin: Ponsonby, 1880.

——, *History of Ireland*: Vol. 1. *the heroic period*. Dublin: Ponsonby, 1878.

——, (pseud. Luke Netterville), *The queen of the world: or, under the tyranny*. London: Lawrence and Bullen, 1900.

——, *The story of Ireland*. Methuen: London, 1894.

——, 'Walt Whitman, the poet of joy', *Walt Whitman critical assessments: vol. 2. The response to the writing*. Ed. G. Clarke. Sussex: Helm information, nd. 141–6.

P.S. O'Hegarty, *A history of Ireland under the Union: 1801 to 1922*. London: Methuen, 1952.

——, *A short memoir of Terence MacSwiney*. With a chapter by Daniel Corkery. Dublin: Talbot, 1922.

——, *The victory of Sinn Féin: how it won it, and how it used it*. Dublin: Talbot, 1924.

Ernie O'Malley, *On another man's wound*. 1936. London: Four Square, 1961.

——, *The singing flame*. Dublin: Anvil, 1978.

M. O'Neill, *Lennox Robinson*. NY: Twayne, 1964.

D. O'Sullivan, *The Irish Free State and its senate: a study in contemporary politics*. London: Faber, 1940.

Seumas O'Sullivan, *Essays and recollections*. Dublin: Talbot, 1944.

Official report: debate on the Treaty between Great Britain and Ireland signed in London on the 6th December, 1921. Session Dec. 1921– Jan. 1922. Dublin: Talbot, 1922.

Janet Oppenheim, *The other world: spiritualism and psychical research in England, 1850–1914*. Cambridge: Cambridge UP, 1985.

A.R. Orage, *An Englishman talks it out with an Irishman*. Dublin: Talbot, 1918.

——, *Readers and writers (1917–1921)*. London: Allen, 1922.

——, *Selected essays and critical writings*. Eds. H. Read and D. Saurat. London: Stanley Nott, 1935.

Oxford annotated Bible. Revised standard version containing the Old and New Testaments. Eds. H. May and B. Metzger. Oxford: Oxford UP, 1962.

Herbert Palmer, *Summit and chasm: a book of poems and rimes (sic)*. London: Dent, 1934.

——, *The vampire and other poems and rimes (sic) of a pilgrim's progress*. London: Dent, 1936.

Patrick Pearse, *Collected works of Patrick H. Pearse: plays, stories, poems*. 1917. Dublin: Phoenix, 1924.

——, *Poems*. Dublin: Maunsel, 1918.

William Flinders Petrie, *The revolutions of civilisation*. London: Harper & Brothers, 1911.

——, *Seventy years in archaeology*. London: Sampson Low, 1932.

——, *Some sources of human history*. London: Society for Promoting Christian Knowledge, 1919.

Plato, *The republic*. Trans. D. Lee. London: Penguin, 1987.

Horace Plunkett, 'Introduction', *State aid and self-help in agricultural development: being a memorandum submitted by the Joint Board for Agricultural Organisation to the Development Commission*. London: Joint Board for Agricultural Organisation, 1911. 3–6.

——, *Ireland in the new century*. London: Murray, 1904.

——, *The Irish Convention: confidential report to His Majesty the King by the chairman*. Np: np, 1918.

Odon Por, *Guilds and co-operatives in Italy*. Trans. E. Townshend. Introduction by Æ. London: Labour Publishing Co. 1923.

Horace Plunkett, E. Pilkington and George Russell, *The United Irishwomen: their place, work and ideals*. Dublin: Maunsel, 1911.

—*Fascism*. Trans. E. Townshend. London: Labour Publishing Company, 1923.

Robert Lloyd Praeger, *The way that I went: an Irishman in Ireland*. Dublin: Hodges Figgis, 1937.

Hilary Pyle, *Red-headed rebel: Susan L. Mitchell, poet and mystic of the Irish Literary Revival*. Dublin: Wolfhound, 1998.

Forrest Reid, *W.B. Yeats: a critical study*. London: Martin Secker, 1915.

Report of the Committee on Evil Literature. Dublin: Stationery Office, 1927.

Report of the proceedings of the Irish Convention: presented to Parliament by command of His Majesty. Dublin: HMSO, 1918.

H. Ricketts, *The unforgiving minute: a life of Rudyard Kipling*. London: Chatto and Windus, 1999.

Frank Robbins, *Under the starry plough: recollections of the Irish Citizen Army*. Dublin: Academy Press, 1977.

Lennox Robinson (ed.), *A golden treasury of Irish verse*. London: Macmillan, 1925.

——, *Bryan Cooper*. London: Constable, 1931.

——, *The Irish theatre: lectures delivered during the Abbey Theatre festival held in Dublin in August 1938*. London: Macmillan, 1939.

George Russell, *Æ's letters to Mínanlábáin*. Introduction by Lucy Kingsley Porter. London: Macmillan, 1937.

——, 'A plea to the workers: a speech delivered in the Royal Albert Hall, London, Nov. 1, 1913', *The Dublin strike*. London: Christian Commonwealth Company, nd. 1–4.

——, 'A tribute by Æ', *Standish James O'Grady: the man and the writer*. Dublin: Talbot, 1929. 63–75.

——, 'An appeal to Dublin citizens', *The Dublin strike*, London: Christian Commonwealth Company, nd. 7–8.

——, *The avatars: a futurist fantasy*. London: Macmillan, 1933.

——, *The candle of vision*. London: Macmillan, 1918.

——, *The collected poems*. London: Macmillan, 1913.

——, *Co-operation and nationality: a guide for rural reformers from this to the next generation*. Dublin: Maunsel, 1912.

——, *The divine vision and other poems*. London: Macmillan, 1904.

——, *The earth breath and other poems*. London: John Lane, 1897.

——, 'Foreword', *The Trinity co-op. : 1913–1921 and after*. J. Johnston. Dublin: At Plunkett House, 1921. 3.

——, *The gods of war*. Dublin: for the author, 1916.

——, *Homeward songs by the way*. Dublin: Whaley, 1894.

——, *The house of the Titans*. London: Macmillan, 1934.

——, *Imaginations and reveries*. Dublin: Maunsel, 1915.

——, *The inner and the outer Ireland*. Dublin: Talbot, 1921.

——, *The interpreters*. London: Macmillan, 1922.

——, *Ireland and the Empire at the court of conscience*. Dublin: Talbot, 1921.

——, 'Ireland, past and future: being a paper read to the Sociological Society on 21st February, 1922', Np: np, 1922.

——, *Michael*, Dublin: for the author, 1919.

——, *The national being: some thoughts on an Irish polity*. Dublin: Maunsel, 1916.

——, 'Nationalism and imperialism', *Ideals in Ireland*. Ed. Lady Gregory. London: At the Unicorn, 1901. 15–24.

——, *New songs: a lyric selection made by Æ from poems by Padraic Colum, Eva Gore-Booth, Thomas Keohler, Alice Milligan, Susan Mitchell, Seumas O'Sullivan, George Roberts, and Ella Young*. Dublin: O'Donoghue, 1904.

——, *Song and its fountains*. London: Macmillan, 1932.

——, 'Twenty five years of Irish nationality', *Reprinted from Foreign Affairs: An American Quarterly Review*. np: np, 1929.

——, *Vale and other poems*. London: Macmillan, 1931.

——, *Voices of the stones*. London: Macmillan, 1925.

J. Russell, *James Starkey/Seumas O'Sullivan: a critical biography*. London: Associated UP, 1987.

W.P. Ryan, *The Irish labour movement: from the twenties to the present day*. Dublin: Talbot Press, nd.

Saorstát Éireann: Irish Free State official handbook. Dublin: Talbot, 1932.

G. Schirmer, *The poetry of Austin Clarke*. Mountrath: Dolmen, 1983.

'Seacranaide', *Easter week and after*. Dublin: National Publicity Committee, 1928.

B. Sexton, *Ireland and the crown, 1922–1936: the governor-generalship of the Free State*. Dublin: Irish Academic Press, 1989.

Shannon hydro-electric scheme. Limerick: Carroll, 1929.

George Bernard Shaw, 'Back to Methuselah', *Bernard Shaw: the complete prefaces. Volume 2: 1914–1929*. Eds. D.H. Lawrence and D.J. Leary. London: Penguin, 1995. 373–430.

——, *Bernard Shaw: collected letters 1911–1925*. Ed. D.H. Lawrence. London: Reinhardt, 1985.

——, ed., *Fabian essays in socialism. By G. B. Shaw, Sidney Webb, William Clarke, Sydney Oliver, Annie Besant, Graham Wallas and Hubert Bland*. London: Fabian Society, 1889.

——, *Pen portraits and reviews*. London: Constable, 1931.

——, *Shaw on censorship: being an extract from the minutes of evidence before the Joint Select Committee of the House of Lords and the House of Commons on the stage plays (censorship), 1909*. London: Shavian Tract No. 3, 1955.

Percy Bysshe Shelley, *Poems and prose*. Ed. T. Webb. London: Everyman, 1995.

——, *Prometheus unbound: the text and the drafts*. Ed. L.J. Zillmann. London: Yale UP, 1968.

V. Sherry, *Ezra Pound, Wyndham Lewis, and radical modernism*. Oxford: Oxford UP, 1993.

Siemens-Schuckertwerke, *Development of the Shannon water power, Ireland: a guide to the building sites*. Berlin: Siemens, 1927.

S. Sigerson, *Sinn Féin and socialism*. Dublin: Kiersey, nd.

A. Smith, *The New Statesman: portrait of a political weekly, 1913–1931*. London: Cass, 1996.

D. Smyth, *Desperately moral: a biography of H.G. Wells*. London: Yale UP, 1986.

Gerry Smyth, *Decolonisation and criticism: the construction of Irish literature*. London: Pluto, 1995.

Oswald Spengler, *Downfall of the west: form and actuality*. Authorised translation with notes by Charles Francis Atkinson. NY: Alfred Knopf, 1947.

Walter Starkie, *Scholars and gypsies: an autobiography*. London: Murray, 1963.

——, *The waveless plain: an Italian autobiography*. London: Murray, 1938.

——, 'Yeats and the Abbey Theatre', *Homage to Yeats 1865–1965: papers read at Clark Library seminar, October 16, 1965*. Los Angeles, UCLA, 1966.

James Stephens, *Arthur Griffith: journalist and statesman*. Dublin: Wilson Hartnell, 1924.

——, *The insurrection in Dublin*. Dublin: Scepter, 1916.

——, *Uncollected prose of James Stephens: volume 2, 1916–48*. Ed. P. McFate. Dublin: Gill and Macmillan, 1983.

L.A.G. Strong, *Green memory*. London: Methuen, 1961.

Francis Stuart, *Black list, section H*, London: Brian and O'Keefe, 1975.

——, *Lecture on nationality and culture*. Dublin: Sinn Féin, 1924.

——, *We have kept the faith*. Dublin: Oak Leaf Press, 1923.

Henry Summerfield, *That myriad-minded man: a biography of George William Russell 'Æ.' 1867–1935*. Gerrards Cross: Smythe, 1975.

Tailteann games: Irish race olympic. Dublin: np, 1922.

M. Taylor, *Community, anarchy and liberty*. Cambridge: Cambridge UP, 1982.

W.I. Thompson, *The imagination of an insurrection: Dublin, Easter 1916*. London: Harper, 1967.

W. Tomory, *Frank O'Connor*. Boston: Twayne, 1980.

Charles Townshend, *Political violence in Ireland: government and resistance since 1848*. Oxford: Clarendon, 1983.

Katherine Tynan, *The years of the shadow*. London: Constable, 1919.

M. Valiulis, *Portrait of a revolutionary: General Richard Mulcahy and the founding of the Irish Free State*. Dublin: Irish Academic Press, 1992.

Norman Vance, *Irish literature: a social history*. Oxford: Blackwell, 1990.

H. Wallace, 'Æ: a prophet out of an ancient age', *Colby Library Quarterly*, 4:2, May 1955. 28–31.

J. Wallace, *Shelley and Greece: rethinking romantic Hellenism*. London: Macmillan, 1997.

B. Waller, *Hibernia or the future of Ireland*. London: Kegan Paul, nd.

Maurice Walsh. British correspondents and the Anglo-Irish war 1919–1920. Unpublished MRes thesis, 2000.

J. Webb, *The flight from reason*. London: MacDonald, 1971.

H.G. Wells, *The war in the air*. 1908. Np: Gutenberg, 2000.

——, *The world set free*. 1914. London: Hogarth, 1988.

Trevor West, *Horace Plunkett: co-operation and politics, an Irish biography*. Gerrards Cross: Smythe, 1986.

T. White, *Kevin O'Higgins*. 1948. Dublin: Anvil, 1986.

Walt Whitman, *Democratic vistas, and other papers*. 1871. Michigan: Scholarly Press, 1970.

——, *Leaves of grass: a textual variorum of the printed poems. Volume 1: poems, 1855–1856*. Eds. S. Bradley, H.W. Blodgett, A. Golden and W. White. NY: NYUP, 1980.

——, *Leaves of grass: reader's edition*. Eds. H. W. Blodgett and S. Bradley. London: University of London Press, 1965.

William Wordsworth, *The poems*. Ed. J. O. Hayden. London: Yale UP, 1977.

W.B. Yeats, *A vision: a critical edition of Yeats's* A vision *(1925)*. G.M. Harper and W.K. Hood (eds.), London: Macmillan, 1978.

——, *Autobiographies*. London: Macmillan, 1955.

——, *The celtic twilight: men and women, dhouls and faeries*. London: Lawrence and Bullen, 1893.

——, *Collected plays*. London: Macmillan, 1982.

——, *Yeats's poems*. Ed. A.N. Jeffares. Dublin: Gill and Macmillan, 1989.

Calton Younger, *Ireland's civil war*. 1968. London: Fontana, 1970.

Index